Contents

Applications in Basic Marketing

Clippings from the Popular Business Press

1999-2000 Edition

Applications in Basic Marketing

Clippings from the Popular Business Press

1999-2000 Edition

William D. Perreault, Jr.
University of North Carolina

and

E. Jerome McCarthy
Michigan State University

Boston   Burr Ridge, IL   Dubuque, IA   Madison, WI   New York   San Francisco   St. Louis
Bangkok   Bogotá   Caracas   Lisbon   London   Madrid
Mexico City   Milan   New Delhi   Seoul   Singapore   Sydney   Taipei   Toronto

McGraw-Hill Higher Education

A Division of The **McGraw-Hill** *Companies*

APPLICATIONS IN BASIC MARKETING: CLIPPINGS FROM THE POPULAR BUSINESS PRESS, 1999–2000 EDITION

This book is printed on acid-free paper.

domestic   1 2 3 4 5 6 7 8 9 0 QPD/QPD 9 0 9 8 7 6 5 4 3 2 1 0 9
international   1 2 3 4 5 6 7 8 9 0 QPD/QPD 9 0 9 8 7 6 5 4 3 2 1 0 9

ISBN 0-07-561029-9
ISSN 1099-5579

Publisher: *David Kendric Brake*
Sponsoring editor: *Rick Adams*
Coordinating editor: *Linda G. Davis*
Senior developmental editor: *Nancy Barbour*
Senior marketing manager: *Colleen J. Suljic*
Project manager: *Christine A. Vaughan*
Manager, new book production: *Melonie Salvati*
Director of design MHHE: *Keith J. McPherson*
Supplement coordinator: *Mark Sienicki*
Compositor: *Electronic Publishing Services, Inc.*
Printer: *Quebecor Printing Book Group/Dubuque*

http://www.mhhe.com

Preface

This is the tenth annual edition of *Applications in Basic Marketing.* We developed this set of marketing "clippings" from popular business publications to accompany our texts—*Basic Marketing* and *Essentials of Marketing.* All of these clippings report interesting case studies and current issues that relate to topics covered in our texts and in the first marketing course. We will continue to publish a new edition of this book *every year.* That means that we can include the most current and interesting clippings. Each new copy of our texts will come shrink-wrapped with a free copy of the newest (annual) edition of this book. However, it can also be ordered from the publisher separately for use in other courses or with other texts.

Our objective is for this book to provide a flexible and helpful set of teaching and learning materials. We have included clippings (articles) on a wide variety of topics. The clippings deal with consumer products and business products, goods and services, new developments in marketing as well as traditional issues, and large well-known companies as well as new, small ones. They cover important issues related to marketing strategy planning for both domestic and global markets. The readings can be used for independent study, as a basis for class assignments, or as a focus of in-class discussions. Some instructors might want to assign all of the clippings, but we have provided an ample selection so that it is easy to focus on a subset which is especially relevant to specific learning/teaching objectives. A separate set of teaching notes discusses points related to each article. We have put special emphasis on selecting short, highly readable articles—ones which can be read and understood in 10 or 15 minutes—so that they can be used in combination with other readings and assignments for the course. For example, they might be used in combination with assignments from *Essentials of Marketing,* exercises from the *Learning Aid for Use with Essentials of Marketing,* or *The Marketing Game!* micro-computer strategy simulation.

All of the articles are reproduced here in basically the same style and format as they originally appeared. This gives the reader a better sense of the popular business publications from which they are drawn, and stimulates an interest in ongoing learning beyond the time frame for a specific course.

We have added this component to our complete set of **P**rofessional **L**earning **U**nits **S**ystems (our **P.L.U.S.**) to provide even more alternatives for effective teaching and learning in the first marketing course. It has been an interesting job to research and select the readings for this new book, and we hope that our readers find it of value in developing a better understanding of the opportunities and challenges of marketing in our contemporary society.

William D. Perreault, Jr. and E. Jerome McCarthy

Acknowledgments

We would like to thank all of the publications that have granted us permission to reprint the articles in this book. Similarly, we value and appreciate the work and skill of the many writers who prepared the original materials.

Linda G. Davis played an important role in this project. She helped us research thousands of different publications to sort down to the final set, and she also contributed many fine ideas on how best to organize the selections that appear here.

The ideas for this book evolve from and build on previous editions of *Readings and Cases in Basic Marketing*. John F. Grashof and Andrew A. Brogowicz were coauthors of that book. We gratefully recognize the expertise and creativity that they shared over the years on that project. Their fine ideas carry forward here and have had a profound effect on our thinking in selecting articles that will meet the needs of marketing instructors and students alike.

We would also like to thank the many marketing professors and students whose input have helped shape the concept of this book. Their ideas—shared in personal conversations, in focus group interviews, and in responses to marketing research surveys—helped us to clearly define the needs that this book should meet.

Finally, we would like to thank the people at Irwin/McGraw-Hill, our publisher, who have helped turn this idea into a reality. We are grateful for their commitment to making these materials widely available

W.D.P. and E.J.M.

Marketing Strategies: Planning, Implementation and Control

Ethical Marketing in a Consumer-Oriented World: Appraisal and Challenges

Marketing's Role in the Global Economy and in the Firm

Reading the Tea Leaves, China Sees a Future for Coffee

By Ian Johnson
Staff Reporter of The Wall Street Journal

BAOSHAN, China — All the coffee in China is a trifling amount. But now, after long being kept at bay by Chinese politics and poverty, the drink is making two inroads into this nation of tea drinkers.

One is here, by China's lush southern border with Burma, where officials are telling farmers to stop growing tea and sugarcane and start planting coffee, which has greater potential for revenue — and tax dollars.

Meanwhile, in China's crowded cities, foreign coffeehouse chains are gambling they can buck tradition and create a coffee culture in the land of the teahouse.

The change won't come easily. While Beijing wants the coffee from Baoshan and the rest of Yunnan province to sell like Jamaica's high-priced Blue Mountain beans, production has been plagued by corruption, politics and chronic low quality. And while chains such as the U.S.'s Starbucks Corp. and Tully's Coffee and Japan's Manabe Kohikan open new coffee bars by the month, coffee sales have declined slightly over the past four years, according to market researchers. Future growth, they say, is likely to be in low-end instant coffees and presweetened coffee mixes.

But that's not the vision driving coffee's missionaries. Here in Baoshan, a major outpost on the old Burma Road, Mayor Yang Jingjian uses a barrage of statistics and rhetoric to persuade the local populace to switch to coffee, arguing that the hard-to-grow and harder-to-roast beans will make them — and his government — rich.

The region around Baoshan now has 5,000 acres of coffee, Mr. Yang says. He wants to double that within five years and make coffee the region's major cash crop. By then, he promises farmers, coffee will have nearly doubled their annual income.

From missionaries 100 years ago to reform-minded communists in the 1980s, many have been attracted by the bean's potential to earn money. But coffee, first condemned by nationalists as a foreign intrusion and later by communists as the "tail of capitalism," was politically incorrect — until recently.

"Politics and coffee have a long relationship," the mayor concedes. "Now the government is all for it."

Farmers may be another matter. At the bottom of a verdant valley planted with coffee, bananas and papayas, one of Mr. Yang's star coffee growers casually announces that he and many of his neighbors want to abandon coffee in favor of longans, a fruit resembling litchis. Mr. Yang shakes his head in frustration and, as though talking to a simpleton, bellows: "Don't talk to me about longan. You have to stick to coffee, understand?"

The man nods skeptically. He knows it's easier to yield to the pressure of local authorities. But he also knows that coffee plants take three years to mature and must be cut back after seven, while longans bring rich harvests almost immediately.

In fact, this desire for fast profits, widespread among Chinese farmers, has crippled China's coffee-growing aspirations, says Robert Tibbo, with Eastern Strategic Consulting Ltd. in Hong Kong. With most coffee plucked early and processed as cheaply as possible, Yunnan coffee remains inferior. At the end of a busy day touring the countryside, Mayor Yang proudly presents a visitor with what is purported to be a bag of choice green coffee beans. A quarter of these beans later turn out to be too low quality for roasting when inspected by a roaster in Beijing.

While the central government has budgeted funds for advanced processing and roasting equipment, local press reports say much of the money was siphoned off by corrupt officials. Last year, China produced 3,400 metric tons of coffee. Virtually none was fit for export, with almost all being ground into instant coffee. "It's a mess down there," Mr. Tibbo says.

Up north, in China's big cities, coffee has a slightly more promising hold, although the vast majority of people still measure their lives in sips of tea rather than coffee spoons. Most coffee is sold to hotels, and almost all the coffee sold at retail is instant.

Undeterred, gourmet-coffee retailers have moved aggressively into China. Starbucks opened its first coffeehouse last month in Beijing, promising to open up to another dozen by mid-2000. "We're going to create a market that may not exist currently," says Lawrence Maltz, chairman of Beijing Mei Da Coffee Co., which has been licensed to open Starbucks in China.

Starbucks's belief in China is based on a simple certainty: Coffee consumption is directly related to income. Following the pattern of other countries, China's rising income is supposed to mean growing coffee sales — as has been the case in Japan, where the tea

Planet Starbucks
The ubiquitous coffee chain gives a dash of international flair to its cafes in Asia

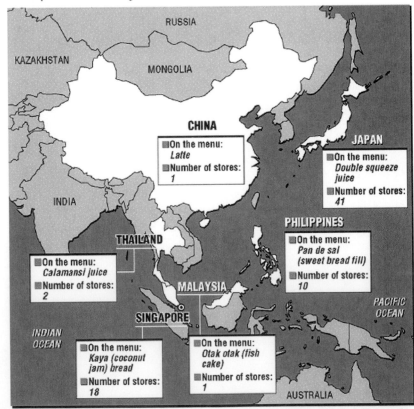

Source: Starbucks Coffee International

ceremony has taken a back seat to street-corner coffee vending machines.

To a degree, this is also true in China. Coffee shops have become popular meeting places and a $2 latte is a status symbol in China, which has a per-capita income of $750. Says Mr. Maltz: "We can't build our business on expatriates and tourists."

For the next few years, however, there may be no other choice. With income levels in China low, coffee consumption has stagnated over the past four years — reflecting a leveling-off in the number of expatriates working in China.

Besides income, a major hurdle is deeply ingrained views toward food and health in China. Traditional medicine views coffee as a "warming" beverage — something that holds true whether the drink is sold scalding hot or as one of Starbucks' iced frappuccinos. Thus, says Mr. Tibbo of Eastern Strategic Consulting, coffee has been slow to catch on in southern China's Guangdong province, the richest — and warmest — part of China. "It's a northern drink and pretty much only in the winter months," Mr. Tibbo says.

The dangers of overestimating China's eagerness to embrace coffee can be seen in its import statistics. When China's economic boom began to gather pace in the early 1990s, foreigners flocked to China and coffee sales began a modest expansion, growing between 5% and 8% a year. In 1996, as experts began predicting that China was the next big coffee market, government coffee traders imported 12,000 metric tons of coffee, almost six times the previous year's imports. That year, however, turned out to be the end of China's coffee-drinking growth period. "I think most of those beans are still sitting in Chinese warehouses, waiting to be roasted and ground," says a Beijing coffee roaster.

Why Foreign Distillers Find It So Hard to Sell Vodka to the Russians

The Market Seemed Ripe, But Cost Matters a Lot, And So Does Patriotism

No 'Drink-the-Label Market'

By Ernest Beck

Staff Reporter of The Wall Street Journal

MOSCOW — Roman Drenovich marches down the cluttered liquor aisle of his neighborhood supermarket and discovers that in today's Russia, all vodkas are not created equal.

Picking his way along the shelves, Mr. Drenovich fingers a fancy frosted-glass bottle of Absolut, selling for $25. He scrutinizes the sleek reindeer on an equally expensive bottle of Finlandia. He moves past a $12 bottle of Smirnoff. Squinting at prices, the 58-year-old finally reaches for a local brand called Komdiv. Made by Moscow's Cristall Distillery, it has a flimsy twist-off cap and a picture on the label of a famous Russian actor. The price: $3.

"I buy only Russian vodka," declares Mr. Drenovich, with patriotic fervor. "It is the purest, the smoothest, the best."

Grandiose Plans

In 1990, when Western companies — like Smirnoff's owner Diageo PLC of Britain and Absolut's V&S Vin & Spirit AB of Sweden — first eyed the vast vodka market here, they believed Russia's voracious drinkers could be lured to their products. With famous brand names and well-honed selling skills, the companies reasoned, they could carry coals to Newcastle, as it were, and overpower stodgy, Communistera products. The goal was to capture consumers eager to trade up to Western brands.

But in a surprising role reversal, Russia's private and state vodka producers are challenging Western marketers and even beating them at their own game — pouring new niche brands onto the market and hawking them with clever, eye-catching packaging and advertising campaigns. After nearly a decade, the newcomers have little to show for their efforts — except a bad hangover and a combined market share estimated at less than 1%.

The setback is frustrating because Russia is by far the world's largest vodka market:

Consumption reached an estimated 250 million cases in 1996, industry watchers say, though exact figures aren't available. That compares with 33.4 million cases in the U.S., the largest market outside Eastern Europe, according to Impact International, a trade-research company. While vodka sales are declining world-wide, about 80% of Russians drink vodka on a regular basis, surveys indicate, and consumption is increasing. Russian drinkers could help power much-needed growth for distillers and their distributors in a crowded, global spirits sector.

Humbled, foreign companies now concede that it may be years before they can grab a big share of the market, but they insist that they aren't giving up. "We're not here to make a profit now — that might only come in five, maybe 10, years," says John Kamviselis, country manager of Seagram Co., which distributes Absolut in Russia. "This is a strategic market, and we're still in the early stages of the game."

'Strategic' Industry

To be fair, not all the problems of the Western companies are of their own making. In many ways, what went wrong in Russia is a classic tale of a risky emerging market, with the usual problems of creaky infrastructure, economic turmoil, low incomes, a poor distribution network and quickly shifting consumer tastes. Yet Russia posed other obstacles: a government determined to protect the "strategic" vodka industry by imposing high taxes and import duties. Another blow came in 1994, when alcohol-advertising restrictions — including a ban on television ads — began to be phased in, in a bid by health authorities to cut the high rate of alcoholism.

What's more, organized crime infiltrated the vodka trade and today is said to control the market for cheap, illicit hooch. About 50% of the Russian vodka market is said to be "illegal," that is, untaxed, counterfeit or bootleg, according to industry officials. While police have cracked down on moonshine merchants, sales still flourish in alleys. One winter night in Moscow, an elderly woman in a threadbare coat plies her wares on an upturned banana box. "Real Russian vodka!" she screams in a raspy voice, offering a suspicious bottle with an unsealed cap to a group of men standing nearby. They fork over rubles worth about $1 and swill the stuff while swaying down the street.

Drinking Objectives

"Russia isn't a drink-the-label market yet," remarks Leon Stelmach, an analyst at Canadean, an alcohol-industry research company in London. "Russians aren't fussy: The goal is to get drunk."

Selling any foreign vodka to Russians was never going to be easy. Most Russians believe vodka, a colorless spirit distilled from grain or beets and potatoes, originated here in the 12th century — although the Poles dispute that. So for many Russians,

vodka is like mother's milk — a native drink from the sacred Russian soil that makes you feel warm in winter, bonds friends, enlivens family celebrations, and nourishes the legendary Russian soul. "Vodka is a *Russian* product," notes Vladimir Korovkin, planning director at Smart-Communications, a Moscow marketing consultant. "Just try selling whisky to the Scots."

But in the early 1990s, the market seemed ripe for the taking. Trade liberalization had opened the borders to importers. And vodka was, basically generic product. Few real brands — in the Western sense — existed here, though Russians knew names like Cristall, a distillery, and Stolichnaya. (Five distilleries make the popular Stolichnaya for export.) Sensing a great opportunity, popular brands like Smirnoff — the world's best-selling Western vodka — and Absolut arrived, hoping to capitalize on the rage for Western products — from Mars bars to Tide laundry detergent. Initially, they proved popular as bribes or trophy gifts, kept on display in the buyer's home, or as status symbols for the brash, free-spending new Russian rich.

For the most part, though, marketing strategies that worked well in London or New York were simply plunked down in Moscow, with only minor tinkering.

Absolut, trying to communicate directly with Russians, adapted its famous global ad campaign to include Absolut *dacha* and Absolut Bolshoi, but it kept its high prices. "We aim for the rich, and aspiring middle classes," explains Andreas Berggren, vice president of Russian operations for Absolut. Indeed, less than 2% of the population can afford to buy a bottle of Absolut, the company estimates. It is Absolut's policy never to produce outside Sweden, officials insist, and even Russia's mind-boggling potential didn't change that.

Smirnoff had a rough ride in Russia, too, after an initial surge of interest as a status brand. At first, it was available only in foreign-currency shops. But by 1993, consumerism was booming and Smirnoff felt emboldened to import and sell via a joint venture on the retail level. However, the company didn't carefully consider important factors like income levels, distribution and a swing away from pricey, foreign-branded goods, says a company insider who didn't want to be identified. A move to become more Russian — by launching an inexpensive brand, called Bread Vodka — was rejected because the low end of the market was overcrowded. Ads weren't customized to the local market; instead, global campaigns were deployed.

Limited-Success Story

While Smirnoff and Absolut struggled with their high-priced products, one company went after the mass market and — at first — did reasonably well.

White Eagle, a brand owned by American United Distilled Products Co., in Minneapolis, Minn., in a joint venture with Archer-Daniels-Midland Co. of Decatur, Ill., launched a big advertising and marketing campaign in 1992. Ads were geared to Russian tastes, featuring a stumbling, drunken American Indian that Russian consumers considered funny, says a company official. "We couldn't do that in America," he adds. Lightweight plastic bottles were used to cut shipping costs. A large variety of vodkas — including cranberry and lemon-flavored ones — were introduced, creating a family of related products. The strategy worked: Sales of White Eagle soared to between three million and four million cases annually, according to the company.

But in 1994, the government started raising import duties to help local vodka producers compete with imports from the West and former Soviet republics. Further tax increases followed, as well as strict rules requiring that all duties be paid in advance. For White Eagle, that meant adding about $9 in costs to a liter bottle of vodka that cost 60 cents to produce in the U.S. White Eagle subsequently pulled out of direct sales and marketing in Russia.

"Russia is a wonderful market, and we were making money, but basically, the government prohibited us," grumbles Douglas Mangine, chief executive of American United. The company also looked into building a production site in Russia but backed away. "You can't invest in bricks and mortar when laws change every day," Mr. Mangine says.

Something for Everyone

Meanwhile, Russian marketers grew savvier and began outmaneuvering the Westerners. Maverick businessman Vladimir Dovgan jumped into the value-for-money vodka sector and backed the launch of myriad midprice vodka brands with packaging and advertising featuring the chubby entrepreneur as pitchman.

His food-and-spirits company currently markets 25 brands — each with his picture on the label. "The foreigners fight for the money of the wealthy, and I flood the market and let the people choose," boasts Mr. Dovgan, a self-styled consumer populist. Bolting around his modern Moscow office, Mr. Dovgan shows off a glass case crammed with bottles of Dovgan vodka. Among the offerings are a mild-tasting Lady brand, a robust Imperial variety and a hardy Winterone. Re-

tail prices are from $5 to $10.

Such saturation marketing, which cuts across price points and niche categories, appears to be working. After two years, Mr. Dovgan claims he will have sold 2.5 million cases in 1997. The Western companies refuse to disclose sales figures, but their shares are estimated to be significantly lower than Dovgan's.

For consumers, the market is awash with vodkas, known here as the "water of life." At a small, well-kept store in a Moscow suburb, vodkas of all shapes and sizes, labels and prices can be found next to a deli counter stuffed with sliced meats and slabs of smoked fish. On the shelves are odd, local brands like Sibirskaya, in a bullet-shaped bottle, and Narkom, short for People's Commissar. "This probably appeals to crazy old Communist drunks," scoffs Leonid Tarasov, director of Ansdell Russia, a consultant to United Distillers & Vinters, the new Diageo beverage unit, in Russia.

New Brand Loyalty

Despite the wide selection, Irina Maximova, the store manager, says Russians are sticking to brands — mostly Russian ones — and closely comparing prices. In other words, they are evolving from being "buyers and users," in marketing-speak, to brand-loyal consumers. "Five years ago, customers would wander around and didn't know what to buy. Now, nobody is confused," Mrs. Maximova explains. According to Gallup Media in Russia, leading Russian brands like Moskovskaya and Russkaya score over 70% in brand awareness surveys, while Smirnoff is at 28.7%. White Eagle scores an impressive 43.7%.

With few self-service retail stores, clever packaging is essential, and Russian distillers like Cristall are learning from their Western competitors. State-owned Cristall's new range includes Priviet, which sports bold black lettering and silver foil wrapping over the cap. "Made with water from Russia's icy glacial lakes that are perfectly clean," attests the label, in an appeal to Russian fears of pollution. And then there's a premium range for around $13 — roughly on a par with Smirnoff — with bold black-and-gold labels. The Cristall name is daubed in elegant script.

"Russians are coming back to Russian vodka, and we're helping with attractive new

brands," says Edward Kusmitsky, deputy director of Cristall. He shows off a limited edition Cristall vodka to commemorate Moscow's 850th anniversary.

The explosion of vodka brands — there are more than 400 now — took Westerners by surprise. (Even Vladimir Zhiranovsky, the right-wing politician, launched his own vodka.) But for Smirnoff, there was another woe: Boris Smirnov, a Russian namesake, launched a vodka and sued Smirnoff for trademark infringement.

Going Local

While the case is still tied up in the courts, Smirnoff is implementing a new marketing gambit: After years of turbulence as an importer, it has gone local. Since March 1997, the brand has been produced in Russia at a St. Petersburg distillery.

"This should make Smirnoff seem more Russian," suggests a Smirnoff official, who asked not to be named because of security and legal concerns. Indeed, the revised strategy — which includes made-in-Russia labels, a Smirnoff telephone hot line and ads that underline the brand's "international quality" and Russian roots — is an attempt to convince consumers that Smirnoff is indeed a Russian brand. "We want Russians to realize that Smirnoff came to Russia to produce for Russians," adds the official. New print and poster ads highlight the double "ff" in Smirnoff, to mirror the way the rulers of Imperial Russia, the Romanoff family, spelled their name.

So far, though, Smirnoff's gamble hasn't paid off: The company says sales volumes haven't budged, although its price has fallen 15%, to around $11 a bottle, because of lower costs.

Sergey Koptev, chairman of ad agency DMB&B in Moscow, which has the Cristall premium account, believes foreign brands will eventually find a niche in the huge market but will never capture a major share of it — or the Russian soul. "Vodka was, and is, a matter of love and trust for us. It's our national brand," says Mr. Koptev.

MEXICAN MAKEOVER:

NAFTA creates the world's newest industrial power

Surfing for clients on the Internet, a Mexican entrepreneur in Monterrey has turned a small metal-working company into a $10 million-a-year exporter to General Electric Co. and Siemens in just five years. In Guadalajara, a 26-year-old high school graduate earns more than $500 a month inspecting silicon components that will help power IBM computers around the world. Across the country, in the city of Puebla, 15,000 Mexican workers churn out Volkswagen's new Beetle for export to the world, including Germany.

Mexico's economy is undergoing a stunning transformation. Five years after the launch of the North American Free Trade Agreement (NAFTA), it is fast becoming an industrial power. Free trade with the U.S. and Canada is turning the country from a mere assembler of cheap, low-quality goods into a reliable exporter of sophisticated products, from auto brake systems to laptop computers. Since 1993, exports have more than doubled, to $115 billion. Manufactured goods now make up close to 90% of Mexico's sales abroad, up from 77% five years ago.

Oil, by contrast, makes up 7% of Mexico's exports, down from 22% in 1993. Mexico's manufacturing sector pulled the economy along at 4.5% growth this year—even though the government still depends on oil for 35% of its budget revenues. President Ernesto Zedillo has been forced to slash spending and raise taxes to make up for the shortfall. That squeeze could slow growth to 2.5% next year, economists say, and helps explain why Mexico's bolsa is down 40% this year in dollar terms. Still, NAFTA has helped protect Mexico from both the plunge in oil prices and the fallout from the global emerging-markets crisis. "This is a completely different economy than Mexico had a decade ago," says sociologist Federico Reyes Heroles.

Mexico's industrial surge also means that North America is winning back thousands of jobs that had been lost to Asia as U.S. and Canadian companies shifted production to lower-cost production sites in the last decade. Now, for example, IBM is making computer components in Guadalajara that were formerly made in Singapore. And clothing retailers such as Gap Inc. and Liz Claiborne are increasingly buying garments from Mexican contractors, who can offer faster delivery than Asians.

The shift back from Asia is just part of a boom in foreign investment in Mexico. As companies from Samsung to Daimler Benz to DuPont open factories or expand existing operations, foreign direct investment has soared from $4 billion in 1993 to an average $10 billion per year. Moreover, the foreign units are no longer mainly maquiladoras, assembly plants huddled along the U.S.-Mexico border. Now, many are more sophisticated factories scattered throughout the country.

The foreigners are attracted by Mexico's low-cost labor—averaging $1.60 an hour in manufacturing, compared with $6.11 in Taiwan and less than 40 cents in China—and by duty-free access to the U.S. market. Just as important, however, NAFTA guarantees foreigners the same rights as Mexican investors and reassures them that Mexico will continue on its free-market course. "When we invest, we consider political stability," says Young M. Kwon, president of Samsung Electromechanics in Tijuana.

But the makeover of Mexican industry goes far beyond export and investment numbers. From small entrepreneurs to executives of the country's new multinationals, Mexican managers are becoming more confident as they respond to heightened competition at home and to the tough demands of foreign customers. NAFTA "has given Mexicans a new vision of the world," says Clemente Ruiz Duran, an economist at the National Autonomous University of Mexico.

To be sure, Mexico still faces huge problems. Indeed, it seems there are really two economies, with free trade benefiting only one. Despite a sharp increase in manufacturing employment, Mexico still suffers from a chronic shortage of jobs, with millions subsisting on part-time work in the "informal" economy. Mexico needs to generate 1 million new jobs each year just to absorb young people entering the job market. To achieve that will require even more investment and better training.

The Wonders of Free Trade

MANUFACTURING Mexico is becoming an industrial dynamo with manufactured and other goods accounting for 90% of exports, spurring new jobs

- -

INVESTMENT Access to the North American market entices Asian and European companies to pour billions into auto parts, electronics, and textiles

- -

GLOBAL MINDSET An increasingly confident business community has abandoned its fear of foreigners and is structuring operations for world markets

Data Business Week

(Cont.)

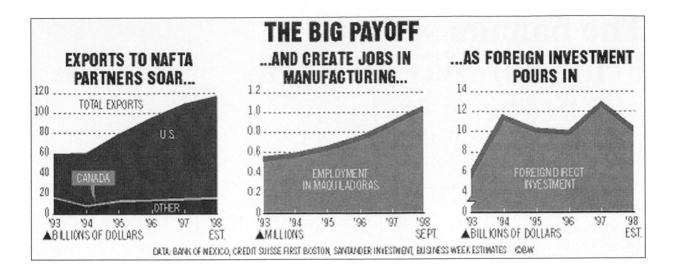

THE BIG PAYOFF

EXPORTS TO NAFTA PARTNERS SOAR...

...AND CREATE JOBS IN MANUFACTURING...

...AS FOREIGN INVESTMENT POURS IN

DATA: BANK OF MEXICO, CREDIT SUISSE FIRST BOSTON, SANTANDER INVESTMENT, BUSINESS WEEK ESTIMATES

Nevertheless, Mexico is laying a solid foundation for economic growth and employment in the years ahead. Increasingly, Mexican engineers are designing products and testing them in multimillion-dollar research and development centers. NAFTA has also given a boost to more traditional industries. Agribusinesses are exporting frozen products to markets as far away as Sweden. And Mexican service businesses are processing U.S. credit-card data and airline tickets as well as creating custom-made software for U.S. clients that once farmed out such work to India.

But the auto industry stands out as Mexico's single most important manufacturing business. It has become integrated with the U.S. industry as parts and vehicles shuttle back and forth across the border. Half a million Mexicans make parts and assemble vehicles for eight of the world's auto makers, including Detroit's Big Three. NAFTA's rules of origin, requiring high North American-made content in cars, have forced European and Asian auto makers to bring their foreign parts suppliers to Mexico as well as buy from local companies. In Puebla, 70 parts makers cluster around Volkswagen's sprawling plant, which produces 600 Beetles and 900 other VW cars per day.

BEETLE POWER. One supplier is Refa Mexicana, a metal-stamping plant started by Canada-based entrepreneur Klaus Reithofer four years ago with a $4 million investment. Today, he employs 1,300 people working three shifts and generating $57 million in annual sales. "We were only supposed to be 130 people, but VW has thrown so much stuff at us, and we took it," Reithofer says. "It's miraculous."

Similar explosive growth is happening in Guadalajara, the country's second-largest city. A joint government-business effort has lured 25 foreign suppliers to set up there

since 1995. Taiwan's Universal Scientific Industrial Co. (USI) this year began producing 2,900 computer motherboards daily for IBM in a new plant employing 270 people. Before, the boards were shipped in from Taiwan.

At the IBM complex nearby, workers produce magnetic readers for computer hard-disk drives. The parts used to be made in Singapore, Taiwan, and Malaysia. Now, IBM ships them from Guadalajara by air each day to San Jose, Calif., where hard drives are assembled for IBM's laptops, desktops, and servers worldwide. Plant Manager Alfonso Alva Rosano says NAFTA helped persuade IBM to shift some operations from Asia to IBM de Mexico, which in five years has boosted exports from $350 million to $2 billion. "If we weren't making the subassemblies here," Alva Rosano says, "chances are the whole process would have moved to the Far East."

Mexico's textile industry is also bringing factories and jobs back from Asia. NAFTA rescued Mexico's declining textile makers by eliminating U.S. tariffs and quotas on fabric and garments made with yarn produced anywhere in the three member countries. In 1996, Mexico overtook China as the largest supplier of textiles and garments to the U.S. Now, U.S. mills are rushing to invest. In Altamira on the Gulf of Mexico, for example, Guilford Mills Inc., based in Greensboro, N.C., is building a $100 million knitting, dyeing, and finishing plant. In Puebla, several Mexican families set up a venture, Skytex, that is turning out two million yards of polyester fabric per month. Half of it goes to the U.S. "This plant was conceived for NAFTA," says Deputy Sales Director Alberto Serur. "I can ship to the border in 18 hours, while the Asians take 21 days."

As the border becomes more porous, many top Mexican executives say they now consider their companies to be North American corporations. Take Monterrey-based

Grupo IMSA, a $1.5 billion maker of steel, auto parts, and construction products. In the U.S., it makes insulated panels and ladders, and it has merged businesses with Johnson Controls to manufacture and sell batteries in Mexico and South America. "For us, NAFTA is a single market—we feel we're an American company," says General Director Eugenio Clariond Reyes.

EDUCATION GAP. In Mexico, though, free trade is exposing more starkly than ever some of the failures of Mexican society, particularly in education. Many analysts believed NAFTA would generate years of demand for Mexico's masses of unskilled, poorly educated workers, who average only 5½ years of schooling. Instead, many employers are leapfrogging to high-tech operations that require a high school education even for assembly-line operators. Since 1993, the gap has widened between wages at local manufacturers and those at top export manufacturers, which are up to 67% higher.

Still, Mexico has achieved a lot in five years. The country's new efficiencies and export mentality should help diversify its trade beyond NAFTA to new markets in Latin America and the rest of the world. "Businesspeople are looking outside the country and into the future," says political scientist Luis Rubio of the Center of Research for Development, a think tank in Mexico City. For companies that have succeeded in Mexico's open market, "it's no longer, 'Those darn gringos,'" Rubio says, "but 'How can we beat them at their own game?'" In a dog-eat-dog global economy, that kind of attitude should serve Mexicans well.

By Geri Smith in Guadalajara, with Elisabeth Malkin in Puebla

The banana split: Fruit war may hike price of European luxuries

By James Cox
USA TODAY

WASHINGTON — In the coming war over bananas, look for collateral damage in unlikely places.

The United States and the European Union, the world's two largest trading entities, are heading for a high-stakes showdown over a fruit that, for the most part, neither grows or exports.

Opponents of the Clinton administration's hawkish banana policy say a trans-Atlantic fruit feud will leave a battlefield littered with the corpses of innocent bystanders — from cheese lovers to industrial adhesive makers.

In recent weeks, critics have warned of catastrophic consequences for groups as diverse as fur-bearing mammals and Greek Americans. The fallout, various opponents have claimed, could include a surge in illegal drug trafficking and the destabilization of fragile Caribbean democracies, not to mention the smuggling of vintage port wines and a rise in anti-Americanism among small-town Swedes.

The doomsday rhetoric comes from individuals, companies and countries that stand to lose if the U.S. follows through on its threat to impose 100% tariffs next month on $520 million worth of European goods. The U.S. says that's how much the EU's restrictions on banana imports are costing the big U.S. banana distributors — Chiquita, Del Monte and Dole.

The administration's determination to punish the EU has special interests large and small scrambling to keep from being squashed between the trade behemoths.

Dozens of lobbyists and corporate executives showed up in Washington last month to testify at a public hearing about 42 products targeted for punitive duties. Hundreds of other companies appealed to U.S. Trade Representative Charlene Barshefsky in anguished letters.

The nation's cheese lobby, dismayed by proposed duties on crumbly, white feta, invoked the proud history of goat's milk cheese.

"Feta is one of mankind's oldest cheeses," testified the general counsel of the Cheese Importers Association of America. If tariffs are imposed, "The economic pain will be born almost entirely by an innocent group of ethnic Americans." Immigrants from Greece and other European and Middle Eastern countries eat feta "quite literally morning, noon and night," Richard Koby said.

Waterford Wedgwood, the maker of fine Irish crystal, appealed to the patriotism of the government panel that heard testimony. Panel members, the company said, should be aware that the Declaration of Independence was signed beneath a Waterford chandelier.

Others argued that to deprive U.S. consumers of certain European products would be to rob society of something inherently good. German-made model trains, for instance, "can help keep our children away from drugs," insisted Ronald Schroeder, a Kennesaw, Ga., railroad enthusiast.

New York City wine merchant Michael Aaron warned that the U.S., by targeting port and Spanish sherry, was headed down the slippery slope from after-dinner drinks to fine wines. "The next time they decide to blackmail a nation they might use Beaujolais or Chianti, and then Bordeaux and Burgundy, 'etcetera, etcetera, etcetera,' as Yul Brynner said in *The King and I*," he wrote.

WHERE IT STANDS

Despite last-minute negotiations over the weekend, the U.S. government plans to ask the World Trade Organization today for authorization to retaliate against the European Union for a banana-import system that the U.S. says violates WTO rules.

The U.S. intends to put 100% duties on 16 types of European products — from candles to coffee makers.

WTO rules make approval of the U.S. request likely. The EU can appeal the tariffs' amount. By appealing, the EU can delay the starting date from Feb. 1 to March 3. WTO chief Renato Ruggiero proposed a compromise Sunday that could delay sanctions further.

(Cont.)

Seven-year war

The banana spat has raged for almost seven years. U.S. officials want the 15-nation EU to change import regulations that have twice been ruled discriminatory by the World Trade Organization (WTO). The EU's banana rules carve out preferences for Caribbean bananas that are distributed mainly by French and British companies, at the expense of Latin American bananas sold by U.S. distributors.

The administration's critics say it has picked a lousy issue to go to war over. They say U.S. economic interests in the banana case are insignificant, confined mainly to powerful fruit distributors Chiquita, Dole and Del Monte.

"Just the word 'bananas' usually brings a smile to people's faces," Barshefsky concedes. But she is deadly serious about the implications of the case, which she says could forever undermine the WTO.

A war over bananas may sound absurd, "But it's more absurd that the EU has failed to comply with its international obligations," she says. "If the EU doesn't comply, it's an invitation to every country to ride roughshod over our rights."

The U.S. and EU have clashed before, notably in the so-called Pasta War of 1985, which began over citrus but resulted in higher duties on imported European noodles.

Picked by bureaucrats

Still, many U.S. companies were horrified last fall to find that a panel of bureaucrats from the USTR, Commerce and other departments had zeroed in on them.

"Toys, dolls and festive articles clearly are not bananas," griped the Toy Manufacturers of America.

"Why not let the produce industry carry the load?" asked Hayward, Calif., wine merchant Paul Lessig.

Barshefsky says the U.S. strategy is to retaliate in a way that does the least harm to domestic businesses and consumers while inflicting "maximum pain" on Europe. A hit list composed solely of fruit and related products wouldn't do the job, she says, so that means targeting a range of goods.

A preliminary list put out in November singled out 42 categories of goods and brought howls of protest.

Mattel, the world's largest toy manufacturer, said the proposed duties on dolls would price its American Girl collectibles — made in Germany — out of the market. Whirlpool warned of devastating consequences for its line of European coffee makers. The National Trappers Association predicted a loss of precious habitat for fur-bearing animals, which are trapped and skinned in the USA, made into garments in Europe, then shipped back for sale in this country.

16 goods on import hit list

The list of European imports that could soon face 100% tariffs in the USA has been cut from 42 categories of products to 16.

The products are:

Pecorino and feta cheese
Sweet biscuits, waffles, wafers
Bath preparations (not salts)
Candles
Plates, sheets, film, foil and strips of propylene polymers
Plastic-covered handbags
Plastic-lined handbags, wallets and other articles
Felt paper and paperboard
Folding cartons, boxes and corrugated paper cases
Greeting cards
Lithographs
Cashmere sweaters
Cotton bed linen
Lead-acid batteries
Electric coffee makers
Chandeliers and wall lighting fittings

The Westlake, Ohio, city council said tariffs on imported sewing machines would imperil plans by a Swedish manufacturer to set up shop in their town. Sweden's trade minister angrily noted that the list also included wooden toys and cookies made in his country. He demanded to know how the USA "could possibly benefit in any way from creating unemployment in Osby, Tyreso or Husqvarna."

Furriers and model train shops complained loudest. Duties on toy trains would have "a devastating impact" and "literally put us out of business," said Reynauld's Euro-Imports of Geneva, Ill.

There were questions about fairness. Upscale retailer Neiman Marcus and others argued that the USTR's hit list was an assault on the stylish and well-heeled because it took aim at designer clothes, cashmere sweaters and leather goods.

(Cont.)

"While there are certainly U.S. designers that have solid reputations in the eyes of consumers, these companies are not even in the same league" as Italian fashion icons Armani, Valentino and Ungaro, said GFT USA, a U.S. importer.

"These cases always produce apocalyptic claims," shrugs Barshefsky, who says luxury goods are deliberately targeted because they aren't essential.

PROXY WAR

Several U.S. industries see the banana clash as a proxy war. They have not been shy about lobbying for duties on their European competitors.

The California olive growers wanted to zap Spanish olives. The Tile Council of America asked for duties on European tile. The National Potato Council urged U.S. officials not to allow the EU to destroy the multilateral trading system.

U.S. pork producers were especially indignant. They argued — successfully — that Barshefsky should slam European pork products. The industry's lobbyists vowed that domestic substitutes would make U.S. consumers forget all about succulent Danish hams and Italian prosciutto. "We frankly feel we have the best hams in the world," boasted pork industry lawyer Nick Giordano.

In the end, the hit list was whittled to 16 types of products. Model trains, port wine, fruit juices, furs, dolls, sewing machines, pens and wooden toys were spared.

Feta cheese was not so lucky.

How Legend Lives Up to Its Name

The state-owned PC maker aims to become a Chinese IBM

The shiny new research center for Legend Holdings, China's leading PC maker, is teeming with activity. Young hipsters and nerds alike bustle down corridors or clack on keyboards. While two-thirds of the 120 researchers are designing new computers, the rest are testing everything from how smoothly they run software to what happens when they fall off a desk to how well they hold up in the 100F-plus sizzle of China's summer.

So far, Legend—and its PCs—are holding up just fine. Even though its research center can't match the resources of Compaq or IBM, it is Legend that's turning up the heat on those rivals and others. The $758 million Beijing-based computer company saw its sales grow by 106% last year, making it the biggest seller of PCs in the fastest-growing computer market on earth—a title that foreign rivals had hoped to capture. But with 15% of China's sales, Legend has twice the market share of its closest competitor, IBM. "We plan to be among the top 10 PC manufacturers in the world by 2000," vows Yang Yuan-qing, general manager of Legend Computer Systems Ltd. Legend's goal: to sell 1.5 million computers in 2001, up from 800,000 units today.

How did Legend dash the dreams U.S. PC makers had of dominating the Chinese market? Credit the company's low prices, broad product range, helpful software, and vast distribution network. Just as important have been Legend's strong links to the Chinese government, which accounts for 25% of Legend's sales, and the decision to push state-of-the-art PCs, not yesterday's models. That helped remove the stigma associated with buying a local computer. Consumers "stopped being ashamed of buying a Chinese brand," says Sean Maloney, senior vice-president for sales and marketing at Intel Corp., which urged Legend to sell the more powerful PCs. "Legend has become synonymous with high tech."

LOCAL HERO. The computer maker is also benefiting from China's love affair with the PC. Desktop-computer sales there are expected to swell 30% this year—double the growth that's forecast for the U.S. market. If this torrid pace keeps up through 2002, some 10.3 million PCs will be sold in China that year, making it the No. 3 market in the world following the U.S. and Japan. (Sales are higher in the U.S. and Japan.)

But Legend's ambitions go well beyond the PC. The company is aiming for nothing short of becoming China's version of IBM—a full-service provider of computers, software, and high-tech knowhow. In the past 12 months, Legend has parlayed its local savvy into development and marketing alliances with Microsoft Corp. and IBM, among others, to take the company into new markets, including software and systems-integration services for China's businesses. This month, Legend plans to sell in China a handheld computer that will challenge 3Com Corp.'s popular Palm computer. "As a local company, we have much more insight into the needs of Chinese customers," says Legend's Yang.

In China, hand-holding is need No. 1. After all, it is a population of PC newbies with only 1 out of every 175 Chinese currently owning a computer. Legend understands this better than foreign PC makers do. The company has developed a variety of software products for first-time customers that are bundled with its PCs, including tutorial programs on everything from using the World Wide Web to mastering home finances.

Legend will test just how well that formula works in a new market: palm-size computers. After one year of development work with Microsoft, Legend's palm-size computer, called Tianji, will appear this month running Microsoft's Windows CE software. As with PCs, Legend has tailored the product to the local market by including a stylus for entering Chinese characters and English letters and by installing a powerful English-Chinese dictionary. Legend and Microsoft also are working with 10 local software companies to develop applications for the product. And with a price of around $540 in China, the Tianji is $60 less than the price of 3Com's Palm computer.

HEMORRHAGE. Just two years ago, Legend might have been viewed as the least likely to survive. The company, founded in 1984, was hemorrhaging $25 million a year and lagging behind multinational rivals IBM, Hewlett-Packard, and Compaq. Then Legend launched a vicious price war, cutting prices three times in one year. With lower production and distribution costs than its foreign rivals, Legend now sells its desktop PC with a Pentium II chip for about $1,200, or 30% less than IBM or Compaq.

State-owned Legend, which is listed on the Hong Kong stock exchange, has something else going for it: a strong distribution network. That's what has stymied foreign competitors. In the past 10 months, Legend has added 800 distributors and now has close to 1,800 across China. It also has its own retail stores that sell Legend products, make repairs, and offer free training for China's often first-time users—including home visits. With 11 shops now open, Legend plans to have more than 50 by yearend. "They have an extremely well-developed distribution network," says Tony C. Leung, director of

LEGEND'S SALES ARE LEAPING AGAIN...

...AND PROFITS ARE BACK

▲ MILLIONS, TRANSLATED TO U.S. DOLLARS EST

DATA: BLOOMBERG FINANCIAL MARKETS, ABN AMRO ASIA

(Cont.)

Greater China marketing for Compaq in Hong Kong. "It will take a lot of time to catch up."

That's why no foreign company can afford to ignore Legend. Its superior distribution network and strong government connections spell opportunity. Last summer, Legend inked a deal with IBM to pre-install Legend PCs with IBM software, including a Chinese-language version of IBM's ViaVoice 98 speech-recognition software. IBM and Legend also are developing software for China's telecom, finance, and aviation sectors. "On the one hand, we compete with Legend," says D.C. Chien, general manager of distribution for IBM's Greater China Group. "But on the other hand, they are our second-largest partner in China."

ACHILLES' HEEL. Despite its standing in PCs, Legend needs foreign help to expand into corporate software and service. Last fall, for example, the company signed deals with Lotus Development Corp. and Oracle Corp. to resell groupware and database software to Chinese businesses. "They still are relatively weak in R&D and in software," says Jay Hu, managing director of the U.S. Information Technology Office, an industry association in Beijing.

For now, that is. In late November, Legend and Computer Associates International Inc. agreed to a $3.5 million software joint venture. First task: to create a software development tool to compete with Microsoft's Visual C++. The software will be available in the Chinese market this summer.

Legend isn't relying strictly on the kindness of foreigners to create a software stronghold. It recently invested $4.5 million to become the leading shareholder of Kingsoft, a Chinese software company. The two will develop Chinese word processing, dictionary, and game programs. And in November, the government announced it would send more than 400 researchers from the Chinese Academy of Sciences—a national think tank—to work at Legend's research labs. The move gives Legend much-needed brainpower in its quest to develop better software and more powerful computers.

With China's computer market the lone bright spot in a now-battered region, competition is bound to be intense. It will take more than frenetic nerds and hipsters to keep Legend on top.

By Dexter Roberts, with Joyce Barnathan, in Beijing and with Bruce Einhorn in Hong Kong

Foreign Rivals vs. the Chinese: If You Can't Beat 'em...

Humility is not a word normally associated with Compaq Computer Corp. After all, you don't get to be No. 1 in PCs by being humble. Yet when it comes to cracking the market in China, Compaq is conceding that it has a lot to learn. Having tried for five years to operate a joint venture with Beijing's Stone Group—in what is now one of the world's fastest-growing markets—the Houston-based company has little to show for its effort but an anemic 4% market share.

Now, Compaq is trying to reboot. As part of its new strategy, the company is cutting deals with personal computer manufacturers around the country—but it's making sure this time that partners will focus on improving Compaq's market share. In October, for example, Compaq signed an agreement to put its brand name on computers made by Dawn, a small PC maker in the grimy city of Shenyang in China's northeast, a part of the country better known for its hulking heavy industry than its high-tech prowess. No matter, says Tony C. Leung, Compaq's marketing director for Greater China. "We are working with someone who understands the market better than we do," he says.

CATCH-UP. Think of it as the Legend lesson. Foreign PC makers have discovered the hard way that local companies have established distribution networks, provide better service, and offer lower prices. Compaq is just one of many foreign PC makers playing catch-up in China. From IBM to Dell to Toshiba, companies that dominate other global markets are taking a second look at their strategy for the world's largest emerging PC market. Beijing's recent crackdown on smuggling has changed the landscape for foreign PC makers: They can no longer rely on producing low-priced machines in other parts of Asia that can then be brought into China by third parties. Now, PC makers are working more closely with Chinese partners and are decreasing their reliance on imports.

It wasn't supposed to happen this way. A few years ago, most analysts were convinced that the global powers would gobble up the Chinese market, with locals like Legend stuck in second-tier status—at best. Instead, the foreigners are trailing Legend (table). Moreover, the foreigners are steadily losing market share. Locals enjoyed sales growth of 65% in the first three quarters of 1998, far outpacing the meager 14% of major foreign players Compaq, Hewlett-Packard, and IBM. Indeed, the top four foreign PC makers command just 19% of the market, down from 21% the previous year. That compares with 23% for the top four local players, according to International Data Corp.

HIGH BARRIER. The grim numbers are making many foreign PC makers recognize the need for a change. Take Toshiba Corp. Like Compaq, the Japanese giant is expanding its ties with local partners. It recently announced a new joint venture with Chinese PC maker Tontru Information Industry Group Co., which is tied with Compaq for fourth place in the Chinese PC market. Meanwhile, IBM has expanded its joint venture with Great Wall Group in Shenzhen, increasing its stake to 70% from its original 51%.

Companies also are trying to break through one of China's biggest barriers: the distribution system. With China's notoriously inefficient transportation system, companies rely on a vast number of local distributors to get their computers to customers, who often turn to the distributor for help with service. Dell Computer Corp. figures that its trademark direct-sales model can help it overcome that disadvantage. It opened a manufacturing plant in the southern city of Xiamen last year and has 300 people working in China. Manufacturing locally, rather than importing machines from a factory in Malaysia, helps Dell compete better with Legend and other Chinese companies. Until Dell opened its Xiamen plant, it had to pay 17% import duty on all its computers sold in the country. Meanwhile, to overcome the idea that foreigners can't offer the kind of service that locals do, Dell also has set up toll-free hot lines to offer technical support. The company even started selling computers over the Internet in China.

For beleaguered foreign PC makers, moves like that may turn out to be the key to the China market.

By Bruce Einhorn in Hong Kong

Way Out in Front in China

Total 1998 estimated sales: 3.9 million units

	MARKET SHARE
LEGEND	13%
IBM	7
HP	6
COMPAQ	4
TONTRU	4

DATA: INTERNATIONAL DATA CORP.

MARKETER OF THE YEAR: VOLKSWAGEN OF AMERICA

Led by the runaway success of the new Beetle, carmaker again rides high

by Jean Halliday

When Clive Warrilow arrived at Volkswagen of America in January 1994 as its new chairman-CEO, "There was a lot of despair here," he recalled. "People were very broken in spirit. Everything was so buggered up."

The Bug marketer was, indeed, "buggered up." VW had just suffered its worst year, selling less than 50,000 cars in 1993, and was bleeding red ink. By comparison, VW sold more than 500,000 cars in the U.S. in 1970, its peak year. The brand's advertising and positioning were also weakened; the carmaker struggled with a tarnished identity as post-Beetle models failed to excite U.S. consumers.

Executives at German parent Volkswagen AG, also on its knees with huge losses, considered pulling out of the market. But a decision was made to stay, and Mr. Warrilow parachuted onto the scene from the same post in Canada. He admits to having his fingers crossed.

VW's German bosses "told me to turn around the brand and stop the bleeding," he said. "Then, they shook my hand. They let me do it my way."

DRAMATICALLY TURNS CORNER

In partnership with marketing honcho Steve Wilhite—who carried the odd-for-the-U.S. title of core process leader—and Liz Vanzura, director of marketing and advertising, VW turned the corner in dramatic fashion. Earlier this month, it announced sales of 201,729 cars in the U.S. through November, a 63% jump from the same period a year ago. The red-hot new Beetle, which arrived back on the market early in '98 after a 19-year absence, accounted for 48,326 of that 75,960 unit-sales jump.

For this turnaround—reincarnation, really—Volkswagen of America has been named Advertising Age's Marketer of the Year for 1998.

With the modest Mr. Warrilow in the driver's seat, VW of America has virtually returned from the dead. Perhaps most incredible is that the marketer's comeback started a few years ago without any new product—well before the new Beetle's launch.

Also, it has rebounded by selling only small cars, running counter to the U.S. truck trend. VW has overtaken

competitor Mitsubishi Motor Sales of America in unit sales through November and sold more cars in that 11-month period than Mazda North American Operations (although truck sales gave it a higher total).

"We knew by 1996 we were going to be OK," said Mr. Warrilow. "When we got the Beetle, we really knew." Looking back, "the VW brand got kind of buried," he added. "But once we were able to dust it off, the inherent goodwill came back."

BEETLEMANIA

Public and media response to the new Beetle have been overwhelmingly favorable since VW first showed it as a non-production concept car in 1994. The Bug's modern metamorphosis captures the styling of the original but introduces nifty new technology, including standard air conditioning and an optional CD player. It's the first VW to offer standard side air bags in the front seat.

The cute-as-a-bug Bug gets lots of attention, and dealers enjoy the added traffic. Houston VW dealer Ben Hulsey reported earlier this year that consumers pressed their noses against the glass of his closed showroom to glimpse the Beetle before it went on sale.

There seemed to be almost no consumers in the early '90s, the bottom of a slide that started in 1975, when Toyota Motor Sales USA displaced VW as the top-selling U.S. import.

VW had stopped selling Beetles in the U.S. in 1979, and buyers quickly became disillusioned with VW's Rabbit model. In 1982, sales dropped below 200,000 for the first time since the early '60s. In 1991, sales slipped below 100,000.

The brand's cars, designed in Germany, just didn't meet North America's needs at the time, Mr. Warrilow said.

RABBIT RUINED REP

There were other problems. The poor quality of the Rabbit ruined the brand's dependability reputation. At one point, the quality of cars from the company's Mexican plant was so abysmal VW of America refused to accept

(Cont.)

vehicles. For 18 months starting in late 1992, VW had few cars to sell; it actually paid dealers cash to stick around.

Mr. Warrilow, who said he believes in empowering staff, quickly restructured upon arrival, combining North American operations. He let go 47% of corporate staff in the U.S. and Canada, including the research and business management units. The money he saved was poured into sales, marketing and customer service.

Quality at the Mexican plant improved. Once the new cars started arriving in '94, Mr. Warrilow kicked off a leasing incentive deal to spur sales—$199 monthly with no money down. The tactic worked; VW sold 92,368 vehicles in the U.S. in 1994, more than doubling sales from the prior year, according to *Automotive News*.

AGENCY SWITCH

Despite the rise in sales, in December of that year VW dismissed ad agency Berlin Cameron Doyle, New York, a now-defunct spinoff created 16 months earlier by former VW agency DDB Needham Worldwide. A predecessor agency, Doyle Dane Bernbach, had handled VW's advertising in the U.S. since 1959, and had created the original Beetle phenomenon in the '60s—sparking the ad industry's creative revolution in the process.

In early 1995, Boston's Arnold Communications was tapped as VW's new agency.

"We really hit if off with Arnold," said Mr. Warrilow.

VW wanted to return to its simple, honest roots and focus on the German-engineered driving experience, said Mr. Wilhite, who will leave VW at yearend.

The brand campaign, pitched by Arnold during the review, broke in July 1995. It announced: "On the road of life there are passengers and there are drivers." The tag: "Drivers wanted." The ads showed the Jetta sedan and Rabbit's successor, the Golf.

The theme "isn't just about driving a car. It's about being a participant in life," Mr. Wilhite explained. The VW brand is "the antithesis of cocooning. Our owners open the windows and they're smiling, and our customers tend to not be awfully concerned about what other people think."

INNOVATIVE PROMOTIONS

With no new product in 1996, the marketer initiated innovative promotions. That spring, VW started advertising a co-promotion with mountain bike maker Trek USA. The car marketer offered a limited-edition Jetta Trek sedan, complete with a 21-speed bike and roof rack. That winter, VW marketed the Golf K2, a similar package with snowboard and ski maker K2.

The offers were continued in 1997, when VW also launched advertising supporting a national test drive offer.

For 1997, Arnold developed memorable, amusing ads for the brand. The series of commercials included "champion car breeder," which spoofed a cattle rancher who herded VWs and also the award-winning "Sunday Afternoon" commercial, with two, bored 20-something guys driving around in a Golf.

New product finally arrived in fall 1997 with the larger Passat sedan. VW recently announced Passat sales were 3,194 in November, a 116% jump from November '97.

Next year, VW will launch two dramatically redesigned models of the Golf and Jetta, its best-selling U.S. car. Last month, VW kicked off a series of teaser spots that don't show the cars. The executions, airing through yearend, are meant to create excitement for the Jetta and Golf coming in '99.

And Arnold flexed its creative muscles again. One spot shows a guy at a backyard barbecue shifting a chicken leg in the dip.

FERTILE SOIL, NOT DRY EARTH

VW's marketing tactics, combined with Arnold's creative, "laid the groundwork for the brand rejuvenation, so when the new Passat and new Beetle came, there was fertile soil—not like a seed landing on dry earth," said Philippe Defechereux, a former VW advertising executive and former staffer at DDB Needham who now writes motorsports books.

He described VW's turnaround as "truly remarkable," and called the new Beetle "the symbol of the transformation of VW."

The brand has a unique "magnificent history of being this trusted friend—more than a car, and people have such affection for it, even people that had bad experiences with the Rabbit," said John Slaven, a former VW ad executive who now runs a marketing consultancy bearing his name.

No other car brand in this country has that "magic," he said, noting that no other car marketer can boast that one of its models starred in three Walt Disney movies. (The original Beetle was featured in the series that included "The Love Bug" and "Herbie Rides Again.")

The restyled Bug, the first VW ever sold first outside Germany, created a new kind of Beetlemania deja vu; it is basically sold out for this year.

It has been "the magnet to the brand," said Mr. Warrilow, "a huge boost that has rocketed VW back to respectability."

BACK TO THE '60S

Arnold's simple, clean Beetle advertising harkens back to DDB's original '60s work. Representative of those original ads, a DDB print ad featured small photos of the car surrounded by white space, with the headline "Think small." Another carried the headline, "Lemon."

The Arnold work shows the new Beetle with such headlines as "Less flower. More power" and "0 to 60? Yes." Arnold created five TV executions for the Bug, and although separately developed for Gen Xers and older consumers, all seem to have a universal appeal. Three were aimed at baby boomers, including one that states "If you sold your soul in the '80s, here's your chance to buy it back."

"We wanted people to make their own personal emotional connection with the car," Mr. Wilhite explained.

VW's ad spending has risen with the brand's popularity. In 1993, the car marketer spent $42.7 million in measured media, according to Competitive Media Reporting. Spending rose to $70.5 million in 1994; was flat in '95 at $70.1 million. It increased to $85.2 million in 1996, and again last year, to $106.6 million. In the first half of 1998, VW spent $84.4 million on measured advertising.

BUYER ENTHUSIASM

As for the consumer: "VW buyers tend to be more enthusiastic about their cars" than other buyers in the seg- ment, said George Peterson, president of consultancy Auto Pacific.

In his company's 1998 customer satisfaction survey, VW's Jetta and Passat were tops in their respective classes, showing dramatic improvements from Auto Pacific's first survey in 1995. Passat beat out American Honda Motor Co.'s hotter-selling Accord in the survey.

VW's cars are now the most aspirational of all small cars sold, Mr. Peterson added.

Mr. Warrilow expects VW's success to continue, but cautioned against over-confidence.

"Arrogance is the beginning of the end, and this industry is full of arrogance," said Mr. Warrilow, who also leaves VW on Dec. 31, after 36 years, in a changing of the guard. His successor is Gerd Klauss, currently VP and the top executive of VW's sister brand, Audi of America. Mr. Klauss has tapped David Huyett as VW's new marketing executive.

Mr. Warrilow isn't sad over his departure. "I can leave here very happy," he said with a smile. "I built the basement and they can build the roof."

Paddling Harder at L.L. Bean

Can the catalog outfitter catch up with the times?

Terri Wise grew up with the catalog from L.L. Bean Inc. as a staple in her house. Her parents regularly called Bean to order clothes and Christmas gifts. But these days, the only tie the 24-year-old Wise has to the Maine outfitter are some wool socks and flannel pajamas. She doesn't even bother to get the catalog. "Their stuff is just so traditional," she says. "It doesn't seem very Nineties."

That's an understatement. In everything from management to fashion, privately held Bean in Freeport, Me., is a company firmly stuck in the past. Although Bean racked up double-digit revenue growth as it rode trends such as the outdoor-sports craze of the '70s and the preppy look of the '80s, it failed to follow suit in the '90s. Today, the average customer is pushing 50. The styling of its khakis, parkas, and sweaters has changed little, and the Bean Boot, the company's very first product, is still one of its best-sellers. "Bean fell into the trap of becoming enamored with its own status while the rest of the world moved forward," says Kurt Barnard, president of *Barnard's Retail Trend Report*.

Indeed, even though strong international sales early in the decade helped mask the problems at home, Bean's numbers in recent years have been little to write home about. Despite having what many see as the strongest brand franchise in the catalog industry, sales are foundering. After dropping in 1996, revenues grew a scant 2.9%, to $1.07 billion, in 1997. Analysts say the company, which doesn't divulge its earnings, will see a similar sales performance in 1998.

WIDE GAP. The slowdown appears to have shaken the outfitter out of its hibernation. Bean President Leon A. Gorman, the grandson of L.L. himself, vows he'll "dramatically change L.L. Bean as we know it." Initiatives ranging from opening stores to updating its clothing to branching into a women's fashion catalog are planned. His goal: add $300 million in sales by 2001 and triple pretax profits. Outsiders, however, wonder if Bean's efforts will be too little, too late. "It used to be that Bean was the only player on the block," says Glenda Shasho Jones, president of Shasho Jones Direct, a full-service catalog agency. Now, "they're playing catch-up to their competitors."

And it's a wide gap to close. For years, Bean, led by Gorman since 1967, has prided itself on shunning the practices of an increasingly cutthroat mail-order industry. It was the last major catalog to start charging for shipping—holding out until 1994. At headquarters, company lore revolves not around financial success or marketing coups but around tales such as the Christmas of 1996, when an incoming shipment of toboggans arrived late at the Maine warehouse. In its anything-for-the-customer tradition, Bean ordered a Federal Express Corp. 747 jet up to Freeport, filled it top-to-bottom with toboggans, and flew around the country making drop-offs at FedEx hubs. "It was a fairly hefty expense," says Lou Zambello, Bean's senior vice-president, "but we wanted the kids to have the sleds for Christmas."

But while Gorman stayed true to his principles, the competition moved in. The overall number of catalogs mailed out each year in the U.S. has jumped from 7.8 billion in 1982 to 13.9 billion currently. "Where the arrival of the Bean catalog used to be a big event," sighs Gorman, it is now "just one of a dozen or so" in the mailbox. More competition came from traditional retailers such as Gap Inc. and Recreational Equipment Inc. (REI), which have copied and updated the casual outdoorsy look once owned by Bean.

Yet even as his core business eroded, Gorman hesitated in expanding the brand. For example, he debated for years with his managers the merits of moving into children's clothing, while rivals such as GapKids sewed up the market. In retail outlets, competitors such as REI grew rapidly, while Gorman held Bean's presence to its one giant store in Freeport—because he felt catalog sales were strong enough. "We discussed the growth we might achieve by opening up more stores," says one former Bean executive. Certainly, such a move would by no means have been risk-free: Mail-order companies such as J. Crew Inc. have demonstrated that the leap from catalogs to stores is not always smooth. Still, industry watchers say he goofed. "He was a fool to pass this up," says catalog consultant William Dean.

SHAKE-UP. Nowadays, Gorman is trying to make up for lost time. Plans are to add one 100,000-square-foot superstore in the mid-Atlantic region—exact location yet unnamed—plus several smaller satellite shops nearby. If those are successful, a national rollout is on the drawing boards. Freeport Studio, a new casual-clothing catalog aimed

---

L.L. BEAN'S FRESH SPURT

OPEN STORES Will add a 100,000-sq.-ft. superstore on the East Coast, along with several smaller satellite stores.

BOOST ADVERTISING A new TV advertising campaign—Bean's biggest ever—started in November. Fresh print ads will appear next spring.

GET INTO FASHION In January, will launch Freeport Studio, a catalog aimed at boomer women, featuring dressier clothes.

(Cont.)

at boomer women—offering dresses, skirts, and jewelry—will be launched next year, as will a full fashion update of Bean's regular line. And he'll double marketing spending, to $26 million, next year to make sure shoppers know that changes are taking place.

Changes are also under way back at headquarters. Gorman is breaking up his hierarchical management in favor of business units responsible for such areas as sporting goods. Most important, he's telling managers that "the 'P' word [profit] is not a bad word."

Concedes Gorman: "Profit has not been a cultural value."

Will Gorman's fixes be enough? Despite legitimate strengths—its service and state-of-the-art warehouse continue to set the industry standard—most of Gorman's moves will simply allow Bean to catch up to rivals rather than surpass them. And skeptics warn that Bean will have a tough time coming up with fashion upgrades bold enough to distinguish itself from such competitors as J. Crew and Lands' End Inc. Wendy Liebmann, president

of consultants WSL Marketing, warns that there are now "110 people offering khakis and oxford-cloth shirts." After years of hesitation, Gorman is fighting a rear-guard action to reclaim Bean's relevance. This time, he won't have decades to figure it out.

By William C. Symonds in Freeport, Me.

Brand Builders: Dunkin' Etcetera

Not long ago, one might have likened Dunkin' Donuts to an early morning coffee hound before the first cup of Joe, barely aware of the world. Starbucks and its clones loomed on the horizon. Bagel chains were popping up like dandelions on a spring day. Even c-store chains like 7-Eleven and Wawa were radically improving their own foodservice programs. A rapidly changing landscape threatened to sap the market relevance of the 50-year-old brand.

"Our competitive set changed dramatically by the early 1990s," said Eddie Binder, vp-marketing. "Throughout the '60s, '70s, '80s and even into the early '90s we were positioned as 'America's finest donut shop.' Everything we did pivoted off of donuts because we were in the business of making donuts. We had a real manufacturer's outlook."

Now Dunkin' has awakened to smell the coffee and serve a new consumer quick to pay anywhere from $2.50 to $4 for a coffee. The Randolph, Mass.-based chain set about repositioning itself as "America's finest coffee and baked goods retailer," in effect, shifting emphasis "from the back of the house to the front of the house," as Binder put it, creating a more inviting retail environment that tenders contemporary products competitive to its proliferating competition.

Binder joined the system in 1995, when, in the face of an influx of flavored coffees into the market, Dunkin' still offered two basic choices—caf and decaf. Soon, Dunkin' launched the first flavors in what is now a java menu of 15 different, rotating varieties such as French Vanilla, Irish Cream and Swiss Almond. To put a more premium face on the longtime Dunkin' staple, Binder moved prepacked coffee beans up front on a merchandising rack. Next he played a quick game of catch-up with its hugely successful Coffee Coolattas, rich, frozen coffee drinks. The line has turned a once slow sales window between May and August to its biggest profit window, and followed in its second season this past summer with Fruit Coolattas. It is suspected the line will produce with a tea-extension this summer.

More significantly, Dunkin' almost singlehandedly took the steam out of the growth of the upstart bagel chains by rolling out its own bagel in 1997. In less than a year, facing the boutique charm of the Einstein's, Bruegger's and other bagelries popping up across the country, Dunkin' abruptly was selling the classic New York nosh in 3,700 stores.

To tie its offerings together, Binder added a centerpiece menu board that spotlighted a handful of no-brainer bundles, such as: coffee and bagel; coffee and muffin; and, coffee and donut. The move has driven check averages up about 30%, to just under $3, in the last two years, while per-unit sales have gone up 20% to $600,000. "We had to go all the way back to the beginning and look at what the concept was founded on, and Bill Rosenberg founded Dunkin' Donuts on coffee," Binder said. "The name of the game in the restaurant business is high volume, high profit, and nothing compares to coffee. If we can get customers on the coffee part of it and get them on a baked good, then the profitability of the franchise owner increases dramatically."

> ## "The name of the game is high volume, high profit, and nothing compares to coffee."
> ### —Eddie Binder, Dunkin' Donuts

The refocusing claimed the job of longtime ad spokesman, Fred the Baker, under previous agency Messner Vetere Berger McNamee Schmetterer/Euro RSCG, N.Y. "Fred personified the back of the house," Binder said. In March 1998, Dunkin' also switched agencies, to Hill, Holliday, Connors, Cosmopulos of Boston.

Unlike other restaurant operations in which the marketer usually faces the same risks and operational issues as franchisees, Dunkin'—a subsidiary of British-based Allied Domecq—is strictly a franchisor and marketing organization. Before going to test with a new product, such as the outcoming Omwich omelette sandwich (*Brandweek, Dec. 7*), Binder will poll franchisees and talk with them about new product trends to see if the thinking in Randolph is on track.

"One of the best things that has come out of Randolph lately is open-mindedness," said Bill Galatis, a 47-unit franchisee and member of the National Leadership Council, co-chair of Market Leadership Council in New England and member of the Boston Advertising Committee. "We have established numerous leadership councils that are good conduits of information for what is going on

(Cont.)

with customers. Eddie is really our champion in Randolph and he walks the walk and talks the talk when it comes to listening to franchisees."

Binder's 60-person team divvies up the Dunkin' menu by category manager, a packaged goods approach he became familiar with during his agency days at DMB&B and Young & Rubicam, both N.Y., when he worked on Procter & Gamble and General Foods. The structure makes the marketing department equally as accountable for driving traffic and profits, and for communicating effectively to franchisees through the Dunkin' intranet, where local and national program specs can be accessed.

"Even in marketing, we had to talk about how to present this to the customers and to reorient the operating system to allow franchisees to make more product, more easily, more consistent and more profitable," Binder said. "If someone wants to run a bagel promotion they need to show how profitable it is going to be for the franchisees."

The approach helped the chain enjoy same store sales increases of 9.7% for fiscal 1997 and 10% for fiscal 1998.

"None of this could be overthought," he said. "We needed it to be dead simple. It is important to know exactly who you are."

Love My Brand

Marketers today are trying to foster true relationships between their brands and their customers. At the center of the process are direct marketers that have left "junk mail" behind on the scrap heap. *By Daniel Hill*

Brian Evans is a 43-year-old investment counselor, living in Worcester, Mass., and he commutes to his office in Boston every day. In the car, when he isn't on his hands-free cell phone, he is listening to opera CDs, not the radio. At home, he says, he spends maybe three hours a week watching TV, and when he does, he is usually multi-tasking, making out bills or leafing through catalogs or a business magazine. The rest of the time is spent "doing stuff" with his wife, Amanda, and their 5-year-old daughter, Anna. He also spends about six hours a week online, doing research, checking email and general surfing.

"I think I must be hard to reach for companies," says Evans. "I get so much stuff via the mail and email that has nothing to do with my needs or wants that my reflex has become to shut *all* of it out."

Evans, with his six-figure salary and family, and others like him, are becoming maddeningly difficult to reach for marketers in all categories. Just reaching them, and getting the Brians and Amandas of the world to open a piece of direct (i.e., junk) mail used to be the goal. Today, the objective for companies like Radio Shack, Saturn, Sears and Gateway is not merely to sell, but to have a "relationship" with their customers. And that puts direct marketing agencies at the center of the storm, trying to figure out not only how to tickle a customer into a date, but how to keep them interested for the long haul. It's no longer, "What do you have to sell me?" but "What can you do for me?"

"It's not like 25 years ago when you bought a spot on *Bonanza* and hoped people went to the showroom the next day," says Jim Julow, Chrysler's executive director of corporate marketing.

The drift toward relationship marketing (RM) is in the numbers. Direct advertising in the U.S. grew by an annual rate of 8% (versus 7% for total advertising growth) from 1992-97, reaching $153 billion last year. That was 57.8% of total U.S. advertising expenditures. From 1997-2002, the Direct Marketing Association projects, expenditures for direct marketing will increase by 6.9% annually. The DMA also estimates U.S. sales attributable to direct to be $1.2 trillion in 1997. And what it refers to as direct marketing employment reached almost 23 million workers in 1997.

Not all Americans, though, welcome these figures as good news. Don Peppers, president of marketing 1:1 in Stamford, Conn., complains that, "I get 10 catalogs a day, and I've never bought anything from any of them." Meanwhile, Julie Highsmith, a New York designer, gets numerous, lavish stock photography catalogs (some a couple of times a year) that she pegs at costing five or six bucks a pop. They've never gotten a dime from her. That's an extremely wasteful use of wood pulp. But no one ever got fired for doing what they've done in the past.

As more consumers resist traffic jams down at the mall, and more surfers yawn at their televisions or forsake it for games or the Net, big money is available to companies who develop (and more crucially, manage) cost-effective databases that indicate who to contact and, rather than why, *how* they should be contacted and when.

Pamela Larrick, executive vp of McCann Relationship Marketing Worldwide, cites numbers from Strategic Marketing Institute, Cambridge, Mass. showing a high commitment to RM yields a return on sales 12 times greater than low RM, and an ROI that's six times greater.

That may be, because, as Wendy Riches, North American chairman of OgilvyOne Worldwide, notes, it has traditionally cost six times as much to acquire a customer as to retain one. The trick, says Peppers, is to con-

> **"The frequent flyer model is one that tries to achieve economic loyalty," says agency boss Bob Lieber. "Relationship marketing strives for emotional loyalty. If you got 'em first with coupons, you'll probably have to continue with coupons."**

sider customers' lifetime value and to start a cost-efficient dialogue, so that, based on past purchases, a book store cashier, for example, can steer someone to the new Elmore Leonard novel. That may sound creepy to some—that a stranger would know what authors they like—but companies right now are struggling with this issue of where the line between the "creeps" and helpful customer handling is.

(Cont.)

"It can't be a faux intimacy," says Peppers, who quips that he is still looking for a dry cleaner he can call his own, one that will store the little swatches of spare material for his suits. Just playing back things they've said, or repeating their name, he says, is a poor way to begin. That was the strategy of Blockbuster Video last year, which, at some of its stores, instructed store workers to say, "hello" to everyone who came in the store, and then address each customer by name when they came up on the computer, as in, "Mr. Hill, that will be $3.99. Enjoy the movie Mr. Hill. That's not due back until Monday night Mr. Hill."

A few companies at the forefront of RM are Dell Computers and Radio Shack. Scott Nelson, research director at the GartnerGroup, says from the very start Dell used surveys and ordering contacts and re-contacts to go beyond capturing names and addresses to asking why customers chose particular configurations, what other systems they looked at and what they might have paid elsewhere. Dell concentrates on what its customers look like over time, so it can upgrade them to multiple usage.

Since over 99% of customer households have purchased something at Radio Shack over the last three years, "We don't need new customers, we need to increase the frequency of our existing customers," says David Edmondson, senior vp of marketing & advertising at Radio Shack. That's understandable when you have 119 million customers in 89 million households. The company, the butt of jokes on occasion for its compulsive quizzing of customers, captures copious data on over 80% of its in-store transactions. It started its current database around three years ago, but using archival data, took only 30 months to achieve historical data on five years of behavior. Radio Shack, says Dennis Duffy, president of

MINING THE DATABASE

Perhaps you've seen the Saturn TV commercial that humorously touts its database, to the point of showing a customer profile on a computer screen: a guy who drives from dealer to dealer with various fabricated complaints just to nab the free jelly donuts.

Now part of the zeitgeist, databases have been key to relationship marketing since the outset. Seemingly dozens of vendors are pushing new products, all with their own bells and whistles. Marketing database software sales in 1997 were just over $1 billion, up from $100 million in 1993. David Raab of Raab Associates outside Philadelphia notes an explosion of software offerings, perhaps a dozen in the past year alone. He published a guidebook in April, and laments that it was obsolete by August.

Vernon Tirey, president of DiaLogos, Boston, cites the decidedly biased claim of the Data Warehousing Institute that a successful data operation can increase a company's customer base by well over 200% within two years of implementation. Less that sound too fantastical, the equally-biased Tirey thinks less than 30% of all data warehousing efforts are successful. Tirey figures 10–15% of the data collectd usually answers 80% of the questions. He recommends companies concentrate more on product attribute information that's easy to get, but often ignored.

The next big thing, says Scott Nelson, research director at the GartnerGroup, is a third-generational, enterprise-wide model that captures on a single platform information from all points of customer contact, be it from the Internet, call centers, blow-back cards or store questionnaires. Say, for instance, someone calls in complaining your shampoo has left his hair oily. Rather than just send him a free sample, the operator can use his age, profile information and past dealings with the company to craft a specific response.

Ideally, says Nelson, such systems will allow companies to focus on issues broader than direct marketing, i.e., "channel management," where—no matter the time or place of contact—the customer receives a consistent message and response. Only about 2% or 3% of all companies are even thinking this way, according to Nelson, and less are up and running. He maintains there's not one off-the-shelf, third-generational system available. Companies pursuing them turn to systems integrators such as DiaLogos, Naviant in Philadelphia or Tessera in Boston. Most companies won't tackle them until they've solved their year 2000 problem and dealt with any snafus associated with the European Monetary Union's common currency, he concludes. Raab feels some computer and financial service firms are taking baby steps in this direction, but no one's really doing it.

The cost? Raab figures it takes $1 million for any sizable firm to buy, modify and get these latest programs flying. And that's if you don't need front-end modifications to your call center, which can cost $5,000 a seat. Tirey puts the cost at up to $3 million. Nelson prices it differently: a typical marketing database costs around 5% of the overall marketing budget; an aggressive program clocks in at 7–10%, he says.   —D.H.

(Cont.)

Cadmus Communications, N.Y., is better positioned than virtually any other company in the category for direct relationship marketing. "What Radio Shack has been doing for years, you couldn't get anyone to start that today," Duffy said.

Consumers exercise tremendous control over how they want to shop, says Chrysler's Julow. They shop at their own speed, at the location they want, in an information-friendly manner, with the right amount of information, he says. Along with rivals Ford and General Motors, Chrysler is building a massive database with new "black-box" artificial intelligence to make the carmaker less reliant on mass media advertising and to make its direct efforts more productive. Right now, most of the direct efforts done by each carmaker are little more than mailed ads, or perhaps an invitation to a special event. But the company has no way of knowing where a recipient is in the car buying cycle or what he or she has responded to in the past. They may be inviting someone to a regatta who is only one month into a 36-month lease on a competing make. Julow has been managing his data internally for around three years. "When it crashes in a year, we'll know we have too many fields," he says. As to his database, he figures he's still perhaps a year-and-a-half from knowing "how high up is up."

Many marketing executives are chary with the details of exactly what RM has achieved. But you get a few gleanings. Julow says RM has enabled Chrysler to raise response rates from 1% or 2% "up into the teens," in some cases, for a corporate or dealer initiative. Lifecycle marketing is in full force in autos, he says, whether it employs a free oil change or free wiper blades for folks with older cars. Three years ago, a customer might have gotten a card from one dealer one week, another from a second dealer the following week and then a catalog from Chrysler. Now the company is hooked up by satellite to all its dealers to prevent this sort of annoying overkill.

Another big-ticket company that is well underway with RM is Mercedes-Benz of North America, which has had a program up and running for 18 months. One initiative was an old-fashioned multi-vehicle launch event, involving food and wine and a dramatic undraping of new models. In Los Angeles, they sent out 100,000 invitations to customers and prospects, and they had to close the highway down. In another instance, Mercedes and its dealers invited customers to the symphony, with 2% of the invitees attending. Last fall, Mercedes sent out one million invitations for customers and prospects to attend one of an array of events at dealerships. Called the "Fall in Love" event, it was supported by a national ad with the same theme. And, two years before the introduction of the

> "Relationship marketing allows companies to minimize the spiral of price cutting, an inevitable war of attrition," says OgilvyOne's Wendy Riches.

M-class sport utility vehicle last fall, Mercedes began polling luxury car owners on what they were looking for in a SUV. The company achieved its goal of a dialogue with 100,000 potential customers and sales of 25,000. It's commitment to RM is in the company's numbers. In 1996, Mercedes' RM budget, which included creative, production, lists, postage, etc., was 8.2% of Mercedes marketing budget for the year. With 800,000 pieces mailed, the response rate (leads) was 225% over 1995's controls and the conversion rate (sales) was 65% better than the controls. Incremental sales were between 30% to 40% higher than those who would have bought anyway.

One tool that companies are using today to make their RM programs more efficient is more powerful and often cheaper computerized capabilities to segment their prospects and tailor their message.

Bob Lieber, chairman and CEO of Lieber Levett Koenig Farese Babcock, New York, describes four criteria for "actionable" segmentation. Consumer segments have to be: "Groupable" (sharing "like attitudinal, behavioral, and/or demographic characteristics"); "Influenceable" (their behavior changeable by communications); "Reachable" (targeted by existing media); and "Measurable" (as to the communication's impact).

One of Lieber's clients, *Readers Digest,* will implement a value-added, segmentation strategy starting this spring. Subscribers will have identified particular health issues of interest, basically "inviting us into their home," says Lieber. Their copy of the magazine will include an advertorial section with news regarding specific maladies.

Jim Ramaley, vp of circulation systems at Ziff-Davis Publishing, which puts out *PC Week* and *Computer Life,* among others, segments his subscribers by whether they paid a discounted or full price initially, whether they subscribe to any related Z-D publications or attend trade shows, hit the company's Web site or avail themselves of any of its online "courses." This enables him to identify different price breaks and change the offer as time elapses. Most importantly, it enables him to drop poor prospects sooner. To similarly keep an eye on her ROI, Denise Tarantino, vice president of marketing for Repp's Big & Tall Stores (a catalog and retail outfit with 200 units

(Cont.)

nationwide), slices her customers into 12 segments, according to response rates, average sales and the like. Some get 6-to-8 pieces a year, some 3-to-5, some only 1-to-3. Repp tries to steer low-volume catalog shoppers into a nearby store they may not even know existed. And infrequent store shoppers might be offered an extra incentive, such as 15% off, for a particular weekend. Repp also has a Web site that gathers data, and its enrollees get short emails from time to time advising them of sales and discounts.

Tarantino gets a 6% response rate to her mailings, far superior to what she describes as a typical, huge non-RM mailing of maybe 750,000 pieces that might get a 0.5% response rate. She also boasts a whopping 30-40% response rate for VIP special events that feature appointments and wardrobe consultations and steep discounts of 20% off a $200 purchase and 30% off $300 tallies.

Some companies mine their transactional data better than others. Barry Blau, chairman of Barry Blau & Partners in Fairfield, Conn., says that though Blockbuster Video Stores has huge amounts of transactional data, "They sent a promotion on a new Nintendo game to every customer they had, though 10% of kids buy 90% of the computer games."

Likewise, some financial services are still sold by simple zip code data. Along with affluence and number of adults in a household, long-distance phone companies look at things like "foreign" surnames or recent immigration to indicate likely high-volume prospects. By not going beyond traditional geodemographic data, says Blau, marketers don't capture what stage people are at in their lives and how that affects their income and spending.

As companies establish relationships, they're able to retreat somewhat from the rewards, coupons and discounts that erode margins. Companies like hotels, airlines and telecommunication firms with high fixed and low variable costs can earn big profits from incremental increases in business. The frequent flier model works for airlines, and they go to great lengths not to fly with empty seats. But it's a model that tries to achieve "economic loyalty," says Lieber. But RM strives for emotional loyalty; getting a customer for life. "If you got 'em first with coupons, you'll probably have to continue with coupons," he says. And even the airlines are now offering some upgraded seats and special boarding lines rather than freebies. Riches at OgilvyOne asserts that RM "allows companies to minimize the spiral of price cutting, an inevitable war of attrition."

Cadmus' Duffy declares, "AT&T threw money away with its True Rewards program. Points and prizes are a fad whose time has passed." He also figures people buy Eddie Bauer for the quality, not some 2% reward program, and that the preferred shopper program launched by Waldenbooks and copied by B. Dalton "is just a margin erosion."

But how do you manage RM, and what the heck does it all cost? It has to emanate from the CEO, say the experts. "You can't have a random act of marketing," says Duffy. "A lot of companies want a quick behavior hit, like you get with a promotion or a sales drive. But that's not RM."

Another reason it has to come from the top is the dedicated personnel to analyze all this data don't come cheap. "You can't just pile this onto the circulation managers who are already up to their necks in alligators," says Ziff-Davis's Ramaley. He sees a particular challenge in asking the right questions, since even with the most sophisticated data mining, the answers don't leap off the page. He'll have hired between 5 to 10 new people by the time he's through.

Finding Target Market Opportunities

After Years of Trial and Error, A Pickle Slice That Stays Put

BY VANESSA O'CONNELL
Staff Reporter of THE WALL STREET JOURNAL

On a recent afternoon, Frank Meczkowski stood in a vast vegetable patch on the Mid-Atlantic coast. Around him were rows of tomatoes and eggplant, but his attention was fixed on cucumber vines — seven acres of them. "Not as green as we would like," he said while inspecting a foot-long, pale-yellow cucumber, "but we can work on that."

Mr. Meczkowski knows his cucumbers. He is a product-development manager for Vlasic Foods International Inc., the biggest player in the $850 million pickle business

> *Hurricanes and insects wreaked havoc in the cucumber patch, impeding the quest for a blockbuster pickle.*

and today's talk of the industry. Yesterday, Vlasic introduced the Hamburger Stacker, a three-inch-in-diameter pickle slice, or "chip," large enough to cover the entire surface of a hamburger. Sliced horizontally from a new breed of cucumber 10 times larger than the standard 3A pickling cucumber, the pickled chips are stacked a dozen high in jars and will appear on supermarket shelves before the end of the year.

These are palpably exciting times at Vlasic, which was a unit of Campbell Soup Co. until it was spun off this past March, and culminate years of effort. Vlasic scoured the globe for rare seeds and spent two years crossbreeding them; and a close look at the process shows the lengths to which food companies must go to spark demand in mature product categories.

Pickle consumption has been falling about 2% a year since the 1980s; but following successful new-product introductions, pickle sales generally get a prolonged boost. Vlasic began its quest for just such a blockbuster pickle in the mid-1990s after Mr. Meczkowski discovered in focus groups that people hate it when pickles slip out of their hamburgers and sandwiches.

By slicing average 3A or 3B pickles horizontally into strips, Mr. Meczkowski created a new pickle concept: long pickle planks intended to be placed between slices of bread. Dubbed Sandwich Stackers, the new pickles racked up more than $60 million in sales in their first year and sparked a rash of copycats

with names such as Pickle Planks, Sandwich Slices, Pickle Slabs and Sandwich Builders.

Mr. Meczkowski knew his pickle slices weren't perfect. Sliced lengthwise, many of the strips consist mainly of the cucumber's seed cavity, the part that gets soft during the pickling process. Aiming to include more of the surrounding flesh — the crunchy part — Mr. Meczkowski set out to create a giant pickle chip, an effort that came to be called Project Frisbee.

At the time, most farmers grew only the standard varieties of cucumbers, no longer than six inches. Bigger pickles tend to get too soft, turning to mush during the pickling, as Mr. Meczkowski discovered. In search of a new cucumber variety, he spent four months poring over catalogs of big seed companies around the world and boning up on the latest research on experimental cucumber varieties.

By 1995, he had found seeds for what seemed the perfect breed of cucumber at a small seed company in the Netherlands. The variety, which Vlasic is calling 5B, is used today in Europe to make relish and melon-ball-like cucumber snacks. Vlasic says the supplier, which it declines to name, had the seeds on hand in case a buyer was looking to adapt some of its traits, such as its whitish yellow color, in crossbreeding with other cucumbers.

More than 15 inches long, with an extra-small seed cavity, the fruit would be large enough to produce three-inch chips and solid enough to withstand pickling. Vlasic bought the supplier's entire inventory of 5B-10 seeds-and researchers planted them at an Ohio greenhouse and lab.

The result was disappointing. Only a few of the plants bore fruit, most of them unsuitable for pickling. Mr. Meczkowski recalls that one of the plants was shaped like a snake. Only one cucumber was straight and large enough for Vlasic's specs.

In 1996, Vlasic's seed supplier began mixing the 5Bs with seeds of a smaller cucumber variety and collecting the seeds of the resulting fruit. Vlasic then sprinkled these seeds across 10 acres in secret sites on the Mid-Atlantic coast and other parts of the world in hopes of producing prototypes of the pickle chips. But failures of biblical proportions ensued. All 10 acres planted were damaged by hurricanes and insects, or produced barren fruit.

By 1997, things began looking up — momentarily. Vlasic had 10 bushels of the new cucum-

bers, enough for the project to get under way. Just as Vlasic was creating its first giant pickle chips, rival Claussen Pickle Co. of Woodstock, Ill., rolled out Super Slices for Burgers, large pickles cut diagonally into oval-shaped slices. "Consumers were having a problem keeping the pickles on the burger," says Claire Regan, a spokeswoman for Claussen, part of Philip Morris Cos.' Kraft Foods Inc.

These two companies have battled over crunch bragging rights for some time. According to Vlasic, the diagonal cut results in a large amount of the seed cavity exposed, and thus a softer pickle. But Ms. Regan responds that Claussen pickles "have that cold, fresh, crisp taste" because they have never been cooked, only refrigerated. "You know when you cook a vegetable what happens to it," she adds.

By this past summer, Vlasic had 2,000 bushels of cucumbers, enough to begin manufacturing the giant chips, but there were still some problems. The new cuke is more susceptible to diseases than older varieties because it hasn't yet had any disease-resisting traits added. The Mid-Atlantic patch, for instance, suffered plant diseases from angular leaf spot to powdery mildew. And the new species bears less fruit than other varieties. Each acre of the new cucumber variety yields a few hundred bushels of fruit, compared with the 500 bushels typical with standard pickling cucumbers.

Harvesting them isn't easy. Because they are so heavy, with a lot of water weight, they are also very fragile. A group of hired farm workers must pick them by hand and then gently transfer them into the bins on a truck for delivery to a plant in Millsboro, Del., where employees are waiting to soak them in vinegar and take them to supermarket shelves.

In the next few weeks, Vlasic executives at the company's Cherry Hill, N.J., headquarters will begin to see if they have a hit on their hands. Robert F. Bernstock, Vlasic's chief executive officer, says he is counting on the jumbo pickle chips to deliver at least $20 million in sales.

Vlasic's new supersize pickles—3 inches in diameter—are packed 12 to a jar

If It Looks Like a Truck but Rides Like a Car, It's Hot

By Joseph B. White
Staff Reporter of The Wall Street Journal

The RX 300 — a splashy new luxury sport-utility vehicle from Lexus — has a front end that says dirt roads and a back end that says carpools.

Call it a hybrid, a crossover vehicle or an "urban SUV," as Jim Press, the Lexus division general manager, does. Or label it a "mall cruiser," as **General Motors** Corp. Chairman John F. Smith Jr. does.

Whatever the name, most industry executives at the big Detroit Auto Show this week agree the RX 300 and other vehicles that look like sport-utility vehicles but ride and maneuver like cars are the industry's next big thing.

As sales of rugged looking sport-utility vehicles have surged in recent years, auto makers have touted the off-road stamina of their four-wheel-drive trucks. All the while, car makers knew that few customers actually took their Jeeps, Ford Explorers or Chevrolet Suburbans off pavement and that most didn't like the kidney-jarring rides and stiff handling that came with the macho looks and big cargo spaces.

Now, auto makers are rushing to bring out off-road vehicles aimed squarely at the on-road-only driver. If that sounds confusing, it only points up the often contradictory motivations of the well-heeled consumers who have made these products a mainstay for auto makers in the U.S.

"The key issues for people leaving SUVs are ride and price, in that order," says Coopers Lybrand partner William R. Pochiluk. By the year 2000, he estimates, sales of car/truck hybrids like the RX 300 could grow to 500,000 to one million vehicles a year. Americans bought more than 2.3 million sport-utility vehicles last year, most of them midsize and large models.

If the Jeep Cherokee and the Ford Explorer launched the sport-utility craze in the early 1990s, industry executives say vehicles like the RX 300 will define the next generation, particularly in the luxury end of the market where the big profits are.

The RX 300, built in Japan, is scheduled to go on sale in March, with a base price of $31,500 for a front-wheel-drive-only model. A well-equipped four-wheel-drive model will sell for about $35,305, Lexus officials say. That is roughly $2,000 less than the asking price for a comparable Mercedes M-Class sport utility. Lexus officials clearly see the hot-selling Mercedes as their main foe, and at least initially they are keeping sales goals for the RX 300 modest, forecasting annual sales of 20,000 vehicles, well below expectations for the Mercedes.

When Toyota engineers began developing the RX 300 hybrid three to four years ago, Toyota's marketing people in the U.S. and Japan balked, says Akihiro Wada, Toyota's executive vice president of research and development. But he insisted that "much more riding comfort was needed" than Toyota's truck-based sport utilities provided, he says, and about two years ago, marketing officials began to agree.

Rivals agree as well. "It's definitely a market that interests us," says Thomas Elliott, executive vice president of **Honda Motor** Co.'s U.S. sales operations, as he sizes up an RX 300 at Lexus's auto show display.

While they wouldn't disclose specifics, executives at **Chrysler** Corp. — owner of the granddaddy of sport-utility vehicle brands, Jeep — made it clear during auto-show interviews that they have vehicles similar to the RX 300 in the works. Similar hints came from GM executives.

If concern about global warming translates into tougher government restrictions on emissions, the pressure to move away from less efficient truck designs will become even greater. By using car chassis and engines, auto makers can design lighter, more fuel efficient vehicles.

The RX 300 is expected to average 19 miles per gallon of gasoline in the city and 22 miles per gallon on the highway with a three-liter V-6 engine. That compares with 15 miles per gallon in the city and 20 miles on the highway for a V-6 powered, four-wheel-drive Jeep Grand Cherokee.

"The crossover market is the SUV market of the future," says John Smith, the GM vice president in charge of the Cadillac luxury division. Mr. Smith makes no secret of his desire to get a vehicle like the RX 300 in Cadillac's lineup. "Relative to Lexus, we'll be playing catchup," he concedes.

The Lexus RX 300 isn't the first four-wheel-drive hybrid to spring from a car chassis. **Subaru of America** Inc. in July introduced a hybrid called the Forester, based on a small-car design, as a companion to the Outback version of its Legacy station wagon, introduced in 1996. Honda's CR-V and Toyota's RAV4 small sport-utility vehicles also ride on small-car underpinnings.

But Lexus officials argue, and some rivals agree, that the RX 300 breaks new ground with its combination of generous size and luxury amenities.

Mercedes-Benz and **Ford Motor** Co., meanwhile, are scoring hits by engineering four-wheel-drive trucks that offer substantially smoother rides than previous models. Ford's Lincoln Navigator was outfitted with a suspension that borrowed heavily from the plush Lincoln Town car limousine. Mercedes' hot-selling ML 320 also offers a more car-like ride than older models. But both vehicles are still trucks at heart — heavy and greedy for gas.

Other car makers are trying to inject some off-road vehicle macho into their cars and minivans. Sweden's **Volvo** AB, for example, last fall launched a new line of all-wheel-drive station wagons, including one called the V70 XC Cross Country. With a price that starts at about $38,000, the Cross Country sits an inch higher off the road than a regular V70 wagon and puts the driver two inches higher, thus delivering some of the sense of command that attracts many people to sport-utility trucks.

Volvo stresses that the V70 also offers a full array of safety features, such as airbags mounted in the front seats designed to protect

Lots of room for packages for a day off road at the mall

Macho grille and hood design says truck

Four-wheel-drive system is for snowy pavement. No heavy-duty mode for off-road use

Floor is 7.7 inches off the ground —lower than rival sport-utility trucks for easier entry

Suspension based on front-wheel-drive car design

passengers in a side-on crash. Many trucks don't yet offer such amenities.

It probably won't be long before consumers have many more car/truck crossovers to choose from, if the direction of the cars on display at the Auto Show is any indication. Ford has two hybrid prototypes on display, one a small off-road wagon called the Alpe built on the chassis of a subcompact Escort.

And Chrysler raised eyebrows with a prototype model called the "Jeepster" that merged its signature Jeep grill and fat off-road tires with a low-slung sports-car body. Tom Gale, Chrysler executive vice president for product strategy, won't say when Chrysler will field a hybrid vehicle for real. But he makes it clear the question is when, not if. Hybrids are "a natural progression," he says.

Discounter Rebounds By Targeting a Clientele Below the Wal-Mart Set

It Cut Costs and Stocked Up To Sell to Working People, Old People and Big People

Heavy on the Textured Acrylic

BY WILLIAM M. BULKELEY

Staff Reporter of THE WALL STREET JOURNAL

ROCKY HILL, Conn. — To Joseph R. Ettore, chief executive of Ames Department Stores Inc., the fate of a rival discount retailer in the Northeast was sealed as soon as it hired a new CEO who started stocking classier goods. "I knew he didn't understand his customers," Mr. Ettore says.

It isn't a mistake that he makes. Ames offers $8.99 acrylic sweaters and $5.99 sweatpants, along with lots of "husky" offerings for kids and few if any petite sizes for model-thin women. It makes stores handy for elderly people to shop in. And while the rival chain has fallen on hard times, Ames is ringing up some of the best sales gains in retailing.

Mr. Ettore has engineered a striking comeback at Ames. After 37 years in the business, he has seen plenty of regional discount chains fall before the advance of Wal-Mart Stores Inc. There were Jamesway and Stuart's, both of which he once ran, and Rich's and The Fair. And there was Zayre's, which Ames disastrously acquired in 1988, leading to its own bankruptcy filing two years later.

Mr. Ettore, who is 59 years old, says the big mistake most made was losing touch with their clientele. "I look for underserved customers," he says. Most of his peers, he adds, "are looking to push up" in prices or in prestige. "We haven't done that."

Of course, giants like Wal-Mart also appeal to customers of modest means. But Mr. Ettore aims a little lower. Although Wal-Mart won't discuss such numbers, Mr. Ettore reckons its core customer base is made up of households with $30,000 to $45,000 in annual income. The Ames chief aims at a cohort between $25,000 and $35,000 — waitresses,

clerks, laborers, retirees. He works overtime to divine their tastes and buying habits.

Bargain Sneakers

Let Gap Inc. stock a deep selection of tops in a few styles and muted colors; Ames goes in for a wide variety and distinctive patterns. Let other discount chains move up to huge, 100,000-square-foot stores; Ames makes a point of staying down around 60,000 feet. Seniors get tired in giant stores, he figures, and working mothers want to be able to get in and out quickly.

"I come here all the time," says Veronica Wilmoth, a 48-year-old liquor-store bookkeeper and mother, as she leaves an Ames in a Medford, Mass., strip mall. "The prices are great." In her bag tonight: $12.99 sneakers, a small picture frame and imitation ivy garlands that are on special at two for $5. Total bill: $26.

Ames's Christmas-season sales were up 10%, exceeding other discounters, including even Wal-Mart, which had a 9.4% gain. Ames's sales are about to get bigger, because last week, Ames completed the takeover of Hills Stores Inc. of Canton, Mass. After digesting Hills, Ames will have $4 billion in sales and 450 stores in 15 states, from Indiana to Maine and south to Virginia. The price of Ames stock is up more than 100% in a year and more than 700% since Mr. Ettore arrived in 1994.

Its recent growth has some observers believing that the epitaph for regional discounters was written prematurely. Ames is "not going to out-Wal-Mart Wal-Mart," says Thomas A. Ferguson, president of Newell Cos., a Freeport, Ill., maker of plastic goods and cookware that sells to both retailers. But Ames is viable, he adds — "large enough to be important" and "small enough to be nimble."

Worsted Case

Founded in Southbridge, Mass., in 1958 in an old worsted mill, Ames adopted its name to save money on signs. Thriving in the early 1980s, it took a shot at the big time, acquiring the Zayre's chain, then in distress but twice Ames's size. Many of the stores in urban areas were losing more than Ames had realized, and their 100,000-square-foot formats proved daunting.

"It was probably the worst deal ever made in terms of synergies," Mr. Ettore says. In 1990, Ames filed for bankruptcy-court protection. By the time it emerged in 1992, its sales were down to $2 billion from $5 billion, more than half its stores were closed, and 37,000 of 60,000 employees were gone. Two years later, it was still floundering, so with the stock price at $3, the Ames board recruited Mr. Ettore from smaller rival Jamesway Corp., where he was leading another bankruptcy reorganization.

When he arrived at Ames's central-Connecticut headquarters, he found promotion costs that were higher than the industry's average; high levels of inventory "shrinkage," which usually means a shoplifting problem;

and a me-too merchandising strategy that, like Wal-Mart's, stressed "everyday low prices."

He closed 28 unprofitable stores and cut the 1,000-person headquarters staff to 850. Eventually, he bought new point-of-sale and security systems to curb shrinkage.

He also changed the marketing tack to what he calls a high-low strategy — deeper discounts on selected goods offered through weekly circulars, and higher prices on the other items. He also sought to expand unadvertised apparel specials so that customers could encounter surprise bargains. To acquire such goods, he hired merchandiser Denis Lemire from Marshall's, a subsidiary of TJX Cos. in Framingham, Mass., that specializes in finding brand-name close-outs and overruns.

Last May, when order postponements by retailer Toys 'R' Us Inc. suddenly stuck toy makers with a glut, Ames offered to take its normal Christmas order then rather than in August if it could get extended payment terms and steep discounts. Industry officials say Mattel Inc. and Hasbro Inc. agreed, although they won't comment. Ames rented a warehouse to hold the toys.

Joseph R. Ettore

Mr. Ettore told Mr. Lemire to replace most apparel buyers and start reshaping the inventory. The new buyers stopped stocking petite sizes. "The glamour thing is to go after the thin customer," Mr. Lemire says. "But there's a correlation between lower income and heavier weight. In our stores, you see, we have a big customer." A quarter of the women's clothes Ames sells, or about double the industry average, are size 12 or larger.

In 1997, Ames added a department for heavyset men called "One for the Big Guy." Now it is ordering "chubby" and "husky" sizes for overweight girls and boys. "A lot of the time," Mr. Lemire explains, customers' "children are big kids."

(Cont.)

Just in Time

Merchandising to lower-income people has other quirks. While the more affluent buy seasonal items long before they need them, "our customers will buy, literally, right after the need," Mr. Lemire says. Winter coats at Ames don't sell until the weekend after a cold snap. And Ames keeps stocking bathing suits well into August.

Ames customers tend to like clothes with bold patterns "where a lot is happening," says Mr. Lemire. So women's racks are full of textured acrylic sweaters, sweatshirts dubbed "fashion fleece" with flowers or snowmen on the front and "satin look" and "velvet look" holiday tops and dresses. The stores also carry lots of ready-to-assemble furniture and a broad selection of crafts, a legacy of their experience with frugal women who sewed and made their own holiday decorations long before anyone heard of Martha Stewart.

Mr. Ettore set out to woo seniors. Other discounters were also offering senior discounts, but Mr. Ettore cut the qualifying age to 55 from 65 to attract people who still work and thus have more income.

In focus groups, he discovered that many older shoppers were embarrassed to show their driver's licenses each time they wanted a discount. The older the customer, the higher the resentment. So in 1996, Ames launched the "55-plus gold card" — requiring proof of age only once. It confers 10% discounts on everything every Tuesday, and check-out clerks don't learn exactly how old the customer is. The cards also help Ames gather demographic information on its customers.

Eleanor Brown, an elderly shopper from Freeport, Maine, turns up at the Ames in Brunswick one Tuesday before the holidays and picks up two $14.99 shirts and some Christmas lights. She says she shops often on 55-plus day, when cookies are served and music oldies are piped in. She finds the store "neat and clean," Ms. Brown says, and easy to get around in because of its size. Ames has given some stores a "racetrack" aisle circling the central apparel area, making it easy for seniors or hurried shoppers to get the merchandise they want.

Stores open at 8 instead of 9 on Tuesdays, since many elderly customers are early risers. "They're concerned about security and driving at night. You have to understand those kinds of issues," Mr. Lemire says. Tuesdays have become Ames's highest-sales day after Saturday, with a spike in sales of prune juice and of toys purchased by doting grandmothers. Further accommodating elderly customers, some Ames stores sent buses to old-age homes during the recent holidays.

Model Trains

To bring down ad costs that were well over the industry average of 3% of sales, Mr. Ettore reduced circulation of weekly fliers by 10% after identifying unproductive zip codes. He cut the size of some circulars to save on paper. And he chopped $1 million in production costs by building a photo studio at headquarters, eliminating use of expensive New York photographers. Once a week, Ames sends a car to New Haven to pick up the models, who take the train up from New York.

The circular items account for half the chain's sales, so Mr. Ettore meets with merchandising staff every Tuesday to fine-tune them. At one meeting, he eyes a $199 price planned for a vacuum cleaner that Ames normally sells for $229. "Can you go sharper on the vacuum?" he asks a staffer.

No, "that's the MAP," she replies, meaning the minimum advertised price at which the manufacturer will share ad costs. Mr. Ettore does succeed in nixing a sale on wireless intercoms (low customer appeal). He is pleased with satin-sheet sets and dish sets, both 33% off at $19.99. The "killer item" of the week, he proclaims: a mission-style kitchen set — a table with two tall stools — at $47.99, down from $119.99. A depreciated currency in Malaysia, where it comes from, makes the low price profitable.

Mr. Ettore is keeping an eye out for acquisitions in the South and Midwest. He plans to add 20 to 30 stores a year, beyond the recently acquired Hills outlets. His marketing plan for those: Hills "going out of business" sales in all of the stores in coming months — followed by Ames "grand openings."

With Hills, Ames will add $1.6 billion in annual sales for a cash outlay of $117 million, although assumed leases and remodeling will boost that to $330 million. Hills was burdened by debt and in danger of bankruptcy, and its stock was badly depressed. In other words, it was a perfect opportunity for Ames: a close-out bargain on distressed merchandise.

NOW, TENNIS BALLS ARE CHASING THE DOGS
Penn Racquet Sports courts canine customers

Suppose your industry were in free fall. What would you do to find more customers? Would you go global in search of sales? Try the Internet?

How about switching species?

That's the drastic move made by Penn Racquet Sports, the nation's No.1 maker of tennis balls, which is suffering from flat sales and a decade-long lull in recreational tennis. This month, Penn begins marketing its familiar, fuzzy orbs to some undeniably loyal customers: dogs. R.P. Fetchem's is a traditional tennis ball that has been gussied up as a "natural felt fetch toy" for pooches. "Ten times more people own pets than play tennis," explains Penn President Gregg R. Weida, owner of a schnauzer named Jake.

NO DYES. Penn is teaching an old ball new marketing tricks—and hoping to bounce its estimated $70 million in sales up by 5% to 10%. For the benefit of four-legged consumers, Penn has made the balls dye- free. They sport the Ralston Purina Co. logo, thanks to a licensing deal with the dog-food giant. The biggest change is the price: $4 to $5 for a can of two Fetchem's vs. $2.50 for three old-fashioned tennis balls. That hasn't deterred retailers. PetsMart Inc. will test them, ordering 400 cases for its 413 stores. "The fact that it's got the Ralston name and the natural felt are pluses," says Greg Forquer, PetsMart vice-president for merchandising.

But that won't attract more tennis players. For Penn—a small Phoenix- based division of chemical and defense conglomerate GenCorp Inc.— making a move into dog toys may be one indication that tennis shows no imminent signs of a comeback. The game has a base of 5 million hard-core players, but it's losing the weekend whackers, explains Brad Patterson, executive director of the Tennis Industry Assn. Recreational play is down almost 20% over the past

decade. Ball sales have dropped 29% since 1991. "Twenty years ago, there was no inline skating, no Blockbuster Video, no home computers," rues Patterson. "It's harder to grab mind share."

Like other ballmakers, Penn has been unable to duck the force of the tennis devolution. Midwest Research analyst Mark E. Koznarek, who follows Penn's parent company GenCorp, forecasts zero growth for Penn and tags the unit a "below-average part of the business" that is ripe for a sell-off.

The dog-toy solution had been kicking around Penn for years. But in 1996, it found a champion in Laura Kurzu, who directs

TENNIS BALL BUST

SALES

110
100
90
80
70
0

'91 '92 '93 '94 '95 '96 '97

▲ MILLIONS OF DOLLARS

DATA: TENNIS INDUSTRY ASSN. ©BW

Penn's account at Veritas Advertising, a St. Louis agency. Kurzu had connections at Ralston Purina and was convinced the two should enter into a licensing deal. "I was laughed at from both sides," recalls Kurzu.

"CHEAP." But Penn may get the last chuckle. Tennis may be stalled, but pet-pampering is booming. Human beings will shell out $5.95 a box for doggie pasta and will pay $59.95 for a pet canopy bed. Most important to Penn, they buy toys: Last year, owners lavished $41.7 million on dog toys sold in pet stores, says the Pet Industry Joint Advisory Council (PIJAC).

While $5 a can might make tennis players gasp, it's no barrier for dog lovers in search of the perfect treat. "That's cheap," says Jim Sweeney, regional manager in Chicago for Pet Supplies Plus, a 145-store chain. He sells dog toys for as much as $25.99. Sweeney hasn't been pitched by the Penn sales force but predicts he could move 1,000 cans of Fetchem's a month. New York dog owner Joel Katz didn't balk at the Fetchem's price tag. "This guy will do anything for a ball," he said of his cocker spaniel, Max. "He loves them more than food."

But while Penn knows the tennis ball world, it will encounter a pack of new competition in the pet toy business. Indeed, Penn already has a rival. Melia Luxury Pet Products makes six flavors of dog tennis balls, including "zesty orange" and "PB&J" (peanut butter and jelly), and sales are in the "hundreds of thousands," says President David Voldandt. Pet watchers aren't surprised to see more entries. "Everyone and their brother wants to get in," says Geri Mitchell of PIJAC. Fetch, anyone?

By Dennis Berman in New York

Sneaker Company Targets Out-of-Breath Baby Boomers

By JOSEPH PEREIRA
Staff Reporter of THE WALL STREET JOURNAL

BOSTON — **New Balance** Inc. has been spending a scant $4 million a year to advertise its athletic shoes. Its best-known endorser is a marathoner named Mark Coogan, who placed 41st in the last Olympics. Its logo is a prosaic NB.

And its shoes are jumping off retailers' shelves.

While **Nike** Inc. and other sneaker makers struggle to eke out gains in shoe sales, New Balance is riding a boom — specifically, the baby boom. Using a flashless formula that includes moderate prices, links to podiatrists and an expansive range of widths tailored to an aging population's expanding heft, the company gobbled up market share last year while recording a 16% gain in sales to $560 million.

President Clinton wears New Balance. So do Steve Jobs, Dustin Hoffman and Richard Templeton, who puffs as he works out on a StairMaster at the YMCA in Quincy, Mass. "My doctor told me to do something about my weight," says the 44-year-old insurance adjuster. "So I got myself a pair of New Balances for Christmas, and here I am."

New Balance "is becoming the Nike of the baby-boom generation," says Mike Kormas, president of Footwear Market Insights, a research firm based in Nashville, Tenn. Mr. Kormas, whose firm polls 25,000 households every four months on footwear-purchasing preferences, reckons that "the average age of a Nike consumer is 25, the average age of a Reebok consumer is 33 and the average age of a New Balance consumer is 42."

New Balance's gains come at a time when manufacturers' U.S. athletic footwear sales climbed less than 3%, to $7.7 billion, in 1997. The industry sales forecast for 1998 is for more of the same, as the inventory-laden retailers are expected to unload some poor sellers at deep discounts. New Balance, meanwhile, is projecting sales of $700 million, up 25%.

It's a triumph of demographics over razzle-dazzle. While industry leaders like Nike, **Reebok International** Ltd. and **Fila Holdings** SpA jump through expensive hoops to court youngsters, New Balance is quietly tracking America's changing population. U.S. Census figures show that while the number of 20-to-34-year-olds in the country has declined by 5.3 million in the past seven years, the population of 35-to-59-year-olds has jumped by 16.5 million.

Although a youngster tends to buy more sneakers than a middle-ager, New Balance's older-age niche has some potent marketing virtues. Customers are less fickle, so the company doesn't worry as much about fashion swings.

Thus, while competitors come out with new models about every six weeks, New Balance introduces one about every 17 weeks. That lets retailers hold onto inventory longer without needing to discount it to free up space. And with fewer models and fewer expensive updates, the company believes it can risk skimping on marketing and big-name endorsers.

"You won't find a poster of Michael Jordan hanging in the bedroom of a New Balance customer," says Jim Davis, New Balance's president and chief executive. The $4 million the company spends on advertising and promotions is less than 1% of Nike's $750 million or Reebok's $425 million.

Another tactic: While most companies offer shoes in two widths — medium and wide — New Balance offers consumers five choices, ranging from a narrow AA to an expansive EEEE. About 20% to 30% of the population has narrower, or wider, than average feet, and retailers say that they sell more EE and EEEE New Balances than any other widths offered under the brand.

Now the company wants to stretch its appeal to include younger consumers. As it is now, New Balance loyalty pretty much ends with the baby boom. Among Gen-Xers and younger age groups, awareness of the brand plummets, according to New Balance market studies. This year, the company will more than triple its marketing budget to $13 million and venture into television advertising for the first time.

It's a calculated risk: The company has courted youth before, without much success. In the 1980s, when sales were stuck at about $100 million a year, New Balance made a full-court press into the teen-basketball market, hiring former Los Angeles Laker James Worthy as its marquee endorser. Efforts were disappointing, partly because Mr. Worthy was arrested for soliciting prostitution in 1990. (He pleaded no contest to two misdemeanor charges.)

"We learned our lesson," says Mr. Davis. "We chose not to be in a position where we live and die by basketball. We'd just as soon pass the $10 to $15 a pair we need in superstar endorsement to the customer." New Balance shoes generally carry a moderate price tag, behind Nike, Reebok and Fila, though overlapping price ranges muddy the comparison.

For now, the company maintains a small stable of athletic endorsers, most of whom are runners with contracts ranging from $2,000 to $50,000 a year. But they are used mostly for product research, Mr. Davis says. None appear in the company's advertisements.

Instead, New Balance has a less glamorous but powerful way of promoting its sneakers. Just as toothbrush companies work with dentists, New Balance frequently networks with podiatrists, who use the roominess of the wide models to insert foot-support devices.

The Eneslow Foot Comfort Center, a shoe store in New York that specializes in "pedorthics," or therapeutic shoes, carries only New Balance among its sneaker selections. Its chief executive, Robert Schwartz, is the former president of the Pedorthic Footwear Association.

Many New Balance wearers buy the same models again and again and go into stores knowing exactly which pair they're looking for. Last month, President Clinton entered a Foot Locker store in the Pier 17 mall in downtown New York seeking a walking/running New Balance model. When informed that the store didn't have that particular model, the president turned to leave. The store manager, Stacey Lighty, refused to let the president leave empty-handed and pressed a pair of New Balance running shoes into his hand as he exited the store.

SPAM THAT YOU MIGHT NOT DELETE

Marketers are discovering that personalized E-mail pitches work

Janniece Martin's E-mail account has become a two-way shopping street. At least once a week, the 34-year-old Rosedale (N.Y.) sales assistant signs on to find "reminders" from software vendor Parsons Technology Inc. urging her to buy a new label maker or clip-art program. Martin, who first used Parsons' mail-order catalog last year, enjoys the personal feeling of an E-mail pitch. She also finds the service convenient. "If I'm not ready to make a purchase, all I have to do is delete the E-mail," she says. Fortunately for Parsons, Martin doesn't do that often: She frequently spends up to $100 on supplies after receiving an E-mail nudge.

Marketers hope Martin is part of a trend. Although users of E-mail have long complained about unwanted direct marketing—commonly called spam—that hasn't stopped companies from looking for new and improved ways to exploit E-mail as a marketing tool. Now, by using sophisticated data-mining techniques to develop far more tailored messages, marketers may well be succeeding. Lured by the speed, cost savings, and personalized pitches that are possible online, companies such as 1-800-Flowers, Amazon.com, and Macy's are testing the tactic. "If the customer is willing, it's the ideal opportunity for a personalized dialogue," says Kent Anderson, president of Macys.com, the department store's online entity. "It gets us closer to a one-to-one relationship."

SCI-FI ALERT. One of the leaders is Amazon.com, the virtual bookseller that has fast become a rival to brick-and-mortar chains. Order a Star Trek book one month and a Lost In Space volume the next, and you can expect to receive an E-mail containing recommendations for similar sci-fi fare. Amazon.com customers also receive E-mail updates if a favorite author is conducting an online chat or has published new work. The tailored E-mail program helps keep customers coming back: 60% of Amazon's 2.2 million customers are repeat buyers, up from 40% last year. But for Chief Executive Jeff Bezos, the real advantage over more traditional direct marketing is the ability to get people to buy something they didn't even know they wanted. "It's all about accelerating the discovery process," he says. "It's high-tech meets hand selling."

While all of Amazon's sci-fi fans get the same message, some smaller companies have managed to sculpt more personalized E-mail marketing. Consider Streamline Inc., a delivery service in Boston that contracts with local groceries, video stores, and dry cleaners. Customers send in shopping lists, and Streamline fills and delivers the order. But in addition to doing your schlepping, Streamline goes one step further into your personal life. The company keeps a database on what you buy and when. Based on your past behavior, its software creates a profile and automatically sends you E-mail reminders when its records show that you're probably low on cereal, toilet tissue, etc. The E-mail prompt encourages users to reorder through Streamline. The result: Streamline's customers—who spend an average $6,000 a year—come back for more 90% of the time. "We can show the customer products that relate to them on a personal basis," says CEO Tim DeMello, who expects monthly revenues to hit $1 million by yearend.

But is E-mail better than plain old paper junk mail? Does an electronic pitch pack more oomph than a dinnertime phone call? Some users, especially those who do business on the Internet, say yes. Dealaday.com uses E-mail to prospect for customers. The Internet closeout seller of brand-name clothing pays database companies for lists of E-mail addresses. The company sends group E-mail to as many as 10,000 names, all consumers who have indicated they would like to receive E-mail pitches. President Ed Mufson, who spent two decades as a retail executive running traditional chains such as Fred the Furrier, says prospecting via E-mail brings in more customers than any advertising or direct marketing he has used. "In normal direct marketing, if you get a 1% or 2% response, you're happy. With E-mail, I'm getting a 7%, 8%, sometimes 10% response," he says. "I give it a rave review."

Other companies have begun using E-mail to create promotions that could not be executed by slower "snail mail." Travelocity, a travel site on the Web, sends frequent E-mails called Fare Watchers, pitching last-minute cheap airfares. The time-sensitive information would be useless in a traditional direct-mail campaign, says Terry Jones, chief information officer for SABRE Group, Travelocity's owner.

Still more are lured by the obvious lower cost of letting a computer do the selling. No paper and postage costs. No telemarketing staff to hire. A host of new software programs can sift through a company's database

---

THIS ISN'T JUNK MAIL!

How E-mail marketers tailor their messages:

ASK FIRST Retailers such as 1-800-Flowers only send E-mail pitches to customers who request the service

STAY ON TOPIC Book buyers from Amazon.com receive E-mail suggestions based on their literature tastes

GET PERSONAL Streamline, a Boston-based delivery service, monitors individual buying habits of customers and sends tailored E-mail reminders

(Cont.)

and zap out E-mail. Add it up, and that can represent a cost savings of 75% or more, says Chris McCann, senior vice-president at 1-800-Flowers. The national florist chain sent out 250,000 E-mail marketing messages to promote Mother's Day specials, in addition to the usual reminders in the post.

AT&T Capital Corp. has seen similar benefits in using the Internet and E-mail to offer its financing services to business customers. It used to take up to six weeks, using snail mail, to develop marketing campaigns, such as an offer to handle computer leasing contracts. Now, Marketing Information Manager Rick Winterkorn says he can target a group of businesses with such service in a single day—and for 10% less.

PRIVACY FEARS. Despite the early success, many of the biggest users of direct marketing have yet to get into E-mail marketing in a big way. Telecommunications and consumer financial-services companies, for example, are largely absent. The reason? They're afraid customers will hate it, thanks to rising fears over privacy on the Internet. As more and more information about consumers' finances or buying habits gets tracked and stored electronically—often without customers even realizing it—concerns over how such once confidential personal data can be exploited are growing. That's one reason BellSouth Corp., which collects data on its customers from its Web site, still uses the telephone and mail to deliver news of promotions and other offers. "Not all of our customers want us to be their best friends," says John Devlin, manager of customer information and analysis at Bell-South. "We don't want to annoy anyone."

Of course, lots of people hate the junk mail they receive by the post or those annoying dinnertime phone pitches, and that doesn't stop them from happening. But angry consumers can strike back online in a way they can't against more traditional junk mail. With just a quick E-mail to friends or other Web sites, an irate customer can cause offending companies to be blackballed in cyberspace.

The result: Many major marketers fear that a mishandled E-mail promotion will instantly get them a worldwide reputation as Spam King. "Spam is a bad word," says Jeremy C. Jaffe, vice-president for electronic commerce at Boston-based investment advisers Liberty Financial Cos. He worries that if he pesters his customers with unwanted E-mail, "they will ignore anything I send. I won't even be able to get a few good words in."

Those fears remain real, because for every happy E-mail recipient such as Janniece Martin, there are many more who would like to keep marketers out of their electronic mailboxes. "I don't find any of it useful," says Keisha Y. Simmons, a marketing manager in Marietta, Ga., who gets about 10 marketing E-mails a week.

To get around this problem, Liberty Financial and many others target only customers who actively agree to be on E-mail marketing lists. Although this limits the marketing universe, it helps avoid negative backlash. Macys.com, for one, offers its E-mail gift reminder service only to those who ask for it. Customers fill out an electronic form with information such as important family birthdates. Macy's sends out E-mail reminders in advance of the big day. "We don't want to force it," says Anderson. "But if the customers say they want us to recommend a gift, I'm happy to do it." Even if he has to send it out by the post.

By Nicole Harris in Atlanta, with Rob Hoff in San Mateo, Calif.

Xerox Recasts Itself As Formidable Force In Digital Revolution

Copier Giant Is Battling A Challenge From Canon For Top of Office Market

Putting Label 'on Everything'

BY BERNARD WYSOCKI JR.
Staff Reporter of THE WALL STREET JOURNAL

LEESBURG, Va. — On the 110-acre campus of Xerox Document University here, about 250 sales specialists are being trained for battle in the digital age.

"I'm 'change' standing right in front of you," intones Rich Penwell, a Xerox Corp. vice president and part of a parade of senior executives who take the stage in a darkened auditorium to hammer home their scripted message of a revolution in the once-staid world of the copying machine. One by one, they enter the spotlight to speak of complex new Xerox devices that scan, fax, copy and print, all linked by digital networks. And they urge the salespeople in the audience to embrace these advances.

It may be bad theater, but it is hardly theater of the absurd. The changes sweeping the office-machine industry are indeed profound, and they illustrate the opportunities and dangers of competing in the new digital landscape.

At the low end of the copy-machine business, 16 American, European and Japanese companies are duking it out in a quagmire of falling prices and elusive profits — the same price erosion afflicting much of high technology. And it has prompted an urgent quest for the promised land: good growth, pricing power and superior profit margins.

High Ground

Xerox has found it, in the high-end segment of the market, where the company raised prices on top-of-the-line machines, some costing $450,000, by 5% last month. This segment includes not only ultrafast copiers the size of a small car. Increasingly, it encompasses complex networks of digital devices, expensive software and consulting services, creating whole systems that can move documents, paper or electronic, around

a corporation or other institution.

Now, the question is whether Xerox can hold on to its enviable place at the top of the document food chain. In effect, it has decided to fight a two-front war in both the low end and the high end of the market.

Nontraditional competitors, such as powerful Hewlett-Packard Co., are threatening the company from below, from an established base in the printer business. But the most pressing challenge to Xerox hegemony at the high end of the market is coming from the U.S. unit of Canon Inc. of Japan.

Six months ago, Canon declared it was taking on Xerox, and would win $1 billion of what Canon estimates to be a $5 billion-a-year high-end market, by the end of 2000. Facing stagnation in Japan and brutal pricing everywhere, Canon aims to take away a big slice of a fast-growing, high-profit market dominated by Xerox: government agencies, commercial copying and print shops, universities and major corporations.

'Soft Underbelly'

"We think this is where Xerox's soft underbelly is," says Robert Bryson, executive vice president of Canon U.S.A., Lake Success, N.Y.

Nonsense, says Xerox. A spokesman for the company, which is based in Stamford, Conn., says there is no soft underbelly, but only "rock-hard abs." And Xerox Chief Executive Paul Allaire, acknowledging Canon as a worthy opponent, points to Xerox's double-digit U.S. revenue growth, soaring profit and its array of new digital devices.

In a way, this is the late-1990s version of a Japanese challenger trying to move upmarket against the incumbents, just as Japanese auto manufacturers introduced the Lexus, Infiniti and Acura in the late 1980s and grabbed a sizable chunk of world auto markets. But that was then, and the 1990s are far different, at least in the office-equipment business.

One big difference is that the U.S. is the most advanced market in use of digital networks. Japan is way behind in deploying personal computers, servers and Intranets. So the leading edge is in Xerox's home market. Canon, meanwhile, is doing product development on one side of the Pacific Ocean, while the customer is evolving, in Internet time, on the other. The competitive landscape never looked like this in the auto wars.

Marketing Twist

Nor has the auto industry faced this interesting twist: If, like Xerox, you have a top-to-bottom product line, something Canon has yet to develop, you can go into a big corporation, take over the entire document-management function, hire some of its staff as your own and throw out every rival machine. For example, last year Xerox took over the copying function at NationsBank Corp., which merged with BankAmerica Corp. late last year and which had more than 20,000 copiers of various brands. As leases expire on

non-Xerox machines, they are being swapped out.

"The ultimate aim is to have a Xerox label on everything," says Tom Dolan, president of Xerox North American solutions group.

Even more important, Xerox is tossing out Xerox. Rather than clinging to the old "light lens" analog technology, whose forerunners date back to the company's original products of the 1950s, Xerox is willing to cannibalize itself by swapping out older machines for the new digital gear. Last week, Xerox reported fourth-quarter profit rose 17% to $615 million, or $1.69 a diluted share. Xerox said that sales of digital products, which now account for more than half its sales, rose 33% from a year earlier.

Meanwhile, Canon, too, is trying to seize the opportunity — to displace Xerox entirely. The battle rages.

One example: At Case Western Reserve University, in Cleveland, there were 200 old-line Xerox copiers until the fall of 1998. The university wanted to upgrade. It wanted all the machines hooked together, so a staff member could scan a document, store it and send copies anywhere on campus. And by connecting the machines to the university telephone system, it sought the ability to route incoming faxes as e-mails to students, faculty and staff.

"We had a bake-off," says Ray Neff, vice president of information services at Case Western. The two finalists were Xerox and Canon. Each offered about the same deal: a five-year lease, based on about four million documents a month, for about $80,000 month.

The winner was Canon, Mr. Neff says, and one factor was superior software. Xerox concedes the loss, but cites a similar competition at an Ohio aerospace company, where it won.

Canon's victory suggests, of course, that it will be a player in the new digital age of copiers. Canon estimates it will place 10,000 digital copiers in the first quarter of 1999, which it considers good progress in its $1 billion sales quest. The win also suggests its system of selling through large dealers, such as Ikon Office Solutions Inc. isn't an impediment to sales. Ikon, based in Valley Forge, Pa., was a dealer/distributor in the Case deal.

Potential Weakness

To some analysts, however, this heavy reliance on independent dealers is a weakness in a complex sale. And they are dubious that Canon can carve $1 billion of revenue out of this market so quickly. "How?" asks Robert Sostilio, a director at Cap Ventures Inc., a Norwell, Mass., consulting firm. "How are they going to do it?"

Some of Canon's heaviest ammunition is technology itself. In recent years, it has been awarded more U.S. patents than any company except for International Business Machines Corp. Its research-and-development budget exceeds $1 billion a year.

These days, U.S. staff visiting Tokyo find themselves pounded by Canon's engineers

(Cont.)

for market intelligence. Mason Olds, manager of Canon's color-products line in the U.S., says he has been surrounded by 50 Canon engineers in meeting rooms, relentlessly grilling him on customer trends.

Today, nobody doubts that Canon understands the need for documents to go from paper to electronic form, or vice versa, to be stored, manipulated and distributed. Moreover, the Internet is fueling a rise in electronic page counts and a rise in the number of printed copies.

"It's the digital document. That's the key to the whole ballgame," says Jay Ingalls, a research director at Gartner Group Inc.

It is likely to be too expensive for players who can't cope with rapid innovation, forging alliances and providing effective global sales and service as the digital age unfolds.

"A lot of the copier companies aren't going to make the trip," says G. Richard Thoman, Xerox's president. He thinks, however, that both Canon and Hewlett-Packard will still be standing, in addition to Xerox.

Element of Surprise

If so, it is a future in which the archrivals will succeed mostly in driving out some of the secondary brands, which today include Minolta, Konica, Lanier and a dozen others. Still, from Canon's point of view, Xerox is enemy No. 1.

Canon has a long history of surprising its American foe. In the early 1980s, Canon stormed the U.S. market with table-top copiers, and more than doubled revenue to $1 billion between 1979 and 1982. Then, in the early 1990s, it launched an innovative digital color copier.

"That surprised us," says Gilbert Hatch, a longtime Xerox executive. But Canon was very slow to exploit its gains in color copying to penetrate the high-end market overall.

If Canon has been slow to the market with some products, it will soon have another challenge: management turnover at the top. Haruo Murase, president of Canon U.S.A., has been in North America since 1971. "Murase is uniquely American and Japanese at the same time," says Masato Sato, a consultant to Canon, who has known him since their high-school days in Tokyo in the 1950s. Last month, Mr. Murase was summoned back to Tokyo, where he will be in charge of domestic sales in a stagnating Japanese market.

Yet Canon's most worrisome problem is undoubtedly that Xerox is a much tougher competitor today than in the early 1980s. Mr. Murase acknowledges as much. "Xerox has overcome its arrogance of the past. It has really listened to its customers," he says.

That's probably true, but it accounts for just part of Xerox's transformation. Last month, Xerox split its organization in two, acknowledging that the low end of the business is high-volume and low-profit — completely distinct from its high-end, high-profit business.

Rather than abandon the low end, the commodity-like business of peddling machines, Xerox believes the low-end is a source of innovation, volume, brand recognition and supply business. It is bulking up its distribution channels. And Xerox is slashing costs again, in part to be a low-cost force at the low end. Xerox has targeted 9,000 of about 90,000 jobs for elimination, and it took a $1 billion charge last year to get its sales and administrative expenses down to 20% of revenue from about 29%.

"In the old analog world, 6% productivity was magical," says Mr. Allaire, the Xerox chief executive. "In the digital world, if you don't have double-digit productivity numbers every year, you're going to be out of business."

Meanwhile, the high end of Xerox's business is beginning to look increasingly like the business model of a consulting firm. That's by design. Xerox executives see themselves competing against IBM, Electronic Data Systems Corp. and Andersen Consulting in the years ahead, combining hardware, software and services into a profitable package, industry by industry.

The main selling point to the customer is cost savings. If Xerox can take cost out of the business, the logic goes, it can charge a handsome price and won't get bogged down in brutal price wars.

"I'm hunting whales," says Phil Pilibosian, a Xerox senior vice president, as he explains how his staff is focusing on 300 major companies in financial services and health care, moving to an industry-specific focus. "We're moving through the Blues [Blue Cross and Blue Shield companies] like Grant through Richmond," says Mr. Pilibosian, who hails from New England.

At the Leesburg sales meeting, Xerox management sounds a confident note. There are gibes about keeping Hewlett-Packard's chief executive awake at night. And one executive repeats a recent line of Xerox CEO Mr. Allaire, who said, "Our competition is momentarily stunned."

"Momentarily" may be the key word. Commenting on an internal document that shows Xerox gaining share from Canon, Xerox's Mr. Thoman says, "These things can turn. Six months from now the figures could be very different."

Evaluating Opportunities in the Changing Marketing Environment

The E-Corporation

More than just Web-based, it's building a new industrial order. ■ *by Gary Hammel and Jeff Sampler*

Somewhere out there is a bullet with your company's name on it. Somewhere out there is a competitor, unborn and unknown, that will render your business model obsolete. Bill Gates knows that. When he says that Microsoft is always two years away from failure, he's not just blowing smoke at Janet Reno. He knows that competition today is not between products, it's between business models. He knows that irrelevancy is a bigger risk than inefficiency. And what's true for Microsoft is true for just about every other company: The hottest and most dangerous new business models out there are on the Web.

Since the new kinds of organizations being spawned by information technology's rapid reshaping of global business don't yet have a name, FORTUNE's editors have decided to give them one—"E-corporations." As the term suggests, a real E-corp. isn't just using the Internet to alter its approach to markets and customers; it's combining computers, the Web, and the massively complex programs known as enterprise software to change everything about how it operates. Elsewhere in this package of articles, you'll read about two companies in the middle of just that transformation, Schwab and VF Corp., plus assess the current state of the huge and growing war among enterprise software suppliers. But our subject here is the infotech revolution's most immediate demand—confronting the promise and threat of the Internet.

Okay, so the Web has been hyped to the point of absurdity by fanatical true believers, but when you strip away the frenzied predictions of the digirati, you're still left with an inescapable fact: The Internet will change the relationship between consumers and producers in ways more profound than you can yet imagine. The Internet is not just another marketing channel; it's not just another advertising medium; it's not just a way to speed up transactions. The Internet is the foundation for a new industrial order.

The Internet will empower consumers like nothing else ever has. Think about this: Already 16% of car buyers shop online before showing up at a dealership, and they aren't comparing paint jobs— they're arming themselves with information on dealer costs. So forget all the patronizing nonsense about being market-led or customer-focused. The new reality is consumer control, and it's as ominous as it sounds if you're not prepared for this radically different future. Indeed, the Internet represents the ultimate triumph of consumerism. Sure, you know the Internet is going to be important, but if you don't have a deep, visceral sense of how radically it's going to change today's industrial order, you're going to lose.

> **The Internet makes consumers all-powerful. One result: a revolution that threatens malls as profoundly as they threatened Main Street.**

Main Street in the 1950s, malls in the 1970s, superstores in the 1990s—since World War II we've seen a fundamental shift in the retailing paradigm with each new generation, and now we're on the verge of another revolution. It's worth noting that each time the business model changed, a new group of leaders emerged. Woolworth's never really escaped Main Street. Sears, for the most part, remains stuck in the mall. Again and again, incumbents missed the early warning signs because they were easy to ignore. Who was really paying attention when Sam and James Walton opened their first Wal-Mart Discount City in 1962? Who really understood the impact that superstores and category killers would ultimately have on the supply chain? Are you convinced that you really understand the potential impact of the Web? Are you sure that your company will be one of the few that define the new Net-centric industrial order?

Though the Internet still represents a minute fraction of total purchases, its growth is mind-boggling. In a spring 1998 study, Jupiter Communications reported that 10 million people in the U.S. had bought something over the Net in 1997, and it expects 17 million to do so this year—up from virtually none a few years ago. Just three years ago only 4% of Americans used the Internet every day. Today the figure is 25%, says the Pew Research Center. Though most connect from work rather than home, the trend is clear: This is not a rising tide, it's a tidal wave.

There is no other channel where revenues are growing anywhere near this fast. There is no other way a business can grow unimpeded by the need to build commercial space and hire legions of sales staff. It doesn't matter how small the Internet's present base of customers, this kind of compounded growth will change the face of business. Of course the Web won't replace off-line retailing. Main Street still exists, so does the mall, and Wal-Mart and Costco aren't going to disappear anytime soon. On the other hand, the Web will fundamentally change customers' expectations about convenience, speed, comparability, price, and service. Those new expectations will reverberate throughout the economy, affecting every business in eight major ways. So read on—and consider yourself warned.

■ No. 1: When Push Comes to Suck

Increasingly consumers would rather spend an hour exploring cyberspace than sit through another execrable sitcom or overhyped sporting event. This trend is a direct challenge to Procter & Gamble, Unilever, Gillette, and other mass marketers, many of which spend as much as 80% of their ad budgets on television. They recognize that the Net threatens to shatter the mass market into millions of individual consumers doing their own thing online.

The Net is not just another medium; it is a profoundly different experience. The Net is about choice, freedom, and control. It is a place to escape, at least temporarily, the incessant interruptions of vendors whose products are more or less indistinguishable save for the advertising.

Any Net advertiser that tries to revoke this freedom will be viewed as little more than a

(Cont.)

> **The Web will fundamentally change customers' expectations about convenience, speed, comparability, price, and service.**

sophisticated spam merchant. It's not that Web users aren't interested in learning about new products and services or getting a great buy on an old standby, but they want to learn on their own terms. They want the choice to click or not, to view or not, and anything more than the gentlest form of persuasion from an advertiser is likely to be construed as an intrusion.

Online advertisers used to talk about push—the ability to put an ad on your computer screen whether you like it or not. Others tried "buying eyeballs," paying AOL, Yahoo, or some other cyberlandlord millions of dollars to put an ad in a prime place on an oft-visited page. Yet these concepts are in many ways antithetical to the Web. The Web is not about push; it's about suck: Online consumers can suck out of cyberspace whatever interests them and leave behind whatever doesn't. You push stuff at passive users, and Web users are anything but passive. You may be willing to let some uninvited advertiser take your TV screen hostage for 30 seconds, but you'd probably throw a fit if they took over your computer screen. Online customers simply aren't going to be pushed around.

For the online advertiser, the challenge is to educate, entertain, and entice, for no one can be compelled to pay attention online. If you want to advertise toothpaste online, you need more than photogenic lovers with toothy smiles. Unilever has created a Website for Mentadent toothpaste that offers potential customers the chance to order a free sample, get oral-care advice, and send questions to a dental hygienist. Every week American Airlines sends E-mail to more than a million NetSAAver subscribers listing rock-bottom fares for undersubscribed flights on the coming weekend.

When I click on an ad, I should get paid. Why should an advertiser send money to AOL or Yahoo—or to CBS, for that matter—when the money could be sent straight to me? This idea is not as farfetched as it sounds. A company called Yoyodyne calls it permission-based marketing, which stands in contrast to interruption-based marketing. Working for clients as diverse as H&R Block, Reader's Digest, and MCI, Yoyodyne designs games and contests—with prizes—that drive traffic to client Websites. Players must provide an E-mail address and choose Websites to visit or ads to view—helping advertisers build relationships with consumers and learn more about them. Having signed up a million players in 1997, Yoyodyne (just bought by Yahoo) hopes to double this number by the end of 1998.

The Net threatens to invert the traditional logic of advertising. Suddenly, the hunted have become the hunters.

■ No. 2: Just the Plain Truth

As advertisers have pegged the hype-o-meter at 100, consumers have developed ever more sensitive b.s. detectors. No wonder more and more consumers are looking to get their information from someone who is unbiased. Neutrality was the foundation for the success of Consumer Reports, and it accounts for the value consumers find in the rankings of J.D. Power or Morningstar.

In the off-line world, the cost of directly comparing products or services was often prohibitively high. No more. Online, mediocrity will have no place to hide. Typical of the new breed of neutral brokers is CompareNet (www.compare.com). The name says it all: Here's where you go if you want to compare products feature for feature and dollar for dollar. Whether it's lawnmowers, camcorders, or treadmills, skeptical customers can read unbiased product reviews and participate in online discussion groups. In this environment, it's pretty hard for a vendor to spin a second-rate product into a first-rate buy.

Today's consumers demand not just independent advice but also vendor-neutral distribution channels. While Sony's Website languishes—you can buy only Sony CDs—CDnow.com, offering 250,000 titles from all five major labels, grows like crazy. Neutrality also means not being told where to shop. E-commerce visionaries like Junglee and C2B Technologies are developing powerful search engines that allow consumers to search for products and bargains all across the Net. Using a virtual database that integrates information from dozens of online merchants, and intelligent agents that scan that information to find the best deal on a particular product, Junglee aims to let consumers comparison-shop on a scale previously unimagined. Suddenly, instead of searching ten different sites, would-be buyers can view the results of a Netwide search in one easy-to-read table. C2B's shopping platform—being offered for license by the company's new owner, Inktomi—gives Web shoppers information on nearly a million products and connects them with hundreds of merchants. It can also do hard-core bargain-hunting. A partnership with Consumers Digest helps C2B deliver Best Buy recommendations and detailed product reviews. Thanks to companies like Junglee and C2B, online buyers are going to have a very big stick with which to hammer down prices and fend off bogus product claims.

Junglee and C2B are the vanguard of a new generation of information intermediaries that help customers get at the truth. This is not disintermediation; it is reintermediation. Online, brokers rule. They will be the new market makers, and they will call the shots.

■ No. 3: As You Like It

In the off-line world, products and services were designed and built far in advance of customer needs, and there was little customers could do to configure those products and services to their own requirements. No more. The Net currently allows a vendor to build to demand, thus keeping inventory to a minimum. Increasingly the Net will enable building to spec. Already Gateway and Dell let customers configure PCs and servers to their liking. With Dell, customers can specify their choice of sound card, videocard, video monitor, speakers, and memory capacity from a pull-down menu on Dell's Website. Dell will even tell a customer whether choosing a particular part would delay shipment or cause a compatibility problem with some other part. It's no wonder that Dell is selling $6 million of products a day over its Website and believes that 50% of its sales will be Web-based by the end of 2000.

Why should some producer decide which tracks you get when you buy a CD? Why shouldn't you be able to custom-build your own CD, track by track? This is difficult to accomplish when you have to take your music home on a silver disk but will become effortless when you suck music off the Internet and store it in your home audio-video server. In letting customers download specific tracks, N2K.com has been taking the first few tentative steps in that direction.

In many cases consumers don't want products, they want solutions. Say you want to build a backyard deck. Why can't you go online to a do-it-yourself site, review a dozen potential plans, select the one you like best, have it instantly adjusted to fit the dimensions of your house, compile a complete parts list, order the parts, and have them delivered to your home with a step-by-step instruction sheet? Today this is just an E-dream, but solution selling will be de rigueur on the Net, and it will allow online merchants to substantially differentiate their service from that of off-line retailers.

Solution selling and online advice are ways in which online merchants can find some relief from the Web's tendency to drive prices to zero. There are also cost advantages in letting customers construct their own online solutions. Think about the economics of teaching thousands of Home Depot employees to give helpful advice to weekend do-it-yourself enthusiasts. Now think about the economics of making that advice available on the Web. No contest.

■ No. 4: Everything's an Auction

Think about all the purchases you've made this year. How many of them did you put out to bid? Maybe you got a couple of quotes on that new deck you had installed, but that was probably it. In the future you might put just about everything you buy out to bid. The Web will make it possible to hold real-time auctions for just about everything.

Priceline.com allows would-be fliers to name their price for travel between any pair of cities. If an airline is willing to issue a ticket at the requested price, the passenger is obligated to buy. Priceline.com says it has been

> In the future you may put just about everything you buy out to bid. Make no mistake; the Web will drive the last nail into the coffin of set prices.

issuing more than 1,000 tickets a day in recent weeks. Already airlines make millions of fare changes a month in an effort to maximize the revenue they get for each seat. Ultimately, we can expect some enterprising E-broker to link consumers directly to the computer yield management systems of the major airlines in an all-the-time, real-time auction.

One of the most successful online auctioneers is eBay. Essentially a national classifieds listing, where potential buyers bid against each other, eBay claims to have more than 900,000 products for sale in 1,086 categories. The site receives 140 million hits a week. For many years the notion of a list price has been under attack from hungry car dealers, aggressive computer dealers, and department stores addicted to never-ending sales. But even in a world of superdiscounters, it is difficult to know whether you're getting the best possible price on any given item. While retailers may offer to beat any competitor's price, they rest secure in the knowledge that few consumers have the time and patience to shop aggressively for and document the best price on anything but big-ticket items.

Now imagine a world in which you put your weekly grocery shopping out to bid. Who will bring me my Double-Stuff Oreos, Levi 501s, and that hot new Callaway fairway club for the lowest possible price? Suddenly, individual consumers will be issuing RFPs just like the largest industrial buyers. Make no mistake, the Web will drive the last nail

into the coffin of set prices. Customer ignorance—about prices and relative product performance—has been a profit center for many companies. But consumers are about to get much, much better informed—and the consequences will be awe inspiring.

The auction economy will certainly bring benefits to producers. They will be able to instantly calculate whether it will pay to add more capacity. They will be able to slash inventory carrying costs because they will always know the market-clearing price. And they will know that they have maximized the revenue yield on every sale. But like everything else online, the auction economy will be even better for consumers. Through the years producers have made billions of dollars in profits from the inability of customers to compare prices quickly. Which customer can put his hand on his heart and swear he got the best possible price on a refrigerator, a pair of Nike shoes, or a hotel room? Online, customers will be able to get producers to bid against each other in a way that seldom happens in the off-line world. And it will be difficult for industry leaders to enforce any kind of price discipline in a world in which there are no list prices and newcomers are more than willing to underbid established players to win market share. So if your product is anything close to a commodity, prices will trend downward toward variable costs, and margins will be skinnier than an anorexic supermodel.

■ No. 5: The End of Geography

E-commerce breaks every business free of its geographic moorings. No longer will geography bind a company's aspirations or the scope of its market. Amazon.com spans the globe, selling 20% of its books to foreign destinations. A physical bookstore serves an area of a few square miles, and you can't peruse its inventory without getting in your car and making a little contribution to global warming. But whether you're in Albania or Zambia, Amazon.com is a click away.

For every early mover who uses the Web to blow out the geographic boundaries of its business, there will be dozens of companies that lose their local monopolies to footloose online merchants. Customers, as well as producers, will escape the shackles of geography. Until recently, if you needed a mortgage, you'd humble yourself before your local banker. Now you can go to Bankrate.com and shop for the best mortgage rates from financial institutions across the country. It's easy

for a big retailer, with a local monopoly, to mistake captive customers for loyal customers. In a world where customers are no longer hostages to geography, loyalty will, for the first time, really have to be earned.

The death of geography will make it difficult for producers to set different prices around the world. This is already a reality for software that is paid for and downloaded over the Internet. No longer is a customer willing to pay £150 in London for a piece of software that costs $150 in New York City. Online commerce will destroy these anomalies. No company will be able to charge a premium when consumers know precisely what things cost elsewhere.

■ No. 6: Search Economies Rule

Distribution economies drove the growth of superstores like Wal-Mart and Costco, which offer zillions of products in stores the size of small countries. Wal-Mart reaps huge distribution economies from putting groceries, clothing, garden tools, sporting goods, auto supplies, and a plethora of other products under one roof. Consumers benefit from these economies through lower prices.

Bundling all those products together in one location may save Wal-Mart distribution costs when compared with a dozen Main Street retailers, but as a consumer you can waste hours wandering the soulless canyons of Wal-Mart in search of that elusive kitchen pail or can opener. Online, search economies trump distribution economies. The boomers and their progeny—the most harried consumers in history—are flocking to the Net because it's simply the most efficient place to shop for a whole range of goods and services. Say you're looking for a digital camera with a 3X zoom and at least 500,000 pixels. I'll race ya. You drive to your friendly electronics superstore, try to nab a salesperson who knows digital cameras from refrigerators, wait while product literature is dug out from behind a counter, and then make your purchase. I'll visit Netmarket.com and beat you by at least an hour. In a world of single-parent families, demanding jobs, and quality time that's measured in nanoseconds, search economies will become hugely attractive to consumers.

■ No. 7: My Place, My Time

Search economies are one-half of the new convenience equation. Fulfillment is the other half. The goal is not just to minimize the hassle of finding something but to minimize the hassle of getting it as well. While companies have spent a decade optimizing the supply chain that runs backward toward suppliers, the delivery chain that runs forward toward customers has changed hardly at all in the past 100 years. Retailers still tell customers,

(Cont.)

You have to come to us. But online consumers are saying, No way—you have to come to us. My place, my time is the new mantra of consumers everywhere.

A few months ago I was sitting with a group of senior executives from some of America's largest grocery companies. None of the august executives present had yet ordered groceries online. When asked whether a significant share of grocery buying might go online, the universal response was, Nope, it's just too expensive to deliver groceries to every household; consumers will never pay to have groceries delivered to their door. Well, I asked, how much is a customer willing to pay to have a pizza delivered to his door? A pizza (frozen) is about $5 at the supermarket and $10 to $15 delivered. You don't need the Net to order a Domino's pizza, but the point's the same: If consumers are willing to pay this kind of premium for a single pizza, what might they pay to get the week's groceries delivered to their doorstep?

My time will be as important as my place. Think of all the times you've tried to make a phone order or call a tech-support line at the other end of the country and heard a recording that says, I'm sorry, we're closed now—we are open from 8.30 A.M. to 5.30 P.M. Eastern Standard Time. Can you imagine an E-consumer's response to this kind of message on the Web? No one sleeps in cyberspace, and the store is always open.

■ No. 8: Word of Mouse

Word of mouth has an upside and a downside for every company. Both the upside and the downside are magnified exponentially online, where opinions propagate like E. coli in room-temperature chicken.

On the upside, consider Hotmail. Within 18 months of its launch, Hotmail had garnered nearly ten million customers for its free, advertising-supported E-mail service. In December 1997, Microsoft bought Hotmail for an initial payment estimated at more than $400 million. The secret of Hotmail's vertical takeoff? Word of mouse. Every time someone sent an E-mail to a friend, the message carried an offer to sign up for free E-mail. At Hotmail they call it viral marketing: Harnessing word of mouse, Hotmail's message spread like a contagion.

This kind of multiplier effect is every marketer's fantasy, but no amount of hype can produce an online buzz. Viral marketing of the type perfected by Hotmail is the product of an offer too good to refuse multiplied by exponential word of mouse. More modestly, the Web means that potential consumers can always get some kind of opinion—delighted or scathing—from someone who has experience with your product or service. I may not know anyone who's taken the QE2 across the Atlantic, but someone out there is dying to tell me. Edward R. Tufte's lavishly illustrated Visual Explanations: Images and Quantities, Evidence and Narrative is virtually impossible to find in bookstores, yet in 1997 it ranked No. 7 on Amazon's bestseller list. The book's reputation was built almost solely on word-of-mouse buzz.

On the Web all customers have a megaphone, and most are willing to use it. Like the eager combatants who will shout down a bumbling orator on Speaker's Corner in Hyde Park, E-customers will ultimately decide which messages get heard online.

■ Getting Ready for the Revolution

How can your company thrive in the exciting and frightening world of customer control? First, don't fight it. Many of the scenarios painted by fervent Web-heads suggest an apocalyptic future, with consumers huddled in the dark confines of their homes clicking their way through cyberspace. Such obvious hyperbole makes it easy for the uninformed and the fearful to simply dismiss the Web. I'd love to have a buck for every time an exec has said to me, People are always going to enjoy the social experience of shopping. Of course they are! Even a bullish forecaster like Forrester Research sees E-commerce as no more than 6% of retail purchases by 2003. Yet the impact of the Web can't be captured by such numbers.

Imagine two stores in town that have divided the local market for widgets between them. Now, imagine that a newcomer opens a store and immediately drops prices by 20%. The incumbents may not have to match the new price, but they sure as heck can't ignore it and hope to hang on to their customers. Online competitors will undermine the price discipline in cozy markets, even if they don't dominate a segment. They'll also attract the most profitable customers—youthful, tech-savvy, big-volume buyers. Given the high fixed costs of many retailers, it doesn't take a big drop in customers to produce a precipitous decline in profits. So you can't ignore the Web.

Instead, you can—and must—dive into it. In the off-line world it often takes months and millions of dollars to retrain a sales force or adjust prices, and if a company gets these things wrong, it pays a big penalty to put them right again. Not surprisingly, this makes companies highly cautious; any changes have to go through a tangle of red tape. Off-line, it's difficult to get rapid feedback from customers on what part of a company's marketing mix is or isn't working. Increasingly, customers can't be bothered to write a letter or even make a call. Result: Companies are slow to learn from their customers and even slower to act on what they learn. All this changes with the Web.

The Web lends itself to immediate customer feedback and rapid adjustment. Learning cycles are much shorter on-line than off-line. Companies that are quick to try, quick to learn, and quick to adapt will win. Those that learn fastest, and keep learning, will stay ahead. Companies that take months to assess what they've learned, whose internal processes don't run on Internet time, will get left behind. Zipping through the learning cycle creates positive-feedback effects: The faster a company learns and adapts, the more customers it wins; the more customers it wins, the faster it can learn and adapt.

So it's pretty simple. If you don't believe deeply, wholly, and viscerally that the Net is going to change your business, you're going to lose. And if you don't understand the advantages of starting early and learning fast, you're still going to lose.

Producers may have to rethink some of their deepest loyalties. You know that Polo sweater they didn't have in your size? Don't bother trying to order it online. Ralph Lauren and a host of other companies are caught in a quandary: Should they go direct to consumers via the Web or protect their traditional channels?

> **Any company that denies consumers convenience and value to protect an entrenched channel is fighting history: Consumers will not be denied.**

Surprising as it may seem, when some companies talk about customers, they don't mean the people who use their products; they mean the retailers that stock their products. Many of these companies have held back from E-tailing for fear that they'll offend their customers. But this may be shortsighted. Any company that denies its ultimate consumers convenience and value in the interest of protecting an entrenched channel is swimming against the tide of retailing history. Consumers will not be denied.

Before assuming that the Internet will cannibalize sales from traditional channels, companies need to get a better sense of the demand that goes unfulfilled by those channels. Most companies that are protecting their traditional channels have no idea how many sales they lose because of out-of-stocks. When Peapod began offering its pioneering online grocery service, it filled orders by pulling products off of partner grocery stores' shelves. (Peapod is now big enough to run its own centralized facilities.) In trying to fill customer orders for specific brands and products, Peapod found that out-of-stocks were three to four times more prevalent than supermarket managers had thought. Most consumers will grudgingly make a substitution in stores where they can't find exactly what they want. So loyal customers end up buying from a competitor, or simply not buying at all.

You want a squeeze-the-Charmin kind of shopping experience? Get in your car. Know what you need and are in a hurry? Boot up. No customer is going to do all his or her buying on the Web, and very few will do all their buying off-line. Clever producers and retailers are going to develop hybrid models that give customers the chance to combine the best of both online and off-line buying. In a study of 850 consumers, Ernst & Young found that 64% of Internet users research products online and then buy them at stores or by tele-phone. The Gap lets customers have it both ways. If you need to try on a pair of jeans, visit the Gap at the mall. If you have a pair of Gap jeans that fit great and you want to order another pair, just go to www.gap.com.

■ Innovation, Information, Service

So let's review. No more holding people hostage through 30-second commercials. No more hype. No more ignorant customers. No more local monopolies. No more search costs. No more Get in your car and come to us. If you've been paying attention, you're sweating by now.

Sitting atop a 90%-plus market share, it's easy enough for Bill Gates to swoon over the advantages of "frictionless capitalism." But let's be clear: In frictionless capitalism nobody makes any money! So how are people going to survive in the so-called New Economy? Well, ultimately the same way they survived in the old economy—through relentless innovation, unparalleled service, and an attitude of genuine helpfulness, but delivered in new ways.

To thrive in a Net-centric world, a company is going to have to offer consumers products with real performance advantages. Like royalty whose whims are satisfied by simpering servants, online customers will demand flawless service. Consumers will have to be given the information they need to make the best possible buying decisions—in a form that is eminently usable and entertaining to boot. Efficiency advantages and low prices won't be enough—they'll be ruthlessly matched online. The bottom line isn't very complicated. The Net is a noose for mediocrity. But it's a humongous springboard for products and services that are truly great and truly consumer-friendly. Consumers everywhere, stand up and cheer!

GARY HAMEL *is a bestselling author and chairman of Strategos, an international consulting firm specializing in strategy. He is also visiting professor of strategic and international management at the London Business School.*

JEFF SAMPLER *is associate professor of information management and strategy at the London Business School.*

REPORTER ASSOCIATES *Patty de Llosa, Jane Hodges, Len A. Costa*

18

How a Breakthrough Quickly Broke Down For Johnson & Johnson

Its Stent Device Transformed Cardiac Care, Then Left A Big Opening for Rivals

'Getting Kicked in the Shins'

By Ron Winslow
Staff Report of The Wall Street Journal

Four years ago, Johnson & Johnson sparked a revolution in the treatment of coronary-artery disease with a new medical device called a stent.

Few devices have yielded such an immediate eye-popping bonanza for their manufacturer. Doctors rushed to use the tiny metal scaffold to prop open obstructed heart vessels. In just 37 months, the New Brunswick, N.J., health-care giant tallied more than $1 billion of stent sales and garnered more than 90% of a remarkably profitable U.S. market.

Then last fall, Guidant Corp. launched a competing stent in the U.S. "Within 45 days, we had gained a 70% market position," says Ronald W. Dollens, Guidant's president and chief executive officer. J.P. Morgan analyst Michael Weinstein characterizes the shift as "the most dramatic transfer of wealth between two companies in medical-device history."

Sharing the Market

Now, as the annual U.S. market for stents surges past $1 billion, Guidant shares more than 80% of it with yet another competitor, Arterial Vascular Engineering Inc. A fourth maker, Boston Scientific Corp., just won regulatory approval to enter the market. J&J's stent sales, meanwhile, are in free fall. Glenn Reicin, a Morgan Stanley analyst who pegged J&J's market share at 91% at the end of 1996, expects it to plummet to 8% by the end of this year.

"They were acknowledged to be the technology leader and to have an almost insurmountable lead," says David Fish, director of interventional cardiology research and education at the renowned Texas Heart Institute in Houston. "Somewhere along the line, they didn't anticipate the temperament of the marketplace."

How J&J, the revered marketer of baby powder, Band-Aids and Tylenol, won and lost the hottest medical-device market of the 1990s points up both the rewards of innovation and the perils of monopoly. Interviews with dozens of cardiologists and other industry insiders suggest that after doing almost everything right to get a breakthrough product approved by regulators, J&J did almost everything wrong to protect its franchise.

"Their stent changed cardiology and the treatment of coronary-artery disease forever," says Eric Topol, chairman of cardiology at the Cleveland Clinic, one of the world's leading heart centers. But "they didn't sustain the technology. They left the door open for the other manufacturers to come on the market with better designs."

Indeed, J&J was slow to develop next-generation versions of its technology, and left the impression among top doctors that it was banking on a strong patent to protect its product from competition. What appeared to be a master stroke to broaden its cardiology line — its $1.8 billion acquisition of angioplasty-balloon maker Cordis Corp. — also devolved into a culture clash that stalled product development and led to an exodus of Cordis talent.

Compounding these missteps, J&J angered many key customers with rigid pricing for its $1,595 device, balking at discounts even for accounts that purchased more than $1 million of stents a year. For hospitals' catheterization labs, where stent procedures are done, this exacerbated a budget-busting investment at a time when managed care and the national debate on health costs were putting enormous pressure on hospitals.

A Pool of Resentment

With no comparable stent options, many doctors felt gouged. The result was an astonishing pool of resentment among cardiology's highest-profile practices, which came back to haunt J&J as soon as new stents arrived in the U.S. last fall.

"Everybody was at our throats" over costs, says Louis McKeever, director of the catheterization lab at Loyola University Hospital in Chicago. "We were trying to do the best we could for our patients. I expected J&J should have participated in the effort."

J&J acknowledges that it didn't move fast enough to advance its device and that it misread a clientele with whom it hadn't previously done business. It says its Cordis acquisition was troubled by factors typical of the initial stages of mergers. But it staunchly defends its pricing strategy. The main problem, J&J maintains, was that insurers initially refused to reimburse hospitals for any costs beyond the standard angioplasty rate. The company mounted an aggressive and ultimately successful campaign to win higher insurance coverage.

In any event, J&J says it now has a full pipeline of new products that will be competitive in what has become a crowded market. "We know we're getting kicked in the shins right now," says Robert W. Croce, a J&J group chairman in charge of the Cordis business line. "But we're doing a lot to get back in the race."

This is in a market that revolves around a tiny metal-mesh tube no thicker than a pencil lead, crimped on a tiny balloon that is threaded into the heart's arteries. At a blockage site, the balloon is inflated to deploy the stent, creating a scaffold resembling a ballpoint-pen spring that remains to keep the vessel open after the balloon is withdrawn.

When J&J introduced its device, known as the Palmaz-Schatz stent, in August 1994, cardiologists had long been frustrated by a major drawback in balloon angioplasty, their flagship procedure: the tendency of arteries to reclose or reclog after being opened with a balloon. In up to 5% of balloon-only cases, the vessel snaps shut abruptly within minutes or a few days — a life-threatening event that often requires a risky emergency coronary-artery bypass operation. In addition, about 30% of the 400,000 angioplasties done annually in the U.S. fail within six months — due to a renarrowing known as restenosis — leading to further treatment.

J&J's stent all but eliminated the abrupt-closure problem, and cut the longer-term failure rate in half. As doctors leapt to embrace it, they tipped their hats to the company for its seven-year effort to get the device to market: It had persevered in the face of regulatory skepticism about safety and the failure of a competing stent that caused deaths. "The original J&J design had a very good track record that was honorably and painstakingly acquired," says the Texas Heart Institute's Dr. Fish. "J&J absolutely developed this market," adds Mr. Dollens of Guidant. "They took the early risks of whether this therapy would work at all."

And they reaped the rewards. In the first year after the U.S. launch, an estimated 100,000 patients received stents amid a frenzy of enthusiasm that promised soaring future sales. With gross profit margins estimated at more than 80%, analysts figured that a product that, at its peak, provided about 4% of J&J's annual revenue, accounted for about 8% of its bottom line. Moreover, competitors had to mount trials to show their products were as good as the Palmaz-Schatz standard before they could win regulatory approval.

But like most first-generation medical devices, the Palmaz-Schatz has limitations. Its width and rigidity make it difficult to use in narrow or sometimes gnarled coronary arteries of heart patients. It isn't easily visible in the X-ray pictures doctors use to guide them to the site of a blockage. And it comes in just one length — about five-eighths of an inch — requiring the use of two more stents to treat longer obstructions.

At first, these shortcomings were small annoyances. But the nation's 6,000 interventional cardiologists soon became impatient. This small cadre of physicians are medical-technology junkies who thrive on the latest and best products, who often work closely

(Cont.)

with manufacturers to improve existing devices and test new ones.

Since J&J was a newcomer to the catheterization lab, some doctors suspected the stent was a one-hit wonder. Others sensed that J&J was behaving more like a drug company, for which rapid product cycles are less important. "As a physician, I expect products to change every year," says Martin B. Leon, chief executive of the Cardiology Research Foundation at Washington Hospital Center, Washington, D.C., and a consultant to J&J on the device. "As a corporation, they couldn't understand that."

Stent Envy

Moreover, by early 1996, more-advanced stents from Guidant, AVE and other companies were available in Europe, where regulatory hurdles are lower than in the U.S. This led to an epidemic of stent envy among U.S. cardiologists.

J&J's Mr. Croce says the small unit that developed the stent was so focused on getting it to market, and meeting enormous demand, that it devoted little time or resources to the next generation. Once that effort began, he says, developers spent too much time modifying the original and didn't pay enough attention to ease-of-use features that cardiologists wanted.

The other big flaw in J&J's stent, according to cardiologists and hospital administrators, was its price. The stent's popularity provoked an explosion in unexpected costs in catheterization labs, typically crucial hospital profit centers. St. Joseph's Hospital in Atlanta, for instance, spent $2 million for stents in 1995 after buying hardly any the year before, one doctor says. Stent-related technology added sharply to the cost of a routine angioplasty procedure. But insurers generally continued to reimburse hospitals at regular angioplasty rates.

Administrators and cardiologists at high-volume hospitals asked J&J for a break. At Our Lady of Lourdes Hospital in Lafayette, La., Stephanie Mayeaux, director of cardiovascular procedures, first sought a discount based on the number of stents her hospital used. Rebuffed, she pooled the purchases of a three-hospital system. Still no deal. Finally, she tried to leverage the buying power of a 300-hospital purchasing group. "J&J did not bend," she says. Major programs in Washington, D.C., Minneapolis, Chicago, New York and elsewhere were similarly frustrated.

J&J also alienated the prestigious Cleveland Clinic. "In their dealings with catheterization labs, there was a very strong sense of arrogance," the clinic's Dr. Topol says. When he and his associates sought better rates, they say, J&J officials suggested they could help doctors design "care tracks" to make the procedure more efficient. "They were implying that we didn't know how to manage our patient population," recalls Mary Heisler, manager of the catheterization lab.

J&J says the stent was a bargain in the U.S. compared to the $2,400 initially charged in Europe, and the $3,500 sticker price in Japan. And it was only $200 more than another stent on the U.S. market for a very narrow application. "We were never price-gouging," says Marvin Woodall, who headed the unit that brought the stent to the market and is now an international vice president for J&J. Today, the stent sells for about $1,000 in Europe, where competition has driven prices down, and about $3,000 in Japan.

The company says it has been vindicated by its competitors. Comparable stents from Guidant, AVE and Boston Scientific are similarly priced. And Mr. Croce says J&J eventually gave discounts to a dozen high-volume centers, including the Cleveland Clinic. "Doctors have short memories," he says.

When J&J launched its hostile bid to acquire Cordis late in 1995, many heart doctors believed both their technology and economic concerns would be addressed. Cordis had built a $500 million-a-year business in equipment used in angioplasty, including a high-pressure balloon favored by many cardiologists using the stent. Combining the companies, doctors felt, would yield new products and increase prospects for package pricing.

Culture Clash

But the anticipated synergy didn't develop. Former Cordis insiders say that J&J's top-down culture clashed with a more entrepreneurial approach that characterized Cordis under Robert C. Strauss, its chief executive officer. And though Cordis was much more experienced with catheterization-lab technology and in dealing with cardiologists, its managers felt that J&J's views prevailed on essentially all early decisions.

A stent that Cordis was about to launch in Europe was shelved. Efforts to combine J&J's stent with the high-pressure balloon foundered. Cordis's "core teams," adept at rapid product development by integrating marketing, R&D and manufacturing operations around specific business lines, were replaced by a more traditional structure that had such functions reporting to separate managers.

The new Cordis didn't come to market with a significant new product until last January—nearly two years after the acquisition. Called the Crown stent, it was significantly outmatched by Guidant and AVE products when it was launched.

"People always underestimate what it takes to put two companies together," says J&J's Mr. Croce, but he defends the acquisition. "We're past a lot of the troubles," he says. But he readily concedes that the combination of J&J's inexperience with the cardiology industry and struggles with the Cordis integration were big factors in a "lag time" in product development.

By early 1997, the patience of many doctors with the Palmaz-Schatz stent was wearing thin. At the Cleveland Clinic, for instance, Dr. Topol became particularly frustrated after complications during an angioplasty procedure forced one of his patients to undergo an emergency bypass. "Had we had access to new stent designs, that would have turned things around" for her, he says. (The patient recovered.)

Top cardiologists, including Dr. Topol, urged the FDA to expedite approval of competing stents. Last October, the FDA cleared Guidant's Multi-link stent just 112 days after the company filed its application; by the end of December, it accepted AVE's stent. "These new stents are so much hands-down better," Dr. Topol says. "We needed them."

J&J was powerless to prevent the resulting rout. Discounts for what was perceived as inferior technology wouldn't work, and doctors weren't interested in J&J's argument that the Palmaz-Schatz stent had a proven track record.

Meantime, J&J's efforts on reimbursement began to bear fruit. Mr. Woodall headed an intense project to persuade insurers that they were underpaying for stent procedures. "They were benefiting because their patients weren't coming back for second and third angioplasties," Mr. Woodall says. The company's analysis of public data on 200,000 Medicare patients convinced Medicare officials to increase stent reimbursement by $2,300, or 26%.

The Next Wave

The new rate became effective last Oct. 1 — just in time to benefit J&J's competitors. The next day, Guidant's stent hit the market at a list price no cheaper than J&J's device.

Now J&J has several new products in clinical trials, including the "miniCrown," for smaller arteries and a product intended to improve on the stent's track record in preventing restenosis. By the middle of next year, it expects to launch the Cross Flex LC, a "slick" stent, say doctors who have used it in clinical trials. That endorsement comes with irony for J&J — the device is patterned after the old Cordis design the company rejected.

Mr. Croce says these products should convince skeptics the company is committed to the cardiology market. He says the only way the company can put to rest the resentment among key customers is with better products. "You can't sell everybody," he says. "But I think we have a decent following. When our technology matches up, they'll come back."

But Guidant, AVE and Boston Scientific are advancing their already-preferred devices as well. James J. Ferguson III, associate director of cardiology research at Texas Heart Institute, says J&J's road back to prominence in the market it created won't be easy. "J&J went out and poisoned the well," he says. "They have a couple of nice products in the pipeline, but they also have a huge backlog of ill will that is going to take a while to dissipate."

19

WE HAVE LIFTOFF!

The strong launch of the euro
is hailed around the world

The mood was giddy just about everywhere on the Continent as Europe's new currency, the euro, made its grand debut. In Frankfurt, dignitaries ceremoniously launched Germany's first euro-denominated stock trading on the morning of Jan. 4 as strobe lights flashed and the uplifting strains of Beethoven's *Ode to Joy* wafted through the bourse. Stock markets from Frankfurt to Paris to Milan responded to the euphoria by soaring more than 8% over the next three days.

The triumphant music seems appropriate, at least for now. After years of skepticism from critics on the Continent and abroad, Europe has its common currency. To the delight of its champions, the euro is a robust newborn, not the pipsqueak its doubters had expected. The $1.17 kickoff rate set by European authorities already includes a rise of about 10% in major European currencies during the runup to the new currency this fall. According to J.P. Morgan, the euro will climb a further 12% by yearend, to $1.31.

NEW GAME. Even without such a dramatic rise, the euro is a force to be reckoned with. The long-term effects of melding an 11-nation, $6.5 trillion, 290 million-person region into one economic and financial bloc are giving Continental Europe new cachet. Companies around the world are eager to exploit what they hope will become a true single market. If the euro acts as a catalyst for regulatory and economic reform, nudging the Continent away from its socialist-flavored capitalism, Europe could become a competitive power, attracting new investment from around the globe.

Already, the euro has instantly created a $2 trillion government bond market, 20% bigger than the U.S.'s, and should over time expand anemic Continental stock markets and corporate bond markets to nearly U.S. dimensions. That potential makes Europe a compelling investment story for foreigners and locals alike. "Now that there is no fragmentation of European currencies, we expect to see enormous investment flows into the new currency," says Luis Manas, deputy chief financial officer at Spanish oil company Repsol.

That prospect changes the game for Washington as well as Wall Street. From now on, the world's central bankers must watch the euro while setting their own monetary policy. The U.S. Federal Reserve may find that the upstart challenges the dollar as a reserve currency. That could alter monetary

---

Booster A healthy euro would help Asia and trim the U.S. deficit by spurring exports. But if it soars too high, Europe could get clobbered.

---

policy: With every move it makes, the Fed would have to take into account the effect on the dollar-euro rate. Tokyo, instead of monitoring just the crucial yen-dollar relationship that regulates the Japanese export machine, must now keep a nervous eye on the euro-dollar link as well. On the bright side, a strong euro will help Japan export more to Europe.

Underpinning the new currency's initial strength are potent economic fundamentals. Economic growth in the euro zone is expected to rival the 2% rate projected for the U.S. this year. And despite the falloff in Asian demand, Goldman, Sachs & Co. expects the region's current-account surplus to hit $109.6 billion, slightly more than last year. That compares with the punishing $250 billion-plus deficit projected for the U.S. "There will be upward pressure on the euro against the dollar for the next year or two," predicts Richard Portes, president of the Centre for Economic Policy Research in London.

At the same time, the euro virtually ensures that European governments keep their fiscal houses in order. Under euro zone membership rules, national deficits must be less than 3% of gross domestic product. Meeting that rule drove inflation in the region down to 0.9% late last year, compared with 1.7% in the U.S. "I'm still bullish on the European economy," says Leonhard Fischer, a board member at Germany's Dresdner Bank. "Despite all the troubles in the world, I think that in Europe the dynamics of the euro will take over."

POLITICAL BACKLASH? A strong euro would be welcome in most of the rest of the world, too. It would ease the economic crisis in Asia and other emerging markets by helping make companies there more competitive when selling to Europe. It also would lessen the strain of the trade deficit on the U.S. economy by giving American exporters a similar boost.

But there's a dark side to those dynamics.

For Europe to prosper, the euro can't soar too high. A too-strong euro could increase strains inherent in the new monetary union. The euro bloc throws together nations with vastly different financial traditions and growth prospects, under one low interest rate tailored for slow-growth Germany and France. The current boom in fast-growth nations like Spain and Ireland could turn into a Japan-style bust if it lasts too long. And rigid labor regulations mean that pockets of high unemployment could crop up in Germany and France at the first hint of recession.

If that happens, pessimists fear that Europe's new left-wing governments will abandon fiscal prudence and go back to their old tax-and-spend policies. That in turn will undermine global confidence in the new currency and send investors fleeing. "How we manage our economy and how Europe manages its economy will ultimately determine the euro's value," predicts Deputy Treasury Secretary Lawrence H. Summers.

Another danger of a supereuro is political backlash. Leaders in Germany and France, which account for more than half of the euro zone's GDP, fear that by depressing growth, business investment, and consumer confidence, a too-strong currency could stall the Continent's already dicey economic recovery. That's one reason German Finance Minister Oskar Lafontaine is calling for a formal trading band to forestall huge swings between the euro, dollar, and yen. U.S. officials reject the idea, but the Japanese are entertaining it, prodded by the Germans and French.

Indeed, the left-of-center governments that have come to power across Europe in the last 18 months are counting on a euro-related boost to help slash the region's unemployment rate, which averaged 11% last year. A supereuro could slam European exports, slow business investment, and kill off the consumer recovery the politicians are counting on. Goldman Sachs equity strategist Peter Sullivan figures that a 15% rise in the euro, to about $1.35, would be enough to begin stunting corporate profit growth and clobber booming Continental equity markets.

TAKEOVER BINGE. At least to begin with, the euro is likely to energize Europe's economy. Already, restructuring is rampant among its biggest companies. The massive mergers rumored to be imminent in the auto industry—with BMW, Volvo, and others believed to be takeover bait—are just one sign

(Cont.)

of the rush to build greater critical mass. One reason: For carmakers, consumer goods companies, retailers and others, the single currency is suddenly making prices transparent across national borders, unmasking protected profit havens, and forcing the overall level of prices down. Global players such as Volkswagen and DaimlerChrysler can better withstand the strain.

Plus, by boosting the balance sheets and share prices of European companies, a strong euro could accelerate Europe's buying spree in the U.S. Some analysts think Daimler Benz's $94 billion takeover of Chrysler and Deutsche Bank's $9 billion bid for Bankers Trust were signs of a huge takeover binge to come. Germany's Dresdner Bank and the Netherlands' ABN-Amro are already scouting the U.S.

At the same time, U.S. companies in many sectors are mapping massive expansion plans. Investment banks such as Morgan Stanley Dean Witter, Merrill Lynch, and Goldman Sachs have moved whole teams of bankers from New York to Europe. In three short years, they have come to dominate European mergers and acquisitions. In retailing, Wal-Mart Stores Inc. has bought up two German chains and is building a major European presence. Long-entrenched U.S. companies know they have to beef up. "My guess is [the euro] will pull investment capital into Europe," says Mike Burns, the new head of General Motors Corp.'s European operation.

Euro skeptics may be underestimating the new currency's appeal in Asia, too. Tokyo-based Warburg Dillon Read economist Kazuko Mizuno predicts that Japanese life insurers, for instance, will quickly start shifting some of their massive investments into euro-denominated bonds. Toyota and other

Japanese companies have announced big new investments in the euro zone, because they think the new currency will boost the Continent's economy.

WILD CARD. Buying by Asian central banks could also buoy the euro as they swap euros for dollars in their reserve holdings. The central banks say they plan to monitor the euro for now, but "there will definitely be some switching if the euro turns out to be a firm, stable currency," says Friedrich Wu, chief economist for state-owned Develop-

THE FALLOUT FROM A STRONG EURO

THE DOLLAR

If the euro challenged the greenback as a reserve currency, U.S. authorities might need to raise rates to shore up the dollar.

TAKEOVERS

A strong euro would give European companies a powerful weapon to shop for acquisitions around the world.

COMPANIES

U.S. businesses could boost their earnings, and maybe sales, in Europe. But the Continental recovery could suffer.

EMERGING MARKETS

Exporters in Asia and other battered regions could get a lift from selling more goods in Europe.

DATA: BUSINESS WEEK

ment Bank of Singapore. Some analysts think the banks will start buying sooner and faster than expected if the euro shows signs of a sustained rise against the dollar.

The wild card in the euro's prospects is interest rates. With U.S. growth at last projected to slow, to about 2% in 1999 after four unexpectedly strong years, economists figure that U.S. Federal Reserve Chairman Alan Greenspan will continue cutting rates from the current 4.75%. At least initially, the European Central Bank also has been easing. It orchestrated a cut to the current 3% in December, even before it officially took over monetary policy. Many economists expect another cut this year. Deutsche Bank thinks euro zone rates could go as low as 2.5% by midyear. That would make the euro a less attractive investment than the dollar even if Greenspan eases considerably.

But the ECB is trying to use its accommodating stance as a carrot for European policymakers. The bank continues to call for more deregulation and other economic reforms. "When the central bankers eased in December, they were saying to the politicians, 'You have to follow through with structural and labor market reforms,'" says Frankfurt-based Bank Julius Baer economist Gerhard Grebe. European central bankers know that a new currency alone won't cure what still ails the Old World. But for now, it's a pretty good tonic.

By Thane Peterson in Frankfurt, with Margaret Popper in Madrid, Owen Ullmann in Washington, Brian Bremner in Tokyo, Bruce Einhorn in Hong Kong, and Karen Lowry Miller in Detroit

20

JUSTICE'S CARTEL CRACKDOWN

It has 25 grand juries looking into international price-fixing

It sounds like the plot of a paperback thriller. Top executives from competing companies in the U.S., Germany, and Japan jet around the world holding clandestine price-fixing meetings at glittering world capitals. Carving up the world market in a key industrial commodity, they agree to limit production and avoid unnecessary competition. Keeping their activities secret, even from fellow employees, the execs use code names when talking to each other on the phone.

This isn't fiction, though. The Justice Dept. charges that leading manufacturers of graphite electrodes, an important component in steel-mill machinery, followed this script for several years. After a multiyear investigation, the agency joined European authorities in a simultaneous raid on the conspirators' facilities in three countries in June, 1997, and succeeded in breaking up the cartel. In April, UCAR International Inc. in Danbury, Conn., agreed to pay $110 million—the largest fine in antitrust history—for its role in the conspiracy. Japan's Showa Denko K.K. has also admitted participating in the cartel, and Carbon/Graphite Group in Pittsburgh was granted immunity from prosecution in return for helping the Justice probe. At least five other manufacturers are under investigation by U.S., Japanese, and European Commission antitrust authorities.

The case is just the latest of a recent spate of big-time global price-fixing prosecutions. On July 9, Justice launched a criminal suit against former Archer Daniels Midland Co. executives Michael D. Andreas, Mark E. Whitacre, and Terrance S. Wilson in the highest-profile price-fixing case yet. The ADM lawsuit may be getting the headlines, but it's just part of a much broader crackdown. At the behest of the Justice Dept., a record 25 grand juries are investigating international price-fixing in industries as diverse as vitamins, glass, and marine equipment. The agency is also pushing for new cooperation agreements with other countries, boosting the number of Federal Bureau of Investigation agents investigating suspect companies, and conducting special border watches aimed at catching conspirators.

U.S. DAMAGE. Driving the Justice campaign is a conviction that international price-fixing is on the rise—and hurting the U.S. economy. Although there's no hard data on the subject, complaints about the problem have been increasing, according to the agency. Assistant U.S. Attorney General for Anti-trust Joel I. Klein believes that as trade barriers fall, companies that once had national markets to themselves may look to cross-border cartels to fend off competitors that are grabbing market share and forcing down prices. "We're looking at cartels that are doing a billion dollars in business," Klein says. "If you assume that they are inflating prices by 15% to 20%, we're looking at hundreds of millions of dollars sucked right out of the economy."

The new wave of price-fixing may not be igniting inflation, but it is increasing costs in discrete markets, Klein contends. In the ADM case, prosecutors say, the U.S. price for lysine, a livestock-feed additive, doubled in the first three months of the conspiracy. Frequently, the cartels are composed of foreign companies specifically attempting to hike prices in the U.S. The Justice Dept.

Taking Conspirators to Court

The Justice Dept. is going after global price-fixing schemes, which chief trustbuster Joel Klein believes are at record levels. A few key cases:

FEED ADDITIVES The price-fixing trial of three Archer Daniels Midland officials, including Executive Vice-President Michael Andreas, began on July 9. Prosecutors charge that ADM execs conspired with four Asian companies to limit production and allocate sales of lysine, a livestock-feed additive.

MARINE SERVICES Dutch, Belgian, and U.S. companies paid more than $65 million in criminal fines last December for rigging bids for marine services in the North Sea and Gulf of Mexico. Under one agreement for heavy-lift barges, conspirators agreed to divide customers, pool revenues, and split profits—and they put it all in writing.

GRAPHITE ELECTRODES Two companies have pleaded guilty to fixing prices and allocating market shares worldwide for graphite electrodes, used in steel minimills. UCAR International paid a $110 million fine, the largest in antitrust history. A judge recently rejected a $29 million fine against Showa Denko Carbon, a U.S. unit of a Japanese company, as too low.

FAX PAPER Several Japanese paper companies have pleaded guilty to conspiring to inflate the price of fax paper sold in the U.S.

DATA: JUSTICE DEPT., BUSINESS WEEK

(Cont.)

recently won guilty pleas from several Japanese companies for conspiring to raise prices of fax paper here by about 10% (though a mistrial was declared in a case against another manufacturer on July 14th).

Despite its recent successes, Justice can't fight price cartels alone. And winning cooperation from other countries gets complicated in a hurry. Foreign governments have long tolerated price-fixing cartels, believing that they protect local companies and maintain employment levels. When the U.S. asks for permission to interview witnesses and review documents, authorities are often reluctant to help. International cooperation is slowly improving, but federal antitrust cops are frustrated. "In most countries, price-fixing is not a crime," says U.S. Deputy Assistant Attorney General for Antitrust Gary R. Spratling. "It's not seen as very serious, and their procedures for pursuing it are more restrictive."

The price-fixing conspiracies that Justice has prosecuted take a wide variety of forms, says Spratling. Conspirators may set a single worldwide price, or one company will be allowed to set the rate that others must follow in its particular region, as is alleged in the graphite-electrode case. Other times, executives will simply divide up the map, charging whatever they want in their assigned countries without fear of competition.

HOW IT WORKS. Cartel leaders develop sophisticated mechanisms to police the agreement, collecting internal production records from each company. Prosecutors charge that in a citric-acid price-fixing conspiracy, for example, cartel members reviewed the sales of each conspirator at the end of each year; any company that had sold more than its allotted share was required in the following year to buy the excess from a conspirator that had not reached its volume-allocation target in the preceding year. Since 1996, five companies have pleaded guilty in citric-acid prosecutions, including ADM, a U.S. subsidiary of German pharmaceutical giant Bayer, and Switzerland-based F. Hoffmann-LaRoche.

While the primary conspirators are usually high-ranking executives, less-senior corporate intermediaries frequently fine-tune the agreements, Orr says. In the ADM lysine case, for example, prosecutors charge that senior executives attended only those meetings necessary to solve big problems, such as volume-allocation issues, while regional sales managers of competitor companies met to work out details on prices in local markets.

To break up these lucrative arrangements, Justice's most potent weapon has been its "leniency" program, which provides amnesty from criminal charges to the first conspirator in a price-fixing case to 'fess up.' Since the program began in 1993, an average of one company a month in a wide variety of industries has come forward. Amnesty cases have led to a record $210 million in fines in the first six months of 1998. "This has uncovered cases that we probably would never have learned about," says Justice's Director for Criminal Enforcement for Antitrust, John T. Orr Jr.

One such case: A U.S. company tipped off Justice to bid-rigging by a joint venture it owned with a Dutch partner. In December, 1997, the Netherlands-based joint venture, HeereMac, paid a $49 million fine after pleading guilty to rigging prices for heavy-lift marine-construction services. Government documents say competitors divided contracts for projects in the North Sea, Gulf of Mexico, and the Far East.

"STUNNING DEVELOPMENT." Slowly but surely, international reluctance to come down hard on price-fixing conspiracies is changing. Antitrust authorities in Europe played key roles in both the lysine and graphite-electrode price-fixing investigations. On May 27, the Japan Fair Trade Commission raided the offices of four graphite-electrode producers. "It's truly a stunning development," says James R. Loftis III, a Washington antitrust attorney with the firm of Collier, Shannon & Rill. "Historically, Japanese competition authorities had been insular about these issues, rebuffing any requests by the U.S. for forced access to Japanese companies."

Still, huge barriers to cooperation remain. But if Justice can bring some of its current price-fixing investigations to fruition, the agency believes it can make a strong case that cartels are a serious global problem, especially in an era of rising global trade. And that might well force other countries to get on the U.S. bandwagon.

By Susan B. Garland in Washington, with Emily Thornton in Tokyo

21

Female frontier: Financial services firms begin to cater to women

By Gary Strauss
USA Today

Ellen McGirt has made two career changes, mostly, she says, because the financial services industry doesn't get it when it comes to catering to women.

"When I began searching for investment advice in the early '90s, most men I talked to had the attitude 'Don't worry about things, honey, once you get married, your husband will take care of it,'" says McGirt, 36.

An art dealer, McGirt went to work for a brokerage, hoping for an on-the-job financial education. But the pressure-cooker selling atmosphere at the mostly male firm proved frustrating. She decided to teach herself. Now steeped in financial expertise, she's become an investment maven with her own Internet advice Web site, Cassandra's Revenge, which gets 85,000 hits a month.

Targeting women for financial services seems like a no-brainer. They may not be the industry's final marketing frontier, but their rapid building of financial muscle as wage earners and investors makes them the biggest, most promising untapped market. Yet, McGirt is a poster girl for millions of women jaded by a financial world dominated by conservative, middle-aged white men who just don't get how to provide women personal finance expertise.

"When I got into the business in the 1980s, I found the sexism on Wall Street more troubling than the racism. Things have changed somewhat, but the financial world is still sexist," says Lenda Washington, who launched Allison Street Advisors in November to provide asset management to wealthy minorities and women.

"This isn't complex surgery. Women want what men want — performance, service and someone truly interested in solving their problems," she says.

Few understand the market

Except for a handful of savvy marketers, few mainstream financial service companies understand the market.

"Almost everyone is still in a learning process," says Charley Blaine, editor of *Family Money* magazine, which skews heavily to women. "The big problem is cultural. Most male brokers and financial planners don't know how to talk to women. The language, the accessibility, the presentation is as important as the content. Women want it told straight. Without a lot of crap."

OppenheimerFunds launched the mutual fund industry's first women's education program in 1992. Compared with a national survey conducted then, results from a follow-up query in 1997 were startling. Women had substantially boosted their expertise and interest in investing, and far more had become their families' primary financial decision-maker.

Yet 58% of respondents thought stockbrokers and financial planners treated women with less respect than men — virtually the same percentage who felt that way in 1992.

"Men have carried the burden of being financial caretakers for years," says Suze Orman, author of the best-selling *9 Steps to Financial Freedom* and the soon-to-be-released *Courage to be Rich*.

"That's partially why Wall Street, out of its own naïveté, is still marketing to women like they are second-class citizens."

Ignoring ripe markets

Adriane Berg, a financial advice radio and TV host and a writer for several personal finance Internet sites, says financial service providers think most women are the same as the clients they've been dealing with for decades — aging, infrequent traders who inherited wealth through divorce or a husband's death and barely make any moves with their stock portfolios except cashing dividend checks. And that slice of the market tends to require an inordinate amount of hand-holding, annoying most commission-based brokers.

Berg says financial advisers need to get in tune with a far more diverse market captivated by protracted domestic economic growth and a robust bull market.

"Much of Wall Street is still behind the curve. There are an enormous number of women of all ages, color and educational backgrounds who are risk-takers waiting to be cultivated," Berg says. "I get calls from single mothers making $26,000 a year asking about stock options to high-powered executives with lots of money in the bank but nothing in the market."

Salomon Smith Barney began targeting women about three years ago, mostly to broaden a client base that was predominately white, male, age 55.

Through focus groups, the firm learned to tailor advertising efforts to attract vastly different segments of women. It also boosted hires of women and minori-

(Cont.)

ty stockbrokers at 450 branch offices. About 40% of its clients are now women, vs. 28% in 1995, says Mindy Ross, head of Salomon's target marketing programs.

Mutual fund operator T. Rowe Price decided to court women in 1997. It bought female subscriber lists from *Money* and *Kiplinger's Personal Finance* magazines, then tested colorful direct-mail brochures featuring pictures of women on the front. The text was the same as the pictureless, black-and-white general mailers. But the response from women was 40% to 50% higher than with the standard mailer, says spokeswoman Valerie King-Calloway.

EMPOWERMENT

Magazine ads featuring only women — a first for T. Rowe Price — began running in several magazines last month.

As many mainstream firms try to define and court an elusive market, McGirt and other nimble opportunists are capitalizing on the information and service void. How a movement is mushrooming:

▲ **Books.** Nearly 200 financial advice books aimed at women were published in 1998. "The amount of ignorance and passivity among women over managing money is tragic, but one thing that's been missing are role models," Barbara Stanny says.

Stanny, daughter of H&R Block founder Richard Bloch, says she wrote *Prince Charming Isn't Coming; How Women Get Smart About Money*, after her first husband, a compulsive gambler, left her $1 million in debt. "It's about empowering women," she says.

Businesswoman/socialite Georgette Mosbacher says there's a ripe market for financial advice in understandable terms. That's a prime reason behind her just-released book, *It Takes Money, Honey: A Get-Smart Guide to Financial Freedom*. "Most financial advice isn't in plain English," she says. "My book is."

▲ **Magazines.** *Worth* magazine parent Capital Publishing rolled out *Equity* magazine in December. Part *Town and Country*, part *Worth*, the lavish quarterly targets affluent women. "There's a large, dynamic segment of smart, wealthy women," says Executive Editor Jane Berentson. "They want to know how to invest wisely. But in an unpatronizing way."

Women in Touch, a bimonthly, was launched in November. Broader in scope than *Equity*, *WIT* has a strong personal finance focus.

"There's a gap in the magazine market for women between 28 and 49," says publisher Paul Severini. "Two years of focus group research showed us that personal finance and other topics typically under the male domain are just as important to women as fashion and entertainment." Underscoring *WIT*'s potential as a

marketing vehicle, the magazine is published by Gramercy Group, an advertising agency.

▲ **The Web.** The Internet has fast become a vast financial electronic encyclopedia, serving up an array of information that lets women choose what and when they want financial advice.

iVillage, a leading women's Web site, added a personal finance channel in mid-December.

"We heard loud and clear that women wanted a place for centralized information," says site director Lisa Kraynak. Discount broker Charles Schwab is among iVillage's top advertisers.

Rival Web site Women.com also recently developed personal finance advice. Offering basics from car buying to asset allocation, it's quickly become one of the Web site's most popular attractions, says marketing chief Fran Maier.

▲ **Television**. Financial planning programming will be part of the viewing lineup on Oxygen, a women's cable channel debuting in 2000.

▲ **Boutique shopping**. Women's Consumer Network, a new member-based, one-stop consumer service, offers deals on dozens of products and services to

For more info
Investment advice for women:

ON THE INTERNET

▲ www.ivillage.com

▲ www.women.com

▲ www.cassandrasrevenge.com

▲ www.electra.com

▲ www.thewomenscenter.org

▲ www.womenconnect.com

▲ www.wealthbuildernews.com

AT INVESTMENT FIRMS:

▲ Prudential Securities offers "Investment Planning for Women," a reference guide (call 1-800-843-7625, ext. 2697).

▲ OppenheimerFunds offers its women an investing program. 212-323-0628.

▲ T. Rowe Price offers retirement planning, 1-800-831-1037.

OTHERS:

▲ Women's Consumer Network, 1-888-926-2221 or womensconsumernet.com.

(Cont.)

help women manage finances, career and family. "There's a reality that men don't understand," says founder Melissa Moss. "We do what women would do for themselves if they had the time, researching the best products and services." Among WCN's offerings: financial education programs and low-minimum mutual fund investments.

'CONSCIOUS EFFORT'

Several financial services have just begun catering to the women's market. This week, Morgan Stanley Dean Witter's Discover unit launched print ads featuring a woman asking why she should use the discount brokerage. The ad offers 50 reasons. Another current spot features a mother with her infant under the headline: "You are the CEO of your life."

"We've made a conscious effort to recognize women," says Discover spokesman Tom O'Connell. "We want to say, 'You are welcome here.' "

Discount broker JB Oxford recently replaced a TV spot featuring actor Wayne Rogers with new spots, including one showing young women talking about trading on the Net. "Clearly, women have been an overlooked market," says Jamie Lewis, company president. "Over the next decade, they'll become a much larger part of on-line trading. We want a fresh image to attract market-savvy investors."

But to some firms, women just aren't a viable market. Boston-based market research publisher About Women plans to end its quarterly *Women and Money* newsletter, launched last April, because of a lack of Wall Street interest. "There's still some resistance to target women in the upper echelons of the financial industry," says editor Cynthia Tripp. "It's still a hard sell."

That's fine with McGirt. "These dinosaurs have allowed me a new career. I'm loving it."

Pick Up on This: Just Don't Answer, Let Freedom Ring

Odds Are, That Telephone Call Isn't Worth the Bother; Of Slaves and Ms. Masters

BY CHRISTINA DUFF

Staff Reporter of THE WALL STREET JOURNAL

WASHINGTON — The home phone rings. Shelly Masters, a lawyer, reclines on her love seat, flipping channels. It rings again. She cranks up the TV volume and stays put.

And why shouldn't she? Ms. Masters, age 33, is quite comfortable letting a ringing phone ring.

The answering machine clicks on. "Shel? SHEL-LY! Will you pick up the phone? I know you're there . . ." Ms. Masters stares at CNN. A life blissfully uninterrupted.

The caller, a friend, doesn't see it that way at all. Reached later — and on the first ring — Reagan McBride is fuming. "She's like, lying to me," Ms. McBride says. The 32-year-old graphic artist makes a point of answering her phone, and she expects others to do likewise.

A Freudian Possibility

This is a country of callers sadly divided. On one side are those who remain phone slaves. These souls continue to treat each ring like a fire alarm, disrupting dinner, interrupting lovemaking, muting the TV and shushing the kids. Often, experts say, these are anal-retentive types who overly respect authority. They probably don't jaywalk. And no doubt they eagerly rip open junk mail.

On the other side are those who have conquered the 122-year-old device. Growing numbers of people are learning to get an answering machine or voice mail, toss in a Caller ID unit — and get a life. To screen calls is simply to have e-mail that talks. Pick up if your boss is calling, otherwise return messages at your leisure and erase the verbal spam. Let's face it: Increasingly, it appears that these people are on the right side of history; they are winning the battle.

Answering machines were considered "insulting" by many in the 1970s, but by 1987, people were evenly split on their worthiness, says James Katz, social-science director of Bellcore, a telecommunications-consulting firm in Morristown, N.J. Today, two-thirds of U.S. households have them, and of those, fully half use them to screen calls, according to the marketing-research firm Roper Starch Worldwide. Grandparents will always answer their phones. But their kids and beeper-reared grandchildren practice guilt-free screening. The plugged-in crowd wants to know who's calling before picking up, which, after all, is a form of commitment.

"Appalling," says Peter Crabb, associate psychology professor at Pennsylvania State University at Ogontz. He did a two-year study of electronic chitchat. "A ringing telephone," he writes, "serves as a summons to interact." Yet, by screening, "callees appear to ignore the established answering norm and to engage in behavior that violates it." The result: "Social isolation," Mr. Crabb says.

Jingle of Social Change

In truth, phone behavior had to change. The wife used to be home manning the phone. Now, the last thing she wants to do after a day's gainful employment is chew the fat. Telecommuters turn off the ringer after hours to help divide work and home life. And with New Age "team" structures at work, many others are talked out by the time they leave the office.

It's "sheer survival," says Christena Nippert-Eng, assistant sociology professor at the Illinois Institute of Technology, in Chicago. "We're trying to counteract a life under siege." Trained like dogs to jump at a ringing noise, "we must de-brainwash ourselves," Ms. Nippert-Eng says. She herself picks up only when expecting a call, or when "feeling adventurous."

Like potty training, learning phone avoidance can be painful, but the end results are less messy and save time and sanity. Guilt and shame quickly turn to secret delight. Empowerment. Freedom.

Realistically, what are the chances a call is going to be more interesting and rewarding than what you're already doing? "Million to one," figures Roxy Roxborough, head of Las Vegas Sports Consultants, the world's largest independent oddsmaker.

Match that against the odds that the caller is a telemarketer, an in-law, or some other undesirable. "Three to one," Mr. Roxborough wagers.

In Kansas City, Mo., Ben Goodall was having a lovely time sipping a cold beer on his back porch on a balmy spring evening when, brrrring! the phone rang. Mr. Goodall, a 44-year-old roofing contractor and father of three, leapt from his recliner and spun too quickly, sending his Heineken into the geranium and severely spraining his left ankle.

All for a soccer mom wanting cupcakes for the last home game. "The shame," Mr. Goodall laments. Obedient no longer, he now relishes the chance to sit and screen. "It feels so good," he says.

It's also totally fair. Take it from etiquette umpire Judith Martin, a k a Miss Manners. "The wildly condemned practice" of screening "is not rude," though it is hard "to make the irate understand that," she writes in her book "Communication." Actually, Ms. Martin says, "it is no more possible or wise always to accept all calls as they are made than it is to leave one's front door wide open." The caller is rude not to realize that.

Technology has made it far too easy to reach out and smother someone. Look at beepers, multiple phone lines, call-waiting. Consequently, victims of telephone assaults have no recourse but to arm themselves with technology of their own and fight back. If a caller refuses to leave messages, a Caller ID box can still reveal his name and number. It was intended as a safety device. Now, "people use it for the control," says Joan Rasmussen of Bell Atlantic Corp., which took eight years to sell its first million Caller IDs and just one year, 1996, to sell the second million.

Voice mail is a cool option. No more bulky machines. But it has one drawback: Callers can't be overheard leaving messages. To this, too, there is a solution: SoloPoint Inc., in Los Gatos, Calif., makes miniature speakers for the phone so voice mail messages can be heard as they come in. Virginia Yorgin, a 63-year-old retired case worker in San Diego, signed up for a pair. Now, she never answers her phone.

Telemarketers and others desperate to get through can electronically mask their number, and not even Caller ID can decipher it. So for the hard-core screener, there's software. YoYo Call Tracker can actually disable the ring for some, all or just unidentified callers and bump them to a machine.

Technophobes improvise. Advice columnist Ann Landers doesn't even own an answering machine, but she takes the phone off the hook during her sleeping hours: 1 a.m. to 10 a.m. "No one's going to call me until I'm ready," she says.

It's time to recognize that screening transcends society, maybe even time and space. When the phone rings, "the bell creates in us a kind of vibration, maybe some anxiety," says Vietnamese Zen master Thich Nhat Hanh. Who is it? What do they want? Do I owe them money?

Mr. Hanh suggests meditation. When the phone rings, don't move: It's a temple bell. Begin to breathe. "Breathing in, I calm my body. Breathing out, I smile," he says. "This is very beautiful." In the French monastery where he lives, near Bordeaux, Mr. Hanh sucks in air and allows a nun to answer the phone.

Of course, there is an ugly side to this. Jason Fries, a 33-year-old sales manager in Chicago, hates the idle-chat-on-the-phone phase of dating. He tried to sneak a message onto a young woman's answering machine one afternoon when he expected her to be at work, but she was there — home sick — and she answered the phone. Startled, Mr. Fries blurted out the truth: "I just wanted your machine." Screeners often prefer to call at odd hours to avoid conversation.

And after the screening habit is learned, it

(Cont.)

can go too far. Bert Garrett, a family practitioner in Austin, Texas, is often paged in the middle of the night. He rushes to call the patient — and gets an answering machine. That's overscreening. To retaliate, Dr. Garrett quickly spits out, "Doctor called," and slams down the phone. "I mean, hell-oo-o. Who else do they think is calling at 3 o'clock in the morning?" he says. "Why not just pick up and say, 'Hi'?"

Struggling to stay relevant, phone fanatics use a universal scold: "I know you're there." To which screeners respond: I know you know I'm here. I'm still not answering. What phone slaves haven't gotten hip to yet is that screening has rendered the once-powerful telephone practically impotent.

Better it than you. One summer evening in the Freeman family's Fort Wayne, Ind., home, the lights were dim, the wine bottle drained, the James Taylor on. In the middle of a particularly amorous moment with his wife, 30-year-old Kevin Freeman heard the high-pitched ringing of a nearby phone and lunged for it.

Now, Amy Freeman turns off the ringer most nights when she and her husband are home. "I'd be a fool to complain," Mr. Freeman says.

Buyer Behavior

23

West, South are building more population muscle

By Haya El Nasser
USA TODAY

The West and the South will be stronger than ever as population trends reshape the nation's political landscape.

If these trends continue through 2000, nine congressional seats would be picked up by seven fast-growing Western and Southern states, according to an exclusive analysis of 1998 Census state population estimates by Election Data Services Inc., a Washington, D.C., consulting firm. Those states are Arizona, California, Nevada, Florida, Texas, Montana and Georgia.

Seven states — New York, Pennsylvania, Connecticut, Wisconsin, Ohio, Oklahoma and Mississippi — are likely to lose seats.

The analysis, which uses Census state population estimates out today and released to USA TODAY first, gives the most up-to-date look at how states could divvy up congressional seats in the next decade. Population counts are crucial to states because they decide how many seats each will get in Congress. The more representatives a state has, the more influence it has when issues affecting the state come up for a vote.

The population estimates are particularly significant because they come just two years before the results of the official 2000 Census are released. Those numbers will be used to redraw congressional districts.

"It's getting us one step closer," says Kimball Brace, president of Election Data Services. "We're getting a more complete picture of what the 2000 numbers might be."

For example, up until 1996, California was expected to gain no seat for the first time since it became a state in 1850; it gained seven in 1990. But the 1998 numbers show that it might get an extra seat, for a total of 53, because the state's rebounding economy has stopped the exodus of its residents.

The 1998 population estimates show that California grew 1.5% in 1998, its highest rate since 1992 and well above the national rate of 1%.

And up until last year, Illinois was expected to lose a district. Thanks partly to a mere .5% increase in its population since 1997, Illinois could hang on to its 20 seats.

According to the analysis, the big gainers are Arizona and Texas; each will add two seats. California, Florida, Georgia, Montana and Nevada each would gain one.

The big losers are New York and Pennsylvania, each down two seats in a reflection of the continued population drain from these older industrial states. Pennsylvania's population dropped .1% to 12 million in 1998. New York's barely inched up .2% to 18.2 million.

Connecticut, Mississippi, Ohio, Oklahoma and Wisconsin each would lose a seat.

California's gain reflects the turnaround in its economy. The state lost people to other states during the early 1990s recession that plagued California. It now is losing fewer people.

GAIN IS NEIGHBORS' LOSS

As a result, the population gains of nearby Western states is slowing down. Their growth was phenomenal throughout this decade because so many Californians were moving to other Western states.

Hawaii, Idaho, Nevada, Oregon, Utah and Washington all saw lower population growth in the past year, largely because the flow of people coming in diminished.

"At least for Nevada, one-third of the migrants were coming from California during the 1990s," says Marc Perry, demographer with the Census Bureau.

Despite the slowdown in much of the West, Nevada remains the fastest-growing state in the country for the 13th straight year. Its population climbed 4.1% since 1997, down from 4.9% the previous year.

"It's really scary when you can talk about 4.1% growth as a slowdown," Perry says. "But no place can keep growing at 5% or 6% a year." Nevada's population, now at more than 1.7 million, soared 45.4% since 1990.

With this kind of growth, there was little doubt that Nevada would gain a congressional seat.

POPULATION MEANS CLOUT

Election Data Services' findings illustrate how crucial a complete tally of states' populations can be in the struggle for political clout in Washington.

The apportionment of the 435 seats in Congress happens every 10 years, after the official Census is taken. Each state automatically gets one seat. But the allocation of the remaining 385 is based on a complex formula that takes into consideration population gains relative to the size of the state.

Montana, for example, stands to gain a seat on the

(Cont.)

basis of only 9,000 people because its population is just over 880,000. But it takes California, the nation's most populous state at almost 33 million, more than 317,000 people to grab another seat.

"If all else stayed the same and Montana had 9,000 fewer people, they would not gain that second seat," Brace says.

That's why there is such political furor over how the Census should conduct the 2000 Census.

The 1990 Census missed close to 12 million people, according to the Census Bureau. Most of them are minorities, the poor and urban residents, all segments of the population that tend to vote Democratic. At the same time, about 8 million people were counted twice, many of them in more white and affluent areas that tend to vote more Republican.

BIG MONEY AT STAKE

Census numbers are critical. Billions of federal and state dollars for housing, health care and other programs are allocated based on Census population counts. So is funding for roads, schools, law enforcement and other public services that benefit everyone.

Census numbers also play a key role in state and local politics. They're used to draw state districts and city ward boundaries.

The Census Bureau wants to correct past errors by using a new method called statistical sampling.

Rather than trying to reach everyone through questionnaires and door-to-door visits, the Census would try to reach at least 90% of households in each neighborhood and estimate the rest.

But that approach is strongly opposed by the Republican majority in Congress because members say it's not only illegal but unconstitutional. They want the Census to try to count every person in the country.

The issue is now before the Supreme Court.

ACCURACY IS KEY

An accurate count for states that have large immigrant and urban populations could make the difference. Illinois, for example, was on the brink of losing one of its 20 seats in Congress most of this decade (it lost two in 1990). But the 1998 estimates show that it might hang on to the seat, just barely.

"It's still really, really close," Brace says. "There is no guarantee that they won't lose it by 2000. It could be because Illinois has a less-than-perfect count or that other states got better counts."

"Clearly, when you're that close, it behooves the state to be careful and push to get as many people counted as possible."

It's not clear which political party will benefit the most from the 2000 reapportionment.

"The question is whether state legislatures and governors can draw the lines to benefit Republicans or Democrats or whether it will just be a wash," says Curtis Gans, director of the Committee for the Study of the American Electorate. "Nobody knows that yet."

BEHIND THE NUMBERS

Politics aside, the new Census numbers reveal interesting glimpses of the changes in the country's population:

▲ West Virginia was the first state in recent decades to have more deaths than births, pushing its population down .2% to 1.8 million. The state never recovered from the demise of the coal mining industry. Young people left, leaving an aging population behind, says William Frey, a demographer at the Milken Institute in Santa Monica, Calif. .

▲ Kansas was the fastest-growing state in the Midwest, up 1.1% to 2.6 million. The state's meatpacking industry attracted foreign and domestic workers, Perry says. No other state in the region grew faster than the nation as a whole.

▲ Georgia, up 2% to 7.6 million, was the fastest-growing state in the South. A lot of the people leaving the Midwest and the Northeast have flocked to Georgia because of the state's booming economy.

▲ The Northeast continued to be the nation's slowest-growing region, up .3%. But it grew at a faster pace than the previous year, largely because of a healthy rebound in the New England economy.

"Domestic out-migration from New England dropped every year since 1990," Perry says. Once again, New Hampshire was the fastest-growing state in the Northeast, up 1.1% to 1.2 million.

New York, on the other hand, had more people leave than come in. Frey says people are following jobs in the Southeast and the West, regions that are less congested.

▲ The District of Columbia had the biggest drop in population, down 1.3% to just over 523,000. But Perry warns that it is not completely fair to compare D.C. to states because it is not a state. Anyone who moves from D.C. to its suburbs ends up in another state and automatically counts as a loss for the District.

24

Generation Y

Today's teens—the biggest bulge since the boomers— may force marketers to toss their old tricks

At malls across America, a new generation is voting with its feet.

At Towson Town Center, a mall outside of Baltimore, Laura Schaefer, a clerk at the Wavedancer surf-and-skateboard shop, is handling post-Christmas returns. Coming back: clothes that fit snugly and shoes unsuitable for skateboarding. Schaefer, 19, understands. "They say 'My mom and dad got me these'," she says.

At the Steve Madden store in Roosevelt Mall on Long Island, N.Y., parents, clad in loafers and Nikes, are sitting quietly amid the pulsating music while their teenage daughters slip their feet into massive Steve Madden platform shoes. Many of the baby boomer-age parents accompanying these teens look confused. And why not? Things are different in this crowd.

Asked what brands are cool, these teens rattle off a list their parents blank on. Mudd. Paris Blues. In Vitro. Cement. What's over? Now, the names are familiar: Levi's. Converse. Nike. "They just went out of style," shrugs Lori Silverman, 13, of Oyster Bay, N.Y.

Ouch. Some of the biggest brands on the market are meeting with a shrug of indifference from Lori and her cohorts. A host of labels that have prospered by predicting—and shaping—popular tastes since the baby boomers were young simply aren't kindling the same excitement with today's kids. Already, the list includes some major names: PepsiCo Inc. has struggled to build loyalty among teens. Nike Inc.'s sneaker sales are tumbling as the brand sinks in teen popularity polls. Levi Strauss & Co., no longer the hippest jeanmaker on the shelf, is battling market share erosion. Meanwhile, newcomers in entertainment, sports equipment, and fashion have become hot names.

What's the problem? These kids aren't baby boomers. They're part of a generation that rivals the baby boom in size—and will soon rival it in buying clout. These are the sons and daughters of boomers.

Born during a baby bulge that demographers locate between 1979 and 1994, they are as young as five and as old as 20, with the largest slice still a decade away from adolescence. And at 60 million strong, more than three times the size of Generation X, they're the biggest thing to hit the American scene since the 72 million baby boomers. Still too young to have forged a name for themselves, they go by a host of taglines: Generation Y,

> Some of the biggest, most successfully marketed brands of the past decade are facing shrugs of indifference from these buyers

Echo Boomers, or Millennium Generation.

Marketers haven't been dealt an opportunity like this since the baby boom hit. Yet for a lot of entrenched brands, Gen Y poses mammoth risks. Boomer brands flopped in their attempts to reach Generation X, but with a mere 17 million in its ranks, that miss was tolerable. The boomer brands won't get off so lightly with Gen Y. This is the first generation to come along that's big enough to hurt a boomer brand simply by giving it the cold shoulder—and big enough to launch rival brands with enough heft to threaten the status quo. As the leading edge of this huge new group elbows its way into the marketplace, its members are making it clear that companies hoping to win their hearts and wallets will have to learn to think like they do—and not like the boomers who preceded them.

Indeed, though the echo boom rivals its parent's generation in size, in almost every other way, it is very different. This generation is more racially diverse: One in three is not Caucasian. One in four lives in a single-parent household. Three in four have working mothers. While boomers are still mastering Microsoft Windows 98, their kids are tapping away at computers in nursery school.

With the oldest Gen Yers barely out of high school, it's no surprise that the brands that have felt their disdain so far have been concentrated in fashion, entertainment, and toys. But there's a lot more going on here than fickle teens jumping on the latest trend. While some of Gen Y's choices have been driven by faddishness and rebellion, marketing experts say those explanations are too simplistic. "Most marketers perceive them as kids. When you do that, you fail to take in what they are telling you about the consumers they're becoming," says J. Walker Smith, a managing partner at Yankelovich Partners Inc. who

specializes in generational marketing. "This is not about teenage marketing. It's about the coming of age of a generation."

Smith and others believe that behind the shift in Gen Y labels lies a shift in values on the part of Gen Y consumers. Having grown up in an even more media-saturated, brand-conscious world than their parents, they respond to ads differently, and they prefer to encounter those ads in different places. The marketers that capture Gen Y's attention do so by bringing their messages to the places these kids congregate, whether it's the Internet, a snowboarding tournament, or cable TV. The ads may be funny or disarmingly direct. What they don't do is suggest that the advertiser knows Gen Y better than these savvy consumers know themselves.

Soon a lot of other companies are going to have learn the nuances of Gen Y marketing. In just a few years, today's teens will be out of college and shopping for their first cars, their first homes, and their first mutual funds. The distinctive buying habits they display today will likely follow them as they enter the high-spending years of young adulthood. Companies unable to click with Gen Y will lose out on a vast new market—and could find the doors thrown open to new competitors. "Think of them as this quiet little group about to change everything," says Edward Winter of The U30 Group, a

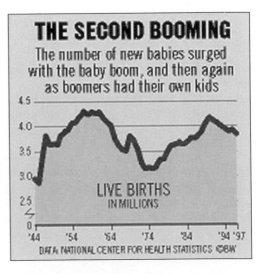

THE SECOND BOOMING
The number of new babies surged with the baby boom, and then again as boomers had their own kids

LIVE BIRTHS IN MILLIONS

DATA: NATIONAL CENTER FOR HEALTH STATISTICS ©BW

COOL STUFF

According to Boomers	According to Generation Y
LEXUS LS400 What to drive when you have your own parking spot. It says you've arrived without the ostentation of a Beemer.	**JEEP WRANGLER** Who cares about gas mileage? It looks great in the high school parking lot.
MAJOR LEAGUE BASEBALL Mark McGwire and the New York Yankees have made the game hot again.	**SKATEBOARD TRIPLE CROWN** Stars compete for glory instead of multiyear contracts.
GAP Those chinos and jeans still look cool. Really.	**DELIA'S** Definitely not your mother's dress catalog.
ER A worthy successor to Marcus Welby, MD.	**DAWSON'S CREEK** High school drama with sizzle.
SUPERBOWL ADS Usually they're more entertaining than the game.	**LILITH FAIR SPONSORSHIP** Supporting the sound of new voices.
HARRISON FORD Tough and fiftysomething. Plus, his action figure is a hot collectible.	**LEONARDO DICAPRIO** Dashing, sensitive, and irresistible to 12-year-olds.
ESTEE LAUDER For the way we ought to look.	**HARD CANDY** For the way we really look.
L.L. BEAN A favorite for decades, but does anyone actually go duck-hunting in those boots?	**THE NORTH FACE** Does anyone actually go mountain climbing in that stuff?
PALM PILOT A Rolodex for your pocket, with a high-tech edge.	**MOTOROLA FLEX PAGERS** Stay in touch anytime, anyplace.
NICK AT NITE All our favorite reruns in one convenient place.	**WB NETWORK** Creating new favorites and a new look for prime time television.
POLITICAL ACTIVISM Make yourself heard.	**VOLUNTEERISM** Make yourself useful.
THE BEATLES Rock 'n' roll as the signal artistic achievement of a generation.	**SPICE GIRLS** Rock 'n' roll packaged and marketed to children.
COKE Water + sugar + caffeine. Besides, it's the real thing.	**MOUNTAIN DEW** Water + sugar + more caffeine. Besides, it's an extreme thing.
DAVID LETTERMAN Late-night TV, slightly mellowed with age. Still among the Top Ten reasons to stay awake.	**JENNY McCARTHY** Think Carol Burnett with a bad attitude.
NIKES From Michael to Tiger, no shortage of sports celebs saying Just Do it.	**VANS** No sports celebs allowed. And they're the coolest shoes on skateboards.

Knoxville (Tenn.) consulting firm.

Nike has found out the hard way that Gen Y is different. Although still hugely popular among teens, the brand has lost its grip on the market in recent years, according to Teenage Research Unlimited, a Northbrook (Ill.) market researcher. Nike's slick national ad campaigns, with their emphasis on image and celebrity, helped build the brand among boomers, but they have backfired with Gen Y. "It doesn't matter to me that Michael Jordan has endorsed Nikes," says Ben Dukes, 13, of LaGrange Park, Ill.

Missteps such as Nike's disastrous attempt to sponsor Olympic snowboarders two years ago and allegations of inhumane overseas labor practices added to Gen Y's scorn. As Nike is discovering, success with this generation requires a new kind of advertising as well as a new kind of product. The huge image-building campaigns that led to boomer crazes in everything from designer vodka to sport-utility vehicles are less effective with Gen Y. "The old-style advertising that works very well with boomers, ads that push a slogan and an image and a feeling, the younger consumer is not going to go for," says James

R. Palczynski, retail analyst for Ladenburg Thalmann & Co. and author of YouthQuake, a study of youth consumer trends.

Instead, Gen Yers respond to humor, irony, and the (apparently) unvarnished truth. Sprite has scored with ads that parody celebrity endorsers and carry the tagline "Image is nothing. Obey your thirst." J.C. Penney & Co.'s hugely successful Arizona Jeans brand has a new campaign showing teens mocking ads that attempt to speak their language. The tagline? "Just show me the jeans."

NET EFFECT. Which isn't to say echo boomers aren't brand-conscious. Bombarded by ad messages since birth, how could they not be? But marketing experts say they form a less homogeneous market than their parents did. One factor is their racial and ethnic diversity. Another is the fracturing of media, with network TV having given way to a spectrum of cable channels and magazine goliaths such as *Sports Illustrated* and *Seventeen* now joined by dozens of niche competitors. Most important, though, is the rise of the Internet, which has sped up the fashion life cycle by letting kids everywhere find out about even the most obscure trends as they emerge. It is the Gen Y

medium of choice, just as network TV was for boomers. "Television drives homogeneity," says Mary Slayton, global director for consumer insights for Nike. "The Internet drives diversity."

Nowhere is that Net-driven diversity more clear than in the music business. On the Web, fans of even the smallest groups can meet one another and exchange information, reviews, even sound clips. Vicki Starr, a partner in Girlie Action, a New York-based music promoter, last year booked No Doubt, a band with a teen following, into a small Manhattan venue. She says that on opening night the house was packed with teenage girls dressed just like the lead singer. "How do they know this? How do they keep up with what she's wearing? It's not from network television," says Starr. "It's online."

The Internet's power to reach young consumers has not been lost on marketers. These days, a well-designed Web site is crucial for any company hoping to reach under-18 consumers. "I find out about things I want to buy from my friends or from information on the Internet," says Michael Eliason, 17, of Cherry Hill, N.J. Even popular teen TV shows,

(Cont.)

such as Warner Bros. Television Network's Buffy the Vampire Slayer and Dawson's Creek, have their own Web sites.

Other companies are keeping in touch by E-mail. American Airlines Inc. recently launched a college version of its popular Net-Saver program, which offers discounted fares to subscribers by E-mail. "They all have E-mail addresses," says John R. Samuel, director of interactive marketing for American. "If a company can't communicate via E-mail," he says, "the attitude is 'What's wrong with you?'"

This torrent of high-speed information has made Gen Y fashions more varied and faster-changing. Young consumers have shown that they'll switch their loyalty in an instant to marketers that can get ahead of the style curve. No brand has done a better job of that than Tommy Hilfiger. When Hilfiger's distinctive logo-laden shirts and jackets starting showing up on urban rappers in the early '90s, the company started sending researchers into music clubs to see how this influential group wore the styles. It bolstered its tradi-tional mass-media ads with unusual promotions, from giving free clothing to stars on VH1 and MTV to a recent deal with Miramax Film Corp., in which teen film actors will appear in Hilfiger ads. Knowing its customers' passion for computer games, it sponsored a Nintendo competition and installed Nintendo terminals in its stores. Gen Y consumers have rewarded that attentiveness by making Hilfiger jeans their No. 1 brand in a recent American Express Co. survey.

Compare that record with Levi's, one of the world's most recognized brands and an icon of boomer youth. It got a harsh wake-up call in 1997, when its market share slid, and research revealed that the brand was losing popularity among teens. With its core boomer customers hitting middle age, both Levi's advertising and its decades-old five-pocket jeans were growing stale. "We all got older, and as a consequence, we lost touch with teenagers," says David Spangler, director of market research for the Levi's brand. Now, Levi's is fighting back with new ads, new styles, a revamped Web site, and ongo-ing teen panels to keep tabs on emerging trends. "We never put much muscle into this sort of thing before, but now, we are dead serious about it," says Spangler. "This is a generation that must be reckoned with. They are going to overtake the country."

Marketers who don't bother to learn the interests and obsessions of Gen Y are apt to run up against a brick wall of distrust and cynicism. Years of intense marketing efforts aimed directly their way have taught this group to assume the worst about companies trying to coax them into buying something. Ads meant to look youthful and fun may come off as merely opportunistic to a Gen Y consumer. That's what happened to PepsiCo in its attempts to earn Gen Y loyalty with its Generation Next campaign, says William Strauss, co-author of the 1991 book Generations: The History of America's Future. The TV ads, in which kids showed off branded trinkets, from jackets to gym bags, fell flat. "They were annoying," says Philip Powell, 14, of Houston. "It was just one long 'Please, please, buy me.'"

'WE ARE GOING TO OWN THIS GENERATION'

The morning after the Delia's catalog arrives, the halls of Paxton High School in Jacksonville, Fla., are buzzing. That's when all the girls bring in their copies from home and compare notes. "Everyone loves Delia's," says Emily Garfinkle, 15. "It's the big excitement."

If you've never heard of Delia's, chances are you don't know a girl between 12 and 17. The five-year-old direct mailer has become one of the hottest names in Gen Y retailing by selling downtown fashion to girls everywhere. Already, the New York cataloger, which racked up sales of $98 million over the past three quarters, has a database of 4 million names, and its fastest growth may still lie ahead: Gen Y's teen population won't peak for five or six years.

TIGHT FOCUS. A lot of thriving Gen Y companies fell into the market by accident. Not Delia's. Founders Stephen Kahn, a 33-year-old ex-Wall Streeter, and Christopher Edgar, his ex-roommate at Yale University, realized that few retailers had taken the trouble to learn this market. So they carefully honed the Delia's concept: cutting-edge styles and mail-order distribution with a Gen Y twist.

Delia's trendy apparel is definitely not designed with mom and dad in mind. "I think the clothes are too revealing," says Emily's mother, Judy. "I tell her I'll buy her anything she wants at the Gap." But Emily dismisses the Gap as "too preppy," preferring Delia's long, straight skirts and tops with bra-exposing spaghetti straps. Delia's order form even includes tips on how to order pants so they conform to the parentally despised fashion of drooping

> **KAHN:** The Delia's catalog offers tips on how to order pants so they droop well below the hips

well below the hips, with hems dragging. In keeping with Gen Y preferences, the catalog illustrates these fashions with models who look like regular teen-agers, not superglam androgynes.

Delia's youthful image isn't just a facade. Most of the company's 1,500 employees are well under 30. And its phone reps—mostly high school and college students—do more than take orders: They offer tips and fashion advice. "Delia's speaks the language of its consumers," says Wendy Liebmann, president of consultant WSL Marketing.

Instead of mass-market advertising, Delia's gets the word out in the ways Gen Y prefers: with local campaigns such as catalog drops in schools and with hot Web sites. In 1997, the company bought gURL.com, a popular fashion, chat, and game site for girls. It also launched its own Web site, with news and entertainment stories, catalog-request forms, E-mail, and online shopping. That effort helped buy some buzz for Delia's stock, which has gyrated between $4 and $32 a share over the past year. In December, buoyed by news of an online shopping venture, the stock shot up more than 50%, to a recent 15.

So far, the company has sold mostly clothing, but it has recently branched out into home furnishings, such as bean bag chairs and throw rugs. "Girls like to do their rooms," says Kahn, who defines his business by its customers rather than by a product category. He foresees a day when Delia's will get these girls their first credit card, first car loan, and first mortgage. "We'll follow them and broaden our offerings," says Kahn.

Next up: boys. The company recently bought TSI Soccer Corp., a sportswear catalog and launched Droog, a catalog for boys. "We are going to own this generation," Kahn says. Or at least a sizable portion of its members' wallets.

By Ellen Neuborne in New York

> Just as network TV has given way to cable, *Sports Illustrated* and *Seventeen* face an explosion of niche magazines.

Ironically, Pepsi already has one of the biggest teen soda hits with Mountain Dew, but the drink's success has little to do with advertising. Instead, kids found out about Dew from their most trusted endorsers—each other. "[Kids] believe—true or not—that they're the ones who figured out and spread the word that the drink has tons of caffeine," says Marian Salzman, head of the brand futures group at Young & Rubicam Inc. "The caffeine thing was not in any of Mountain Dew's television ads. This drink is hot by word of mouth."

Along with cynicism, Gen Y is marked by a distinctly practical world view, say marketing experts. Raised in dual-income and single-parent families, they've already been given considerable financial responsibility. Surveys show they are deeply involved in family purchases, be they groceries or a new car. One in nine high school students has a credit card co-signed by a parent, and many will take on extensive debt to finance college. Most expect to have careers and are already thinking about home ownership, according to a 1998 survey of college freshman for Northwestern Mutual Life Insurance Co. "This is a very pragmatic group. At 18 years old, they have five-year plans. They are already looking at how they will be balancing their work/family commitments," says Deanna Tillisch, who directed the survey.

GRASSROOTS. That means marketers who want to reach worldly wise Gen Yers need to craft products and pitches that are more realistic. To rejuvenate its Gen X hit House of Style, for example, MTV switched the emphasis on the weekly fashion show from celebrity lifestyles to practical information, with segments on decorating your bedroom and buying a prom dress. "We adapted the show to be more of what they wanted to see," said Todd Cunningham, director of brand research for MTV.

To break through Gen Y's distrust, marketers are also trying to make their campaigns more subtle and more local. A growing number, including Universal Studios, Coca-Cola, and McDonald's, use "street teams." Made up of young people, the teams hang out in clubs, parks, and malls talking to teens about everything from fashion to finance, trying to pinpoint trends as they emerge. Other marketers are trying to build grassroots support for their brands. Following the lead of underground rock bands, mass marketers have taken to "wild postings," that is, tacking up ad posters on street corners and construction sites. Others sponsor community events or hand out coupons and T-shirts at concerts and ball games. Golden Books Publishing Co. distributed sample chapters from a new teen book series at movie theaters. The idea is to let kids stumble onto the brand in unexpected places.

Last year, when Lee Apparel introduced Pipes, a line of oversize, multipocketed pants aimed at 10- to 14-year-old boys, it spent its marketing dollars on the Internet, outdoor posters, and skateboard magazines. "As a brand, you need to go where they are, not just pick a fashion statement, put it on TV, and wait for them to come to you," says Terry Lay, president of the Lee brand. Even Coke, a master of slick advertising, looks for more personal ways to reach Gen Y. Last summer, it courted teens with discount cards good for movies and fast food. To build credibility, it mailed them directly to high school sports stars and other leaders first before handing out more at stores.

Of course, plenty of marketers continue to reach for this group with national TV campaigns. The ones that work are funny, unpretentious, and often confusing to older consumers. Consider Volkswagen of America Inc. Although VW doesn't market directly to teens, both its Golf and Passat models show up on surveys as Gen Y faves. Part of the credit goes to the carmaker's quirky TV commercials, which are about as far from the traditional image-building ads Detroit churns out as possible. "We're a little edgier, a little more risk-tolerant, and not so mainstream," says VW marketing director Liz Vanzura. While other marketers fled the airwaves when Ellen DeGeneres came out of the closet on her show last spring, VW used the groundbreaking episode to introduce a new commercial showing two guys in a car who pick up a discarded chair. The ad, funny and oblique, became a favorite among young adults and teens.

With the oldest Gen Yers turning 20 this year, a lot of other companies will soon find themselves grappling with this new genera-

> The biggest change is the Net. Fashion trends that used to spread slowly now hit everywhere instantly.

tion. Toyota Motor Corp., noting that 4 million new drivers will come of age each year until 2010, unveiled the Echo at this year's Detroit auto show. With low emissions and a price well below the Corolla, the new subcompact is aimed squarely at boomers' kids who are buying their first cars. General Motors Corp. is putting together a task force to figure out how to appeal to Gen Y. The auto maker brings teens and children as young as sixth-graders into car clinics, where researchers probe their opinions of current models and prototypes of future cars. Michael C. DiGiovanni, GM's head of market research and forecasting, says Gen Y kids have an entirely different aesthetic from their parents. Their sense of how a product should look and feel has been shaped by the hours they spend at the keyboard. "One of the trends that will manifest itself is computers," says DiGiovanni. "The design of products will be influenced by the way a computer screen looks."

Meanwhile, computers and other high-tech products are starting to look less industrial and more sleek in an effort to attract younger buyers. By using bright colors and cool designs, Motorola Inc. helped transform the pager from a lowly tool for on-call workers to a must-have gizmo for teens. Apple Computer Inc. appeals directly to the same group with products such as its rounded, space-age-looking iMac computer. "For this generation, the computer is like a hot rod," says Allen Olivo, Apple's senior director for worldwide marketing, who says kids are constantly comparing features and styling with their friends' systems.

Apple's stylish iMac may or may not become the computer of choice for this new generation. But Apple and other marketers that attempt to chart the Gen Y psyche now could have an advantage as this generation moves into adulthood. After all, some of the biggest brands on the market today got their start by bonding with boomers early and following them from youth into middle age. Will the labels that grew up with baby boomers reinvent themselves for Generation Y? Or will the big brands of the new millennium bear names most of us have not yet heard of?

THE NEW WORKING CLASS

by Rebecca Piirto Heath

As recently as two years ago, leading newspapers were announcing the death of the working class. That obituary now seems premature. Although the structure of the working class is shifting, its spirit is thriving. What's changing is the working-class stereotype of a hard-hatted, blue-collared, middle-aged, white man. As the industrial age becomes more of a dim memory, the image of the group of people who drive the economy is changing, too. Indicators suggest that the working core of Americans is becoming younger, more ethnically diverse, more female, somewhat more educated, and more alienated from its employers.

> *In a supposedly classless society, nearly half of Americans consistently identify themselves as working class. This group is more diverse than it was a generation ago, and now it includes people from all walks of life. Perhaps the greatest common bond of working-class Americans is their belief in the combined strength of working people — through unions.*

Trying to pinpoint the precise nature of this shift, however, is a prickly proposition. The difficulty comes from our uniquely American view of class. The common belief on these shores is that America, unlike Europe, is a classless society. We admit to racial, ethnic, gender, and cultural divisions. But to class? Most Americans think of class the same way they think of the British monarchy — something foreign.

Economic indicators show a steady polarization between incomes of the top-earning households and the lowest-income households. Only the richest Americans have seen any real income growth in the last decade. Incomes of the top 5 percent of Americans grew 37 percent between 1984 and 1994, compared with a meager 1 percent increase on the bottom.

Despite this evidence, many Americans find it most comfortable to believe that class divisions, if they exist at all, are minor obstacles. Even supposedly jaded baby-boomer parents still teach their children they can be anything they want to be. Despite growing rumbles of doubt, most of us still believe the old adage that an individual with enough gumption can pull himself up by his bootstraps, especially with a little hard work and a good education.

"No one wants to be working class in America," says Peter Rachleff, professor of history at Macalester College in St. Paul, Minnesota. For those who take issue with that statement, Rachleff asks another question: "When was the last time you saw a U.S. film about the working class?" British films, on the other hand, are full of working-class heroes. "We are bombarded by so much popular culture that tells us continually that this is a middle-class society," says Rachleff.

Michael Moore, author of Downsize This and a popular director and producer, has made a name for himself by poking fun at America's "classlessness." Roger & Me was a surprise hit documentary about Moore's attempts to track down General Motors CEO Roger Smith to ask him why the company's auto plant in Flint, Michigan, was closing and laying off thousands of loyal long-time workers. Moore says that getting a distributor for his films has always been an uphill battle. "There's something about working-class satire and irony that seems to be missing from our national language," he says.

This lack is ironic in itself, considering the relative novelty of a large middle class in this country. "The middle class didn't even exist until this century," says Moore. So what's behind all this American denial of its working-class roots? "It all started to change after World War II, when working-class people were able to own a home, buy a car or two, take extended summer vacations, and send their kids to college. Once they got some of the trappings of wealth, they got the illusion that they were like the man who lived in the house on the hill," says Moore.

CLASS IN A CLASSLESS SOCIETY

One reason why many surveys don't reveal the state of the working class is that they don't ask about it. Many definitions of the middle class are based on income. By one definition, the middle class includes households with incomes of $15,000 to $75,000. Such socioeconomic categories rarely include an explicit working-class group.

One survey that does is the General Social Survey (GSS), conducted by the National Opinion Research Center. Since 1972, it has asked Americans to classify themselves as lower, working, middle, or upper class. In

1994, 46 percent of American adults said they were working class, virtually equal to the 47 percent who claimed middle-class status. These proportions have varied little over the past 22 years.

In an effort to get at the characteristics underlying class affiliation, Mary Jackman, a professor of sociology at the University of California-Davis, and her husband, political scientist Robert Jackman, published Class Awareness in the United States in 1986. It was based on a landmark survey conducted by the University of Michigan's Survey Research Center in 1975. The study has been called "the most important study of class identification since Richard Center's 1949 Psychology of Social Classes." The Jackmans intentionally crafted the question to include five class divisions — poor, working, middle, upper-middle and upper. "This way middle was truly in the middle, which is more how people think of it," says Jackman. With this grouping, 8 percent identified with the poor, 37 percent with the working class, 43 percent with the middle class, 8 percent with upper-middle, and 1 percent with the upper class.

The Jackmans went on to analyze why people classified themselves the way they did. They asked them to rate the relative importance of attributes such as income, education, and occupation, as well as lifestyle and attitudes. Topping the list for most people was occupation, followed by education and people's beliefs and feelings. Up to 49 percent rated the kind of family a person came from as not important at all. "It seems that, for most people, social class is a combination of fairly hard-core economic attributes that you can identify pretty quickly and other cultural and expressive attributes that you can't identify quite so quickly — their lifestyles, values and attitudes," says Jackman.

Income turned out to be less valuable a predictor than occupation or education. "Education ends up being so important because it's a piece of social capital that reflects Americans' long-term focus," Jackman says. Occupations also played a role, although a less clear one. "The occupations that caused the most confusion about working- or middle-class status were the upper-level blue-collar jobs or skilled tradesmen," says Jackman. Lower-level clerical jobs also created confusion. But there was no debate over assembly-line workers and seven other solidly blue-collar occupations.

The occupational line is blurring even more today. With more companies downsizing, outsourcing, and turning to temporary workers, some highly qualified workers have been marginalized and are underemployed or working for lower pay and fewer benefits. At the same time, formerly semi-skilled blue-collar jobs demand higher-level skills. Even auto mechanics, a solidly working-class occupation in the 1970s, now require sophisticated knowledge of electronics. "For most functions, you just can't use a mechanic anymore. You really need technicians who can solve problems at a much higher level than in the past," says Myron Nadolski, dean of automotive and technical training at American River College in Sacramento, California.

TODAY'S WORKING CLASS

The work force isn't the same as it was 40 years ago. Neither is the working class. Since the Jackmans' study hasn't been updated and the General Social Survey doesn't ask respondents why they label themselves the way they do, differences between working- and middle-class Americans must be inferred by their answers to other questions.

The average age of working- and lower-class Americans is declining, while the age of the middle and upper classes is increasing in line with national trends. On the other hand, the working class has become more average in its gender mix. The proportion of working-class Americans who are female increased from 48 percent in 1974 to 54 percent in 1994. The other classes have been predominantly female all along.

One of the most significant changes in the working class that is also in line with national trends is its increasing racial diversity. Back in the mid-1970s, Jackman found a clear delineation between the races in class attitudes. "You really have to deal separately with blacks and whites because the distribution is so different," Jackman says. This is because, historically, blacks were left out of the economy altogether and have only recently begun to rise into the working and middle classes.

Racial diversity among the lower, working, and, to a lesser extent, middle class is increasing, while the upper class is becoming less racially diverse. Between 1974 and 1994, the proportion of whites who claimed working-class status decreased 9 percent, while the proportion of blacks grew 3 percent and those of other races rose 5 percent. The shift was even more pronounced for the lower class, and somewhat less so for the middle class. Meanwhile, the proportion of whites claiming upper-class status increased, while the proportion of blacks decreased.

The GSS supports the notion that income level plays an unclear role in class identification. In 1994, 74 percent of the working class and 63 percent of the middle class reported household incomes between $15,000 and $74,999. But 10 percent of the upper class also reported making less than $15,000, and 4 percent of the lower class reported making over $50,000 a year.

Educational level is a more reliable indicator that rises steadily with social class, although educational level for all groups has increased. The upper and middle classes still have the preponderance of bachelor's and graduate degrees, but higher degrees are becoming more common among the working class. The proportion of bachelor's degrees held by working-class adults more than doubled between 1974 and 1994, from 4 percent to 10 percent. The proportion of two-year degrees held by working-class respondents increased by 5 percentage points, to 6.5 percent. Two percent of the working class had graduate degrees in 1994.

Similarly, the occupations that make up the working class are less clear-cut. Between 1988 and 1996, the proportion of managers and professionals in the working class increased by 4 percent, to reach 17 percent in 1996. The proportion of technical, sales and administrative workers also rose slightly. Conversely, the proportions of service employees, farm workers, and craft and skilled workers have declined. (It is not possible to compare occupations before 1988 because the classification scheme changed.) In addition, the number of part-time workers has increased across the board, but part-timers remain most prevalent in the lower and working classes.

What does all this mean? Changes in the working class reflect changes in the work environment itself, says David Knoke, professor of sociology at the University of Minnesota, who is currently conducting a panel study of 1,000 work environments around the country to measure shifts in outsourcing, part-time and temporary employment, and cutbacks. "The number of people involved in non-full-time work has quadrupled in the past decade," says Knoke. Up to 30 percent of all U.S. workers are now "contingent" workers — temporaries, part timers, subcontractors or independent consultants, according to Knoke.

Knoke and colleagues theorize that increased global competition has forced the elimination of companies' internal job markets. "It used to be that if you got a job with IBM out of college, you were set for life," Knoke says. "A series of job ladders was built into the organization that allowed people to count on a slow but steadily rising standard of living."

The likely effect of these shifts on workers is already being seen. "People involved in part-time work have a looser stake in the organization. There's more of a sense of having to fend for themselves," Knoke says. "People see themselves as more working class and having less of a stake in the middle class." Jackman agrees. "I believe there has been a hardening of awareness of class boundaries in the last 10 or 15 years because the situation for American workers has gotten grim, and it's happened so quietly."

The UPS strike last year crystallized these issues for American workers, which is one reason why the 180,000 striking teamsters had such overwhelming support from the public. "Workers across the country could identify with the striking UPS workers because they're all feeling the same pinch," says Deborah Dion, AFL-CIO spokesperson.

UNION RESURGENCE?

Not surprisingly, interest in organized labor is one of the attributes most common among the working class. "You can be working class without being a union member, but it's difficult to think of a union member who is not aware of working-class issues," says Rachleff of Macalester College. This relationship is borne out in GSS data. Union membership is one of the clearest delineators between the working and other classes. Although union membership among U.S. workers has fallen across the board, for the last 25 years it has remained highest among those who claim working-class status.

Unions understand the changing structure of the new working class and are targeting somewhat younger, more ethnic, better-educated workers, and different occupations than they did 25 years ago. Coincidentally, just around the time UPS capitulated to strikers' demands for more full-time jobs and a better pension arrangement, the AFL-CIO launched a five-city pilot ad campaign to help boost sagging union membership. More than one-third of all American workers belonged to unions in 1950. By 1997, less than 15 percent of workers (only 10 percent of nongovernment workers) were union members.

A recent AFL-CIO poll found that 44 percent of the general public employed in a non-supervisory job said they would vote to form a union at their workplace. Another 20 percent were less certain but still positive, saying it was better to join together at a work site to solve problems. "That 20 percent is made up of the same people we're trying to reach with our campaign — minority groups, young people, and women," says Dion.

The ads are four personal stories from real union members. Mike, a construction worker, represents the traditional white, male, blue-collar core of the membership, but with a twist — he's young. A young black nurse named Arthereane talks about her love of helping children and her conviction that hospitals run best when they're run by doctors and nurses, not the profit motive. Erin, a working mother, balances family and her job as a chef with the help of her union. Michael, a worker at a Harley-Davidson plant, sings the union's praises for keeping the company from closing the plant, and making jobs more secure and the company more profitable. The tag line is: "You have a voice, make it heard; today's unions."

"These issues are the key because they are issues that workers everywhere are concerned about. Everything's going up except workers' fair share — the stock market's going up and executive salaries are skyrocketing," Dion says. She believes this is a pivotal time for unions to get this message out to people who may not realize the historic power of unions to raise wages and secure better benefits for workers.

Filmmaker Michael Moore also sees this as a pivotal period. "I think we're going to see a resurgence in interest in unions," he says. "In the last five years, it's dawned on a lot of people that unions have been asleep at the wheel. They really don't have that much in common with the man on the hill."

> **It used to be that if you got a job with a company like IBM out of college, you were set for life.**

Moore features some of the newest members of the United Food and Commercial Worker Union in his latest film, *The Big One*. The 45 booksellers who start at $6 an hour at the Borders Books store in Des Moines, Iowa, voted in the union in December 1996. They are mostly young, with bachelor's or even graduate degrees. Many came to Borders from other professions — teaching, the arts, or independent bookstores driven out of business by the big chains. They say it's not about money so much as it is about respect.

"The way they pay us and treat us is a paradox," says employee organizer Christian Gholson. "On one hand, they say the employees are the reason for Borders' success, then they say this is a transitional job and you aren't worth more than $6.50 an hour." So far only four of Borders' 200-plus stores have organized, but Gholson sees it as a worthwhile struggle. "In my perfect world, I'd like to make $8.00 an hour. That's not so much when you see the volume of business that goes through this store," he says.

The trend toward unionization is growing among health-care professionals as well as among upscale service businesses that depend on younger workers. Stores in the Starbucks Corporation and Einstein/Noah Bagel Corporation chains have also voted for union representation in the past year. As for Gholson, their issues are better wages, full-time hours, health benefits — and respect.

Social scientists see historic similarities between today's labor issues and those of the 1930s. "After the Depression, everybody's job became a lot more insecure," says labor historian Rachleff. "There were a lot of efforts by white-collar workers to unionize. The intervention of anti-communism stopped that and threw the labor movement back onto a much narrower social foundation." Knoke says that the contract between employers and workers has once more ended in the 1990s. "For a lot of people, it's turned into something like it was before World War II," he says. "There is great uncertainty. People are being forced out of jobs that are disappearing."

If globalization is creating a working class with a wider social base, what does a person like Gholson, who considers himself a writer and a poet, have in common with an auto-plant assembly-line worker? It seems like a clash of cultures. "It's very funny watching these enthusiastic young kids trying to get the old fogies of the union to take action and get involved," says Mike Moore.

The Jackmans' study found that beliefs and feelings were an important determinant of class in the 1970s. For today's working class, the commonality just might be age-old issues such as job security, autonomy on the job, occupational prestige, and the belief that hard work should be rewarded. The working class has always been the group most likely to rate job security as the most important reason for taking a job, according to GSS data. "There are differences between us and the old union people," admits Gholson. "But there's a middle ground where we all agree."

The mere fact that working-class identification has stayed so stable over the last 20 years, despite myriad macro economic and social changes, is significant in itself. "If we find people continuing to identify themselves as workers, there must really be something going on socially," says Rachleff, "because there's so much stacked against their doing that."

BEHIND THE NUMBERS

The General Social Survey (GSS) has interviewed a nationally representative sample of American adults aged 18 and older on an almost annual basis since 1972. Questions on social-class affiliation have been asked on a consistent basis throughout the survey's history, as have many other questions about demographic, social, and economic characteristics and attitudes. For more information about the GSS, contact the National Opinion Research Center, 1155 East 60th Street, Chicago, IL 60637; telephone (312) 753-7877. The cumulative database is in the public domain and is available from the Roper Center at the University of Connecticut in Storrs; telephone (203) 486-4882.

Reprinted from *American Demographics* magazine with permission. © 1998, Cowles Business Media, Ithaca, New York.

26

INVISIBLE—AND LOVING IT

Black entrepreneurs find that the Internet's anonymity removes racial obstacles

Often, the slights seem incidental: Customers approach the white store clerk, assuming he's the owner. At other times, the comments Betty A. Ford hears at Mailbox Haven, her suburban Seattle package-delivery business, feel more racially pointed. She recalls one white customer who warned, "I'm going to watch you wrap my package," and another who asked, "Is this business black-owned?" Well, yes, Ford thought. But why did it matter? Such patrons "assume I'm not in control because I'm black," she says.

Mailbox Haven thrives, but Ford wants to sell the operation. She's seeking her fortune now on the Internet, having launched City Boxers, an online retailer of hand-tailored boxer shorts. The product is a natural, filling an attractive niche geared toward the Net's large male audience. Just as important, in the Web's virtual reality, Ford has found some workplace solace. Shoppers "make their decision on what the boxer shorts look like, not on who's selling them," she says.

As President Clinton and his Race Initiative Advisory Board wrestle vainly with racial bias—what W.E.B. DuBois proclaimed the problem of the 20th century—the Net is providing some relief for the 21st. Hundreds of black and other minority entrepreneurs are setting up shop in cyberspace, many with impressive results. Though exact numbers are impossible to nail down, "there's a group of black folk that recognizes the potential to shatter the barriers that physical commerce creates," says Julianne Malveaux, an economist and author of *Sex, Lies and Stereotypes: Perspectives of a Mad Economist.*

COLOR-BLIND. It's an intriguing outcome of the Cyber Age. The Internet has been reviled for isolating Americans via their PCs, encouraging "virtual" communities at the expense of real ones. Cyberspace, moreover, has provided unchecked time and space for race-based hate diatribes. Yet in commerce, the Net's cool anonymity proves an advantage to minority business owners, allowing them to bypass real-life tensions by masking their racial identity. Just as important, Web-based businesses typically require far less capital than comparable physical operations, removing another historical hurdle for minority entrepreneurs.

That's no answer to racism per se, of course. But the Internet's color blindness does allow entrepreneurs to succeed, or not, on their own merits. Roosevelt Gist Jr., a 51-year-old former car salesman, remembers white customers at a large Virginia dealership asking if they could speak to another salesman, clear evidence that his race was a turnoff. On the Net, the question is moot. Gist's four-year-old online service, a forum for buying, selling, and researching cars, gets 40,000 visitors a month—none of whom has a clue that he's black—and collects about $200,000 a year in advertising revenue.

While racial anonymity provides psychic advantages, though, the Net's crumbling of financial barriers is the bigger boon. Carolyn Louper-Morris, a former political science professor, first tried to launch Cyberstudy101 the traditional way, producing study aids on diskettes and shipping them to colleges. But that operation would have required $2.2 million in investment to send 217,000 boxes to 58 universities a year.

BREAKING DOWN BARRIERS ONLINE

The Internet's anonymity and low cost help minority entrepreneurs launch businesses. A few sites:

minority.net Once complete, this business-to-business site will host the largest minority E-commerce mall on the Web, with more than 100 companies. Supporters include Nexgen Solutions, IBM, the U.S. Commerce Dept., the Urban League, and the Asian American Business Development Center.

cyberstudy101.com A new site to help high school and college students prepare for exams has been a hit after less than a month. Since Sept 1, it has grossed $6,000; it expects to generate $4 million in its first year.

twmall.com This Asian-American mall does business in Chinese and English. After one year, it includes some 40 companies and has grossed more than $120,000.

autonetwork.com One of the most complete automotive sites on the Web. It has classified ads, leasing information, broker services, advice columns, and scores of links. From startup money of $6,000, the site now produces $200,000 in annual revenues.

collard-cards.com This site sells greeting cards and cookbooks featuring upbeat black images. Sales in six months have totaled just $500.

(Cont.)

GLOBAL REACH. Instead, Louper-Morris took Cyberstudy101 online, where its operating expenses are dramatically lower. Customers download materials directly from the Web site, so shipping costs have disappeared. The company's operating costs, limited mostly to marketing and Web site management, are expected to be $65,000 the first year. "That's what made me move the product from land to line," says Louper-Morris, who says revenues should reach $4 million. Many Web-based businesses are even cheaper to run, costing as little as $100 a month and "allowing people . . . to build a small business out of passion and interest, whereas before, the barriers were too high," says Barry Parr, director of E-commerce strategies for researcher International Data Corp.

Entrepreneurs can leverage such small investments by reaching instantly across global markets. Gigi Roane created drumand-spear.com on retirement savings of $5,000, offering access to black-oriented books that most mainstream bookstores don't carry. The online business quickly reached customers in Kansas, Oregon, and overseas, grossing

> The low startup and operating costs in cyberspace also are a big boon for minority businesses

$170,000 in 1997 and persuading her to set up a small physical shop for local customers in her Washington home last year.

For a segment of ethnocentric black businesses, indeed, the Internet's vast reach is more compelling than its anonymity. Operations such as Roane's are explicitly race-based: They thrive by serving the Net's growing minority population. Some 5 million black Americans surf the Web, according to a recent study by researchers at Vanderbilt University. And black consumers are just as likely as whites to make purchases online.

More important, black entrepreneurs are moving past small consumer-oriented sites to discover business-to-business applications, which account for two-thirds of all online transactions. One key project: minority.net,

an electronic mall set to be launched in mid-October by Nexgen Solutions Inc., a Silver Spring (Md.) Web-consulting firm, with support from the Commerce Dept.'s Minority Business Development Agency and the National Urban League. Minority.net initially will link 75 small, minority-owned businesses with major companies, including giants such as IBM. By yearend, Nexgen hopes to have 500 minority companies exchanging goods and services with the behemoths—allowing a black-owned software consultant in the Midwest, say, to strike a local consulting deal with IBM.

Ultimately, of course, black entrepreneurs on the Internet still need the same skills and products required to succeed in the physical marketplace. Yet the online world can help: It doesn't eliminate racism—but for some entrepreneurs, it does level the playing field.

By Roger O. Crockett in Chicago

27

Morning goal: Break *faster*
Need for speed drives cereal killer

By Bruce Horovitz
USA TODAY

The breakfast revolution is alive, well and burning in Harry Balzer's toaster.

Balzer isn't solely responsible for breakfast in America being turned on its head. But as breakfast guru at research firm NPD Group, he crunches the numbers that show it. And as a father of a 15-year-old, he lives the life that proves it.

Take this morning. Balzer, as he does every morning, prepares his breakfast by plopping a Pop-Tart in the toaster. Ditto for his son, Christopher. That's it. Along with a glass of grapefruit juice. While the Pop-Tart bakes, Balzer lets his dog out and grabs the paper. Still standing, he gobbles his Pop-Tart while scouting around for toll bridge change.

"I may not eat a very nutritious breakfast, but time is a lot more important to me than nutrition," Balzer says. "That's true for most people."

Is it ever. Breakfast in a bowl has become a soggy concept in America. Just ask Kellogg. Or General Mills. Or Post. Sure, cereal is still the most popular morning meal, by far. But it is slowly losing ground to a cereal killer called convenience.

Cereal once reigned as king of convenience. No longer. Ready-to-eat cereal sales fell 1.3% in 1998 from 1997. During the past three years, sales fell more than $800 million, to about $7 billion last year. New cereal introductions were down about 30% last year.

When 5,000 consumers nationwide were asked to keep diaries on their breakfast habits, they told NPD Group they've been cutting back on cereal for two years. They also are eating less toast. And fewer eggs. All require too much preparation.

Instead, consumers increasingly are eating toaster pastries. And breakfast bars. And bagels. All are low-maintenance meals. And portable, too. You can eat 'em in the car. At your desk. And, yes, while glopping on the shaving cream or mascara. That's why cereal makers are falling all over themselves to produce cereal replacements.

In 1993, not a single cereal bar was introduced in the USA. Last year, there were nine. In 1994, not a single new toaster pastry hit the market. Last year, 23 did. And in 1994, just one new national bagel brand made it to grocery store shelves. Last year there were 78, reports *New Product News*.

"The best to you each morning," says futurist Watts Wacker, in a jaded reference to Kellogg's TV jingle of the 1960s, "is not about dribbling milk on your tie."

"Going from hand to bowl to mouth is out," adds Wacker of consulting firm First Matter. "Going from hand to mouth is much more in sync with lifestyles built on mobility."

There's another factor at play: Eating breakfast at home is becoming passé. Nearly two-thirds of consumers do not eat breakfast at home, the National Restaurant Association estimates. About 26% of consumers eat breakfast at their desks.

"We call it deskfast," says Tom Vierhile, general manager at Marketing Intelligence Service. When it comes to new breakfast products, Vierhile says, he offers this single piece of advice to all clients: "It's the convenience, stupid."

Many consumers can't wait until they're at their desks. They gobble breakfast in the car on the way to work. Automakers are taking note. Within the next five years, several car companies are expected to offer optional microwaves for time-hungry drivers, says Todd Waters, a promotional marketing consultant.

Soon, about the only thing time-wary consumers will need a spoon for at breakfast is to stir cream in their coffee. If that. Coffee consumption at breakfast is falling, too. Who has time to clean the coffee maker?

Certainly not Mom. Moms increasingly are absent from the breakfast table. About half of all breakfasts eaten at home are now served without Mom, reports NPD Group. Dads now prepare about 11% of breakfasts, while 37% of kids younger than 18 prepare their own. That explains why items like toaster pastries and cereal bars are on the grow. "Everyone's looking for the easiest way out," Balzer says.

SOGGY CEREAL SALES

Don't think the cereal giants aren't painfully aware of this. Perhaps none more than Kellogg. To combat a decline of almost 7% in its domestic cereal sales through the first three quarters of 1998, Kellogg recently fired 765 workers, hired a new ad agency and named a new CEO. But the most important move in Kellogg's bowl of tricks may be its new emphasis on convenience products.

It's enough to make Tony the Tiger roll over. Although cereal sales at Kellogg fell last year, the company's so-called convenience breakfast foods grew by more than 15%. Sales of the company's Nutri-Grain Bars, introduced in 1991, grew 17% last year. Kellogg last year introduced Nutri-Grain Twists, which combine items such as strawberries and cream.

Even sales of Pop-Tarts, which were introduced 35 years ago, grew more than 10% last year. Kellogg, which now makes 25 kinds of Pop-Tarts, did some serious Pop-Tart rejiggering last year. It introduced Pastry Swirls, adult-oriented Pop-Tarts. And it even developed kid-targeted Wild Magic Burst Pop-Tarts, which turn colors when heated.

"Convenience is a subject vital to our hearts," says John Forbis, vice president of global convenience foods at Kellogg. "A mobile world is fueling breakfast-on-the-go."

Last year, portable breakfast foods accounted for $1.4 billion of the company's sales. That's about 25% of its worldwide revenue. Yet Kellogg only recently began to take the segment seriously. While Forbis declined to discuss portable products in development, marketing consultants say all the cereal makers are searching for ways to blend best-selling cereal brands and baked goods into cereal-coated pastries.

Post Cereal is only beginning to discover the importance of portability. "Car-seat dining has become a reality," says Mike Polk, general manager at Post Cereal. "Many moms now have to feed their kids in the car."

That's why Post last month introduced Post Snackabouts — small, potato-chip-like bags of Post's most popular cereals. While Snackabouts mark Post's first entry into the convenience sector, "It won't be our last," Polk says.

General Mills, meanwhile, doesn't think lack of convenience is the cereal world's biggest problem. It doesn't make any cereal bars or toaster pastries, and has no immediate plans to, says spokeswoman Pam Becker. "The real issue," she says, "is the category's lack of innovation." In its bid to innovate, General Mills is about to introduce its first line of organic cereals.

NOT JUST CEREAL

The growing demand for convenience at breakfast is leaving its mark well beyond the cereal aisle. Pillsbury's dry pancake mix has been in a rut for nearly a decade. So Pillsbury's new-product gurus were called in to brainstorm convenient breakfast concoctions. More than a decade ago, they came up with Toaster Strudel to compete with Pop-Tarts.

And recently, they devised Toaster Scrambles — a frozen, flaky pastry wrapped around eggs, cheese and bacon or sausage that is prepared by plopping it in the toaster. Within a year, sales of Toaster Scrambles should exceed $160 million annually, says Heidi Thom,

vice president of breakfast at Pillsbury.

With sales of eggs on the skids, an unexpected victim is being dragged down with them: toast. Consumers told NPD Group that in the past five years, they have eaten 2.2% less eggs, but 5.1% less toast.

"It's a losing battle," says a frustrated Mark Dirkes, senior vice president of marketing at Interstate Bakeries, maker of Wonder Bread.

That's one reason Interstate introduced bagels several years ago. And, last year, its first cereal bars: Hostess Fruit & Cereal Bars. That line will be extended this year, Dirkes says.

The breakfast battle extends well beyond the grocery store. Fast-food titans McDonald's and Burger King have made a science out of concocting hand-held breakfast creations.

In 1971, a McDonald's franchisee tried to figure out how to make eggs benedict portable. By substituting cheese for hollandaise sauce, and folding the creation inside an English muffin, the Egg McMuffin was born. It has since become a multibillion-dollar business. So big that one-third of McDonald's revenue now comes from its breakfast business. Franchisees are currently testing easy-to-handle bagel sandwiches and breakfast burritos in some areas.

Meanwhile, Burger King doesn't sell a single breakfast product nationally that requires silverware. Last year, it introduced Cini-minis — bite-sized cinnamon rolls in packs of four. "When you're navigating the freeways, you don't want to juggle a huge dish over the steering column," says Sherad Cravens, director of breakfast marketing.

DENNY'S TO GO

Even Denny's, the casual dining chain famous for its $1.99 "Grand Slam" breakfasts, is in the process of rethinking how to serve a convenient breakfast.

Several years ago, Denny's installed take-out dessert counters so people could quickly grab a piece of pie. In a few markets, Denny's is preparing to convert them into breakfast-to-go counters with take-out bakery items. "We need to respond to our customers who don't have time in the morning," says Denny's President John Romandetti.

Which brings us back to Balzer and his daily Pop-Tart.

When Balzer was a kid, he dutifully ate a bowl of Cheerios every morning. But he can't recall having so much as a spoonful of cereal in at least two years.

"When it comes to breakfast, never bet against how lazy we Americans can be," Balzer says. "The remote control breakfast can't be far behind."

28

ARE TECH BUYERS DIFFERENT?

Marketers say new consumer categories are needed

To the bright young founders of WebTV, it looked like a home run: hook televisions up to the Net and tap into the vast market of couch potatoes curious about this new thing called the World Wide Web. But after burning through an estimated $50 million to advertise the new service during the 1996 holiday season, WebTV and partners Sony and Philips Electronics counted a disappointing 50,000 subscribers.

The problem, WebTV now acknowledges, was the wrong marketing message. Couch potatoes want to be better entertained, while computer users are content to explore using small PC screens. A revamped campaign now emphasizes entertainment over education.

WebTV's marketing myopia isn't unique. As the $280 million consumer market for technology soars, companies that sell stuff ranging from cellular phones and computers to software and Internet services have some surprising blind spots about who their customers are and what motivates them.

Enter market researchers, sniffing opportunity. Unlike soup or soda, technology products are often complex and evolve rapidly. And the failure of a few well publicized products, such as WebTV or Kodak's PhotoCD, to hit it big with a mass market has convinced a growing number of companies that when it comes to high tech, conventional marketing research doesn't go far enough. "The traditional approach pretty much always falls back on the ancient taxonomy of early adopters and followers," says Peter M. Winter, president of Cox Communications Inc.'s Interactive Media unit. "That's not precise enough."

MOTIVATION. The result has been a scramble among researchers to find out what makes technology customers tick—and whether consumers behave differently when they buy technology than when they purchase other consumer products. Of course, consumer-goods makers figured out long ago the value of understanding consumer habits, even for seemingly mundane stuff such as toothpaste. But to gain similar insights into technology consumers, some marketers argue, research must go beyond demographics and buying patterns—it must capture how people really use technology day to day, and how they feel about it.

Some market-research firms, such as San Francisco-based Odyssey Research and pollster Yankelovich Partners' Cyber Citizen, are focusing on the way consumers use the Internet. Others, such as SRI Consulting Inc., are using traditional market-research methods that combine demographics information with an analysis of consumer emotions to predict how tech buyers will behave.

But the most ambitious effort so far is a scheme from technology consultant Forrester Research Inc., which contracted with polling and research firm NPD Group to survey 131,000 consumers annually about their motivations, buying habits, and financial ability to purchase technology products. Dubbed Technographics, the first survey results won't be completed until later this month. But already, some big-name clients, including Tele-Communications, Sprint, Visa, Ford, and Bank of America, have signed up for a look. "Technology is not just changing the way consumers spend time," says Gil Fuchsberg, director of new media for ad agency Interpublic Group, a Technographics client. "It's also changing the way nearly every company is making, selling, and delivering products. We've got to understand that."

Of course, plenty of technology companies have prospered without such tools. But Jim Taylor, who ran Yankelovich before he became senior vice-president for marketing at computer maker Gateway 2000 Inc. in 1996, thinks technology-specific research will be increasingly critical as PC makers and others learn to segment their markets to keep up growth. The difference, he says, is that traditional consumer research will tell you who bought a computer. But it won't tell you that four different people in a household use it—or how their needs differ. Marketing to the wrong member of the household can sink a product, he says. "In this business, you don't have to screw up much to screw up a lot," he says.

To help companies zero in on their target customers, Forrester's scheme separates people into 10 categories. Some, such as career-minded "Fast Forwards" who own an average of 20 technology products per household, and their less affluent colleagues, known as "Techno-Strivers," are at ease with technology and use it at home, in the office, and at play. Others range from "New Age Nurturers" who spend big bucks on technology, though primarily for family use, to "Hand-Shakers." These older, wealthy consumers—often managers—let younger assistants handle computers and other technology in the office (table).

CLEAR TARGETS. Some Forrester clients have already started identifying products and services they're likely to rework. At Cox Interactive, for example, Winter plans to use Technographics to identify more clearly the target viewers for his Web sites. Once he has a stronger handle on who they are, he'll reshape content to better draw them in.

To get a glimpse of how it will work, consider Cindy Williams, 46, an administrative secretary for a health-maintenance organization in Tulsa, Okla. She and her husband Gary, a 44-year-old maintenance supervisor, have one PC they bought three years ago and no Internet connection. They are mulling an upgrade since their sons, ages 11 and 12, want speedier games than their sluggish machine can play.

Thanks to their family status and income—two traditional signposts—a conventional consumer-research profile would highlight them as promising technology buyers. But Forrester claims those factors are misleading and that any tech company pitching sophisticated products to the Williams would likely be wasting its money. Technographics pegs the Williams as Traditionalists—family-oriented buyers who are relatively well off but remain unconvinced that upgrades or other new techno-gadgets are worth buying. Why? A key factor in the Williams profile is the age of their PC. Three years old is ancient by tech standards.

So an online grocery service starting up in Tulsa might use Forrester's information to bypass the Williams, despite their superficial demographic fit. Unlike other family-oriented consumer groups such as New Age Nurturers or Digital Hopefuls, Traditionalists "wait a long time before upgrading. That's not a very fertile part of the online market," says Forrester analyst Josh Bernoff.

But Technographics should also help a company find new buyers. Carol Linder, 46, is a customer-service manager for Ameritech Corp. in Milwaukee. She and her husband Robyn, a 53-year-old CPA, already have three school-age children, two pagers, and three PCs. By the end of the month, they plan to buy two more computers. Robyn spends time online for work. Although similar to the Williams family in income and family status, they are light-years away in how they use technology. The Linders are classic Fast Forwards, using computers and other gadgets for job, family, and individual pursuits. So a

(Cont.)

company selling ISDN phone lines that speed computer connections might use the Technographics profiles to target the Linders while avoiding the Williams.

Such distinctions should also come in handy as tech companies struggle with marketing to a broader audience as they shift away from early adopters. That's the challenge facing Tele-Communications Inc. The cable-TV giant wants to use Technographics to help develop and sell new products as its cable-modem business goes mass market. "How we market the product initially, and how we target and talk to our customers changes over time," says John Najarian, director of consumer research for TCI.

TECH CUSTOMERS: THE OPTIMISTS . . .

☐ MORE AFFLUENT   ☐ LESS AFFLUENT

FAST FORWARDS
These customers are the biggest spenders, and they're early adopters of new technology for individual use.

NEW AGE NURTURERS
Also big spenders, but focused on technology for home uses such as a family PC.

MOUSE POTATOES
They like the online world for entertainment and are willing to spend for the latest in technotainment.

TECHNO-STRIVERS
Use technology from cell phones and pagers to online services primarily to gain career edge.

DIGITAL HOPEFULS
Families with a limited budget but still interested in new technology. Good candidates for the under-$1,000 PC.

GADGET-GRABBERS
They also favor online entertainment but have less cash to spend on it.

DATA: FORRESTER RESEARCH INC. ©BW

. . . AND THE PESSIMISTS

☐ MORE AFFLUENT   ☐ LESS AFFLUENT

HAND-SHAKERS
Older consumers—typically managers—who don't touch their computers at work. They leave that to younger assistants.

TRADITIONALISTS
Willing to use technology but slow to upgrade. Not convinced upgrades and other add-ons are worth paying for.

MEDIA JUNKIES
Seek entertainment and can't find much of it online. Prefer TV and older media.

SIDELINED CITIZENS   Not interested in technology.

DATA: FORRESTER RESEARCH INC. ©BW

more traditional researchers argue that it's doing little more than putting old medicine into new bottles. "Consumers," says Bill Guns, director of SRI Consulting's business-intelligence center. "Nothing in the data we've seen over 20 years suggest that somehow people are different beings when they are buying technology." SRI's research, called Values Lifestyles Survey, leans more on emotions, delving into whether or not customers like technology or are intimidated by it.

But retail consultant Wendy Liebmann, president of WSL Strategic Retail, says the slow start of Net shopping and the frustrated expectations of many consumers new to online services clearly show the need for more targeted technology marketing. Companies are providing services that consumers ignore. Meanwhile, consumers sign up for other services and are disappointed. With a mountain of data on tap, Forrester is hoping it can carve out a new category for itself: techno-matchmaker.

By Paul C. Judge in Boston

TCI knows that speed and performance have been important to early users of cable-modems. But that's not necessarily what will appeal to new types of buyers. So Najarian says it might use Technographics to help create kid-friendly Internet marketing targeted to family-oriented New Age Nurturers, for example. Or it might develop ways to download TV clips that appeal to entertainment-hungry Mouse Potatoes.

NEW BOTTLES? Similar plans are under way at Delta Air Lines. The Atlanta-based carrier hopes that by analyzing its own customer database using Technographics' categories, it can better target online ticket sales. Delta plans to create marketing campaigns aimed at time-strapped Fast Forwards and New Age Nurturers, for example. Just as important, it figures to save a bundle by using Technographics to eliminate customers who appear to be technology pessimists from its solicitations. High income or not, they're unlikely to use such a service. "Traditional marketing research gives you a picture of the universe but doesn't focus on the people more likely to book online," says Paul Lai, manager of marketing research for Delta.

Despite the interest Forrester has sparked,

29

Adding U. S. Soybeans To India's Spicy Diet Faces Big Roadblocks

Protein-Loaded Legume Could Help the Hungry, If Only They'd Eat It

Hiding 'That Beany Taste'

By Jonathan Karp

Staff Reporter of The Wall Street Journal

NEW DELHI — Virgil Miedema thinks he can do wonders for Indians' health, and American farmers' wealth, by sneaking a little blandness into South Asia's famously spicy cuisine.

The 52-year-old North Dakotan is traversing this land of curry and onions, chatting up millers, farmers and housewives in near-fluent Hindi, to spread the gospel of the soybean. "This is the only area of the world where soy isn't consumed as food," sighs Mr. Miedema, South Asia director of the American Soybean Association and the son of a soybean farmer. "It's being fed to chickens, but we're missing a huge opportunity by not marketing it as human food."

Why care? India swells by 16 million people a year, but its farm output of cereals and lentils isn't keeping pace. Indians face a protein shortage. Meanwhile, the U.S. grows many more protein-rich soybeans than Americans can digest. U.S. farmers need big, new export markets. With nearly one billion people, India is a perfect match. Except for two problems: India already grows so many soybeans that it exports them, paradoxically shipping out protein it could use at home. And the reason it does this is that Indians, poor yet discriminating diners, hate soy.

"It's that beany taste," grimaces food scientist V.D. Devdhara, rubbing his thumb and forefinger together as if handling a loathsome legume.

But he shares Mr. Miedema's mission. So, in an act of nutritional subterfuge, Mr. Devdhara is pioneering a way to get soy protein into Indians' diets in the guise of the lentil, a national staple. After years of research, the government dairy board where he works is close to commercially producing faux lentils made of soy and wheat flour. The brown pellets are designed to look, cook and taste like the real thing, known locally as [dal]. But they can pack at least 60% more protein bang for the buck.

Apart from taste, soybean boosters must overcome the biases of a famed food culture, the ghosts of previous soy failures and xenophobic activists who wildly accuse "powerful soybean interests" of conspiring — and even killing people — to open the market, dominate Indian farming and wipe out indigenous crops. Yet powerhouses such as DuPont Co. and Monsanto Co. have joined the soy fray in India.

Research suggests soybeans lower cholesterol and may slow cancer growth. For India, the issues are more basic. Swift population growth is devouring the gains of the 1960s Green Revolution, when highyield seeds boosted India's grain output. Today, production of lentils, a main protein source in the largely vegetarian diets of most Indians, is stagnant. Per capita availability of lentil protein is half its level at India's independence in 1947. And lentil prices have doubled this year.

In a country where 53% of children under five years old are malnourished, soybeans, backers say, are a perfect way to help plug a growing protein gap. Soybeans are an extremely rich 40% protein by weight. Mr. Miedema sees the makings of a huge market for soybeans from the U.S., producer of nearly half the world's soybeans. But cracking India, the fifth-largest soybean producer, entails more than overcoming high trade barriers. "The goal is to sell them our commodity. But we can't dream of doing that until we get Indians to consume their own," says the clean-cut Mr. Miedema in his New Delhi office above a chaotic shopping arcade.

The St. Louis-based American Soybean Association, which is partly funded by the U.S. government, set up an Indian beachhead in 1996. It hired Mr. Miedema, who had spent 17 years in South Asia with the Peace Corps and U.S. Agency for International Development. His mission is to repeat the soy lobby's success in China. In just 15 years, it helped turn that soybean producer into an importer. In 1997, China bought $657 million of U.S. soy products.

Of course, the Chinese have been eating soybeans — as soy sauce and tofu, among other things — for millennia. In India, Mr. Miedema is starting almost from scratch. His recipe doesn't directly challenge India's food culture. Instead, he's prodding companies to add soy to everyday Indian food, such as wheat flour used to make [chapati], the flat bread eaten at most meals in northern India. "You've got to stick with tradition," says Mr. Miedema.

Not everyone is ready for it. At a recent New Delhi trade fair, salesman Ashish Jain can't get passersby to check out his Mealmaker-brand chapati mix and soy chunks, a spongy meat substitute. But he's swamped with business for his other product: toilet freshener that smells like mothballs. Over in Hall 13, though, Chetali Gupta of AFM Foods Ltd. is making progress. She wins over housewife Neelam Sareen with a pitch that

AFM's new soyfortified flour for chapatis has 35% more protein than wheat and can reduce the risk of cancer and the aches of menopause.

AFM, which makes a best-selling wheat flour, is Mr. Miedema's first partner for promoting wheat-soy blends. By wooing topnotch millers with technical and marketing assistance, he hopes to create a market amid surging demand by middleclass Indians for high-quality flour. The soybean association estimates Indian consumption of soy blended with wheat flour could rise from virtually nothing today to 1.8 million metric tons a year in 2010. (A metric ton equals 2,204.62 pounds.)

India has dashed soy hopes before. A decade ago, the U.S. association backed three local companies that failed after trying to popularize soymilk. RJR Nabisco Inc. abandoned making soy oil, and Swiss giant Nestle SA recently withdrew its soymilk powder and soy-based baby food because of poor sales.

The soy crusaders believe this campaign can be won with aggressive marketing, smarter products and higher technology to remove that beany taste. "There's a percolation of soy through the Indian food chain," says Sanjeev Chaudhry, who was involved

Virgil Miedema

with Nabisco's soy-oil factory. Today, he is India chief for Protein Technologies International, a St. Louis company at the forefront of developing turbocharged soy extracts. Its Supro brand, which is 90% protein, is so successful in the West that DuPont bought the company last year for $1.5 billion.

In India, the business is small but growing fast. Mr. Chaudhry sells about 100 tons a year to 25 customers, ranging from Bombay's

(Cont.)

leading bread baker to a healthclub owner who recently launched India's answer to Slimfast diet drink. He plans to hit the mass market through fortified flour, and has data showing his imported product makes a better chapati. Still, some major Indian food marketers, who operate on paper-thin profit margins, balk at the marginally higher cost, and others remain haunted by soy's past flops.

A different anxiety hangs over Protein Technologies' experimental soy program in southern India. Field trials are under way to demonstrate for the government the advantages of soy-fortified foods. Mr. Miedema's soybean association is also a sponsor, but plays down that role for fear of provoking backlash from a small coterie of very loud antiforeign activists.

Leading the crusade against U.S. soybeans is Vandana Shiva, a self-styled guardian of India's biodiversity.

Seated in an office adorned with indigenous plant samples in glass jars, Ms. Shiva calmly states her objections: Free trade in agriculture, inevitably controlled by multinationals selling expensive genetically engineered seeds, will destroy India's farmers and local foods, she says.

For her, soybeans exemplify this evil. They're alien and were planted at the expense of traditional crops. Large-scale cultivation in India began in the 1970s to reduce dependence on imported edible oil. Soy oil still isn't popular, but Mr. Miedema and other lobbyists keep pushing to open the market. In late August, the government decided to allow soybean imports and slash customs duty on edible oils including soy oil, a move that Ms. Shiva says paves the way for foreign food domination.

That decision closely followed a curious calamity that added fuel to her fire. New Delhi residents started dropping dead in August from contaminated mustard oil, the most popular cooking oil in northern India. Eventually, more than 50 people died, prompting the government to ban the oil until safer packaging was introduced.

To many, the incident was a reminder that poor quality control imperils India's public. To Ms. Shiva and her allies, the poisoning appeared to be part of a conspiracy by the U.S. soybean industry to discredit traditional cooking oil. "The mustard-oil tragedy thus serves as a perfect market opening for U.S. agribusiness corporations," she says.

Ms. Shiva went on the offensive, claiming that a main beneficiary is Monsanto, which is expanding aggressively in India and hopes to sell genetically engineered soybean seeds here. As a running barb against Monsanto, she likes to remind people that the firm made the notorious Vietnam War defoliant Agent Orange. Monsanto vehemently denied it had any role in the mustard-oil contamination.

In the western town of Anand, Verghese Kurien, another ardent nationalist, is joining the soybean forces. As head of the National Dairy Development Board, Mr. Kurien made India self-sufficient in milk and the world's biggest milk producer, while thwarting foreign dairy firms. He branched out into edible oil to help his country cut costly imports.

More recently, he launched what could be India's most ambitious soy-food project, making faux lentils. The paradox is that Mr. Kurien, who retired late last month, is decidedly anti-multinational but is using U.S. technology to make his soy lentils. And, if the project succeeds, it could serve Mr. Miedema's aim of boosting soybean demand.

The idea has been germinating for a decade, starting with U.S.-funded soybean research at an Indian university. The dairy board, whose sister organization, Amul, is one of India's largest food marketers, took on the challenge of developing a cheap, uniquely Indian protein alternative. "Soy can be made into chickens and bacon, why not dal?" says Mr. Kurien.

But the synthetic lentil has been tough to master. Mr. Devdhara, the scientist leading the soy project, has traveled back and forth to the U.S. for the past three years to work out kinks in a $2 million food processor for the lentil pellets. Back in India, he brought in flavor chemists to get the soy taste out and put in the aroma and subtle flavor of lentil. The hardest part has been fine-tuning a synthetic lentil that can satisfy India's many regional cooking styles.

After eight months of trial production, launch appears at hand. Mr. Miedema, who isn't connected to the project, may be the most eager to see the faux lentils in Indian markets. He thinks they could open the market to a second wave of soy products, made with U.S. beans. In time, he believes marketers can try again with soymilk and tofu, which looks and feels like Indian cottage cheese, called paneer. But he doesn't have the gall to sell tofu on taste. "Indians say that tofu is not as good as paneer," he says, "but it's better for you."

30

OUTSOURCING
IS MORE THAN COST CUTTING

It's also a way of conserving capital, tapping into other companies' production expertise, and getting new products to market fast. ■ *by Philip Siekman*

The one thing agricultural equipment giant Deere ought to know how to do, it might seem, is paint something green. So it should, but it usually doesn't. The company that once brought steel in the back door and rolled combines and tractors out the front sends out for most of its painting. And at five of its plants, including its newest in Fuquay-Varina, N.C., it doesn't send very far. The paint shop designed, owned, and staffed by MetoKote Corp. is just on the other side of the wall.

The North Carolina plant, opened last year, builds big mowers like those multigang affairs that tend your golf course. Pieces of the machines move 45 feet a minute to and from MetoKote on more than a mile of conveyor. Deere operatives like Judy Meister, once a touring golf pro, load parts on a hanging rack, set switches that signal green or black coatings, and then see them off on their journey up and across the plant and through an opening in the east wall.

On the other side, now in MetoKote territory, the conveyor slows to travel through tunnels for automated washing, application of a powder coat primer, and top coating. The workers include Cheri Carroll, who had 25 years at MetoKote's hometown plant in Lima, Ohio, before she wangled a transfer last year to get out of the snow. Cheri stays in touch with Judy and other Deere people by radio and, when required, uses a hand gun to apply a finishing touch by leaning out into a coating tunnel so advanced in containing stray paint particles that she needs neither mask nor protective clothing. Four hours after loading, the now-gleaming parts are back at Deere where they started.

Deere and MetoKote did their first contiguous-operations deal in 1991 in a new light-tractor plant in Augusta, Ga. Recalls Bob Zippay, then plant manager in Augusta and now running Fuquay-Varina: "I was challenged by corporate as to what we could do to preserve captial." Getting MetoKote to

pay for the paint section not only answered that but also eliminated shipping costs and all the packing, paper, and boxes needed to protect parts painted off the premises. Just as important: "They really understand paint. If we were in charge, we would need technical people to support it and stay on top of all the EPA regulations and what is going on in paint these days." From Augusta the idea spread, and the arrangement got refined as Deere pared down from what was once nearly total vertical integration, outsourcing lots more than painting so that it could concentrate on those things that add competitive advantage. New plants like Fuquay-Varina are little more than welding shops and assembly lines.

Deere is hardly alone in doing what it does best and buying the rest. Some other examples of the latest and most imaginative forays in outsourcing:

■ Archcompetitors Kodak and Polaroid, which once made almost everything themselves, are farming out more and more. Ironically, both are turning to the same minuscule U.S. firm to make their latest mass-market cameras in China.

■ The ultraconservative pharmaceuticals industry is spawning a handful of specialized biotech production firms that brew new compounds for small biopharmaceuticals houses and for giants like Lilly.

■ After contracting out parts and pieces for years, the big brands in personal computers, including IBM, Hewlett-Packard, and Compaq, are starting to send bare-bones machines to distributors, which finish assembling them only after orders come in.

Outsourcing, of course, is old hat in many industries. Some clothing companies, even those whose cachet is high-quality, extra-durable wear like California's Patagonia Corp., have never owned a factory. Switzerland's Nestle Corp. owns 495 plants around the world, but somebody else turns out more than half its production and almost all the packaging. Outsourcing is the tinder of labor

disputes in Detroit, where assembly plants are increasingly supplied by subassemblers that combine components they themselves have outsourced. The ultimate so far: a "rolling chassis" being delivered by Dana Corp. to Chrysler's new $315 million Dodge Dakota pickup-truck plant in Campo Largo, Brazil. The chassis arrives on inflated tires complete with brakes, steering components, gas tank, and other parts supplied by 70 companies, including ITT, TRW, Eaton, and Bosch.

Not everybody's doing it. It's tough to outsource a portion of the process in oil refining, steel production, or pulp and papermaking. "In industries like shipbuilding," says Richard Grotheer, a KPMG partner in Chicago, "a lot of guys are very skeptical." There can be uneasiness about falling behind in technology if somebody else is doing the manufacturing. And, says Peter Robb, director of global process control at Dow Chemical, "everybody struggles with loss of control." Nor is it ever easy. As Robert Hershey III, a New York City KPMG partner, points out, outsourcing means "moving from a capital-based business to an information-based buiness. You need a much different kind of management and a different person leading the organization." Some of the companies cited in this article, despite their enthusiasm about outsourcing, continue to make certain products under their own roof.

Still, concerns about "How can anybody do it better if we've been doing it for 50 years?" are fading. A 1997 study by the Outsourcing Institute in New York City found firms planning projects that would double their outsourcing of all types, including services as well as production of parts. This year, companies covered by a Dun & Bradstreet survey said they would increase manufacturing outsourcing alone by 25% in the next 12 months. That's partly because it's easier to do. A couple of years ago there might not have been an

(Cont.)

outside source of a given component.

The aim is not just to cut direct cost. When the Outsourcing Institute asked companies to name the top three reasons for going extramural, "costs" showed up on 64% of the lists. But "improve company focus," "access to world-class capabilities," and "free resources for other purposes" were each mentioned more than 40% of the time. Often, another goal is to shrink the time and distance between a supplier's parts bin and a retailer's cash register, reducing the amount of product inventoried along the supply chain. Whatever the reasons, unless a manufacturer has a plant in place and a market that will absorb enough output so that it can operate at optimum rates and costs, the burden of proof has shifted from "Why outsource?" to "Why make it here?"

For sellers of lower-price consumer products, the chief impetus remains cutting labor costs, often by shifting production to the less developed world. In a huge, 57-acre plant just outside Shenzhen in China's Guangdong province, Windmere-Durable of Miami Lakes, Fla., makes 24 million small appliances a year—blenders, coffeemakers, fans, irons, mixers, waffle irons—sporting such brands as Hamilton Beach, Philips, Proctor-Silex, and Sunbeam, plus private labels of U.S. retail chains. Reflecting its low labor costs, the factory employs 14,000 people in peak seasons who do just about everything on-site, including winding small motors and molding plastic parts. This year Windmere-Durable got its own first-class brand by buying Black & Decker's small-appliance business. It might keep the U.S. and Mexican plants that came with the deal, but it will make much of the line in China.

Elsewhere in the Shenzhen area, there's a 600,000-square-foot camera factory in which Concord Camera, a tiny, $103-million-a-year company in Avenel, N.J., is turning out Kodaks and Polaroids almost side by side. Concord, with some 4,000 employees in China, produces 25 million cameras a year and shipped $28 million in product to Kodak in its last fiscal year. The Kodak model it's making is the entry-level Advantix 1600, which sells for about $50 and uses the advanced photo system now attracting users after a miserable start in 1996. Outsourcing a high-volume, relatively inexpensive product is a sharp change for Kodak, which has often bought in more expensive cameras but has kept for itself the low-price descendants of George Eastman's box. Nor is this a case of simply hiring acres of fleet fingers. Kodak tweaked performance and added some special touches, but Concord did the camera's basic design in its Hong Kong offices and uses it for other brands.

Mark Schneider, Kodak's director of research, development, and manufacturing of cameras, says the company has become more sophisticated about "what stays inside vs. what goes out." The camera business, he points out, is a low-margin, "pretty difficult industry to compete in." Kodak still makes disposable cameras in hometown Rochester, N.Y., and at a plant in France. It also assembles some conventional cameras at its own factories in China and India. But it's now talking about new camera projects with several suppliers, including Concord.

Letting go isn't always easy, Schneider makes clear. He worries about "outsourcing everything with what may look like an attractive cost upfront, but finding after a period of time that you let your commercialization skills erode to the point that you really cannot be a good buyer of product because you don't bring anything to the party. If you're not careful, you end up with undifferentiated product. You just become a commodity."

Schneider thinks the answer is to work with several suppliers so that none get complacent and, most important, to keep some design work in-house. "It doesn't have to be a whole camera. It may be a lens design, a viewfinder design, something that adds a unique, recognizable differentiation." He also wants to have enough in-house production so that Kodak doesn't "generate designs that are inefficient to produce. That's the beginning of the end."

Over in Cambridge, Mass., Polaroid also is starting to mix in-house and outsourced production as part of a mighty effort to transform an inward-looking company into a svelte consumer marketer. Haunted by the ghost of its genius founder, Edwin Land, Polaroid has long focused on "heroic" projects: dramatic new products devised, developed, and put into production internally and released to the market at fairly long intervals. That approach changed in 1995 with the arrival from Black & Decker of Gary DiCamillo, the first outsider to become CEO. If it hadn't, says Sandy Posa, an executive vice president and head of marketing and new-product development, "we'd be gone."

The new philosophy could be summed up as waves of new products, with different kinds of cameras and different kinds of film targeted at different users globally. This translates into a half-dozen introductions a year, which consumes engineering, design, and manufacturing talent at rates that make outside help indispensable. Explains Posa: "We need to leverage our real core capabilities and partner in areas where other folks have better capabilities." One of those better capabilities is Concord's command of churning out cameras with low-cost labor. Its first product for Polaroid is PopShots, the only disposable camera with instant film and potentially a big seller. Now in production at Concord at an initial rate of 108,000 a week and about to hit the stores, PopShots cameras will be priced at less than $20. They come preloaded with ten-exposure film packs that are being assembled in a Polaroid plant in the Netherlands using film made by the company in Waltham, Mass.

PopShots has some innovations, though hardly the heroic kind that would have impressed Land. None of the half-dozen other new Polaroids in the latest crop, some made in-house and others farmed out, boast real changes. One is a restyled version of a camera in the standard instant-photo line that the company makes itself either in Scotland or in Shanghai. Another is a reloadable PocketCam that takes photo-booth-size pictures and is being manufactured by Japanese toymaker Tomy Corp. In early production in a U.S. Polaroid plant is a cost-reduced, tarted-up-for-teens version of an older Polaroid that will be introduced first as the JoyCam in Japan. It it takes off, chances are good that production will be outsourced.

Keeping the tough ones at home and sending out for the rest looks like the future at Polaroid. Says Posa: "The criterion is where do we add value and real expertise in the design and manufacture of a product, and where do others add more value than we do?" Deciding what goes where, Posa continues, is the search for "the sweet spot between cost and quality." Besides divvying up conventional camera production between its own and outside factories, the company buys in its entry-level digital camera and makes a $2,000 version itself. It is also developing a combination instant-film-and-digital camera that does verge on the extremely innovative and will almost certainly be produced internally.

Polaroid is also mixing partnerships with go-it-alone as it probes for new opportunities. It has a deal with Sterling Diagnostic Imaging for the development and marketing of instant diagnostic-imaging systems, and has turned to Sony for key parts of a self-serve Make-a-Print kiosk, where retail shoppers can make copies and enlargements of photographs. At the same time, Polaroid on its own is coating paper for photographic quality output on inkjet printers and building its ColorShot Digital Photo Printer, a $299 small box driven by a computer or digital camera. It spits out four-by-four-inch prints in 15 seconds that, Polaroid insists, are "photo quality."

When it comes to buying outside, the pharmaceuticals industry has an understandably cautious approach. Quality errors can kill more than sales. As Manny Silva, vice president of corporate engineering for Glaxo Wellcome, points out, regulators and others "look at you a lot more closely if you are outsourcing. The assumption is that you are trying to cut costs and, possibly, reducing reliability and safety." As a result, major drug houses have turned to outsiders for services and even filling and packaging but have kept a firm hand on production.

(Cont.)

Recently, says Silva, things have changed. Improved research methods not only have yielded a flood of potentially useful new compounds, straining the drug companies' internal capabilities, but also have compressed the time between regulatory approval of a new drug and the day a competitive product gets to the market. It still takes years to bring a product from the laboratory through clinical trials and the FDA approval process, but being able to produce and market it quickly in the weeks and months immediately following approval can be critical.

The problem is compounded for new drugs that result from rearranging proteins through genetic engineering. A river of interesting molecules is now flowing through development labs. But producing recombinant proteins by bacterial or yeast fermentation and making more complex molecules by mammalian cell culture involves batteries of tanks and extraction apparatus interconnected with lots of stainless-steel piping. In such plants, entry-level jobs require B.S. degrees. Most big drug houses have plenty of capacity to synthesize small molecules and turn out billions of tablets and capsules, but often lack command of the process, the plant, and the people needed for biopharmaceuticals. Certainly, the price tag for such facilities is beyond the reach of smaller biopharmaceuticals houses with more talent and expectations than capital.

Some large firms, including Abbott Laboratories, Boehringer Ingelheim, and Hoffmann-La Roche, make biopharmaceutical materials for other companies, mostly to cover the rent until they need the space for their own production. However, a new subindustry of manufacturers that want to be nothing other than outsourcees is competing for the business.

All but one of these contract biopharms are subsidiaries or divisions of larger firms with some connection to pharmaceuticals. The exception is Bio Science Contract Production Corp. in Baltimore; the company's principal owner, CEO Jacques Rubin, has already built and sold one other biopharmaceuticals plant. The rest are a Montreal operation owned by Gist-Brocades, the Netherlands' large producer of pharmaceutical chemicals, including penicillin; Lonza Biologics in Portsmouth, N.H., which is part of Alsuisse Lonza Holding, a Zurich conglomerate; and, in a sparkling new, 109,000-square-foot lab on the south edge of North Carolina's Research Triangle Park, Covance Biotechnology Services.

An offshoot of a Princeton, N.J., contract research organization spun out of Corning in 1996, Covance Biotechnology shipped its first materials to a customer last year. A visit to its new plant conveys a sense of the barriers to entry. The place has cost $70 million so far and still has lots of empty space to fill with additional costly tanks, plumbing, and instrumentation.

All four of the specialists are cooking stuff for both major pharmaceuticals houses and a collection of smaller biochemical specialists. Typical of the latter is Corvas International in San Diego, which was started 11 years ago by a group of scientists with some research findings and intuition about what causes blood to coagulate, nobly stanching a wound or ignobly forming a fatal clot. Corvas earned its first dollars with a diagnostic tool picked up by Johnson & Johnson, traded an interest in some other compounds for help from Schering-Plough, and got Pfizer involved with a discovery that could lead to a drug used following strokes. Now it has enough cash, momentum, and investor interest to chance at least early clinical trials on its own and has Covance building the molecules.

Partly because outsourcing is still not quite respectable, and mostly because they don't want to tip off competitors, the majors say little about arrangements with contractors even though there are lots of deals. Bio Science is working on a cancer drug with Britain's Zeneca Pharmaceuticals. Switzerland's Novartis has a contract with Covance. At its last annual meeting, in an exception to the general reticence, Eli Lilly touted its deal with Lonza for the production of Activated Protein C, which appears effective in the treatment of sepsis and is about to enter the final phase of human clinical trials. The arrangement, said Lilly CEO Randall Tobias, is intended to get the drug to market faster.

So far, none of the contractors is producing a product for market; everything is being used for trials. All these operations were founded, however, on the hope that production will be left with them if and when the molecules they are brewing turn into profitable, efficacious drugs. That empty space at Covance is waiting for the big 2,000- or even 5,000-liter tanks needed for full-scale commercial production of something.

A change in the FDA approval process has improved the contractors' prospects. Prior to 1996, a biotech drug was effectively approved along with the way it was made and where it was made. Changing the process or plant took time, money, more clinical trials, and more federal filings. That's no longer the case: The product, not the process, is approved. As a result, drug developers are more willing to outsource, since their products won't necessarily become captives of the outsourcees. If demand is sufficient, the drug developer can always build its own facility. However, the contract manufacturers argue that economics are in their favor except for the rare billion-dollar molecule that clearly supports a dedicated plant.

The contractors' argument includes the usual benefits for outsourcing: Conserve capital, get access to expertise, and cut costs through economies of scale. Then there's the capability to get to market quickly. A pharmaceuticals company may be reluctant to start work on a plant well before FDA approval when the future is tough to read. "At that point," rhetorically says Charles White, vice president for business development at Covance, "you don't know what the market is. You don't know how effective it is. It could fail in clinical trials. So you are taking a big risk in building anything." Lilly apparently agrees with this kind of reasoning. It expects to leave its Activated Protein C with Lonza after approval.

The realities that drive White's spreadsheets differ little from those in another industry that increasingly lets others do its manufacturing: infotech devices, particularly personal computers and related hardware. The extent of outsourcing by the industry leaders varies from Compaq, which still makes its own circuit-boards for desktop computers, to IBM, which does less and less of its own PC manufacturing, to Hewlett-Packard's printer and computer divisions, which have largely been cut down to development and engineering in the back and marketing and sales in the front with outsourcees in between.

In its printer divisions, HP has almost arrived where its competitors probably have to get. Last February the company's consumer-products group in Rancho Bernardo, Calif., whose main product is inkjet printers, announced that it would "redeploy" 1,000 of its 1,800 manufacturing employees in the U.S., shifting production to contractors such as Solectron Corp. Later in the year another HP group, the laser-printer division in Boise, which has always relied on Canon for engines, sold its U.S. and Italian circuitboard assets to a contractor, Jabil Circuit, and thereby got rid of the last of its manufacturing operations.

Sniffs one HP executive: "Putting parts together? Others can do that." That's a big change, observes Phil Faraci, head of operations for HP's consumer-products group. "When I started working at HP 20 years ago, we used to make screws, anneal steel, and wind motors." Back then, Faraci says, when HP printers were so-called *XY* plotters, "the ability to acquire many components did not exist. Buying subassemblies was totally impossible. And we had ourselves spread very thin." Today the group initiates production internally, usually in Vancouver, Wash., but then moves it out to a contractor as quickly as possible.

The new era didn't arrive without pain. Says Antonio Perez, vice president and general manager of the consumer-products group: "It hasn't been a natural act for us. It was an incredible revelation to find that others could do things as well as we were doing, even better, for a lot less." HP had no choice. Perez

(Cont.)

reckons that his group, with annual sales estimated by outsiders at more than $8 billion, has an annual volume of 20 million units, or nearly half the world market for inkjet printers. But each of the group's new products is quickly copied, and a hungry competitor can come up with a new or cheaper version just as HP is ramping up.

Staying ahead requires constant product development. Perez estimates that "probably 70% of our revenue or more comes from products we introduced in the last three years." Given that, he adds, the group outsources production only partly because it needs a lower cost structure. "More important is the fact that we have to dedicate our own people, who are better trained and more capable, to the next challenge. We have to get rid of the less-value-added activities as soon as we can so that we can start with the next innovation immediately."

HP and its peers are also under severe pressure to cut manufacturing costs and shorten the supply chain in personal computers. What's shaking up the PC industry: Dell Computer's build-to-order and direct-distribution system is more cost-efficient than mass manufacturing and distribution by middlemen and retailers. One response by HP and others has been to cut production costs around the world by selectively farming out work to the regional plants of electronics contractors such as Solectron and SCI.

The next step, for HP and other brands that continue to use middlemen, is to push some of the assembly and inventory costs down to the distributors. For some time, in response to pressure from big retail chains such as CompuCom, CompUSA, and Micro Warehouse, distributors have been opening the boxes and installing additional ware, hard or soft, before shipping the PCs to stores. Now the large PC distributors are going a long step beyond this by setting up assembly lines to which the original equipment manufacturers, or OEMs—HP, IBM, and others—ship barebones, stripped computers, often without price-volatile memory chips and microprocessors. As orders are received from retailers, the machines are built. Ordered on Monday. Shipped on Tuesday. Or sooner.

In today's supply-chain argot, this kind of manufacturing in the distribution pipeline is called "in-channel assembly." Big PC distributors such as Ingram Micro, Tech Data, and MicroAge are on the way to becoming big PC assemblers. In March, Ingram Micro opened a 488,000-square-foot facility in Memphis to put together desktop machines for IBM, Compaq, HP, and Acer. In June, Tech Data, already assembling in a small Indiana facility, started up lines at its distribution center in Swedesboro, N.J.

Says Jerre (pronounced "Jerry") Stead, Ingram Micro's intense CEO: "This industry's moving from a push vendor model to a pull customer model." It's also shifting risk. Ingram Micro and its peers once got unlimited price protection. If the value of the computer or board they had purchased and put in stock declined—as it is wont to do, given the industry's numbing rate of obsolescence—the brand-name OEMs took the hit by issuing an offsetting credit. No longer. The deals vary, but the protection period now expires in a couple of weeks. Turn inventory, or else.

Besides sharply reducing inventories, in-channel assembly also ought to help the brand-name holders capture a chunk of the largest piece of the U.S. personal computer market, the white boxes or unbranded clones that are assembled by thousands of mom-and-pop computer stores in strip malls and that account for four out of ten PC sales. With prices below $1,000 including monitor and printer, branded products are now invading white-box territory. And with in-channel assembly, PCs can be built to satisfy consumer whims about as quickly as they can at the local clone shop. Hedging its bets, Ingram Micro also assembles white boxes in Memphis.

The question is whether anybody can make money in the hardware business. Ingram Micro, with headquarters and telemarketing offices that sprawl across 34 acres of expensive Santa Ana, Calif., thinks it can. Certainly it has the heft: 13,000 employees in 31 countries and an inventory of 145,000 products, parts, and pieces supplied by 1,400 manufacturers. Last year the company made an after-tax profit of $199.6 million on sales of $16.6 billion and a nice 19% return on equity. Sales are likely to top $20 billion in 1998.

Ingram Micro, which serves 100,000 computer retailers, has the potential to be the gorilla of PC marketing. However, it was a June announcement that really raised industry eyebrows—a deal between Ingram Micro and Solectron Corp. of Milpitas, Calif., one of the largest electronics contract firms and a leader in circuitboard production. The plan is to ally the two companies' facilities and capabilities to provide "build to order" from 11 sites on four continents. Nobody at either company seems quite sure how this is going to work, but the benefits of joining a manufacturing expert with the world's largest infotech distributor are so obvious that brand owners are starting to ask why they have any assets tied up in manufacturing.

Doug Antone, who heads up in-channel assembly for Ingram Micro, says, "We're not there today. But an evolution in thinking is going on. Some of the brand-name OEMs are saying, 'We can see the day when we're in the research-and-development business, the branding business, and the end-user-demand business, but we're not really in the product business.'" However, as Antone notes, that raises the question of how the OEMs get paid for their efforts. He continues, "If an order is placed that stimulates this virtual company, and we pull the parts from our warehouse, who are we buying the computer from?" Some sort of royalty or license fee might be one answer. But until the system evolves, nobody's sure.

Like the MetoKote paint shop that adjoins Deere, the Ingram Micro and Solectron arrangement illustrates how the boundaries of U.S. manufacturing are getting blurred and rearranged, with overlaps all along the way from parts to subassemblies to final production to distribution. As the open question of profits in PCs illustrates, more's at stake than who makes what. Moreover, the new tie-ups are creating what Earle Steinberg, co-leader of supply-chain manufacturing practice at A.T. Kearney, calls "virtual *keiretsus*," or marriages for which annulment may be more difficult to obtain than it is in Rome. Says Larry Chang, head of the worldwide supply chain for Hewlett-Packard's PC business: "If something goes wrong at an electronics contractor like SCI, I can't fire them. I've got to go in there and help them fix it. These suppliers are like my brothers and sisters." That's a long way from traditional easy-come, easy-go outsourcing.

Getting Information for Marketing Decisions

31

WHAT'VE YOU DONE FOR US LATELY?

Data mining is pinpointing which customers are profitable

Like most companies, Federal Express Corp. has some customers that are losers: The cost of doing business with them is greater than the profits they return to the shipper. But FedEx has an edge that most companies lack—it knows who those customers are. That knowledge has kicked off a marketing revolution inside FedEx, where customers sometimes are rated as the good, the bad, and the ugly. "We want to keep the good, grow the bad, and the ugly we want nothing to do with," says Sharanjit Singh, managing director for marketing analysis at FedEx.

It's relatively easy for companies to recognize who is spending money with them. But surprisingly, identifying which customers are profitable for them requires a quantum leap in sophistication. Confounded

> **Often, efforts focus on prodding customers who aren't quite profitable but could be**

by technical difficulties and the high cost of software and data storage, many businesses muddle along with only a rough approximation of which customers make them money. "Not too many people have actually done this yet because it's difficult to pull off," says Wayne Eckerson, a principal analyst at Data Warehouse Institute.

But those few that have begun are finding that determining each customer's profitability can pay big dividends. Savvy companies are conducting behind-the-scenes beauty contests to determine who they like and who they wish would go away. Companies such as U S West, Bank of America, and The Limited are creating vast information warehouses stocked with customer data that allow them to compare the complex mix of marketing and servicing costs that go into retaining each individual consumer, vs. the revenues he or she is likely to bring in. "Some companies are building a profit-and-loss statement for each customer," says Mike Caccavale, president of Aperio Inc., a consulting firm that specializes

in customer-relationship management.

Of course, companies have been using large databases to help refine their marketing efforts for years. But previous attempts focused on the average behavior of large demographic groups, while the newer efforts allow marketers to target individual customers with pinpoint accuracy. And the latest techniques go well beyond determining whether a marketing campaign encourages a consumer to buy—they focus on whether or not that consumer spends enough to make a campaign worthwhile.

At FedEx, customers who spend a lot with little service and marketing investment get different treatment than, say, those who spend just as much but cost more to keep. The "good" can expect a phone call if their shipping volume falters, which can head off defections before they occur. As for the "bad'—those who spend but are expensive to the company—FedEx is turning them into profitable customers, in many cases, by charging higher shipping prices. And the "ugly"? Those customers who spend little and show few signs of spending more in the future? They can catch the TV ads. "We just don't market to them anymore," says Singh. "That automatically brings our costs down."

The power of such an approach lies in a company's ability to determine how much to spend on marketing campaigns—and where to direct those dollars. Twice a year, U S West sifts through its customer list looking for money-losers who have the potential to be more profitable in the future. The starting point is a database containing as many as 200 observations about each customer's calling patterns. By looking at demographic profiles, plus the mix of local vs. long-distance calls, or whether a customer has voice mail, they can estimate a customer's potential telecom spending.

Next, U S West determines how much of the customer's likely telecom budget is already coming its way. Armed with that knowledge, "we can set a cutoff point for how much to spend marketing to this customer before it begins to deteriorate our profitability," says Dennis J. DeGregor, chief database marketing executive for U S West. Those savings fall straight to the bottom line.

Seems like the kind of information mar-

keters would die for. But so far, only a handful have taken the plunge. For one thing, it's expensive. Fleet Bank, one of the few big companies to break out its costs, is spending $38 million just to get started. Also, details about which customers are profitable and which aren't is not always welcome news. "It means the things you did in the past were wrong," says Scott Nelson, an analyst at Gartner Group. "Big advertising campaigns, product introductions—all might be mistakes because you find out they didn't contribute profit."

WRONG REVENUES. That's what executives at Glasgow-based Standard Life Assurance, Europe's largest mutual life-insurance company, discovered earlier this year. They were stunned when the first cut of a profitability survey showed that the insurer was loading up fast on policyholders who held little or no potential for making money. Instead of bringing in the affluent customers Standard Life wanted, its direct-mail marketing campaign was encouraging elderly couples and stay-at-home mothers to sign up for costly home visits by sales agents. Revenues were up—but they were the wrong kind of revenues. "It was an exact mismatch," says Graham Wilson, Standard's database and statistics manager. "These are people who love to sit down and have a cup of tea with someone, but they typically buy only one policy, and margins are small."

Even motivated companies may find mining for profitable customers a tough task. The mechanics are demanding. To get a true picture of customer profitability, Bank of America calculates its profits every month on each of its more than 75 million accounts. Mortgages, for instance, have different costs than checking accounts, car loans, or home-equity credit accounts. And service costs vary by how customers bank—whether they use ATMs, tellers, or the Net.

By wading through all that data, however, BofA is able to zero in on the 10% of households that are most profitable. It assigns a financial adviser to track about 300 accounts at a time. Their job: to answer questions, coordinate the bank's efforts to sell more services, and—perhaps most important—watch for warning flags that these lucrative customers may be moving their business elsewhere.

(Cont.)

If the bank's computer notes a change in the customer's normal pattern of transactions or a falling balance, for example, it alerts the account manager, who may post a flag to the tellers at the customer's branch warning that the account is in danger of moving.

The next time the customer walks into the bank, a teller asks if they have any concerns about the account and offer them a chat with the bank manager. The heavy intervention seems to be working. Since BofA launched the program 18 months ago, customer defections are down, and account balances in the top 10% have grown measurably. "When such a small percentage of customers generate such a large percentage of profits, this kind of program is critical," says Christopher Kelly, senior vice-president for database marketing at Bank of America. "We view it as a strategic weapon."

HANDHOLDING. Often, the strategy is used not to jettison low-spending customers or to reward the cream of the crop. Efforts are focused on those in the middle—customers who aren't yet profitable but whose demographics suggest that they could be. Consider Joseph Taylor, a 62-year-old minister in the United Church of Christ and a professor of pastoral theology at Howard University in Washington. When First Union Bank bought Signet Bank in 1997, Taylor's accounts moved, too. As First Union combed through

---

ARE YOU WORTH IT?

Savvy companies are sorting their customers to see who gives them the most bang for their marketing buck. How you can tell where you rate:

◆ Alter your spending and you get a call: Chances are you are profitable and the company is making sure you're not preparing to jump to a competitor.

◆ You're pitched new services: You're on the fence, and you are being "upsold" to nudge you into profitability.

◆ You're getting fewer catalogs: You may have been blacklisted. As a low-spender, you're not worth the company's marketing dollars.

Signet's records looking for customers with higher profit potential, up popped Taylor. Soon, a marketing push to profitability began.

First Union's buyout of Signet was the third time Taylor's bank had been acquired, and he was fed up. But he dropped his plans to switch when he received a phone call from a First Union marketer. "He talked as if he had known me, even though we had never met," Taylor says. Taylor maintained high balances in his bank accounts, frequently writing large checks to help church members in need. The marketer suggested that Taylor consolidate his checking and savings accounts in one interest-bearing account, providing income to Taylor while reducing the bank's servicing costs. First Union also per-

suaded Taylor to sign up for a home-equity loan, and he brought over the accounts from his ministry as well.

Customers who cost more to lure than they're worth aren't likely to see the same pampering. For those who enjoy browsing through catalogs without buying much, the days of receiving free reading material may be numbered. Mail-order retailers such as Victoria's Secret are winnowing their lists to focus on the most profitable recipients. "Some we expect to drop—those we don't get any return from at all," says Frank Giannantonio, chief information officer for Victoria's Secret.

"Free money" offers are already on the wane. MCI Communications, Sprint, and AT&T have largely dropped their once-omnipresent offers of cash for customers who switch their long-distance service. "They were offering $20, $30, $50 to all takers, without any understanding about whether they actually would want to retain those customers once they had won them," says Thomas Tague, chief operations officer for Tessera Enterprise Systems Inc., a data-warehouse builder. Now, focusing on profitability gives the phrase "valued customer" a whole new twist.

By Paul C. Judge, in Boston

32

Stalking the Elusive Teenage Trendsetter

BY MICHAEL J. MCCARTHY
Staff Report of THE WALL STREET JOURNAL

NORTHBROOK, Ill. — Two researchers peer through a one-way mirror, tapping notes into a computer and observing a most exotic and mysterious subject, the American teenage girl.

Seven of them sit at a table, checking their hair in the mirror, clawing at bowls of M&Ms, firing off opinions. The 44-year-old moderator, Paul Zollo, steers the talk to Taco Bell, a unit of Tricon Global Restaurants Inc., and its talking Chihuahua, whose commercials have been a hit in high schools for about a year. What's the latest on the dinky dog? "Way old," declares 16-year-old Lisa Walsh.

Every word is being tape-recorded, every gesture videotaped here at one of the roughly 1,000 focus groups that Teenage Research Unlimited, a market-research firm, will hold this year. From its headquarters outside Chicago, where it has pioneered the business of picking the teenage brain, the company divines what's in and what's out for such clients as Coca-Cola Co., Levi Strauss & Co. and Microsoft Corp. Celebrities including Michael Jackson have ordered its reports and services, which cost on average about $10,000 a year.

Teenage Research is closely tracking the popularity of baggy clothes (down), sunglasses (up) and funky nail-polish colors (down). On the way in are kick-boxing, girls' snowboarding clothes, and swing music. Headed out: used jeans, coffee houses, video arcades, and "all that."

Prying rich, candid information out of teens isn't easy. In focus groups, they tend to clam up, cut up, or gang up on the moderator. "It always amazes me how much easier this is with adults," says Mr. Zollo, who also is Teenage Research's president.

Marketers hear a demographic drumbeat: The current bulge of 27 million teens is expected to swell 10% by 2010. So companies are rushing to quantify every aspect of the adolescent lifestyle. Teenage Research can tell them teens watch 11.16 hours of TV each week on average and gab on the phone 6.18 hours — nearly double the time they spend cracking books. They spend about $84. Fully 20% carry a beeper, the same proportion wearing a class ring.

Working with Teenage Research, ad agency Bates USA is immersed in a yearlong study, hoping to probe deep into teens' lives. Says Janice Figueroa, a Bates senior vice president, "We want to understand them from the inside out."

Last spring, Bates sent disposable cameras to 36 teens on a national panel and asked them to document their favorite people, places and possessions. The kids sent back snapshots of everything, including the kitchen sink. One caption, from a 16-year-old named Jason, reads, "This picture is of my kitchen sink, which I have to clean every weekend, along with all the other sinks and the bathtub." Another photo shows his toilet. "This is where I go for pure isolation from my family."

A ninth-grader named Amy sent in a shot of a hockey stick. "I have two brothers who are both awesome athletes, and making the field hockey team was my way of proving that I am also a good athlete."

The insight? "We've seen the statistics showing girls are participating in sports more," says Ms. Figueroa, "but this revealed to us that sports may really be more about self-confidence — a powerful motivator marketers could use."

Teens, who live and breathe fads, are a precious source of information and inspiration for the adult marketers in corporate America. Bates doesn't flatly ask them which clothes are popular. Instead, it instructs them to pretend to be a costume designer for the teen TV hit "Dawson's Creek," and then describe how they would dress characters. To figure out what would prompt teens to chew more gum, they are supposed to play "mad scientist," set loose in a lab to dream up innovations. One 16-year-old boy suggested adding sprinkles or cutting sticks into dinosaur shapes.

With clients including Wendy's International Inc. and Estee Lauder Inc., Bates assembled a panel representing the nation's 13- to 17-year-olds, covering cities and suburbs, several ethnic groups, and middle-class and affluent economic groups. Since April, Bates has been sending surveys to its panel every two months or so. It pays the panelists about $60 each to fill them out.

Bates, a unit of Cordiant Communications Group PLC, wanted to uncover how teens really feel about fast food. It asked its

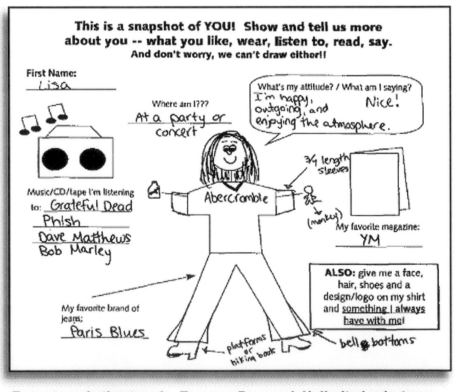

To spot marketing trends, Teenage Research Unlimited asks teens to complete a drawing

Coolest Brands

Teenagers' picks:

Nike	**38%**
Adidas	**19**
Tommy Hilfiger	**18**
Sony	**11**
Gap	**10**
Pepsi	**9**
Coca-Cola	**8**
Levi's	**7**
Ralph Lauren/Polo	**7**
Nintendo	**6**

Source: Teenage Research Unlimited

panel to match a list of restaurants with celebrities likely to eat there. One 17-year-old boy said the Spice Girls, Ally McBeal and Puff Daddy would eat at McDonald's, while Martha Stewart and the cast of the TV sitcom "Golden Girls" would go to Wendy's.

Teenage Research has been fine-tuning its techniques for studying teens since it was founded in 1982 — when the population of adolescents was shrinking and few research firms specialized in them. In the early 1990s, the firm detected the budding popularity of "extreme" sports and passed the tip on to Pepsi-Cola Co., a PepsiCo Inc. unit, which went on to shoot ultrahip Mountain Dew commercials featuring skysurfers.

The researchers expect to be surprised: In a recent survey, teens' single favorite store turned out to be J.C. Penney (chosen by 16%), followed by Old Navy.

Teenage Research produces a twice-yearly report based on its own national teen panel. A search firm recruits teens in malls and by telephone. Teenage Research screens recruits in a second round of phone interviews, looking for "influencers," or the kids most other kids copy. "Who decides what you and your friends do on a Saturday night?" the company asks. Influencers tend to make the plans.

Once they start talking, teens can show detailed knowledge about consumer-product marketing and retailing. When Mr. Zollo asks the girls to list their favorite stores, in a matter of minutes they come up with three dozen retailers, classified into 11 categories.

Unprompted, the girls called one group, Trendy, and put Urban Outfitters and Abercrombie & Fitch there. They put T.J. Maxx, Target and Wal-Mart under Discount. Says Dee Perkins, "I like the changing mix of clothes at Express stores."

In another recent panel, a backpack company wanted to get feedback on a new pocket. Several teens immediately pointed out it was too small for a Walkman.

Teenage Research typically conducts separate sessions for boys and girls, to eliminate cross-gender horseplay. Participants come from different high schools, so they won't worry about having what they say repeated back in their hallways.

At the opening of the recent session with the seven girls, Mr. Zollo works to warm them up. "I'm definitely not a teacher," he says. "So just speak up — there are no wrong answers."

Before arriving, each girl had been asked to bring a recent purchase she "really liked." Their picks included a Kodak Advantix camera, a ticket to a Phish concert, a Garth Brooks compact disk and $65 contact lenses that make eyes a wild blue. "Oh, my gosh!" Lisa Walsh exclaims. "Those are are *so* cool."

In another exercise, each girl fills out a page showing a stick figure, a radio and a blank magazine cover. Carol Hoffman, 16, draws herself wearing wide-cuff jeans and a Tori Amos T-shirt, listening to the group Soul Coughing and reading Rolling Stone and Sports Illustrated.

And as for that commercial with the chatty Chihuahua — the one the group seems to think is getting tedious — Dee spouts off a suggestion: "Taco Bell should give him a friend."

33

Retailers in search of customers for life

by Bruce Horovitz
USA TODAY

Kids want everything. The right clothes. The right Christmas and Hanukkah gifts. The right car to be driven to school in.

Because so many kids seem to want so much so often, it is kids who have become wanted. They are wanted by virtually every major company in America. As customers. For life.

Right now, between Thanksgiving and Christmas, is when the drumbeat of marketing to kids sounds loudest. "The influence of kids goes up when the jingle bells ring," says James McNeal, author of *Kids as Customers*.

But even after the holidays are over, kids will be followed, observed, scrutinized and lured by familiar brand names — such as Levi's, Sega, Mattel and even General Motors — in ways unimaginable just a few years ago.

There's no kid-glove protection from this effort. Just a grinding need for new customers that forever has changed the way many of the nation's biggest marketers treat kids as young as pre-schoolers.

Once upon a time, kid marketing was limited to toys and breakfast cereals. Now, marketers realize kids as young as two can influence everything from where the family will vacation to the next car in the garage.

By age 2, kids are nagging their folks for the latest gizmo they saw hyped on TV, says Dan Acuff, author of *What Kids Buy and Why*. And this is just the beginning of kids' struggle for control over what once were solely parental decisions. It should be no surprise that many of the nation's biggest marketers are siding with the kids.

In many families, this power struggle reaches a crescendo when the Christmas tree goes up and the Hanukkah candles are lighted. That's why toys ads are hogging the airwaves. The typical Saturday morning television viewer is seeing a TV spot for a $110-plus toy, K'NEX Hyperspace Training Tower, four times a week right now, estimates Paul Kurnit, president of the ad agency Griffin Bacal, which created the ad.

"Kids like frequency," says Kurnit, an expert in ads that target kids. "This is the time of year to be in sight and in mind."

But critics say there's no proper time of year to chase kids. "It's hard to believe that so many marketers are sitting around thinking of ways to invade young peoples' space at a time youngsters are just trying to figure out who they are," says Marianne Manilov of the Center for Commercial Free Public Education, a consumer group.

Driving this youth frenzy is one thing: economics. And the amount of money kids spend or influence is far, far greater than most marketers have previously believed.

Until now, it was widely believed that kids were spending or influencing spending of about $150 billion annually. But new research by McNeal, who many regard as the nation's top authority on kid spending, dwarfs earlier estimates. In 1997, the nation's estimated 34 million children age 12 and under will have spent or influenced spending of a record $500 billion, says the marketing professor at Texas A&M University.

That $500 billion is about what Americans will spend on all forms of legalized gambling this year.

But marketing to kids is no gamble. It's regarded as a must. Overall spending for kids is growing at a torrid 20% annual clip, says McNeal. At that rate, it could surpass $1 trillion in less than five years.

KIDS VIEWING 20,000 ADS PER YEAR

It's no accident, then, that the typical American child sees 20,000 ads a year, says the American Academy of Pediatrics. And marketers are aware that TV spots targeting kids lead to peer pressure as early as age 3, says Victor Strasburger, professor of pediatrics at University of New Mexico.

Marketers also know that kids form brand loyalties early — sometimes as early as 2, says Debbie Solomon, senior researcher at the giant ad firm J. Walter Thompson. The majority of American adults, she says, still use the same toothpaste, peanut butter and canned soup that their folks bought.

"There is not a company on the globe that does not have some vested interest in marketing to kids," says Devorah Goldman, senior editor of the *Selling to Kids* newsletter.

Perhaps that helps to explain why, like never before, major marketers are stepping over the invisible line that once separated them from the private lives of America's youngest consumers. Consider:

▲ They're in the bedroom. Mattel commissioned a global study in a dozen countries — from the United States to China — where it looked at everything that

(Cont.)

youngsters had hanging on their bedroom walls. One purpose of the study was to see what brands kids were using, says Gene Del Vecchio, who creates Mattel ads for Barbie at Ogilvy Mather.

▲ They're taking pictures. Levi's supplies kids with throw-away cameras and video cameras and asks them to record diaries about how they and their friends spend their time. "Kids serve as reporters for us by showing us what's going on in their own world," says Andre Richards, marketing research manager for Levi Strauss Co.

▲ They're spending the night. While consulting for Esprit, teen marketing expert Marian Salzman had three girls — all about 14 — stay with her in a guest bedroom of her New York apartment for six weeks. The girls also worked as interns at her teen research firm. "This gave me an incredible insider's perspective," says Salzman, now at Young Rubicam.

▲ They're watching on weekends. Several years ago, Pepsi's ad agency, BBDO, arranged for about 30 high school kids to spend an entire weekend at a posh hotel in New Jersey, along with adult chaperones. The agency talked to them about new Pepsi ads. Many of the sessions were videotaped.

▲ They're using the schools. Grade schools in Connecticut have, for a $5,000 fee and some real-world courses in media, given marketers wide access to interview 10- to 12-year-old students after school inside classrooms. The money funds after school activities.

▲ They're following on-line. Every Wednesday afternoon, Nickelodeon has on-line chats with 150 kids between 7- and 11-years-old. The most recent was about their favorite movies. The network even has asked kids to send photos of their pets. "Knowing what kids want is critical to our success," explains Cyma Zarghami, general manager of Nickelodeon.

▲ They're amassing huge databases. Sega of America has dialogues on-line with kids, capturing thousands of names every day for future prospects. Since the program began this year, Sega has been capturing 2,000 names per week of kids aged 12-17, says Anne Moellering, director of marketing.

▲ They're getting kids to do the work. Many marketers, including Eveready's Energizer battery, have retained the research firm Kid2Kid, which hires kids as young as 14 to moderate focus groups of peers. Four years ago, Kid2Kid was one of the first to test this controversial format. Now, says Kid2Kid president Jim Holbrook, "it's become just another tool."

▲ They're paying for information. Some marketers, including Levi's, have handed kids $50 to $100 cash, then asked the kids to record how they spent every nickel of it.

KIDS ON THE COMPANY PAYROLL

All of this is happening with parental approval.

Levi Strauss has tapped 700 kids nationwide — ages 11 to 19 — to report to the jeans' giant on their habits, hangups and day-to-day lives. Kids are recommended to the company by other kids Levi's already talked to. They're paid $20 to $100 to complete a research project.

Renee Cruz, a 15-year-old 10th grader from Miami, Fl., was paid $75 to photograph her outfits every day and glue the pictures in a scrapbook. To make sure the task was done right, Levi's even sent her the gluestick.

When the project was done, two Levi's representatives came to her house and spent about an hour talking to her in her bedroom. They mostly wanted to see the clothes in her closet. And they videotaped the session.

"I think of it as an even exchange," says Cruz. "I got $75," she says, "and they got a lesson on what's cool."

Never mind that Cruz doesn't own a single pair of Levi's.

Across the country, in Santa Monica, Calif., Levi's also has 14-year-old Valerie Adeff, a 9th grader, on its trends panel.

She's convinced that Levi's listened closely to her advice. Less than a year after she showed Levi's a pair of funky, baby-blue corduroy bellbottoms that she bought at a thrift store, she spotted a remarkably similar Levi's version of the same pants at the mall near her house.

But this kind of research is not foolproof.

That's why many companies, without letting parents know, are collecting personal information from kids who browse Internet web sites. In a Federal Trade Commission survey of 126 Web sites, 86% were collecting names, e-mail and postal addresses and phone numbers, the agency reported this week. But only 4% asked for parental permission.

That's one key reason why the FTC plans to review Internet information-collection practices for a report to Congress in March. The agency will investigate the extent to which Internet sites, including children's sites, are posting privacy policies.

This new arsenal of sophisticated marketing weaponry is not kid's stuff. But many marketers convincingly claim that children are empowered — not exploited — by being brought into the decision-making process at every level. When kids help decide the look of the next style of blue jeans or the tone of some video game ad, that's giving them a vote, they say.

"You can't force a trend to kids," says Rena Karl, executive editor of the *Marketing to Kids Report*, a monthly newsletter out of Encinitas, Cal. "Kids are the tail that wags the dog."

(Cont.)

Kids grouped by their advertising ages

All youth marketers want to know how to raise kids' eyebrows.

There is no single answer. But Dan Acuff, co-author of *What Kids Buy and Why*, offers these tips on how marketers target kids through the years.

▲ Birth to age 2: Appeal to Mom and Dad. Parental agendas for gifts for their kids rank in this order: safety, love, stimulation.

▲ Ages 3 to 7: The "nag" factor begins. Kids nag parents for things they see advertised on TV. The influence of kids on parental buying decisions increases. This is an age of fantasy, and a time when kids seek more power and control. Cabbage Patch Kids and Power Rangers were hits because they appealed to those needs.

▲ Ages 8 and 9: Kids get attracted to "causes," and seek toys and games that fulfill these goals. It's why Johnson & Johnson is developing Endangered Species shampoo for kids.

▲ Ages 10 to 12: There's a new interest in games of challenge, and sports are important. Figures like Michael Jordan are featured in ads.

▲ Ages 13 to 15: Kids have a growing need to "fit in" with friends. At the same time, there is a push for self-identity. Brand-consciousness takes over. Apparel and music become enormously important.

▲ Ages 16 to 19: Childhood's over. No more toys and games — unless they're CD players or pagers. There's a longing for controversy — sensed by marketers like Calvin Klein.

EVEN SANTA GETS INTO THE ACT

Critics charge it's all turning the nation's kids into the sum total of their spending power.

"It's not about love or caring," says Alex Molnar, author of *Giving Kids the Business*. "It's about selling."

At some of America's biggest malls, Santa isn't doling out candy canes. Instead, at several malls in Northern Virginia, he's handing out samples of Post Cereal's new Honey Nut Shredded Wheat cereal. In a gift bag, of course.

"We could have put 20 more ads in the bags," brags Clarke Green, merchandising director at the White Flint mall near Bethesda, Md., "but we didn't."

As Wall Street pressures companies for bigger profits, many firms are reaching out to a segment of the population they previously ignored.

Also driving this youth marketing mania: parental guilt. A new world of dual-income families has left parents anxious to make up for so much time away.

Laments Donald F. Roberts, professor of communications at Stanford. "The dominant message kids in this country hear is, 'Buy, buy, buy.' "

Especially on Saturday mornings.

The cost of 30-second commercial slots on network Saturday morning kids shows can increase 50% during the hectic fourth quarter. Ad industry executives refer to these last eight weeks of the year the "Hard Eight" because toy makers and others fight so hard for the key Saturday morning time slots.

Some ads, such as Mattel's spot for the Workin' Out Barbie Doll, can take four months to create. The ad, which opens with a life-size, life-like Barbie exercising on the beach, is made with the aid of computerized graphics imagery.

"Some may cry exploitation or materialism," says adman Del Vecchio, "but for a little kid — on a cold, dark night — who gets to hug her Barbie doll, this is just a fantasy fulfilled."

No detail is too small when it comes to kids marketing. Ask McDonald's. The giveaways in its current Happy Meal promotion for the re-release of Disney's *Little Mermaid* were the result of intensive research. That included interviewing hundreds of kids as young as 4.

Interviews convinced McDonald's executives to sprinkle some Happy Meals with special gold-painted versions of the *Little Mermaid* characters. Most of the Happy Meals get the characters painted the same color they are in the film.

Some parents have had it with all this marketing to kids madness.

Take Sloane Smith Morgan, of Oakland, Calif. Her 2 1/2-year-old son, Paris, recently received a birthday gift from Aunt Fern. The gift: a book on counting.

But it's not about counting numbers. It's about counting M&Ms. The book, *The M&M's Counting Board Book*, looks exactly like a package of M&Ms. Each page is dotted with photos of M&Ms.

Morgan threw out the book. She didn't want her son to learn to count M&Ms. "My son can learn to count using grains of sand, beans or his fingers," she says, "but he's not going to learn with M&Ms."

Novel P&G Product Brings Dry Cleaning Home

BY YUMIKO ONO

Staff Reporter of THE WALL STREET JOURNAL

Procter & Gamble Co., the laundry detergent powerhouse, wants to take a spin with all those clothes that normally get sent to the dry cleaner.

In February, the consumer-products giant plans to begin test-sales of a product it hopes will open up a huge new market: home cleaning kits to be used in household dryers. Dubbed the Dryel Fabric Care System, the kit contains pieces of moist cloth which are tossed into an accompanying nylon bag along with dirty clothes.

As the dryer tumbles, P&G says, heat-activated vapors emerge from the cloth, penetrate the clothes and "volatilize," or remove, odor molecules. Instructions urge consumers to remove spotty stains first with stain remover, provided in a separate bottle.

The stakes are high for P&G, which has been searching for the next blockbuster to add to its annual $35.8 billion sales, but has recently been criticized for reacting slowly to emerging trends. Research for Dryel (pronounced "Dry-ELLE" stretches back five years, P&G says — including testing the product with 10,000 consumers and 36,000 loads of clothing.

One challenge will be marketing Dryel without setting off alarms in consumers' minds about toxic fumes and other potential health hazards sometimes linked to conventional dry cleaning. P&G officials say Dryel doesn't use perchlorethylene, or "perc," the toxic solvent used in most of the nation's 37,000 professional dry-cleaning plants. They won't say exactly what Dryel does contain, other than "biodegradable wetting agents" commonly used in other household products.

P&G officials stress that Dryel isn't meant to replace the corner dry cleaner, especially for really tough stains. "We view this as a great complement, to let consumers care for their [dry clean-only] products at home," says Jamie Egasti, a marketing director for P&G's laundry and cleaning products division.

But the $8 billion professional dry-cleaning industry is already sweating. Dryel "will have an impact — how big or small depends on how good their marketing is," says William Seitz, executive director of the Neighborhood Cleaners Association International, a New York trade group. "Procter, when it comes to marketing, knows its way around the terrain," Mr. Seitz adds.

Mr. Seitz, a 53-year veteran of the industry, says that while Dryel may not clean clothes as thoroughly, it could steal away the business of clothes that are merely stained by cigarette smoke or need to be freshened up.

Mr. Seitz says P&G officials approached him yesterday about working together to expand the entire business for dry-clean-only clothes, and perhaps even sell Dryel through professional dry cleaners. He doubts his members would want to sell a competing product in their outlets, but says he plans to discuss the issue.

The maker of Tide and Cheer says its research revealed that only 40% of Americans regularly go to the dry cleaners — another 40% never go. And as many as 70% of consumers, P&G's statistics show, avoid buying dry-clean-only clothes because they are such a hassle to care for.

Interviews found that some people go to interesting lengths to avoid the expense and trouble of lugging garments to the dry cleaner. Some consumers simply wash and iron clothes meant to be dry cleaned. Some people wear the same sweater or suit time after time before dropping them onto the dry cleaners counter.

To persuade consumers to break with tradition by throwing silk shirts into the dryer, P&G plans to bombard consumers in its test market, Columbus, Ohio, with samples and product demonstrations in shopping malls. Ads, created by Chicago's Leo Burnett, are expected to carry the tagline, "A fresh new choice for dry clean only fabric care."

A starter kit will cost $10 to $11 and can be used for 16 garments. By contrast, dry cleaners can charge $5 or more per garment.

Other companies have been trying to develop similar dry-cleaning alternative products for years, with spotty results. During the 1970s, some manufacturers created do-it-yourself dry-cleaning machines that looked like washing machines, and installed them in laundromats. But the effort fizzled after people discovered their clothes came out smelling of solvent — and not much cleaner.

For the last three years, a company called Creative Products Resource Inc. in Fairfield, N.J., has been selling its own dry-cleaning kit, first through the QVC shopping network and now through supermarkets and drug stores in East coast cities from Maine to Baltimore. Custom Cleaner, as it is called, also uses the dryer, and includes a plastic bag and moist cloth containing ingredients found in a window cleaner and a seaweed extract called carageenan. Custom Cleaner sales are expected to reach $4 million this year, the company says.

Business breeds shady strategies

Ethics lost to competition

By Tom Lowry
USA TODAY

NEW YORK — The Microsoft antitrust trial is pulling back the curtain on a realm of business that most executives would rather keep in the shadows — cut-throat competition.

CEO Bill Gates' e-mail calling for the demise of his competitors pales in comparison to the lengths some executives are going to gain market share, corporate investigators and ethics specialists say.

"Remember the Watergate break-in? Those tactics are common in the business world today," says investigator Joel Gross, owner of consulting firm Risk Strategies International. "There are so many different ways it's going on out there, from whisper and negative buzz campaigns against competitors to dumpster diving."

Undermining the competition is as old as capitalism, but the boundaries between proper and improper activity are being stretched to new limits.

"Companies need to be competitive globally, and that has stressed management. You say to yourself, 'I need to do what it takes.' Sometimes that means you cross the line," says William Boni, a director in the forensic investigations unit at PricewaterhouseCoopers, an accounting firm.

South Carolina textile and chemicals maker Milliken & Co. is accused of using consultants from Atlanta to pose as investment bankers and graduate students to steal trade secrets from rivals NRB Industries and Johnston Industries, according to separate lawsuits filed in the past year by those companies against Milliken.

The NRB lawsuit was settled; the terms were not disclosed. Milliken allegedly paid the investigators $500,000 for detailed information on NRB's customers and manufacturing operations. The Johnston lawsuit is ongoing.

"In the older days, companies operated with honor," says Johnston lawyer Jere Beasley. "But today it's so cut-throat that companies seem willing to do anything to gain a competitive advantage. You're going to see more lawsuits like ours."

Milliken says it plans to defend itself "vigorously" against Johnston's accusations. The company also says it has a policy against unlawfully obtaining information from a competitor, and that it has fired the Atlanta consulting firm.

Sometimes executives look no further than their own families to gain an edge.

In his 1996 book *Staples for Success*, Staples CEO Thomas Stemberg wrote, "The message was clear: Spy or be spied upon."

So Stemberg had his wife, Dola, apply for a job at the Atlanta delivery-order center of competitor Office Depot. Staples was not offering delivery service at the time, and Stemberg says he wanted to learn how Office Depot's delivery system worked.

Dola stopped the application process before she was offered a job, but not before Staples got the information it wanted, Stemberg says.

"Any time you have an action that a company is not willing to have known to the public at large, ethics have been breached," says professor Daniel Diamond, who teaches a course in business ethics at New York University. "There is a lot of gray area these days. Society has raised the bar on what's acceptable."

FBI agent Chris Graham, an economic espionage specialist, says the bureau is being tipped off to more cases of trade-secret theft. Competing companies appear to be fueling a lucrative black market, he says. "People are definitely doing it for the money," Graham says.

PricewaterhouseCoopers' Boni says 90% of what companies can learn about their competitors' operations is in public records. "Executives are obsessed with getting the last 10% but get lazy about obtaining it through proper channels. It's become increasingly common to induce someone to sell trade secrets."

EUROPE'S PRIVACY COPS
The EU wants others to protect electronic data as it does

Germany's data police, the Datenschutz, considers itself a kind of anti-Gestapo. Whereas Hitler's secret police used files on German citizens as tools of terror and control, the Datenschutz protects people's personal data. Inspectors trek from Berlin to Sioux City, S.D., to Citigroup's giant data-processing center, where computers store financial information about millions of German credit-card holders. The Germans, says Stefan Walz, a Datenschutz commissioner, pay regular visits "to make sure that the data are being handled according to [German] law."

Citi accepted the supervision four years ago in return for permission to market a credit card in Germany. But soon, U.S. companies could be dealing with Europe's privacy inspectors whether they've bargained for it or not. On Oct. 25, when the European Union Directive on Data Protection goes into effect, commissioners in Brussels will have the legal tools to prosecute companies and block Web sites that fail to live up to Europe's exacting standards on data privacy.

The directive, which was negotiated among the EU governments over six years, guarantees European citizens absolute control over data concerning them. If a company wants personal information, it must get that person's permission and explain what the information will be used for. It must also promise not to use it for anything else without the citizen's consent. A company selling birdseed, for example, can't use its mailing list to hawk Audubon calendars. Citizens have the right to know where information about them came from, to demand to see it, to correct it if wrong, and to delete it if ob-

jectionable. And they have a right to file suits against any person or company they feel is misusing their data.

One piece of the law is particularly stringent. Article 29 demands that foreign governments provide data protections every bit as rigorous as Europe's, under a similar regulatory structure. Those that fail, the EU warns, could find their data flows with Europe, the world's largest economy, outlawed.

EU officials maintain that they would target certain companies or industries, not entire nations. Yet the new directive marks the first concerted initiative of a united Europe to dictate its norms to the rest of the world. It also takes Europe's regulatory reach into the vital organs of the Information Economy—computer databases and the Internet. "A global system requires global regulations," says Walz.

The question is whether governments outside Europe will stand for the law. As the global leader in online business, the U.S. is a particular target of the directive. So Washington finds itself negotiating on behalf of the entire non-European world.

At the root of the battle is a philosophical chasm nearly as wide as the Atlantic. Europeans look to democratic regimes to protect their privacy. Americans, meanwhile, tend at first to leave information flows unregulated. Later, they slap controls on objectionable areas, such as child pornography on the Web. "In Europe, people don't trust companies, they trust government," says Emanuel Kohnstamm, a Time Warner Inc. vice-president in Brussels. "In the U.S., it's the opposite way around: Citizens must be protected from actions of the government."

"BALKANIZATION." Data exchange, already a critical issue for business, is a key to marketers' global ambitions. Their plan is to plumb databases of buying patterns, develop thousands of detailed customer profiles, and then hit buyers with finely tuned pitches—preferably online. This targeting is at the heart of E-commerce, an industry that totals only $32 billion in annual sales now but is expected to reach $425 billion within four years, according to International Data Corp. Execs on both sides of the Atlantic fret that it could be throttled in its cradle by zealous regulators. "This could mean the Balkanization of E-commerce," warns John E. Frank, European legal counsel for Microsoft Corp.

Europeans respond that E-commerce can't grow without consumer confidence. Only a fearless or foolish consumer, they say, would venture into unregulated digital malls. Europeans abhor the American habit of planting "cookies," the data tags that hook into a log-in name, track the Web sites it has explored, and send back consumer profiles. They are outraged that U.S. prosecutors and insurers use the Web to unearth facts that people would rather keep to themselves. Brussels claims it can protect Europeans from such intrusions.

As Oct. 25 approaches, negotiators in Brussels and Washington are working to reach a practical compromise. The Europeans have dropped demands for a new privacy department in Washington. And the U.S. team, led by Commerce Under Secretary David L. Aaron, is proposing a self-regulation scheme that has the backing of bluechip companies from Procter & Gamble Co. to Microsoft. Companies would certify before a nongovernmental privacy group that they are meeting European standards on data management, much as companies worldwide meet European industrial-quality standards with the ISO 9000 certification.

The betting now is that Americans will offer at least enough to forestall a rash of European legal actions this fall. "We won't shut off the general flow of data," says one European Commission official in Brussels. "We will judge on a case-by-case basis and bring suit if necessary."

But even as EU officials promise restraint, privacy activists in Europe are preparing to go after U.S. companies that

HOW THE NEW LAW WILL CRAMP SALES STYLES

◆ No company will be able to transmit personal data about European Union citizens to countries whose privacy laws don't meet European standards

◆ Companies will have to show customers their complete data profiles on demand and make all changes that customers request

◆ Web-site owners will not be able to use data tags known as "cookies" to track customers' preferences and movements without their permission

◆ Cross-marketing without customer permission will be illegal

(Cont.)

violate the new directive. Privacy International, a London-based advocacy group, says it is investigating privacy practices at 25 leading U.S. companies, including Electronic Data Systems, Ford, Hilton International, Microsoft, and United Airlines, and vows to sue alleged offenders in January. That would force EU regulators to take legal action, too. For their part, the target companies say they are hurrying to meet Europe's new privacy requirements.

That has created opportunities for software makers and other high-tech companies. Microsoft, for example, is developing programs to quiz consumers, through a series of pop-up menus and mouse clicks, about what products or services they want and how much data they' re willing to share. NCR Corp., a major producer of data-storage software, is marketing a host of new products to meet privacy needs, allowing companies to juggle digital warehouses of consumer data. For example, a

> The cross-marketing ban means a birdseed company can't use its mailing list to hawk Audubon calendars

user would have access to personal information for benign purposes, such as anonymous market surveys. But the same user could not access that data to launch a direct-mail campaign for a new product—unless consumers had given the O.K. for such pitches.

PRICEY RETOOL. Companies that rely on cross-selling are scrambling to comply with the new rules. Airlines, for example, pitch their first-class passengers everything from limousine rentals to bargains on luxury suites. Now, such cross-marketing is forbidden without the customer's consent. British Airways PLC has been revamping its software to ask questions the right way—explaining to customers why it wants birth dates (to distinguish one John Smith from another) and nationalities (to whisk people through immigration). "We haven't even put a cost on that yet," says BA data-operations executive Tricia Ade.

It may seem ironic that Europe, which is playing catch-up in the entire digital arena, from personal computers to E-commerce, has taken the lead in policing data on the Internet. But privacy is a burning issue of the New Economy and one that cries out for regulation. The question is whether together, Europe's regulators and America's free marketeers can devise a scheme to patrol the Net without dragging it down.

By Stephen Baker, with Marsha Johnston, in Paris and William Echikson in Brussels

Product

37

Bank With a Giant, or Bank With Merton Corn

BY MATT MURRAY

Staff Report of THE WALL STREET JOURNAL

In Manhattan, bank presidents spend their days pondering huge acquisitions, monitoring overseas markets and lobbying for financial reform.

Across the bay in Staten Island, Merton Corn is making sales calls.

"Here's my calling book," he mutters, tossing a volume onto the desk. It is the Yellow Pages. "I'm calling every company on the Island." There are 8,000 of them.

He flips to "Auto Detailing," as far as he has gotten in the A's. He has checked off every company in the book so far. Not long ago, for novelty's sake, he started making calls in the M's as well. He's up to "Marble."

Mr. Corn is a New York City bank president, too. But his office is small and sparsely decorated. It is located just off the banking floor of Victory State Bank, where most of his 12 employees are working. His office walls don't even reach the ceiling, and a glass window leaves Mr. Corn as exposed to the lobby as a monkey in a cage. Almost every customer waves to him on their way to the teller window.

"You see?" Mr. Corn says wryly. "How many bank presidents have to say 'hello' to every customer that comes in?"

Not many—and that's the point. At a time when banks are merging into vast, multinational networks, Mr. Corn and Victory State Bank are riding a surprising counter-trend and building a new community bank.

Community banking is supposed to be going the way of blacksmithing in an era of consolidation and increasing financial sophistication. Yet the number of start-ups has been rising for nearly six years. There were 207 new bank charters issued last year, the most since 1988, according to the Federal Reserve.

Besides Victory, the upstarts included Home National Bank in Scottsdale, Ariz., Pelican National Bank in Naples, Fla., and two separate institutions called, simply, the Bank, one in Jennings, La., and one in Springfield, Mo.

As those homey names suggest, many of the newcomers paint themselves as friendly, local alternatives to menacing out-of-state intruders. They woo customers distressed at losing their hometown bank, or dismayed by the impersonal veneer of banking by telephone and automated-teller machine.

Jim Catalano, a customer at Victory, is a typical convert. A semiretired contractor of heating, ventilation and air-conditioning systems, he recently switched his account to Victory after closing a Citibank account

which had racked up $300 in fees.

"I am sick and tired of the way the big banks operate," he gripes one recent morning, after stopping in Mr. Corn's office to visit. "They pick you apart, looking for ways to take as much money as they can." (A spokeswoman for Citibank, a unit of Citicorp, says it works hard to accommodate small-business customers and adds: "We're sorry when any customer is unhappy with our service.")

The mergers that have created banking giants have also created a pool of laid-off or retired executives, many of whom wind up running small banks. Mr. Corn, who is 63 years old, is one such banker. For nearly 20 years, he was president of Gateway State Bank, a Staten Island institution founded in 1977. Gateway had five branches and $300 million in assets when it sold out to rival Staten Island Savings Bank in 1996.

Mr. Corn spent a brief, unenjoyable stint as a senior vice president at Staten Island Savings, before running a bank in Brooklyn, N.Y. He was lured to Victory last summer, after a former founding director of Gateway, Joseph J. LiBassi, and a group of local businessmen launched an effort to start a new community bank.

"After we sold Gateway I never expected to be involved in banking again," Mr. LiBassi says. "But I was constantly reminded by customers that they missed the Gateway style of banking — personal, hands-on service."

The group raised $7 million in capital, the minimum amount required by state regulators. They rented a shuttered Chase Manhattan Corp. branch in a strip mall, convenient because it already had a vault and teller windows. They redecorated with green carpet and marble. The "Victory" name popped up in a brainstorming session; it refers to Victory Boulevard, one of the main local thoroughfares.

Mr. Corn, who earns a base salary of $135,000 a year, recruited some of his former co-workers from Gateway. In his low-key but blunt manner, he tries to fire them up with pep talks. He reminds them that when supermarkets arrived, pundits predicted that the days of the local deli were numbered.

His philosophies are simple: "Keep the bank safe. Know your customer. Deal with people you trust." He instructs his staff to be straightforward. "I've trained people, 'Don't use the word policy,'" he says. "I don't want someone ever to say, 'It's our policy.'"

Mr. Corn, who arrives to work by 7:30 most mornings, spends about half his time making sales calls. Often he introduces himself by asking, "When's the last time a president of a bank came out to see you?" That, he says, "is a sure-fire line."

One recent day, he visited an appliance store, a tool-and-dye maker, a nonprofit organization that sells T-shirts, an attorney and a detailing shop. Only one wanted a loan. But Mr. Corn believes a hands-on approach plays well in this close-knit community of small business owners, many of whom work in the home-building industry.

"They go home and tell their wife, 'Hey, Mert Corn came to see me today,'" he says. "She tells the next-door neighbor, who is also an entrepreneur. Word spreads."

Principally a commercial bank, Victory isn't trying to attract consumer accounts. It targets a niche of small-business owners with limited needs. It can't make loans greater than $650,000 unless it teams up with another bank. It isn't the bank for a company that needs foreign-exchange trading. It doesn't do home mortgages, and doesn't have an automated-teller machine.

So far, Victory has opened about 400 corporate accounts. It hasn't yet made money, but losses have steadily declined, to $34,000 in July from $166,000 in December. Mr.

"I Know Their Faces"

Victory State Bank in Staten Island has only 13 employees including the president.

Name	Position	What the job's like
Michelle Barretta	Teller	'It's a lot less pressure. Nobody really waits that long.'
Richard Boyle	Vice President, Chief Lending Officer	'They literally come in straight to see me. It's one on one. No branch officers, no centralization.'
Sheila Martinez	Customer Service Representative	'You can always go straight to the president with a question — and I do.'
Betty Tesoriero	Operations Assistant	'I greet everyone by name. I know their faces. It's something.'

(Cont.)

Corn expects to turn the corner in the next few months. Assets, meanwhile, recently topped $25 million.

To try to nurture long-term relationships with customers, Victory doesn't fuss about making small loans, which can cost more to service than the bank earns in interest. Unlike most big banks, Mr. Corn eschews the current trend of generating revenue by slapping fees on an array of services.

"There's a conventional wisdom now that banks should make money on fee income," he says. "We have a different philosophy. Our philosophy is that we should make our money on the interest-rate spread between what we borrow and what we lend out."

That self-consciously old-fashioned approach also applies to those services Victory does offer. The bank grants customers instant credit on deposited checks, for instance, an admitted risk. It makes decisions on loans quickly. At big banks, a small business might wait two weeks after submitting an application. Mr. Corn and his senior executives can authorize any secured loan as much as $300,000 themselves. Higher requests are reviewed by a directors' committee that meets weekly.

"A quick 'no' is better than a drawn-out 'yes,'" says Richard F. Boyle, Victory's chief lending officer.

Eventually, Victory hopes to grow to have four or five branches, all on Staten Island. But Mr. Corn says his bank has no higher ambitions — even in an age of global finance. "It's an anachronism," he admits, shrugging his shoulders. "But it fills a real need."

38

BRANDING ON THE NET

The old rules don't apply. So how do you hustle those wares online?

Devotees of Troy and Linda will never know how their romance turned out. Bell Atlantic Corp. has pulled the plug on its online soap opera, which revolved around the yuppie newlyweds. The weekly installments ran on the Bell Atlantic corporate Web site last year. The serial had lots of fans. It won rave reviews from entertainment critics. But the Baby Bell's research showed Troy and Linda didn't do a thing to build the Bell Atlantic brand. No bounce in brand awareness surveys. No spike in consumer loyalty. "Creative is fine," says Janet Keeler, vice-president for brand management at Bell Atlantic. "But that kind of creative just didn't pan out. We want to build our brand on the Web."

She and everyone else in the marketing community. Harnessing the reach and interactivity of the Internet to build and maintain brands has become the Holy Grail of marketing. It's the focus of conferences. The subject of committee meetings. The talk of the consultancy circuit. The tantalizing prospect of pushing a brand name and stoking consumer loyalty in the one-on-one setting of the personal computer attracts everyone from carmakers to newspapers. But as Bell Atlantic discovered, branding tactics that work in the real world don't always translate online. "It's the biggest issue facing the marketing community in 25 years," says Elliott Ettenberg, CEO of Bozell Retail Advertising. "What keeps us all up at night is the idea: Is my competitor going to figure it out first?"

The buzz about branding on the Net has intensified in the past year, in part because Procter & Gamble Co., the nation's second-biggest advertiser, mobilized interest with its Internet advertising summit in August. More important, the first handful of legitimate, recognizable brand names have emerged from the chaos of the virtual world. As companies such as America Online, Amazon.com, Yahoo!, and Netscape Communications graduate from obscure virtual businesses to those that score in the 50% range on unaided brand-recognition surveys, marketers have begun to salivate. The potential is there, they say. A brand can grow and secure customer loyalty on the Net. And as today's huge generation of computer-savvy kids matures, that

power will only increase. "That has all of us wondering how can we do it, too," says Joel Anderson, who heads up Internet marketing for Toys 'R' Us Inc. "To do it well is worth millions."

Marketers, who have used TV and print ads for decades to imbue even cigarettes and dish detergent with an emotional aura, know full well the value of a strong brand. "A brand is the emotional shortcut between a company and its customer," says Ted Leonhardt, principal of Leonhardt Group, a brand-marketing firm. But as the older mass media of TV and print become more fragmented and crowded, their ability to build brands has weakened. The advertisers whose real-world brands grew up with TV worry they'll be left out if they don't solve the enigma of marketing on the Net.

For companies whose businesses are based on the Internet, forging a recognized brand name is even more important. With nothing to pick up or touch and hundreds of similar-sounding sites to choose from, online consumers have little to go on besides a familiar name. In cyberspace, anyone with enough resources to rent space on a server and build some buzz for their brand is a potentially dangerous competitor.

NO POP-UPS. But just as the need to build brands on the Internet is spiking, there's a growing recognition among marketers that the tactics they have tried so far have been ineffective. The emotion-laden vignettes that work so well on TV simply don't woo viewers in cyberspace. Meanwhile, the established methods of Internet advertising don't do much better. Interstitials, ads that just pop up on the screen, are tagged as annoying interruptions to the online experience. Spending on banner ads is expected to drop next year as companies conclude that computer users are ignoring them. "You're not allowed to say or market anything online unless the customer wants to hear it," says Chan Suh, CEO of Agency.com Ltd., an interactive consulting firm. It's the central theme differentiating television from Internet marketing, he says. "In this kind of marketing, the customer is in charge."

That means marketers set on building their brands in the online world have to per-

suade consumers to participate in their marketing efforts. The latest theory of how to do that involves something called "rational branding." The idea is to marry the emotional sell of traditional brand marketing—the pitch that links "Disney" with "Family" or "Volvo" with "Safety"—with a concrete service offered only online. Rational branding strives both to move and help the online consumer at the same time. In essence, the advertiser "pays" the consumer to endure the brand message by performing some kind of service. But the tactic poses a real challenge to makers of consumer products. There are

---

A TWO-WORLD STRATEGY

The biggest brands on the Internet craft distinct images in both the real and virtual worlds. For many, real-world ads are a softer, more emotional sell. Online, the consumer gets individual attention.

AMERICA ONLINE

SNAIL MAIL. AOL is famous for its nonvirtual marketing, such as mass-mailing sample disks of its service with computer magazines and using TV and print to lure more subscribers. It also does some online marketing, linking to popular search engines.

SATURN

LIKE ORDERING PIZZA. GM's revamped Saturn Web site is all business. It helps serious car buyers with projects such as selecting a model, calculating payments, and finding a dealer online. Offline, the Web site is the star of Saturn's humorous TV commercial showing a college student ordering up a car over the Internet. The successful television commercial has tripled visitors to the Saturn Web site.

(continued)

(Cont.)

A TWO-WORLD STRATEGY
(Concluded)

COCA-COLA
JUST PASSING THROUGH. Coca-Cola still pours most of its advertising effort into televison and print. It uses its Internet site to tout promotions and to appeal to niche groups such as collectors of vintage Coke products. Early experiments linking Coca-Cola.com to Internet entertainment sites sent consumers away too quickly. Revised Web marketing is designed to let Net surfers linger.

TOYS `R' US
MAKING A LIST. The toymaker fired up an online shopping site in time for this year's holiday rush. The effort was not just aggressive marketing but also a preemptive tactic aimed at staving off cyber-ambushes by small Internet upstarts. The site offers services such as online gift registry and E-mail reminders. Offline, marketing messages in stores and on TV emphasize wide selection and low prices.

logo all over the hottest new online shopping sites. It also gives the company a chance to promote its Internet image. While the TV pitch is clearly about using MasterCard to achieve a peak experience, online the image is about security, trust, and service. "The TV user is looking for entertainment. The Internet user is online for more practical reasons," says Debra Coughlin, of the company's Internet marketing team. "Our brand efforts reflect that end-user goal."

LESS HYPE. When General Motors Corp.'s Saturn revamped its Web site to offer more help and less hype, it was easy to measure the improvement. Site visits over the last year tripled to as many as 7,000 a day. An astounding 80% of Saturn's customer leads now come via the Internet, almost double a year ago. Saturn's old site offered the usual car specs and dealer referrals, but last year the carmaker began adding features that were actually useful, including a lease-price calculator, an interactive design shop for choosing options, and an online order form. Then it highlighted the new online features with a TV commercial that delivered an old-fashioned emotional brand appeal. The humorous TV ad features a college student in his dorm room using the Internet to order a Saturn, as easily as one might order a pizza. The site quickly took off. "This improves our brand position in a way an online brochure could not," says Farris Kahn, Internet coordinator for Saturn marketing. "By giving the consumer something they want, you are helping them and promoting your brand message at the same time."

How did marketers figure out the potential of offering consumers a practical benefit online? By watching the Internet brands build their businesses into powerhouses. The common thread running through the successful online technology sellers, such as Dell Computer Corp., and such retail and service companies as Yahoo!, Amazon.com, and America Online, is that they help the Web-surfing consumer do something.

BUILDING BLOCK. Dell lets customers configure and price a computer system online. Yahoo! and AOL offer a slew of options for customizing their services. David Risher, senior vice-president for product development at Amazon, says that more than any ad or sponsorship, the Web site itself is the crucial building block for his brand. And he says that "70% to 80% of the feeling people have about the brand is from the experience they have online at our site." Much of Amazon's effort at brand building is therefore focused on improving the site with frills such as one-click ordering and software-generated book recommendations.

The success stories are reverberating through the online-marketing industry. Two top Net consultants, Jupiter Communications and Forrester Research Inc., have released studies examining the practical turn of Net marketing. Jupiter coined the phrase "rational branding." Forrester's Jim Nail calls the

frighteningly few ways to make soap or soda useful in the virtual world. Indeed, of the top five buyers of TV advertising, most are nearly invisible online.

But companies that can provide a time saver or money saver online are diving in. MasterCard International Inc., in search of a rational branding plan, has transformed its Web marketing from one that simply hypes the card to one that offers a helping hand to the online shopper. While MasterCard pumps out shamelessly schmaltzy TV commercials—such as one with Mark McGwire sending No. 62 over the fence under the tag line "Priceless"—its online branding efforts take a different tone. The company is pushing Shop Smart, a sort of MasterCard seal of approval given to E-commerce sites that use advanced credit-card security systems.

The program lets MasterCard slap its

WHAT WOULD MAKE NET CONSUMERS CLICK

Ads More Informative	71.4%
Sweepstakes or Contests	33.8%
Make Ads More Creative	33.1%
Offer Awards/Cash	20.5%
Affinity Programs	3.4%
Don't Know	12.1%

DATA: NFO INTERACTIVE FOR JUPITER COMMUNICATIONS.

TV AD LEADERS PALE ONLINE

BIGGEST SPENDERS ON TV

➤ General Motors

➤ Procter & Gamble

➤ Johnson & Johnson

➤ Philip Morris

➤ Ford Motor

BIGGEST SPENDERS ONLINE

➤ MicroSoft

➤ IBM

➤ Excite

➤ Yahoo!

➤ Netscape Communications

DATA: COMPETITIVE MEDIA REPORTING

(Cont.)

tactic of adding an interactive service "experiential marketing." "Experiences—not advertising-induced perceptions—will drive brand attitudes," he says. He expects spending on experiential marketing will grow from $1.1 billion this year to $11.2 billion in four years, while spending on banner ads will top out at $300 million in the next year and begin to decline.

But for most packaged-goods marketers, who have little to offer online, the trend toward rational branding poses a huge dilemma. More than half of consumers surveyed by Jupiter say they never visit a consumer-product Web site. Even the most popular ones pale in comparison to truly high-traffic locations. In May, Budweiser.com, among the top five most popular consumer-product sites, drew 180,000 visitors, according to a study by Jupiter Communications. Meanwhile, Netscape.com welcomed 10,828,000.

It's not that the packaged-goods makers haven't tried. But they are rapidly discovering that what made them powerful on the TV screen does not easily translate to the computer screen. Consider Coca-Cola Co. Recognizing its slick TV commercials wouldn't play well on the Net, Coke tried a different tactic—one that works beautifully in the real world. It acted as sponsor for entertainment. For example, the company rigged its Cherrycoke.com site as an entertainment gateway, filled with links to interesting sites around the Internet. Coke executives thought the site was fine until they realized consumers were spending an average of 90 seconds on it before moving on. That might be a long time on TV, when consumers are passively letting an ad wash over them. But for a consumer searching for something else, it's far too short to make an impact. "We wanted to use the site to capture our consumer and provide a unique brand experience," says Scott Brannan, Coke's manager of interactive communications. "But all we were getting to do was say, 'Thanks for coming.'" Now the soft-drink maker's site focuses more on promotions, which keep the Internet consumer looking at the Coke logo a little longer.

WAIT FOR VIDEO? Others have tried the service proposition, with only mixed results. P&G offers the Stain Detective at tide.com; Unilever's Ragu brand has a popular site filled with recipes; and Bristol-Myers Squibb Co.'s Clairol site allows consumers to scan in a personal photograph and experiment with different hair colors. The idea is to let consumers "try on" a brand online. But even as these sites win praise from consultants, the brands continue to get most of their boost

WHERE THE NET USERS ARE

CONSUMER PRODUCTS WEB SITES	VISITORS PER MONTH
KODAK.COM	184,000
KRAFTFOODS.COM	182,000
BUDWEISER.COM	180,000
REVLON.COM	178,000
COCA-COLA.COM	153,000

MOST VISITED WEB SITES	VISITORS PER MONTH
AOL.COM	19,179,000
YAHOO.COM	18,300,000
GEOCITIES.COM	11,341,000
NETSCAPE.COM	10,828,000
MICROSOFT.COM	10,455,000

DATA: MEDIA METRIX, PC METER CO., JUPITER COMMUNICATIONS

from traditional marketing. "In direct marketing or traditional ads, it's much easier to show a return on investment," said Peggy Kelly, vice-president of advertising services at Bristol-Myers, at an industry conference in August.

Does all this mean that the Internet is simply the wrong place to advertise cereal and soda pop? The answer may be yes...for now. Some big name brands are settling for a dollop of consumer attention online while they wait for the Web to grow up. McDonald's sports a Web site with everything from financial data to kids' games. But David G. Green, senior vice-president for international marketing, says Web marketing will only be a sliver of the McDonald's game plan, until the technology allows for more video and audio programming. "It is more difficult for those of us who do not have a good or service that is transferable to a virtual experience," says Green. But while TV and print are more powerful now, tools such as full-motion video will someday be more available online. "That makes it important for us to be in touch with the Internet," Green says.

He, like others, acknowledges that de-

spite current difficulties in marketing online, in the long run no one can afford simply to ignore the medium. The Net offers an extremely attractive demographic mix that will only get better. Already, the online world is losing its status as a boys' club; women now make up 38% of Web surfers. With a median income of $63,000 and a heavy tilt toward the professions, Internet users are a brand marketer's dream. Most compelling of all, the current generation of children is the largest since the baby boom, and they are growing up with the Net as a given. As they mature into the next great consumer generation, no marketer will be able to ignore one of their favorite media.

The hope among the traditional TV advertisers is that new technology will give them a way to present the emotional visual pitches that have worked so well for them elsewhere. IBM just unveiled Hot-Media, a new Java-based product that aims to make banner ads and other online marketing tools more visually gripping while still leaving them quick and easy to use, even by consumers with slower modems. But the real anticipation is for the day when consumers can command all the wizardry of the Internet from their living-room entertainment centers. "Eventually, this medium is going to hit our business," says Denis F. Beausejour, P&G's vice-president for worldwide advertising. "It's critical that we be in this space, experimenting, trying to develop our own business models."

Interestingly, one industry that's already getting the hang of the Internet is retailing—an industry experts predicted would be especially threatened by the medium's emergence. Stores have begun to use their Web sites as both a sales channel and a place to build consumer loyalty and extend brand awareness. Macy's online services, for example, offer a gift registry and personal shopping assistance via E-mail. Visitors to the site, drawn by TV and print ads, are younger than the average store shopper and are more likely to be male than the average. "It's clear the Internet presence is extending our brand to shoppers we were not reaching with our stores," says Kent Anderson, president of Macys.com. "To us, that's classic brand building."

The retailer success stories hold a lesson for all marketers: The Internet cannot build a brand alone. Macy's credits the combination of Internet and other ad vehicles for its success. And even the pure Internet companies agree. The most successful and well-known Internet companies have sought significant publicity in the real world as they've struggled to build their brands. America Online is

(Cont.)

famous for distributing free disk samples through computer magazines and the mail. Yahoo! has recently embarked on an aggressive real-world brand-marketing campaign featuring television and print advertising and a slew of licensing deals, from a co-branded Visa card to T-shirts.

CAR TALK. Internet car seller Autobytel.com. Inc. goes even further. It has used mostly real-world marketing to build itself into the top car-shopping service on the Net. To woo new customers, it relies on the most traditional of marketing methods: public relations. Anne Benvenuto, Autobytel's senior vice-president of marketing, travels the country with her laptop, talking up the site to the media, to Wall Street analysts, to anyone who might talk about car buying to consumers. The company has set up publicity stunts such as car giveaways to lure press coverage. "You can't build a brand solely on the Internet. Not yet, anyway," she says. Brand marketing, she adds, must be done even when the consumer is not thinking about buying your product. "The Internet consumer is already thinking about car buying. We also have to plant our seed in the mind of the consumer not yet in the market for a car."

That need for real-world brand building may increase as rival Internet companies begin to fight for dominance within product categories. Just look at the bruising battle shaping up between Barnes & Noble Inc. and Amazon. Amazon, like most of the strong Net-based brands, achieved dominance because it was first to offer a high-quality online service. That has created enormous brand equity for the bookseller—but for the first time ever, it faces a rival with an equally strong brand name and the financial wherewithal and marketing skills to match. Expect Amazon to hammer home its message of superior selection and online knowhow, while Barnes & Noble plays up its authority as the nation's No. 1 bookseller.

The battle of the booksellers has already created fallout. Determined not to get caught in the same bind as Barnes & Noble, for example, Toys 'R' Us is opening a new online shopping site in time for the holidays. Does the toy giant see visions of huge online profits? Not exactly. The move is at least in part defensive, to counter branding efforts by online upstarts such as tiny eToys. "Barnes & Noble learned it the hard way," says Anderson. "If you are not online, your competition is out there alone talking to the online customers."

That highlights another lesson for marketers. The fact that such heavyweights as Barnes & Noble and Toys 'R' Us are responding to rivals a fraction their size speaks to the leveling power of the Net. If the retailers were competing in the nonvirtual world, the smaller companies would barely register as a threat.

That power, the ability to turn upstart pygmies into mighty amazons almost overnight, is what keeps marketers coming back to the Net. Will rational branding prove the best way of harnessing that power? One thing is certain: Surfing the Net, whether for fun or for business, is going to become an increasingly sponsored experience.

By Ellen Neuborne in New York, with Robert D. Hof in San Mateo, Calif.

CAN I TRY (CLICK) THAT BLOUSE (DRAG) IN BLUE?

Those Star Trek replicators that dispense food and clothing on command aren't here yet. But retailers are getting closer. This week, Eddie Bauer Inc., the 78-year-old Seattle-based casual-apparel maker, is testing an online service that lets customers mix and match styles on the computer screen.

It's the latest attempt to build the Bauer brand over the Internet. Visitors to EddieBauer.com will find the same khaki, denim, and knit basics found in the retailer's catalogs and mall stores. But the site is more than just an electronic sales flyer. Want to see how that holiday sweater will look with the khakis? Or maybe try the sports jacket with those plaid pants? Just click and drag in Eddie Bauer's virtual dressing room. "It's fun," says 28-year-old Cally Raduenzel, who tried the service recently at Screenz, a Chicago cybercafe. "I like being able to put the boots and shoes and stuff up there and change the colors."

Since half the consumers who visit the Web site have never before shopped at Eddie Bauer, their experience online is an important first contact with the brand. The company won't release profit and revenue figures for the site, casting it as a marketing tool to lure new customers and keep current shoppers interested. Like other online marketers, Bauer is betting that a potpourri of services will keep those new online customers coming back. "We knew from the beginning that they didn't want to see a poster," says Judy Neuman, who created Eddie Bauer's Internet site. "They want to be able to do something."

Besides the virtual dressing room, Bauer offers online customers a reminder service that alerts them by E-mail to upcoming birth dates, anniversaries, and holidays. It lets them create electronic wish lists of products they want friends or relatives to buy for them. And it sends them targeted E-mail messages offering special sale prices on items, based on their past buying patterns. All offer the online shopper something other catalog giants can't match, says Lauren Freedman, president of e-tailing Group, a Chicago-based consulting group. "They have leveraged technology to do something that can't be done in a traditional retail environment or within a catalog."

These are just the latest refinements. A year ago the retailer offered free software that allowed shoppers to plug in the floor plans for their homes and see how Eddie Bauer furniture looked in the living room or bedroom. This year's Java-driven dressing room is faster and easier, with no software to download. In both instances, the idea is to give online customers more "hands-on" ways to try out its stuff.

Perhaps most important, Eddie Bauer has worked to integrate its Web site, catalog, and stores so that all three supplement one another and boost the overall brand. The Eddie Bauer catalog promotes the online service. The online service lets visitors know they can take products they're unhappy with back to bricks-and-mortar stores. Store cash registers sport the Web address.

NO BANNERS. But even the coolest Web site isn't worth much if no one knows about it. Besides pitching its online service in its catalogs and stores, Bauer advertises on the Internet—but not with traditional banner ads.

It gave banner ads a test run in the fourth quarter of 1997 and again this spring but didn't get much joy. Says Neuman: "They're expensive, and conversion [to sales] is low."

Instead, the retailer is using its Internet advertising to seek customers who are outside its traditional customer base of casual baby boomers. It boosted its back-to-school push this year by promoting campus gear on popular teen sites such as student.com and dogpile.com. Normally, Bauer doesn't squander ad money on prospects outside its core boomer group. "But this was easy to do, and inexpensive," says Neuman.

The real payoff for Eddie Bauer will come if it builds a base of customers used to shopping at Eddie Bauer online and off-line, 24 hours a day, seven days a week. As round-the-clock shopping catches on, Bauer wants to make sure its brand name is leading the way.

By De'Ann Weimer in Chicago

39

AT&T Joins Wave of Marketers Hiding IDs Behind New Brands

LUCKY DOG DIAL-AROUND SERVICE AIMS FOR VALUE-CONSCIOUS CROWD

by Beth Snyder

When AT&T decided to introduce a new service to cost-conscious consumers last month, it realized it had to give up its identity.

The familiar blue-and-white logo, which perennially ranks as one of the country's best-known brand icons, was too stodgy to attract a new class of customers. To court the value-oriented crowd, AT&T Corp. concluded it would have to toss its 113-year-old brand name in favor of a new one.

Several months later, the $52 billion company whelped Lucky Dog Phone Co. In the new, fiercely competitive telephone communications market, the move was a case of desperate times calling for desperate measures.

JOINING THE FRAY

For years, dial-around players—such as Telecom USA's 10-10-321 service—nibbled away at AT&T's long-distance profits. AT&T even attributed a recent third-quarter decline of $171 million in long-distance revenue to such competition, leaving the telecom giant little choice but to join the dial-around fray.

Analysts estimate the dial-around market will reach $2 billion by the end of this year. AT&T predicts the market will total $3 billion in 1999.

"Lucky Dog has a different value proposition than AT&T service," said Stephen Graham, AT&T VP-marketing and communications worldwide. "The Lucky Dog Phone Co. is a way to characterize that difference."

The technique of spinning off a brand to distance a new company from the too-established positioning of an older one—or to avoid tarnishing a carefully polished image—is not new.

Retailers, brewers and carmakers all have tried the strategy for a host of reasons. When The Gap wanted to reach out to cost-conscious students and young families, it created Old Navy. Alternatively, Miller Brewing Co. targeted specialty beer drinkers by spawning Plank Road Brewery, marketer of Red Dog, Southpaw and Ice-House beers.

LUXURY CAR LINES

And when Toyota Motor Sales USA wanted more affluent consumers, it debuted the Lexus line of luxury cars. It was soon followed by American Honda Motor Co. with the Acura line and Nissan Motor Corp. USA, with Infiniti.

"Most other industries do this. In telecommunications, why for so long have we been a one-brand industry?" said Brian Adamik, director of consumer communications for consultancy Yankee Group. "The fact is, AT&T can't be all things to all people."

Lucky Dog Phone Co., a wholly owned subsidiary of AT&T, was launched with one product, a dial-around service called 10-10-345. AT&T executives hint that other products will be added to the Lucky Dog portfolio.

Currently, the service allows customers with any long-distance provider to tap into Lucky Dog discounts by dialing the seven extra digits. Lucky Dog also offers prizes and cash as incentives to use the service.

In the telecom world, spinning off a company or "flanker brand" has been a sleeper strategy for several years. MCI WorldCom bought Telecom USA and its 10-10-321 dial-around service in 1996, promoting it heavily, along with the non-MCI branded 1-800-COLLECT product.

Sprint Corp., too, has hit on spin-off success with its prepaid calling cards, especially its non-Sprint branded Spree cards. Sprint has its own dial-around service, 10-10-777, but is still only test marketing the service in three cities.

ATTRACTING CRITICISM

Meanwhile, Lucky Dog's supporting ad campaign has been taking some criticism. Ads from Y&R Advertising, New York, feature real dogs dressed in human clothing and use well-known actor voice-overs—people such as Larry Hagman and Kathleen Turner.

The ads are a departure from AT&T's usually more refined and subtle messages.

Mr. Graham, who said he likes the commercials,

(Cont.)

defended them: "Lucky Dog is not designed for everyone, and neither are the commercials. But there are people who are going to love them."

Mr. Adamik and some AT&T insiders said it was about time AT&T established a foothold in the dial-around category.

"It's about damn time. AT&T has finally realized that if you can't beat them, join them," said Jeff Kagan, president of Kagan Telecom Associates. "It's a departure from the way long distance has been marketed, but Lucky Dog will probably be successful."

LOSSES TO DIAL-AROUNDS

AT&T Chairman-CEO C. Michael Armstrong first hinted at the possibility of creating a dial-around product earlier this year. At that point, however, AT&T had already endured years of diminished profits attributed to dial-around competitors.

In fact, before MCI launched its 10-10-321 service in 1996, AT&T's then-president, Alex Mandl, told analysts and reporters the company was beginning to see losses from dial-arounds and vowed to fight back. But he never followed through.

Analysts said part of the reason AT&T may have been slow to react was the possibility of cannabilizing its existing sales.

But, according to Yankee Group statistics, AT&T has a better chance of grabbing customers away from competitors than of cannibalizing its own sales. The consultancy found only about 15% of AT&T customers use dial-around services, while 26% of MCI customers and 24% of Sprint customers use them.

"This is a signal to people that AT&T is waking up and taking on the challenge," said Mr. Graham. "And it's the signal of a new aggressive attitude at AT&T."

Who said you can't teach an old dog new tricks?

40

CEREAL-BOX KILLERS ARE ON THE LOOSE

New packaging and products are ripping into Kellogg's share

The contrast speaks as loudly as Tony the Tiger's roar. In the last month, the Kellogg Co.—the nation's largest cereal maker—has announced it's considering a big layoff at its headquarters in Battle Creek, Mich., and the chiefs of both its North American and European divisions have quit. Earnings have missed their target in each of the last two quarters, and the stock, at 34, is down more than 30% this year.

Meanwhile, at the Quaker Oats Co.—a relatively small fourth player in the industry—cereal volumes have increased every quarter for the past two years. Market share is up two percentage points in the last two years, and the stock is trading near its all-time high.

So what's Quaker's secret? It's in the bag—the cereal bag, that is. For the past three years, Quaker has been rolling out a line of bagged cereals that are cheaper versions of its rivals' national brands. By skimping on packaging and marketing costs, Quaker can sell bagged products for about $1 less than boxed counterparts. And Quaker is not alone. Malt-O-Meal Inc., a smaller Minnesota company that has long produced boxed knockoffs of the national brands, also now offers its cereal in bags. Since 1995, bagged cereals have skyrocketed from virtually nothing to account for 8% of all cereal packages sold. "The taste is similar, and it's probably a dollar or two less," said Jim Buchner while buying a bag of Malt-O-Meal's Golden Puffs at a store in Overland Park, Kan.

Bags are just the latest sign that the ready-to-eat cereal industry is going through wrenching changes. Over the past decade, industry leaders, particularly No.2 General Mills Inc., have jacked up the cost of a box of branded cereal to as much as $5. But while prices have gone up, demand has gone down, as hectic lifestyles have Americans looking for breakfast to eat on the run. "A Pop-Tart or a bagel or a muffin is a lot easier to eat while you're driving a car than a bowl of cereal," says Merrill Lynch & Co. analyst Eric Katzman. The result: U.S. cold-cereal sales fell by 15% in real terms, or more than $1 billion, between 1994 and '97.

Almost the only players to make any headway against those forces are the ones that have offered consumers a lower-priced alternative. Malt-O-Meal's market share has more than doubled, to 4%, in the past five years. Quaker's share of cereal sold in the U.S.—including its boxed brands, such as Life—is 10.1%, up from 8% two years ago, says Donaldson, Lufkin & Jenrette Inc. analyst William Leach.

Whether they're in a bag or a box, the cheapo cereals show just how tired consumers are of paying ever higher prices for a relatively unexciting product. The knockoffs—with comically ripped-off names like Rice Crisps and Frosted Flakers—are stealing market share despite some major disadvantages. Not everybody agrees with Kansan Buchner about the taste. Kids sometimes complain that they don't have a box with games or cartoon characters. And the zipper-like bags can be difficult to close or store. The growth of these low-end products shows how out of step cereal giants have been with shoppers' preferences. In fact, few consumer products have suffered more in recent years than ready-to-eat cereals.

For Quaker, bags are to some degree an admission of defeat. Referring to the industry's habit of pushing expensive cereals backed by costly ad blitzes, Quaker CEO Robert S. Morrison told an industry conference earlier this year: "The days of 'high price, high spend' in the cereal category are perhaps over." That's bad news for the big marketers. Margins on bagged cereals are thin as a corn flake, about 3% to 5%, vs. 15% for branded, boxed products.

PAINFUL SLIDE. Still, what it has lost in margins, Quaker has more than made up in volume. Brisk sales of its bagged products helped push its second-quarter operating income from ongoing businesses up 14%, to $199 million. During the same quarter, Kellogg's profits fell by 17%, to $143 million.

The inventor of "Snap, Crackle, Pop" has a new plan to fight back, but unlike Quaker, it's not willing to dent margins by adding a cheaper cereal line. In June, 44-year-old Carlos M. Gutierrez, a 23-year Kellogg veteran who had headed up global business development, vaulted over execs at bigger units to become president—and the leading candidate to replace Arnold G. Langbo as CEO. Kellogg plans to cut $100 million in annual costs, probably through layoffs, and use the savings to boost ad and promotion spending. It recently invited five ad agencies to submit new marketing ideas. Kellogg executives declined to comment on their plans.

Kellogg's painful market-share loss, from 38% to 32% since 1994, has left industry-watchers skeptical it can persuade more consumers to pony up for stagnant brands like Fruit Loops and Corn Flakes. Since 1995, Rice Krispies has lost more than a third of its market share and Apple Jacks about one-sixth.

To make its marketing blitz pay, Kellogg hopes to come up with some

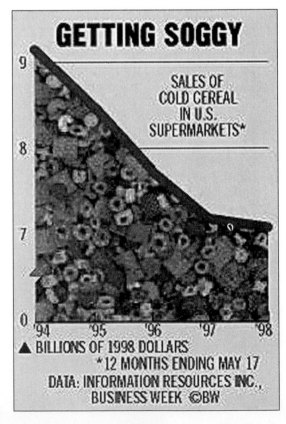

GETTING SOGGY

SALES OF COLD CEREAL IN U.S. SUPERMARKETS*

9

8

7

0

'94   '95   '96   '97   '98

▲ BILLIONS OF 1998 DOLLARS
*12 MONTHS ENDING MAY 17
DATA: INFORMATION RESOURCES INC.,
BUSINESS WEEK ©BW

(Cont.)

blockbuster products. Kraft Foods Inc.'s Post unit—the No.3 cereal maker—is the only one of the Big Three to show a sales gain over the past year, according to Information Resources Inc. Post got a boost from new products like Oreo O's, launched this summer with a bigger-than-normal $40 million campaign.

The pressure on the big marketers is not likely to let up soon. Private-label cereals, which right now come mostly in boxes, have grown almost as fast as the bagged versions in the last five years, but still have room to grow. Altogether, generic products are re-

> **Kellogg's strategy:** Cut costs, boost ad spending—but hold the line on price

sponsible for less than 12% of the cereal segment—compared with about 20% of the cracker, cookie, and nuts category.

Indeed, generic powerhouse Ralcorp Holdings Inc., which now holds a 55% share of the private-label boxed category, may try to muscle in on the bag market. Said Ralcorp CEO Joe R. Micheletto, speaking to a group of analysts in June: "We are seeing more and more retailers asking for store-brand bags." That could soon mean even more no-name rivals for Tony the Tiger.

By David Leonhardt in Chicago, with bureau reports

41

IT WAS A HIT IN BUENOS AIRES—SO WHY NOT BOISE?

U.S. companies are picking up winning product tips from consumers in faraway places

In June of 1997, Haagen-Dazs began serving a new flavor called *dulce de leche* at its sole ice cream shop in Buenos Aires. Named after the caramelized milk that is one of the most popular flavors in Argentina, the locally developed line was an immediate hit. Within weeks, the supersweet, butterscotch-like confection was the store's best-seller.

Just one year later, consumers from Boston to Los Angeles to Paris can find *dulce de leche* at the supermarket or in one of Haagen-Dazs's 700 retail stores. In U.S. stores that carry it, only vanilla sells better. In Miami, *dulce* sells twice as fast as any other flavor. In the U.S., it does $1 million a month in revenue. And in Europe, it will soon move up from a seasonal flavor to year-round status.

FERTILE FEEDBACK. The dessert is just the latest example of an emerging two-way trend among American marketers. No longer does the shrinking of the globe mean simply that U.S. companies pump out hamburgers, sneakers, and movies for the world to consume—or that Asian and European companies readily sell their goods in the U.S.

In globalization's latest twist, American companies from Levi Strauss & Co. to Nike Inc. are lifting products and ideas from their international operations and bringing them home. Although U.S. companies have long exported their products, a few have now begun using their international operations as incubators for the next big hit. "As the world becomes smaller—relentlessly, if slowly—the interchange and exchange of ideas is becoming much more commonplace," says Simon Williams, chairman of the Sterling Group, a New York-based brand consulting firm.

It's not just happenstance, either. Companies are reorganizing so that hot products from one region of the world can be more readily spotted and shipped elsewhere—either to the U.S. or other international markets. Reliance on the home office for product research, development, and ideas is shrinking. Within companies, says Jane Fraser, a consultant in McKinsey & Co.'s global practice, "the importance of the product is rising, and the importance of the country is beginning to decline."

Take Pillsbury Co., which owns Haagen-Dazs. After consolidating its international division last year, it now invites U.S. executives to training seminars to swap ideas. North American executives who had tried *dulce de leche* at a brand conference in January, 1997, realized it might fit with the company's recent move to target Latinos in the U.S. But the product did more than that. Today, U.S. sales of the flavor are growing by about 27% monthly—compared with 6% for another specialty flavor, coffee mocha chip. "It's remarkable and unusual to have a new flavor do so well," says Vivian P. Godfrey, Haagen-Dazs vice-president for North America.

BUYING NON-AMERICAN. Quaker Oats Co., too, made strategic changes in its management to encourage the exchange of ideas across international borders. In March, the company cut a layer of management and merged some of the operations of its Latin American and Asian divisions. One goal of the changes: to build better communications between regions.

There are good reasons for the shift. An increasingly diverse U.S. customer base has companies searching for ways to connect with fast-growing ethnic groups. Rising levels of immigration also have brought salsa, soccer, and Thai food into the mainstream. At the same time, Americans of all backgrounds have become increasingly willing to choose more adventurous products. Altoids, a 200-year-old British product originally used to calm upset stomachs, now holds 17% of the $281 million U.S. breath-mint category, having edged aside tamer candies such as Certs. "The popularity of stronger, more intense flavors has soared," says Liz Smith, general manager of Callard & Bowser-Suchard, a Kraft subsidiary that owns the Altoids mint. "What used to be daring and experimental is now broad-based and mainstream."

Moreover, the vast increase in imported products in the U.S. over the last two decades has made consumers and marketers far more comfortable with the idea of products with international roots than they once were. With U.S. households increasingly buying Japanese electronics and German cars, the "Not Invented Here" impulse no longer applies. "Most Americans who buy a Mercedes or Toyota don't think they're buying a value system along with a product," says Richard Pelles, a history professor at the University of Bonn who has written about the cultural effects of international trade.

To be fair, the trend is in its early stages. A good number of giant marketers, such as Coca-Cola Co. and RJR Nabisco Inc., say they have never taken a product or ad campaign from abroad and brought it into the U.S.

But others are happy to take the plunge. Nike has found success with shoes that don't appear to jibe with U.S. tastes. A soccer boot, designed with and worn by Brazilian national team member Ronaldo, was a hit at stores, especially during this summer's playing of the World Cup. Two running shoes have also been imported to the U.S. A long-distance running shoe called the Air Rift, which fits like a mitten with the big toe separate to better simulate running barefoot, was designed with the help of Kenyan runners. And the Air Streak was introduced first in Japan and a year later in the U.S.

The reason for the moves? Nike based them in part on an internal consumer study, which shows a decline in nativistic consumer sentiment in the U.S., especially among

---

GLOBAL PRODUCTS HIT THE STATES

DULCE DE LECHE
Haagen-Dazs developed the caramel-flavored ice cream for Argentina. Now its popularity is second only to vanilla in U.S. stores where it's sold

HARD JEANS
Levi's newest American product, made of darker, stiffer denim, is based on a hit product in Japan

SOCCER BOYS
Nike says its Brazilian-designed boot is selling faster than expected in the U.S.

(Cont.)

young buyers. That has inspired Nike to look abroad more often for new ideas. "All of our products used to be driven almost 100% by consumers in the U.S.," says Juliet Moran, Nike's director of international marketing. "But we're now finding we're getting insights from around the world."

Other companies are hoping for similar outcomes. Levi Strauss, famous for exporting the all-American look of blue jeans to the world, is hoping to bring an offshore trend to U.S. consumers. For three years, a dark version of Levi's denim has been the hot seller in Japan. This year, Levi's is launching an offshoot called "hard jeans" that will be darker and stiffer than typical denim. Levi's has told its U.S. managers that looking abroad for ideas is part of their job. "Three or four years ago, that would have been inconceivable in this company," says Robert Holloway, Levi Strauss's vice-president for business development. "People had a much narrower view."

> Americans are more diverse— and more open to new foods and products

The tactic does not always work, however. Sometimes, companies discover a product was successful abroad thanks to a dearth of competition. While Keebler Co. was owned by British-based United Biscuits PLC, it tried to import favorites from Rose's marmalade to Panda licorice to Kame cooking oils into the U.S. in the early '90s. But Keebler was not able to make the pricey products distinct from established rivals, and the imports languished.

That hasn't discouraged a host of new candidates already waiting at the border. Cereal partners General Mills Inc. and Nestle have successfully invaded Canadian stores with a popular European chocolate breakfast. General Mills CEO Stephen W. Sanger says

he thinks some products from the joint venture will eventually find their way to the U.S. And as new McDonald's Corp. CEO Jack M. Greenberg figures out how to perk up his struggling U.S. division, he says he'll look for help in the company's international outlets. Already, he has reorganized McDonald's American management structure to resemble the decentralized setup overseas, and the company says ad campaigns and tie-ins may cross borders in the future.

Meanwhile, Haagen-Dazs isn't finished. If it can figure out how to import the ingredients, Godfrey says, it will soon sell its most popular Japanese flavor—green tea—in the U.S. Just imagine the possibilities for cross-cultural sundaes.

By David Leonhardt in Chicago

42

Umbrellas made skies brighter

Entrepreneur wasn't afraid to take a chance

By Bill Meyers
USA TODAY

Gangs attacked her on the way to school. They beat her up in the hallways between classes. They snatched her books, money and homework at will.

Things became so bad that she had to ride the elevators with her teachers to avoid the violence at Taft High School in the South Bronx. But Deborah Rosado Shaw was lucky. The studious minister's daughter from New York's Spanish Harlem was determined to survive.

Today, 26 years later, that courage has helped her become an entrepreneur worth $1 million.

"I confronted enormous fear back then, and there's not a lot that could scare me as much today," says Rosado Shaw, 38. "In business, I believe if you're not doing something that makes you shake in your shoes, you're not doing enough."

ABOUT UMBRELLAS PLUS

Founder: Deborah Rosado Shaw
Based in: Chester, N.J.
Estimated 1998 revenue: $10 million
Full-time employees: 19

Over the past decade, she's done plenty. Starting with $300,000, the Hispanic executive has built her New Jersey-based company, Umbrellas Plus, into a $10 million enterprise with a client list that includes such powerful retailers as Wal-Mart, Costco and Toys R Us.

"There's nothing sexy about our business," says Rosado Shaw. "We sell beach umbrellas, sand chairs and tote bags, the portable stuff you take to the beach."

But it's a brutal business, with shrinking margins and ferocious competitors that dwarf Umbrellas Plus.

"They'd love to remove me from the landscape," says Rosado Shaw. "But I'm not going anywhere. I've always played in a game that's too big for me."

HARD KNOCKS

That kind of passion and pride has inspired many up-and-coming entrepreneurs in the USA.

"Deborah's story is one of those positive, land-of-opportunity stories," says Manuel Mirabal, president of the National Puerto Rican Coalition. "She started with nothing, and then she used lots of her energy and intelligence to end up where she is."

The land of opportunity seemed far away when Rosado Shaw entered elite Wellesley College at the age of 16.

During her first week on campus, her roommate's parents wanted to toss her out of the dorm room.

"I was devastated," says Rosado Shaw. "I had fought so hard for this dream."

The dream was in tatters after Rosado Shaw dropped out of Wellesley and returned to New York in search of a job.

"I had no skills or experience," she says. "And I didn't know anyone in business except the corner bodega owner, and he was a thief."

Commuting from New Jersey, Rosado Shaw formed a tenant's group to make sure her apartment building had heat and hot water. The group's attorney introduced Rosado Shaw to his wife, who worked at a company that made umbrellas and tote bags.

Rosado Shaw was hired and quickly fell in love with business.

"It was incredible," she says. "The orders came in. The stuff got made. It was creating something out of nothing."

Rosado Shaw wanted to be a salesperson, but the company wouldn't let her sell. So, the 19-year-old dynamo took a sick day and called on marketers at the Museum of Natural History.

She came away with a $140,000 order.

"I went to the president of the company after that," recalls Rosado Shaw, "and I asked him, 'Are you guys going to let me sell now, or what?' "

They did, but two years later, at age 21, she defected to a rival firm. Soon after, she moved to California to expand her new employer's umbrella business.

DREAMING BIG

In 1987, Rosado Shaw scratched together $300,000 to buy a controlling interest in the company.

By then, she was married and the mother of two children.

"I was in shock," says Rosado Shaw. "All of a sudden, I was an entrepreneur without a salary. But I didn't have a choice. There was no way, no how, that a large

(Cont.)

corporation would ever let me do what I wanted."

Freedom didn't translate into easy profits. Rosado Shaw had never seen a balance sheet before. She had no idea how to calculate her return on investment. And she lost money on late deliveries.

"I was one of those seat-of-the-pants, didn't-know-what-I-was-doing entrepreneurs," she says. "Most people think success is a straight line. It's not."

When orders finally started raining down, however, Rosado Shaw was able to get Umbrellas Plus cranking.

And to better serve her retail customers, the entrepreneur re-tooled her company and moved it to New Jersey three years ago.

Instead of creating a line of beach gear ahead of time, sticking it in a warehouse and then waiting for orders to arrive before distributing the merchandise, Umbrellas Plus now custom manufactures its products for large retail chains after lengthy consultations with them.

This new business model cuts way back on inventory and killer overhead costs, but it doesn't eliminate risk altogether. If Rosado Shaw's products don't sell at retail, she must take them back and swallow the cost.

That hasn't been a problem in her dealings with Wal-Mart, which purchased and sold about $1 million worth of merchandise from Umbrellas Plus last year.

"They are an entrepreneurial mecca," says Rosado Shaw. "And they have supported me and opened a lot of doors."

The relationship began two years ago, when Rosado Shaw, then an unknown at Wal-Mart, was invited to address the chain's top 1,500 executives at one of their weekly Saturday morning meetings. The experience was intimidating. But she performed.

And Wal-Mart vice chairman Don Soderquist was impressed.

"(Rosado Shaw) is the kind of person you'd like to have as a friend or neighbor," he says. "There are unlimited opportunities for her."

All those opportunities may not be in the umbrella business.

"I've made so much money," says Rosado Shaw, "that I can exit at any time."

Indeed, the entrepreneur is in the process of becoming a much-sought-after inspirational speaker.

Coca-Cola, for example, has asked her to deliver a series of motivational talks to children. Rosado Shaw also wants to start a foundation called Dream Big, which would impart skills for entrepreneurial success.

"I want to tell people they have the same power I have, that they can live a dignified life, too," she says.

In the end, however, perhaps the best advice Rosado Shaw can give appears on her PC as a screen saver: "Don't let fear stop you."

How Sony Beat Digital-Camera Rivals

BY ALEC KLEIN
Staff Reporter of THE WALL STREET JOURNAL

It's costlier, clunkier, doesn't produce the sharpest pictures — and it is the top-selling digital camera in the U.S.

It's Sony Corp.'s Mavica, and the explanation for its 41% market share is simple: It's a snap to use. The Mavica stores its pictures on a standard floppy disk. To make photographs after taking the shot, you just remove the disk, pop it into your personal computer, and print. "A child could figure it out," says Ron Glaz, a market researcher with International Data Corp. in Framingham, Mass.

By comparison, competing digital cameras either require cables that connect from a port in the camera to the computer (if you can figure out which port goes with which cable), or they use a floppy-disk converter system, sold separately.

Introduced in August 1997, the Mavica, like all digital cameras, requires no film. Instead, it etches images on electronic sensors and translates them into computer-readable binary data to create photos that can be printed out from a desktop PC. Thanks to its pop-in-and-print feature, the Mavica let Sony vault over the likes of Eastman Kodak Co. and Casio Computer Co., the earlier market leaders.

"No one had foreseen the Sony Mavica taking off as it did . . . because we were all concentrating on the resolution," or image quality, says Gary Rado, executive vice president of the U.S. unit of Japan's Casio.

Last year, led by Sony, digital-camera sales were up about 50% and accounted for 1.1 million of the estimated 12 million point-and-shoots sold in the U.S., according to the Photo Marketing Association.

Sony, although previously a minor player in still photography, was helped in its rise to the top of the digital heap by its esteemed brand name and its broad distribution channels. But the Japanese giant also took a page from history: In the early days of camcorders in the 1980s, consumers opted for the models with large-format tapes that could be played on standard videocassette recorders. They shied away from smaller but more complex recorders, like a Sony model, requiring cable hookups or adapters to view the images.

Things are even more complicated among Mavica's digital competitors, where there are at least five noninterchangeable storage systems, and none are as PC-friendly as Sony's. "We looked at an industry that had no standard...where consumers complained that it was a product that was hard to use," says Daniel P. Nicholson, national marketing manager for digital imaging at Sony's U.S. unit. "People like it easy and quick."

The Mavica's various models sell at an average price of about $665, while other companies' digital cameras generally go for between $300 and $500. But Mavica's key attribute, its floppy disk, costs the consumer less than a dollar and comes with 1.44 megabytes of memory storage. That is enough for about 20 pictures on average, each with under a million pixels, or dots of light that determine the image quality. The more dots, the better the picture.

Kodak, Casio, Canon Inc., Seiko Epson Corp. and Matsushita Electric Industrial Co. all use CompactFlash, a smaller storage card that costs about $70. Although CompactFlash cards hold eight megabytes of memory, the system also yields only about 20 pictures-but each picture has more than one million pixels (or more than one megapixel), hence a sharper image.

Meanwhile, Olympus Optical Co., Fuji Photo Film Co. and Toshiba Corp. employ a memory card called SmartMedia, which costs about $30 and also contains eight megabytes of memory that can produce about 20 megapixel pictures. SmartMedia cards can be inserted into a floppy-disk adapter that plugs into a PC.

"So many products out there, so much clutter," says Ed Pullen, a senior industry analyst at research firm ZD StoreBoard in La Jolla, Calif.

And so many Sony competitors playing digital-camera catch-up. Olympus and Po-

An easy-to-use floppy-disk system propelled the Mavica to top spot

laroid Corp. have each recently introduced printers that directly connect to their own digital cameras via cable, eliminating the need for a PC. (Sony has a Mavica printer that accepts a floppy.) In December, Lexmark International Group Inc. began shipping to retailers the only printer on the market that can directly accept both CompactFlash and SmartMedia cards.

Many analysts believe the industry will ultimately gravitate to a single storage standard to gain wider consumer acceptance. They say it won't be Sony's current system — since floppy technology won't allow enough storage for the kind of high-quality images consumers are used to from traditional film.

Sony acknowledges it consciously sacrificed image quality with its floppy strategy as a way to establish a leadership position. But Mr. Nicholson says the company is moving into the next phase of its digital strategy. Before the end of this week, Sony plans to introduce an $1,800 digital camera that uses the Memory Stick, a removable device with lots of storage space and higher resolution, much like those used by Kodak and other competitors.

Eventually, Sony says, it expects the Memory Stick to be its dominant storage device, not only compatible with lower-priced digital cameras but also with several other company products, including PCs, telephones and TVs.

This, too, has a familiar ring. Once consumers got familiar with camcorders, as Sony well knows, they began flocking to a smaller, non-VHS format with better picture and sound. Betting the same scenario will unfold again, Sony says it is preparing to lure customers up to a more advanced digital camera.

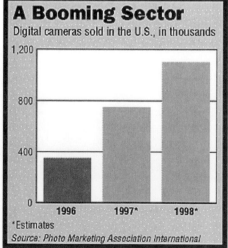

A Booming Sector

Digital cameras sold in the U.S., in thousands

*Estimates

Source: Photo Marketing Association International

8-TRACKS, BETAMAX —AND DIVX?

With DVD catching on, the rival format's outlook is fuzzy

A year ago, it seemed like a gutsy move. Circuit City Stores Inc., in partnership with a Hollywood law firm, announced a new kind of videodisk called Divx, for Digital Video Express. The format was a variant of DVD, or digital video disk—with important differences. With Divx, consumers could buy a movie on a disk for $4.49—versus $15 and up for DVDs. They could watch it during a 48-hour period, starting when they first hit the play button, and then throw the disk away. Or they could build a library of movies on disks and watch them like pay-per-view flicks, for $3.25 a shot. The player, hooked to a phone line, bills them when they watch movies a second or third time. For an extra $15, they would get permanent, unlimited viewing. No more late fees or just-before-midnight return trips to the video store.

Trouble was, consumer-electronics makers, retailers, and some film studios were struggling at that time to launch conventional DVDs. They weren't consulted about Divx and tended to view the new format as a threat. Ordinary DVD machines wouldn't work with the new Divx disks. That raised the spectre of "VHS vs. Beta-max," the ugly format battle that slowed adoption of VCRs.

Well, those fears are starting to look overblown. Ordinary DVD, on sale since last fall, is off to a roaring start. More than 1 million players will be sold worldwide this year, and 2,500 movie and music video titles will be available on DVD by yearend. Meanwhile, Divx players, which can also play DVD disks, face an uphill struggle. Most electronics retailers don't want to stock the players, and video stores won't touch Divx titles. By the time Circuit City finally rolled out Divx nationally, on Sept. 25, the Richmond (Va.) chain was already downsizing its ambitions. Circuit City stock, meanwhile,

slipped 32%, from a July high of 54 1/2 to around 37.

NO GUARANTEES. The Divx saga isn't over. But it has highlighted the pitfalls that new formats face in a environment where almost any digital gadget is possible. Divx' distribution model—a hybrid of pay-per-view, sell-through, and rental—allows users to own a film library with little up-front cost. But as Divx promoters are discovering, cool concepts don't come with any guarantees, even when the price is right.

What went wrong? First of all, technoids and home-theater buffs—the folks most likely to shell out $400 and up for a new player—complain that Divx sacrifices many of the advantages of DVD. Users don't get a choice of wide-screen vs. conventional display formats on the same disk. Nor do they get multiple-language subtitles, directors' commentaries, and theater trailers.

More important, the "digerati" don't like the Big Brother overtones of the technology—the idea that their viewing choices are being monitored. "We've had customers tell us that if we carry Divx, they won't shop our stores again," says Thomas Campbell, a corporate director at Dow Stereo/Video Inc., a nine-store San Diego chain.

A few of the problems should have been obvious from the beginning. Many consumer-electronics chains don't want to sell a product that lines the pockets of their biggest competitor, Circuit City, which gets license fees from player makers and a cut of the revenues as disks are bought and played. By the time Divx went national, only three regional chains had signed up. "Even if Divx rolls out like wildfire, [there will be] less than 1,000 storefronts, compared with 8,000 for DVD," says Ted Pine, president of market researcher InfoTech Research Inc. in Woodstock, Vt. "You're going to have to go out of your way to get it."

DESPERATION. Circuit City, which owns two-thirds of the Digital Video Express partnership, feels the pain. Unable to draw additional investors, it was forced to scale its launch budget back from $100 million to $60 million during the first year. "We're certainly not going to be on every retail store shelf this Christmas, so we'll focus our advertising on retailers carrying the product," says Richard L. Sharp, CEO of both Circuit City and Digital Video Express.

Divx skeptics sniff desperation in the air. Retailers say the $60 million that Sharp is funneling to them as co-op ad funds is the most generous subsidy ever for one product. And Circuit City is pricing the players aggressively as well. The RCA model, which its stores sold for $499 when it was introduced, fell to $399 by the

DIVX' PLUSES AND MINUSES

⊕ Disks sell for just $4.49 and offer a 48-hour viewing period

⊖ They don't do multiple formats and subtitles, or commentaries

⊕ You can hold onto the disks after 48 hours and pay a fee to watch again whenever you want

⊖ Divx disks won't play in a PC or in other DVD machines

⊕ You pay $3.25 for subsequent viewings—a bargain, if you only watch two or three times

⊖ If you trade disks with friends, you must pay the per-view fees

second weekend. (Conventional DVD players start at $299.)

Another bad sign is the dearth of programming. The disks were supposed to be available everywhere, from department stores to the corner drugstore. In fact, there are just 200 titles available, and those only at the electronics stores that sell Divx players. Originally, some studios such as Disney and DreamWorks were attracted to Divx because its antipiracy safeguard exceeded that of DVDs. But those concerns have since faded, and all studios are releasing movies on DVD. Video shops, meanwhile, have always been anti-Divx. Blockbuster Inc. and Hollywood Entertainment Corp., which control more than half the video rental market, say Divx eliminates the need for return visits, which generate impulse rentals.

Perhaps the worst news for Divx promoters is the way their format has galvanized the competition. DVDs were conceived as a sale-only product. Now, Blockbuster and others are adding the disks to their rental racks and stretching rentals out as long as seven days to get rid of the onerous midnight deadline. Stores are also renting out players from Sony, Toshiba, and Philips. "The world has changed in the rental industry," says Douglas A. Gordon, an analyst at NationsBanc Montgomery Securities in San Francisco.

That, to be sure, could work in Divx' favor. Gordon thinks the economics could still attract a small following. People may eventually realize that if they're going to watch a $35 DVD movie only two or three times, then a pay-per-view Divx disk makes more sense. In other words, Divx could survive in a niche, as just another feature on a DVD player. Robert A. Gunst, chief executive of The Good Guys Inc., isn't raring to assist Circuit City. "But that doesn't mean I'm going to deny my customer the right to choose," he says. Besides, there's really no downside for people who buy Divx players. It's not like Sony Corp.'s Beta VCRs, which couldn't play VHS tapes. Even if Divx should flop, you can always use the machine to play DVDs.

By Larry Armstrong in Los Angeles

Reprinted from November 9, 1998 issue of *Business Week* by special permission, copyright © 1998 by McGraw-Hill, Inc.

45

Plot twist for books: Novel trend must prove it's got the write stuff

By Kevin Maney
USA TODAY

Beach reading might soon require batteries.

Electronic books arrive this fall, as first SoftBook then Rocket eBook hit the market.

These books without paper soon will enable you to browse an Internet bookstore using an inexpensive computer about the size of a fat paperback. Find the tome you want, and you can download the contents into the electronic book and read it in a way that's as portable and comfortable as an age-old paper book.

In the long run, electronic books threaten to burn book publishing. But they are, by no means, the only technology hacking at the $72 billion-a-year book industry. Internet bookstore Amazon.com is not just shaking up book retailing but making the notion of the bestseller list almost obsolete. And daring new authors are using the Net to change the way books generate all-important, word-of-mouth demand.

The twist in this plot, though, is that the encroaching electronic age doesn't necessarily mean bad times for the old guard—at least for a while. Savvy publishers see ways to use technology to boost profit margins by cutting such cost-bloating practices as storing acres of books in warehouses and taking back books that don't sell in retail stores. And for now, electronic books cost too much and don't work well enough for mass consumption.

"We don't see somebody getting hit by a train from electronic books," says James Sachs, CEO of SoftBook Press, maker of the SoftBook.

But certainly publishers can now hear that train whistle somewhere down the tracks.

SoftBook weighs 3 pounds, is about the size of *Glamour* and has a leather cover that opens like that of a hardcover book. Under the cover is a black-on-white, touch-sensitive screen. On the perimeter are four buttons: one to bring up a menu of controls; another, a list of books and articles stored in the machine; the third, to go back a page; and the last, to turn pages forward and back.

The touch screen lets readers do many of the things they like to do with paper books: dogear pages, slip in bookmarks and mark up pages. But readers also can search a whole book for a keyword and make type on the page bigger. It runs on a rechargeable battery.

To keep cost low and reliability high, the SoftBook purposely incorporates no new technology, says creator Sachs, who co-designed the first Macintosh mouse and was the designer of Teddy Ruxpin, the 1980s talking bear. When it hits the market next month, a SoftBook will cost $299. But buyers will then have to buy at least $9.95 worth of products each month for two years from SoftBook's on-line bookstore, pushing the total to nearly $540.

To buy a book, plug a phone line into the SoftBook and hit a button from the touch screen menu to dial into the SoftBook store. A typical book will download in about three minutes at today's speed. A SoftBook can hold 100,000 pages, but you can essentially store an indefinite number of books on the SoftBook site. Once a book is paid for, you can download it free any time.

SoftBook initially will target people who read a ton, such as college students, who typically lug around numerous fat textbooks, paperbacks and articles. If all the books were available in the on-line store, then presumably all the student would have to carry would be one electronic device.

The SoftBook also makes it easier to compile hybrid textbooks. "A professor can say, 'You need three chapters from this book, three from that one and four from another one,'" Sachs says.

Publishers like the SoftBook but are wary of its somewhat proprietary bookstore, which would make all publishers funnel sales through SoftBook. So far, they seem more comfortable with the Rocket eBook from NuvoMedia, which takes a more open approach, allowing anyone to sell content for the device. In fact, publishing giant Bertelsmann and bookstore operator Barnes & Noble are among its investors.

The Rocket eBook is smaller, simpler and, on the inside, more technologically advanced than the SoftBook. It has more in common with the 3Com PalmPilot — probably because it was designed by a PalmPilot creator. When it appears later this year, a Rocket eBook will cost $500 but have no minimum monthly charges. To buy a book, the Rocket eBook plugs into a personal computer, which connects to the Internet and then to any on-line bookstore, such as www.barnes&noble.com. Download a book through the PC and into the Rocket eBook. It can hold 4,000 pages. Old books stay stored on the PC hard drive — a nuisance if they hog too much space.

PUBLISHER APPEAL

In a lot of ways, electronic books look good to publishers. The editors at Harvard Business School Press were shown a Rocket eBook earlier this year. Far from flinching, they jumped at it. "We were almost fighting over who could have it," says Carol Franco, who runs the publishing house.

Publishers say Rocket eBook or SoftBook don't yet seem threatening to traditional books. For the next five to 10 years, their expectation is that the market will be similar to books on tape: a niche for avid readers. "In reference categories, we'll see some movement" toward electronic books, says Phil Pfeffer, adviser to Random House CEO Peter Olsen. "Whether or not the great American novel will be downloaded, I just don't know. (Electronic books) don't go to the beach well. You can't fall asleep on them well."

Second, sales of electronic books should mean higher margins and fewer headaches for publishers. The way publishing works now, the publisher gets less than half the cover price of a book. Much of the expense of publishing goes to author royalties, printing, warehousing and distribution. Then, if a book doesn't sell, the retailer returns it. Up to 40% of books shipped get returned. By contrast, there are no costs of printing, storing, shipping or returns with electronic books.

Third, SoftBook and NuvoMedia have done a pretty good job of burying encryption software in their technology. That should keep someone who buys a book from making copies and sending them around the Internet or from loading them into multiple PCs or other electronic books.

But what happens if electronic books hit technology crosscurrents? For instance: What if books become widely available on the Net for free, with no anti-copying code?

That's a question consultant and author Larry Downes and co-author Chunka Mui are asking with their recent book *Unleashing the Killer App*. The book recommends giving away information as a way to build a business. To test the theory, Downes and Mui put the entire contents of *Killer App* on a Web site

---

Electronic book not yet as fit as print

By Kevin Maney
USA TODAY

For the past several weeks, I've been trying out the SoftBook and showing it to colleagues, friends and family.

The first reaction of almost everyone who sees it is amazement. A piece of science-ficiton—the electronic book—is here. People gather around to look and touch and try it out.

Review

The second reaction comes as soon as the SoftBook is put in anyone's hand. It's too heavy. It would be uncomfortable to hold for hours on end. After using the SoftBook for a bit, the third and almost unanimous reaction is that it's cool and fun to try, but it just doesn't seem worth messing with. Paper still wins.

I pretty much fit that mold, too. There's no question the SoftBook, which is the first of a few electronic books to hit the market, is a nifty piece of work. It's what computers should be. Open it up and it pops to life—no booting up. With just four buttons and a simple on-screen menu, it's extremely easy to figure out.

The designers have worked hard to make SoftBook a booklike experience or improve on bound paper. Pages are "turned" forward and back using a rocker button. Page corners can be dog-eared by touching the upper corner of the screen. The page can be found again by hitting a "bookmarks" icon on the touch-screen. You can write in the margins on the screen using a stylus tucked in the bottom of the SoftBook, then easily erase the scribbles.

Yet, you're still looking at a computer screen—black on white, no color—that doesn't match the crispness of the printed word. And a SoftBook book just doesn't seem as easy to navigate as a regular book. If you had a paper copy of *Fodor's Aruba*, you'd flip through and quickly find the hotels or restaurants. Clicking through the SoftBook version of *Fodor's Aruba* is more work.

I came away thinking electronic books are like early cellular phones: too bulky, too expensive and not quite good enough. But if electronic books improve the way cell phones did, a lot of us might eventually be reading screens instead of paper.

(Cont.)

(www.killerapp.com). Anybody could save the $24.95 cover price and read the book free.

"If our theories are true, we'll actually sell more books," Downes says. "We'll lose a few people who read it on line and don't like it or get enough that way. But we'll generate buzz and more people will be interested in the book and we'll sell more." The book, out in May, made *Business Week*'s best-selling business books list, though there's no way to know how much of a role the Web site has played in that success.

For now, Downes says, the risk is small: Few people want to read a whole book on a PC. But what if people get comfortable reading electronic books and could just as easily grab a free version as a copy they'd have to pay for?

There's a chance that the basic content of books might indeed be evolving toward being free, says Nicholas Negroponte, head of Massachusetts Institute of Technology's Media Lab. Project Gutenberg, a not-for-profit Web site, is on a mission to put all public domain books on the Net for free. Titles on the site range from *The War of the Worlds* to *Cyrano de Bergerac*.

Authors will have to come up with imaginative ways to make money off their work, Negroponte says. "Maybe I use the book as a loss leader for lectures, consulting or performances."

Many authors might not feel comfortable with the technological shift. "Maybe it was inevitable that computers would try to replace books, but I don't think they're there yet," says poet Beth Wellington. Then again, many might feel like Harriet Rubin, once a top book editor and now an author and speaker. "Publishers provide no service," Rubin says. "If this hurries their demise, maybe that's a good thing."

Certainly publishers—if they don't want to fade—would have to find new ways to make money from written words. But no one seems to have a great answer as to how. "The longer-term implications I find very difficult to sort out," Downes says.

NEW BUSINESS MODEL

In the meantime, publishing is grappling with the rise of Internet bookstores such as Borders.com, Barnes&noble.com and Amazon.com. On the surface, such stores are just another way for consumers to buy traditional books. But the Net stores raise new questions, too.

"They turn the top-10 best seller list upside down," says Nathan Myhrvold, chief technology officer at Microsoft. Net stores give readers the ability to search for topics and authors while software helps them find books they might like, based on other books or writers they enjoyed. So customers tend to find books they want — not just books that are popular with a mass audience.

If readers buy more niche books, publishers will have to fulfill more one-of-a-kind orders. So publishers are asking questions about the old model of printing thousands of books in anticipation of sales. IBM and distributor Ingram Book are developing a project called Lightning Print, which would allow publishers to print each book as it's ordered. Books could be kept available forever, never going out of print. "All of this is very exciting," says Rubin, speaking of the technology hitting the publishing industry from several directions at once. What she and others find fascinating is that there are clearly so many more developments to come, and no one knows how this story will end.

Place

WRESTING
NEW WEALTH FROM THE
SUPPLY CHAIN

Five companies, with products from microprocessors to salted nuts, have found smarter ways to stock stuff and ship it around. ■ *by Stuart F. Brown*

Electric utility linemen in a rural Alabama garage crack open a shrink-wrapped pallet of hardware and electrical components packed into blue plastic bins and load them onto a bucket truck that hoists workers to the tops of poles. At the job site, the linemen have all the stuff they need to hook up a new customer, replace worn-out components, or restore juice to dozens of homes left in the dark by a storm.

The utility, Alabama Power, "kits" the materials for jobs at one of four regional warehouses and trucks them to the garages where work crews meet to pick up the service trucks. Since it began the practice, the company has slashed the time its workers spend rounding up parts and has reduced the amount of expensive material kept in inventory. With deregulation likely to unleash new competition in its territory before long, moving to centralized warehousing is one of the ways Alabama Power is using supply-chain management techniques to root out inefficiencies that didn't seem so important in the past.

As those prepacked bins demonstrate, the religion of supply-chain efficiency is popping up in surprising places. It's also taking on innovative refinements at companies already converted to this broad doctrine, which encompasses tightening up internal logistics, bolstering upstream links to suppliers, and offering better downstream service to customers. In much the same way that techniques like the late W. Edwards Deming's statistical process control have become mandatory on the factory floor, supply-chain management—which is saving the U.S. economy billions through streamlined shipping methods, faster inventory turns, and lower prices for parts and services—is becoming

the thing for companies facing tough competitors and demanding customers. Among other recent supply-chain successes:

■ Thomson Consumer Electronics is working with a big retailer to improve market forecasts and reduce the time required to build and ship its RCA color TV sets and other products, thus avoiding missed sales and excess inventory.

■ By coordinating production, distribution, and promotional plans several months in advance with a supermarket chain, Nabisco has helped it achieve a 40% sales increase in salted nuts with almost no leftover stocks.

■ Bay Networks, a maker of Internet switching and routing equipment, has winnowed its supplier base to a seventh of the previous total. The survivors, which are deeply involved in the company's product development process, deliver parts faster, generally at lower prices.

■ Intel, though in an enviable position as the dominant maker of microprocessors, has been busily reinventing the way it moves and stores inventory to minimize the quantity of expensive chips awaiting shipment to customers. It's also helping customers in the scrappy personal-computer industry operate with pared-down inventories.

Many companies are in no hurry to share their latest supply-chain brainstorms. "A lot of them see these projects as deeply strategic, and they don't want to disclose what they've been doing," says Barrett Boehm, a partner at Price Waterhouse Coopers in St. Louis. Greg Owens, managing partner of Andersen Consulting's supply-chain management practice in Atlanta, says, "Most of these firms aren't going to tell you what their most innovative strategies are because they involve service-differentiation or cost-structure improve-

ments that give them an advantage over their competition."

Alabama Power

In the power-generating business, it isn't easy to operate with tiny inventories, because cars and trucks will sometimes crash into power poles, and Mother Nature will unpredictably weigh in with thunderstorms and tornadoes, such as the destructive monster that killed 32 people last April near Birmingham. Or Hurricane Georges, which beat up the Gulf Coast in September and caused flooding in Mobile, where 148,000 customers were temporarily without electricity. One of five utilities owned by Southern Co., Alabama Power serves the lower four-fifths of its state. Its 45,000-square-mile territory is crisscrossed with 72,000 miles of lines strung along 1.35 million poles and towers, which bring power to 1.3 million residential, commercial, and industrial customers.

Although the wave of deregulation taking place in the U.S. power industry hasn't yet arrived at Alabama Power's doorstep, the company wants to brace itself for the possibility that it could one day be obliged to deliver juice generated by other companies through its distribution lines. Worried that regulators might permit only a slim charge for this use of its infrastructure, the utility wants to trim fat and make the best use of capital that would be otherwise tied up in inventory.

Brought in to assess things a few years ago, Douglas Castek, an Anderson Consulting expert based in Atlanta, identified materials distribution as an area ripe for improvement. In the past, some regulated utilities let inventories pile up pretty high because electricity rates were calculated on their amount of invested capital, although public utility commissions

(Cont.)

are charged with keeping an eye out for inventory that exceeds a "prudent" level.

Larry Grill, Alabama Power's general manager of materials services, says his challenge is balancing the company's obligation to provide reliable service and quickly recover from mishaps with the business goal of trimming redundant supplies of hardware. While the company keeps about 7,800 items in stock, a fairly short list of common items accounts for most of the flow of goods through the warehouse system: cable, transformers, meters, insulators, switches, and the like. A host of infrequently needed items must also be kept on hand, such as expensive steel high-tension towers like those that replaced pylons crumpled by last spring's tornado.

Alabama Power's logistics system grew up around the six geographical divisions into which its territory is organized. Within each are 56 locations where repair trucks are garaged and work crews report for assignments in the field. Over the years, these local facilities naturally became warehouses for parts and materials.

Now the utility has centralized its stocks of materials, and most inventory is stored in just four distribution centers. The exception to this so-called hub-and-spokes arrangement is that a certain amount of emergency storm-repair material is still kept at work-crew locations. Grill, a soft-spoken man who in his spare time serves as a local judge, says, "When the lower inventory costs achievable with a hub-and-spokes logistics arrangement were compared with the somewhat greater amount of trucking it would entail, the four-warehouse model turned out to be a much cheaper way to do things. Of the $26 million in materials we've brought in from the field, we will soon have eliminated $8 million worth, and the additional trucking cost is only $100,000 a year.

Brock Hornsby, Alabama Power's manager of material distribution, says another benefit of centralization was finding previously uncounted items and keying them into the computerized inventory-management system. Stocks of common items, which in some cases had turned over only three times per year, now score an average of 38 turnovers yearly, he says.

One of the four sites where the utility's materials are stored is a 240,000-square-foot distribution center near the unforgetably named small town of Alabaster, Ala. Outdoors are 40 acres of "laydown yards," where large transformers, heavy cable, and other big items are lined up in rows. Indoors, warehousemen armed with bar-code scanners roam the aisles of parts, picking what's needed to fill orders coming from engineers in the field who have identified installation or repair jobs that need doing.

Linked by radio to the warehouse's computer inventory system, the scanners automatically transmit the identities and quantities of items as they are packed into reusable blue-plastic bins. Commonly needed things—such as crossarms and insulators that reside atop power poles—are located near one another in the aisles to save steps. When inventory of an item falls below a preset threshold, the system automatically sends the supplier an electronic replenishment order.

Warehouse crews stack the kits of items needed for a job onto wooden pallets, which are then shrink-wrapped to make sure nothing gets lost or stolen and put on a truck headed for one of the 56 work-crew facilities nearest the job site. Divisional managers like this system, Grill says, because their crews spend less time rummaging around for hardware and more time climbing poles to keep customers' lights lit. The money that's been freed up through inventory reductions is now available for more profitable investments, such as the 750 megawatts of new gas-turbine generating equipment the company is installing in Mobile.

Despite the concentration of inventory in fewer locations, the new setup hasn't hampered Alabama Power's ability to respond quickly to weather disasters. To augment the limited stocks of emergency items always kept at the local garages, the utility "pre-positions" repair materials in threatened areas when trouble looms. As hurricane Georges moved in on Mobile, for example, the company sent in 39 trucks loaded with 780,000 pounds of emergency materials. It also mustered 2,000 workers and hundreds of repair trucks, both from its own ranks and from contractors and utilities in neighboring states. Though nearly three-fourths of the area's customers lost electricity, Larry Grill reports, service was restored to most within 48 hours—faster than in past hurricanes.

Thomson

Few sectors have more reasons to revamp the supply chain than consumer electronics, where profits can be hard to come by. Monte Chamberlin, general manager of supply-chain management and methods at Thomson Consumer Electronics in Indianapolis, says his industry, impressed by successes in other businesses, is beginning to follow suit. His employer, part of the French company Thomson Multimedia, makes and markets RCA, GE, and ProScan products, of which color TV sets make up the biggest chunk.

Almost a year ago, Thomson U.S. launched a major program called Chain ReAction to galvanize its troops into improving forecasting and customer service while achieving quicker inventory turns. Some of the retail chains that are Thomson's customers have gotten a taste of inventory cost savings through their dealings with computer and appliance manufacturers, which have sophisticated supply-chain programs of their own. Computer makers and retailers, Chamberlin says, early discovered the importance of inventory reduction because their products are more valuable than TV sets yet become obsolete—and lose value—faster.

Chamberlin looks to Dell Computer, with its direct-sales, build-to-order business model, as an ideal. "We believe they operate off of less than two weeks of inventory," he says, "and we use this example to stimulate our people to think about the possibilities." Although Thomson doesn't intend to sell direct to consumers as Dell does, it wants to borrow the PC maker's strategy of assembling a large number of product models from a small number of different components that it owns for as short a period as possible.

In its production-engineering department, Thomson has embarked on a program to reduce by 75% the number of assembly steps that aren't common to a wide variety of models. This will permit far greater manufacturing speed and flexibility. The idea is to bring a limited number of "generic" sets with few differentiating features to near completion on assembly lines. Then, in a last-minute response to customer orders, the sets will be finished by routing them through a relatively small number of steps that add features unique to each model.

This is a TV maker's version of what PC manufacturers already do. If you remove your computer's housing, expect to find a few unused and unexplained connectors that helped the maker postpone as long as possible the machine's final configuration. The small extra cost of the connectors is more than offset by the flexibility and quick turnaround they permit when customer orders arrive. This "postponement" strategy in the assembly process is one of the ways Thomson plans to reduce its response time to market shifts from a few months to just one.

Thomson is also moving to production planning based on one-month sales forecasts from its customers, which are much more accurate than attempts to predict retail sales several months ahead. And it is shifting to receiving orders and shipping goods weekly instead of monthly, as customers get better at predicting demand and trimming their inventories. In a test program with one retail chain, which Chamberlin prefers not to name, Thomson has cut the customer's inventory of 19-inch to 25-inch TVs from two months to one. The retailer has missed few sales: All the kinds of sets the public wants are in the stores 99% of the time.

The highest-value component of TV sets is the picture tube, which Thomson produces at plants in Pennsylvania, Ohio, and Indiana. The tubes are then shipped to plants in Juarez, Mexico, where they are assembled with components from various suppliers into finished sets. In the past, trucks driving northbound from Juarez moved the TVs to distribution centers in El Paso, Los Angeles, and Indianapolis. But now, when a large customer signals that it can handle an entire truckload, the practice is to deliver directly from the factory.

For a weekly ordering and shipping cycle to work, Thomson needs timely market forecasts from retailers. The company asks its customers to supply 26-week forecasts, with frequent updates. Some customers provide new information weekly, some every few weeks, and others monthly. "In theory, if they're really good at saying what they want and we're really good at building it, then we can fill all their orders without a lot of inventory," Chamberlin observes.

Thomson uses a software package called Demand Planner, developed by i2 Technologies in Irving, Texas, to keep track of the delivery dates its customers are asking for. The program generates a forecast each week projecting demand for about 250 different color TV models, and can display point-of-sale information from customers as it arrives via electronic data interchange, in some cases daily. "This system focuses us on what our customers want and tells us what we need to build," says Kimberley Hall, manager of sales planning and analysis.

In the plants, an i2 program called Factory Planner schedules workloads for the production lines. Next year, a third i2 program, Supply Chain Planner, will tie together Demand Planner and Factory Planner, automating the flow of data between the marketing people and the manufacturing people. Price Waterhouse Coopers consultant Gary Van Wagnen has been helping Thomson get these systems running. Chamberlin says: "Our goal is to achieve eight to 12 inventory turns a year, depending on the type of product, instead of the four to eight turns we've had in the psat. And we want to be able to give our customers what they want, when they want it, 95% of the time."

Nabisco

Companies in the ultracompetitive packaged-goods business were among the first supply-chain innovators because they had no choice. With tough customers like Wal-Mart to keep happy, they had to get efficient and responsive or perish. Nabisco is a case in point. Says Joseph Andraski, vice president for customer development: "We've been focusing on the supply chain since the late 1970s. We just called it by different names, like physical distribution, logistics, and then integrated logistics."

The experimentation and fine-tuning have continued to the present. Nabisco has shed operations it once owned, including truck fleets and warehouses, in favor of outsourcing these services to contractors. Using so-

called public warehouses opens up the interesting possibility of filling trucks with goods made by several manufacturers who use the same building for storage. Nabisco is engaged in such a partnership with 20 other manufacturers that serve a West Coast customer, American Stores, from the same distribution center.

Mixing partial loads of different products makes it possible to send out trucks fully loaded, and frequently. Since this year-old program began, Andraski says, American Stores has seen a 30% reduction in its inventory of products supplied by the cooperating manufacturers, while the individual stores have found they can get what they want from the distribution center 99% of the time, vs. 95% previously. "This is a commonsense way to do business," Andraski asserts, "and we're going to see a lot more of it."

In another promising experiment, Nabisco is engaged in close collaboration with Wegmans Food Market of Rochester, N.Y. A well-regarded family-owned supermarket chain, Wegmans has 57 stores in New York and Pennsylvania. Early this year, Nabisco people sat down with executives at Wegmans and devised a program aimed at winning back a small piece of turf the retailer was losing to other stores: snack nuts. The category includes cans, jars, and bags of peanuts, cashews, mixed cocktail nuts, and sunflower seeds, which have a shelf life of about one year.

Nabisco briefed Wegmans in uncommon detail on promotional plans for its Planter's nut products over an upcoming six months. Using its knowledge of shopper preferences and trends at other stores in its area, Wegmans worked together with Nabisco to put together a week-by-week forecast of the amount of nuts it wanted to sell, carefully dovetailing the two companies' promotional plans to avoid duplication or sales missed by not having enough stock on hand when ads or coupons got into circulation. Plans were put in place specifying how Nabisco would replenish Wegmans' inventory, and how many days' supply it would help the supermarket chain keep on hand.

Wegmans and Nabisco turned to Benchmarking Partners, a Cambridge, Mass., research and consulting firm, for help in mapping the steps both parties needed to follow during this venture into what's called collaborative planning, forecasting, and replenishment, or CPFR. Software called Networks, developed by Manugistics of Rockville, Md., ties together the parties via the Internet, so updates to forecasts or revisions in production or shipping dates can be mulled over in advance, and week-to-week plans adjusted accordingly. The Networks software automatically sends each week's order from Wegmans to Nabisco through an Internet link that eliminates paperwork.

The result, says Jack DePeters, Wegmans'

vice president of operations, is a "number so big it sounds like pie in the sky: a sales increase of about 40% in the nut category, including some non-Nabisco brands. And the planning has been so good that at the end of a promotion we've found we served our customers and had very little inventory left over. In the past we probably would have over-ordered. Manufacturers in the past have not been in the habit of sharing their long-term marketing plans with retailers. Next I'd like to try a higher-volume product category that will have more impact on our logistics."

Andraski thinks the inventory discipline inherent in CPFR is not only good for sales and operating costs but may also take a bite out of spoilage. Unsold nuts that have exceeded their shelf life revert to Nabisco for disposal. "Spoilage is a huge problem that costs about $15 billion a year in the U.S.," Andraski says. "The stuff ends up at a reclamation center. I know that manufacturers who have succeeded in reducing their inventory at the retailer have seen spoilage go down commensurately."

Bay Networks

This maker of Internet switching equipment in Santa Clara, Calif., had a different supply-chain goal: taking a supplier base that was unmanageably big and drastically trimming it. Eighteen months ago the company had about 480 suppliers. Now, as a result of its Preferred Supplier Program, there are just 67. In paring down its supplier list, Bay Networks typically kept three companies in each category of goods and services. "That lets me assure each one that they will get about one-third of my business, and that they will participate in our new products," says Jose Mejia, vice president for commodity and supplier management.

Bay Networks quickly brings new products to market, sometimes in just four to six months; last year 58% of the company's $2.4 billion in revenues was from products it didn't offer the previous year. The company uses contract manufacturers to produce most of what it sells, but certain new products felt to be particularly time-sensitive are first produced in-house in low volumes. This allows the design engineers developing something new to work alongside production engineers responsible for manufacturing it. As the prototypes quickly evolve, so do the processes for making them.

During the product development cycle, Bay Networks brings engineers from its contract manufacturers and from key suppliers under its roof to collaborate on the effort. Once a new product's design is set and the pilot production process has been debugged, the job is moved to a contract manufacturer's plant for full-scale production. The transition is usually smooth, Mejia says, because the contractors' engineers are involved from the get-go.

(Cont.)

Mejia thinks Bay Networks, which recently was acquired by Canada's Nortel Networks, is already benefiting from having closer ties to fewer suppliers. "I'm now seeing some outstanding pricing of components that we aren't even buying in large volumes, and I'm able to get application-specific integrated circuits (ASICs) made in just three weeks, which is extremely quick," he says. "There suppliers see themselves as being with us for the long haul, and that's certainly the way we've tried to make them feel."

Intel

Even this mighty company, which has harvested huge profits from Pentiums and their predecessors, found it could not rest content with its logistics. Intel's epiphany came as it saw the life cycle of its microprocessors going from about eight years for the 386 series to less than a year and a half today. The fat years during which the latest-generation chip sells for a princely sum were contracting into a much shorter period, a trend that dictated smaller inventory. Says Jim Kellso, manager of engineering and strategic planning in Intel's worldwide logistics operation: "When the product is being devalued so fast, I want to ship it at today's price, not tomorrow's, and I want to know the right amount of new stuff to build on the right day. Our product, ounce for ounce, is more valuable than platinum, and the cost of inventory is a number beyond anything you can imagine."

Intel decided in 1995 to replace its existing sales-order computer system, which keeps track of pricing, orders, delivery, and inventory management, with SAP's enterprise resource planning software. The old setup actually consisted of four separate systems that handled orders from the U.S., Japan, Asia, and Europe, and rolled them together so that they could be tracked on the domestic system. But this arrangement didn't give a clear picture of exactly where all the inventory was on a given day. Just as serious, it wasn't year 2000–compliant.

Putting in a new sales order system during a period when Intel was growing from $18 billion in annual sales and 40,000 employees to $26 billion in annual sales with 60,000 employees was no small feat. "This is what I call doing a heart transplant during a marathon," says Kellso, "and we did it while improving our delivery performance to customers." The key to a smooth transition was keeping the old setup functioning while phasing in the SAP system. "Now we can see our inventory anywhere in the world, commit it to a customer, and deliver it within three days," Kellso says. "We couldn't do that before."

Order and inventory tracking weren't the only activities Intel sought to improve. Shipping costs were growing steeply because of a shift from selling just packaged chips to selling "single-edge connector cartridges" containing a Pentium II chip, some RAM, a heat sink for cooling, and other components. Developed both for technical and marketing reasons, the cartridges suddenly increased the physical volume and shelf space required for Intel's premier product fivefold. For the whole company, inbound, interplant, and outbound shipping costs threatened to balloon from $300 million a year to over $1 billion by 2001 if something wasn't done about it.

Intel's ultraclean chipmaking plants, or fabs, are located in the U.S., Ireland, and Israel. Chips for European markets go through final assembly and testing in Ireland, but the rest of the company's output is completed at plants in Asia and Costa Rica, where labor is cheaper. Last year Intel decided to reshuffle its global logistics and direct a substantial part of its production flow through three big new warehouses located next to airports in Malaysia, the Philippines, and Costa Rica.

The new facilities are described as "integrated" because they handle both parts and materials coming in from suppliers and other Intel plants, and outbound finished chips on their way to customers. Designed by Lockwood Greene Consulting in Mesa, Ariz., the 225,000-square-foot buildings were built cookie-cutter style from virtually the same blueprints.

Intel chips begin their globe-hopping odyssey at the fabs, where brittle silicon wafers with scores of chips etched on them are packed in sturdy, cushioned containers called boats. These in turn are placed in plain brown boxes, the better to divert attention from their valuable contents—Intel's name does not appear on the carton—and air-freighted to the integrated warehouses. From there they are trucked to nearby plants where they are cut into individual "dies" and tested again. The good chips are encased in plastic frames, and exquisitely tiny lead wires are attached to their microcircuitry. Some of these chips are shipped as is, while others move on to further workstations for assembly into cartridges or motherboards for computers.

By routing its international shipping through these three points, Intel is able to guarantee its air-freight contractors planes that are full or close to it, both coming and going on the ocean-hopping "blue water" flights that account for 80% of shipping costs. Thus the company gets a much better deal on freight rates. Intel has further reduced its shipping costs by redesigning its packaging to nest twice as many cartridges safely in each carton. This "densification" program alone has saved $1 million a week in shipping costs.

Interestingly, the integrated warehouses don't have fancy automated storage and retrieval (ASR) systems, in which unmanned cranes move materials in each aisle. The development of hand-held radio-frequency barcode scanning devices like those at Alabama Power has largely eliminated the "placement discipline" problem those expensive ASR systems were designed to solve. Riding simple bin-picking trucks, warehousemen follow computer instructions, using the scanners to make sure they move the specified item to or from the correct cubbyhole.

Through its various improvements in logistics, Intel has reduced its finished-goods inventory from eight weeks' worth three years ago to four weeks' today. Through production refinements, the chipmaking cycle time also has been greatly reduced, although this varies with the type of chip being made. Now the company is forging electronic links to customers to help reduce their chip inventories. Using an Intel software program called Supply Line Management, the chipmaker has hooked up its sales-order system to the inventory systems of five leading PC makers.

The software automatically triggers a new shipment order when a customer's inventory falls to about four days' worth of Pentiums. During the three-day order and replenishment cycle, that customer's inventory might get as small as a one-day supply before a new shipment arrives. "By cutting them from an average of eight days' supply to only four days', I halve the time they're holding this valuable inventory," Kellso says. "With the price of the microprocessor accounting for the lion's share of the PC's manufacturing cost—not including the monitor and keyboard—that's a lot of money saved. This is trading information for inventory."

Intel wants to extend its computer links into the inventory systems of the big retail chains that are the PC makers' biggest customers, thus getting one layer closer to sensing where the market is going. In another corner of the market, the company is already able to tell exactly what a retail customer has just bought. Many mom-and-pop computer stores, which will assemble a computer just the way you want it, are part of a network of factory-authorized outlets called Genuine Intel Dealers. A customer who buys a PC from one of these stores can plug a phone line into the modem port and ring up a number Intel provides. Intel will then run a remote diagnostic probe and send a printout certifying what's inside the new computer. That way, says Kellso, "the customer knows he got what he paid for, and we know what he bought."

"If I can talk the retailers who aren't Genuine Intel Dealers into doing this too," Kellso adds, "I'll really have instant feedback on what's selling and what I should be building." By its nature, he argues, "the PC industry is probably an easier one than any other for quickly getting detailed inventory data." But as those linemen at Alabama Power are proving as they load up their service trucks, just about any business can find more efficient ways to stock stuff and move it around.

47

Some Big Companies Long to Embrace Web But Settle for Flirtation

They Fear Online Marketing Could Cause Sales Staffs And Distributors to Rebel

A Risk of Getting 'Amazoned'

BY GEORGE ANDERS
Staff Reporter of THE WALL STREET JOURNAL

The Internet commerce boom is posing a tormenting challenge for many of America's biggest companies. They are tempted to move a lot of business online—but they worry that this new way of selling will betray the salespeople and distributors who have long kept the cash registers ringing.

At the medical-products unit of Hewlett-Packard Co., an army of 500 sales representatives and dozens of distributors account for sales of more than $1 billion a year worldwide. For years, this has been a people-centered business, in which face-to-face meetings, handshakes and product demonstrations have built customer relationships that translated into big money.

Now, some leading hospital chains want one-stop shopping on the Internet, says James Cyrier, H-P's head of medical sales and marketing. With a few mouse clicks, these customers could buy everything from ultrasound machines to electrodes without ever seeing a salesman. Mr. Cyrier is intrigued, but if he moves too fast, he risks a mutiny from his traditional sales force and distributors, who don't want to surrender their commissions.

Ticklish Business

Across the U.S., hundreds of manufacturers face the same dilemma. The Internet could prove to be the most effective sales tool since the telephone, letting companies reach millions of potential customers quickly and cheaply. Online commerce is an outright menace, however, to the men and women who do in-person selling or distribution, and who still control 90% or more of most companies' order flow. As a result, jittery corporate strategists are trying to capitalize on the Internet's potential without sabotaging traditional sales channels.

Typically, it is large corporations in highly competitive industries that feel most boxed in, says Vish Krishnan, an assistant professor at the University of Texas business school in Austin, who specializes in Internet applications. Such companies have the most to lose, he says, because they have spent fortunes mastering traditional sales methods. Anything different is a threat to their corporate culture — and next quarter's earnings.

Ignoring the Internet isn't much of an alternative, though. Selling online can slash costs as much as 15% by getting rid of paperwork and sales commissions. Those potential efficiencies are attracting swarms of online entrepreneurs. So if established manufacturers don't sell their cars, catheters or chinos over the Internet, odds are that some upstart will. Those who hesitate risk being "amazoned," forfeiting business to an Internet newcomer, in the way that bookstore chains have lost ground to Amazon.com Inc., the online bookseller.

A Sugar Coating

As a result, producers are engaged in awkward dances with distributors, trying to develop Internet sales channels that won't rock the boat. In some cases, that means launching Web commerce sites with no publicity or limited merchandise offerings. In other cases, it means keeping online prices high, so traditional vendors can lead the way in offering discounts. Some manufacturers are even trying to placate dealers and salespeople with a cut of each Internet sale, regardless of whether they played a role in generating it.

In essence, companies are sugar-coating what may be the most disruptive sales transformation in a generation. Corporate executives insist that online commerce is merely another way to serve the consumer. But sales representatives and dealers privately question whether they will be cast aside someday as relics of a bygone era.

At Hewlett-Packard's medical unit, managers have decided that Internet commerce can't be ignored. In the next few months, they will roll out a Web site that will let major buyers such as Columbia/HCA Healthcare Corp. and the Premier hospital-purchasing alliance place orders over the Internet. At the outset, says H-P's Mr. Cyrier, online prices will be carefully aligned with those available in other sales channels. Online orders may still generate commissions for the sales representatives who usually handle those accounts.

Learning From Experience

"We'll learn as we go," Mr. Cyrier says. "We have a big direct-sales force calling on hospitals, and it would be very demotivational for them if customers placed an order through this new e-channel, and they didn't get paid. At the same time, selling online could be more cost-effective. So maybe we will end up passing the savings on to the consumer."

In the car industry, Internet-assisted commerce is starting to shake up the ties between the Big Three manufacturers and their independent dealers. Traditionally, dealers have enjoyed free rein to boost car prices above cost, generally collecting 3% to 15% of the eventual sales price for themselves. So far, auto makers and Internet car-buying services are merely collecting leads online and sending potential buyers to dealerships. But some industry observers think bigger changes lie ahead.

In Seattle, car dealer Ron Clauden is keeping a close eye on General Motors Corp. So far, Mr. Clauden has been a willing partner in GM's Internet initiatives. He has gained 10 sales in the past year from the Detroit car maker's Web sites, and GM officials say that cooperative approach is all they want from online commerce for now. But Mr. Clauden thinks GM someday might consider taking orders directly and getting rid of middlemen such as himself.

(See related letter: "Letters to the Editor: Business Survival Ploy: Self-Cannibalization"—WSJ Nov. 19, 1998)

"I would be disappointed if GM didn't think about that eventually," Mr. Clauden says. "They've always got to look for better ways to sell cars."

The struggle between old and new sales methods is most intense in the computer industry and related high-technology fields. There, online commerce already is a multibillion-dollar alternative to traditional selling. In Round Rock, Texas, Dell Computer Corp. collects $2.2 billion a year, or 14% of its personal-computer sales, from customer orders placed directly over the Internet. That helps Dell hold down inventories and costs, giving it an edge over rival makers of PCs such as Compaq Computer Corp.

"We can't afford to lose business to anyone," says Enrico Pesatori, Compaq's senior vice president for corporate marketing. In the past few months, Compaq, which is based in Houston, has rolled out its own Web commerce site, selling computers at rock-bottom prices directly to small-business customers and individuals.

A Chunk Out of Sales

PC dealers are seriously unhappy about the switch. "It's taking a chunk out of our business," says Richard Wong, head of Sefco Computers Inc., South San Francisco, Calif. His company sells about $8 million a year of computers, and Compaq used to be a major part of his business. "We still have people ask us for bids on small-business installations, but we don't win the orders anymore," Mr. Wong says. Compaq's Internet site typically underprices him by about $50 a machine, he explains.

Some other PC makers, such as International Business Machines Corp., have tried a gentler approach, using their Internet sites mainly to steer customers to online ordering sites run by long-established dealers. But that approach doesn't take full advantage of the Internet's ability to wring costs out of the distribution system. For its part, Compaq makes no

(Cont.)

apologies for its more aggressive approach; Mr. Pesatori says distributors should recognize that all-out use of the Internet is essential if Compaq is going to stay competitive.

Even technology companies approaching the Internet more gingerly are amazed at how rapidly sales can take off. In May, Radius Inc. began online sales of its software for handling digital photos. The Mountain View, Calif., company did almost nothing to promote its Web site, says Mark Housley, chairman and chief executive officer, because it didn't want to alienate its traditional distributors. Nonetheless, within three months, nearly 10% of its sales were coming from the Internet. "The Web lets us try new promotions quickly, at almost no cost," Mr. Housley adds.

Yet the executive shudders at the notion of trying to turn his Web site into a heavily promoted discount marketplace for Radius software. Distributors still provide more than 90% of his sales, he says, and he doesn't want to risk anything that might hurt their profit—and perhaps lead them to stop stocking Radius products.

Software maker Intuit Inc. shares this aversion to online discounting. "We could decide to market aggressively on the Web," says William Harris, the Mountain View, Calif., company's CEO, "but we don't do that, in deference to our third-party resellers." Intuit for more than a year has offered best-selling programs such as Quicken and TurboTax on its Web site, but only at list price. Discounting is left to the bricks-and-mortar retailers who deliver the bulk of its sales.

Outside the high-tech sector, manufacturers aren't feeling as much immediate pressure to decide their online commerce strategy—but the same tensions loom. "None of them really want to start selling on the Web, but all of them feel compelled to do so," says Trevor Traina, president of CompareNet Inc., a San Francisco provider of online shopping information.

A year ago, he says, most manufacturers viewed the Internet as a way to disseminate product brochures. Now, they increasingly are devising ways for customers to place on-line orders, rather than lose that business to an online rival.

In the airline industry, AMR Corp.'s American Airlines unit has signed up 1.6 million people who get regular e-mail about cut-rate fares available that weekend. John Samuel, American's head of Internet commerce, calls the program "a clear home run." It gives American a quick, cheap way to communicate directly with fliers and generally lets the carrier avoid the usual overhead of about $20 a ticket associated with staffing a toll-free phone bank, as well as travel agents' commissions that run as high as 8%.

As the airline moves into electronic commerce, it must tread carefully to avoid alienating travel agents or hampering its ability to sell seats at much higher prices. "We don't want our site to become a haven for cheap seats," Mr. Samuel says. "But we will use it to manage inventory." In particular, he says, the Internet is a great way to sell "distressed inventory"—the long-haul Saturday afternoon flights unpopular with both business and vacation travelers.

To some companies, even such limited use of Internet commerce is unsettling. Minnesota Mining & Manufacturing Co., St. Paul, Minn., lists hundreds of its products on its Web site, but generally doesn't provide any way to order them directly from the company. That is deliberate, says Peter Jacobs, an Internet strategist for 3M.

"We are very concerned about our distribution-channel structure," Mr. Jacobs says. "We take care not to damage those relationships." Besides, he says, many customer-generated orders would be too tiny to be profitable. A single consumer might want two dozen floppy disks, for example, he says. His company would much rather fill two loading-dock pallets with computer disks and ship them off to a distributor.

One of the starkest contrasts in online strategy is playing out in the home-mortgage market. Many big lenders, such as Chase Manhattan Corp., PNC Bank Corp. and Countrywide Credit Industries Inc., have begun offering consumers ways to execute most of a mortgage application online. Doing so is faster and cheaper than the traditional approach of having a loan officer collect all the paperwork, says Cameron King, head of Countrywide's Internet efforts. Online transactions now account for 1% of Countrywide's loan volume, he says, and could grow rapidly.

Not a 'Threat'

But the nation's biggest mortgage lender, the Norwest Mortgage unit of Wells Fargo Co., is fighting the trend. It has built a 4,000-person sales force, with more branch offices than any of its rivals. Face-to-face contact is crucial in Norwest's business model; even on its Web site, Norwest repeatedly tells mortgage seekers to call a toll-free number and talk to a loan officer.

For now, Norwest's approach is keeping its powerful sales force happy. "When we first started hearing about mortgages on the Internet, a lot of sales people panicked," says Scharol Battaglia, manager of Norwest's Saratoga, Calif., office. "They thought they'd be replaced. But when you take care of customers the way we do, the Internet isn't really a threat."

Online competitors say that's exactly what they want to hear. Seth Werner, chief executive officer of First Mortgage Network Inc., Plantation, Fla., calculates that he can originate mortgages online at a cost of about 0.6% of the loan amount-about half of what traditional lenders spend. The biggest savings, he says, come from eliminating costly sales forces packed with loan officers earning $150,000 a year or more.

If some of the mortgage industry's giants don't want to change their business models, Mr. Werner says, that gives him plenty of room to undercut their rates by a fraction of a percentage point, and still do business more profitably. In the hotly competitive mortgage market, he says, "the Internet is clearly the future."

48

Movies soon could be just a click away

By David Lieberman
USA TODAY

NEW YORK — Slowly and quietly, a battle is starting to build that could revolutionize the way millions of consumers approach home entertainment—and spend billions of dollars.

After years of false starts, several cable operators are making serious plans to offer video on demand. Subscribers will be able to use their remote controls to choose the movies they want, watch them whenever they want, and enjoy the same flexibility they have with videotapes to pause, rewind and fast-forward.

That's tantamount to a declaration of war on 28,000 video stores.

"The threat to Blockbuster is starting to take hold," Salomon Smith Barney analyst Spencer Grimes says.

There's a lot at stake. More than 83 million families own VCRs. They will spend about $8 billion this year to rent videos, and an additional $9 billion to buy them. Video sales account for about 57% of the revenue that Hollywood studios make from their films.

But cable operators and allied technology companies say that video on demand can crash that party.

"By the end of 2000 this should become something that the majority of U.S. homes will have access to," DIVA Systems President Alan Bushell says.

His technology company is first out of the gate, offering about 250 video on demand movies to 1,000 cable subscribers outside of Philadelphia. It reports that each customer orders, on average, more than four movies a month. (Most video renters pay for about three per month.)

What's more, video on demand users often "drastically cut, if not totally eliminate, their use of video stores," Bushell says.

That possibility frightens home-video retailers. But they say movie studios will help them stop cable from taking over.

"Hollywood would be a ghost town if it weren't for the video industry," Video Software Dealers Association President Jeffrey Eves says.

Cable executives counter that Tinseltown's love affair with video stores will cool once moguls see consumers using cable's Godzilla variant of today's pay-per-view service.

FAST-FORWARD TO THE FUTURE

Video on demand (VOD) offers several advantages over rental stores. Advertised films are never out of stock. The pictures and sound can be as clear as a signal from a satellite, which is much sharper than a tape. And there are no late-return fees, because there's nothing to return.

Video on demand was one of the few success stories from Time Warner's interactive Full Service Network in Orlando, Fla., which lasted from 1995 to 1997. Although Time Warner won't disclose specific results, consumers there are said to have ordered as many as seven movies a month.

"Orlando was a time machine," Jim Chiddix, Time Warner Cable's chief technical officer, says. "It gave us a window on what consumers would do with technology that would become cheaper in the future."

That future is here. DIVA's service outside Philadelphia has been running since September. Customers pay a $5.95 monthly charge, and about $3.95 for a recent movie—on top of their usual cable bill.

Although the average videotape rental costs less, at $2.67 a shot, the convenience of video on demand makes it worthwhile says Joseph O'Brien, who has used the DIVA system since March. He has stopped visiting the video store, where he used to rent several movies a month.

"This way I sit back in my recliner and push some buttons," says O'Brien, 68, a retiree who used to work as a machine operator for Scott Paper. "Like anything, you pay for convenience. If I were to get (the video on demand system) taken out, my grandkids would force me out."

Over the next year, operators such as Time Warner, Cox, Comcast, Cablevision Systems and Adelphia are expected to either deploy or test video on demand in about 50 cities, including Austin, Texas; Baltimore; and San Diego.

Video on demand is possible now because cable operators are starting to give consumers the new generation of digital cable boxes. Tele-Communications Inc. CEO John Malone says the devices could be nearly ubiquitous among cable's 65 million subscribers by 2001. Wall Street analysts are more conservative, envisioning about 15 million digital cable homes by then.

Meanwhile, the cost of providing video on demand to the home has plummeted. Cable operators store movies on hard drives in computer file servers. When a subscriber orders a flick, the system transmits the video and audio through the cable as a stream of digital information. "The (equipment) cost three years ago per stream was in the thousands," says Yvette

Gordon, director of interactive technologies for Sea-Change International. "Now it's under $100."

Upcoming tests will determine the mix of prices and services that inspire consumers to dig deepest into their wallets.

"They really don't know how to market VOD," says Scientific-Atlanta's H. Allen Ecker, who's president of the technology company's subscriber systems. "Do you charge $4 per movie, or (a flat rate of) $20 per month? They need trials."

Enthusiasts say video on demand will lure consumers into a bigger world of impulse buying. For example, viewers who settle in for a movie might also buy a pizza via cable TV. When Time Warner and Pizza Hut offered this service in Orlando, they discovered that video on demand customers tended to order more toppings than did phone callers.

NAYSAYERS WEIGH IN

Some operators, including TCI, aren't ready to take the plunge. They believe they can attract nearly as many movie fans by offering dozens of pay-per-view channels and giving viewers lots of different start times for new films.

"We are pushing hot and heavy on near-video-on-demand," says TCI's Tony Werner, executive vice president for engineering and technical operations. He adds that once subscribers have digital boxes it will be simple for TCI to switch to full video on demand when it proves profitable.

The most passionate cheerleader for video on demand, Time Warner, is leaving little to chance. Some of its cable systems won't accept ads from video stores, since that would help a competitor. That policy has hurt Video Hut, a 10-store chain based in Fayetteville, N.C. Time Warner's cable system covers about 85% of Video Hut's market.

Time Warner is "panicking and scared," Video Hut President Thomas Warren says. "They clearly say, you're a competitor of ours so we're not going to sell you these ads."

Time Warner Cable spokesman Mike Luftman says the company does not have a national policy on video retailers' ads, but its local systems have "the right to accept or reject any advertising without an explanation."

Video retailers say that they're unfazed by cable's tough talk about video on demand. After all, they note, VCRs are in 85% of all homes—people won't want that investment to go to waste—and cable's track record with pay per view is unimpressive.

About 32 million subscribers have set-top cable boxes capable of delivering pay per view (PPV). People in those homes are expected to spend a mere $500 million in 1998—about $1.30 per home per month—for movies and events.

That anemic performance is partly due to Hollywood's decision to let video stores offer new releases exclusively for about 53 days before they migrate to pay per view.

THE VIDEO ADVANTAGE

Video stores covet that advantage—and they are maneuvering to protect it. Major chains, including Blockbuster and Hollywood Video, have strengthened their ties to studios by scrapping the system in which stores simply bought videos and kept all of the rental revenue. Studios now give stores extra copies of new releases, and collect as much as 45% of the cash consumers spend on rentals. "We've doubled the number of new releases on our shelves," Blockbuster's Karen Raskopf says.

Since studios have a stake in a video's rental performance, some are spending more to promote them. MGM/UA, for example, bought time in the last episode of *Seinfeld* to push the video of its James Bond flick, *Tomorrow Never Dies*.

Retailers also play to Hollywood's fear that cable customers might crack video on demand encryption codes, make perfect digital copies of films, and sell them on the black market.

"In some parts of the country, you can pay the cable installer a few hundred bucks, and he'll give you the technology you need. It's a serious problem," Eves says. "You're already talking north of $8 billion per year in losses to the cable companies from signal theft. And in some pay-per-view events, such as boxing matches, the (theft) rate can be 50%."

Supporters of video on demand say that is a red herring. If someone cracks a digital encryption code "you just download a new algorithm," SeaChange's Gordon says.

Still, Hollywood seems uninterested in giving video on demand a break at the expense of video retailers—for example by shortening the lead time when a movie will only be available in stores.

"I look at VOD as an enhanced PPV, so I see it as the same window as PPV," says Mitch Koch, who oversees Disney's video distribution in North America. "If consumers want to see a movie first (after the theaters), they'll go to a video store."

All of these uncertainties give forecasters pause in predicting when, or whether, video on demand will create havoc for video stores. "To say the jury is still out is being polite," says Sanford C. Bernstein analyst Tom Wolzien.

49

Nafta Reality Check: Trucks, Trains, Ships Face Costly Delays

Weak Infrastructure Stands In the Way of Free Trade; The Captain's Long Wait

Improvements Take Forever

By Anna Wilde Mathews
Staff Reporter of The Wall Street Journal

Close up, Nafta is not a pretty sight.

Along the Mexican border, some freight trains have been backed up all the way to Kansas, waiting to squeeze through one-track crossings. Seething, honking lines of trucks choke tiny Texas towns with Manhattan-style traffic jams. Even ships have problems: Outside the busiest Mexican port, Veracruz, 12 were at anchor in the sparkling Gulf waters one recent day as they waited for scarce docking space.

"You have to get used to it," sighs Capt. Czeslaw Pacholczyk, whose ship recently sailed from Houston to Mexico.

Trade among the U.S., Canada and Mexico under the North American Free Trade Agreement is hitting a giant pothole: There aren't enough bridges, rails and docks to handle the goods, and the existing structures are often in the wrong places, mired in the traffic of busy downtowns. The result can be hours-long delays for billions of dollars of goods crossing North American borders.

"This infrastructure was built for a different era," says James Giermanski, a professor at Texas A&M International University in Laredo. "It's hamstringing the trade."

Extra Expenses

The stakes couldn't be much higher. Last year, the U.S. had $477 billion in trade with Mexico and Canada, up 13% from 1997. Squeezing the flood through border bottlenecks spreads extra expenses through the economies of all three nations—as much as $2.5 billion a year. But analysts say the real cost may be to Nafta's much-vaunted potential as a truly opentrading milieu, the main selling point for the controversial 1994 pact. Supporters once advertised a powerhouse trade bloc of three closely knit economies.

But "if we're really going to have free trade, you just can't have a truck waiting in line for five miles," says Bernard LaLonde, professor emeritus at Ohio State University. "From day to day, you don't know what's going to happen. It's contrary to the logic of Nafta."

That's a major problem in today's hurry-up economy, where retailers and manufacturers demand clockwork precision in transportation to keep factories running and store shelves full. Many companies complain if freight is just 15 minutes late and can hardly imagine waiting hours for urgently needed goods. Cole-Haan Inc., a unit of Nike Inc., even yanked a shipment of 144 pairs of shoes off a truck that was stuck in Mexico for five days; a retail customer was already running ads for them. The footwear flew by Federal Express—at more than twice the cost.

Consumers Pay the Price

For U.S. auto companies alone, one study put the price of delays at Laredo at almost $3 million annually in wasted time, higher labor costs and extra storage expenses. "There's not a flow-through process at the border," says Stephen Harley, a logistics manager for Ford Motor Co. Ultimately, of course, those extra costs trickle down to consumers; transportation accounts for 5% to 10% of retail prices.

Though the worst delays occur at about a dozen choke points in all three nations, the price tag to fix the infrastructure would be steep: more than $2.5 billion. Some improvements are already on the way, including rail yards, ship berths and bridges. But many other plans are bogged down by complex bureaucratic rules or local resistance. Permission to build a new bridge across the Rio Grande, for instance, requires filings with more than 25 government agencies in Mexico and the U.S.

'If We Build It . . . '

Meanwhile, some bridges and other facilities built in recent years are in little-used places or have bad connections. One span, in Los Indios, Texas, gets less than half the trucks it could handle; it's 20 miles from the major crossing at Brownsville, where the downtown is crammed with freight heading to Mexico. A crossing in Calexico, Calif., waited months for a highway to be built on the Mexican side. For a while, the U.S. road connected to nothing but sand dunes.

"In some places, there's been an 'if we build it, they will come' attitude," says Rob Harrison, an economist at the University of Texas' Center for Transportation Research in Austin.

Nafta itself didn't make any provisions for new infrastructure. Though the federal government has to approve new border resources such as bridges, the initiative comes at the local level, with towns and counties typically raising money and planning their own structures. "The infrastructure is mixed," says M. Elizabeth Swope, coordinator for U.S.-Mexico border affairs at the State Department. It's "good in some places and bad in others."

Of course, a weak infrastructure isn't the only thing holding Nafta back; every agency from customs to immigration to law enforcement has a hand in inspecting and bogging down border trade. U.S. efforts to detect illegal drugs, including searches by trained dogs and drilling holes in truck trailers to find hidden compartments, also slow things down. Cultural variances, including differing work schedules in different nations, can create problems. "We lose half our time with inspections and paperwork," says Larry Fields, president of the Texas Mexican Railway Co. of Laredo.

But it's no customs agency that draws Capt. Pacholczyk's ire on his recent voyage. It's almost 4 a.m. when his big ship, the Renate Schulte, arrives at the Mexican port of Tampico, before going on to Veracruz. He picks up the radio to call for a pilot to steer him into the harbor, a service available 24 hours a day at all U.S. ports. But he gets no response; the port doesn't guarantee late-night pilots unless the shipping line calls ahead.

"It's not professional behavior," complains Capt. Pacholczyk, a meticulous man who sports a neatly pressed shirt on the bridge even in the middle of the night.

Not until afternoon the next day can his ship, operated by Crowley Maritime Corp. of Oakland, Calif., finally ease through the narrow channel, with tiny fishing boats darting around it. The dock is crowded and chaotic, with workers on bicycles dodging cars, trucks and forklifts. Corn unloaded from another freighter is scattered across the pavement where it missed the opening of a rail car. Tampico has no modern cranes for lifting truck-size cargo containers, the way most U.S. and European ports do, so vessels use their own cargo lifters, which can take twice as long.

"There's hardly any space," says Rinus Schepen, a Crowley vice president, adding that his ships have waited as long as 10 hours for a berth at Tampico.

Stalled in Laredo

Cargo can wait even longer than that in Laredo, by far the busiest U.S.-Mexico crossing point; last year, an average of $65 million in goods funneled through the city each day. There, the trucks form lines as long as four miles through the center of town. One City Council member even suggested setting up roadside toilets for the stranded drivers. While waiting for trailers to cross from Mexico to the U.S., where they can be switched to American tractors, U.S. truckers crowd movie theaters and restaurants; a few have even become regulars at the local Casa Blanca Golf Course.

The problem: Much of the freight flows over two aging bridges in the center of town. Last year, after decades of heavy use, a 3-foot hole opened up in one of them. "You could see the river," says Rafael Garcia, manager of Laredo's bridges. The problem has been fixed.

(Cont.)

Trains don't do much better there. The most heavily used border rail bridge is a one-track structure that was built four decades ago and rattles with 1,250 rail cars crossing every day. Traffic over it is controlled by Simon Medina Jr., an unflappable Texas Mexican Railway employee who works in a dilapidated shack with a plastic-foam cup plugging a hole in the door. Sometimes, Mr. Medina speaks into two phones, to one in Spanish and the other in English; often, he must referee between rival railroads. The companies "act like babies," he says. "They say, 'Why can't my train go? I was here first.'"

On a recent night, a mile-long train of coffee, tar and steel crawls through downtown Laredo, past the public library and rows of small houses, blocking annoyed truck drivers and blasting its horn to warn pedestrians. Suddenly, a gauge inside the locomotive plunges: An impatient teenage bicyclist has unhooked some cars. Brakeman George Dabdoub leaps out to fix it, returning a few minutes later, relieved that drivers aren't swearing at him.

Help on the Way

Railroads, shipping lines and transportation officials say part of the problem is the time lag between planning construction and actual building. Even in faraway Chicago, where southbound Canadian rail shipments can wait for days, Canadian National Railway Co. and Illinois Central Corp. plan to merge their systems, so trains can go through the city without stopping. Texas Mexican is building a 480-acre facility where government inspections will be held, to avoid blocking the Laredo rail bridge, while both Laredo and Brownsville plan to build new bridges.

The port of Veracruz is investing more than $300 million to modernize, creating new docking space and fixing up cargo cranes, but shipping lines say it can't keep up with the relentless growth in traffic. One problem: protected historical monuments such as the 400-year-old stone fortress that was built to repel pirates but now takes up a chunk of prime waterfront land. And one central dock is blocked by two turn-of-the-century warehouses, which also have historical-landmark protection.

The U.S. Congress also is stepping in to speed things up, as part of the big six-year transportation bill passed last month. The bill allots $700 million for border projects and major road corridors for north-south trade. Although states have to compete for the money, winners will probably include California, Texas and Michigan.

But such legislation won't solve the problem of the Peace Bridge in Buffalo, N.Y. There, officials have been fighting for four years to build a new bridge to supplement the 70-year-old, three-lane structure, which on an average day is crammed with 4,000 exhaust-belching trucks crossing the Niagara River between the U.S. and Canada. Locals oppose the somewhat-chunky green-painted project that the bridge authority designed; they want a more-graceful suspension bridge.

An engineering class at a local university prepared six designs for an assignment, while a local architect suggested colorful awnings that would protect the bridge from the elements. "We've had people weigh in with almost every kind of plan imaginable," says Steve Mayer, operations manager for the bridge.

What's more, potential border crossings face a complex international government approval process that has mired one group, in McAllen, Texas, for six years. There, officials have spent nearly $2 million and filed a 14-foot pile of documents with U.S. and Mexican officials for permission to build seven miles of road and a four-lane bridge. The research included everything from interviews with car drivers (to determine traffic patterns) to an archaeologist who went over the site with a shovel and a spoon (looking for Indian relics) to a naturalist (plans now incorporate three bus-size tunnels under the road to help ocelots cross safely).

There may be at least one simple reason why governments are slow to move: Some projects have failed to shift traffic. Los Indios, Texas, for example, has a well-lit crossing with four lanes and a highway sign promising that the Free Trade Bridge is open 6 a.m. to midnight. The chamber of commerce in nearby Harlingen, Texas, which helped finance the bridge, has even offered gift certificates at shops for locals who cross over.

But the bridge is nearly deserted at 7:30 one recent evening, with a trickle of cars and just one 18-wheeler parked at the U.S. end. Though bridge officials say traffic is growing, Gary Nichols, marketing director at Contract Freighters Inc. of Joplin, Mo., one of the biggest U.S. cross-border trucking companies, says he can't remember one of his rigs ever using the crossing.

"It's the bridge to nowhere," he says.

50

READY TO SHOP UNTIL THEY DROP

Central Europe's rising middle class is on a buying binge

Philosophy professor Nina Gladziuk thinks carefully before shelling out her hard-earned zlotys for Poland's dazzling array of consumer goods. But spend she certainly does. Although she earns just $550 a month from two academic jobs, Gladziuk, 41, enjoys making purchases: They are changing her lifestyle after years of deprivation under communism. In the past year, she has furnished a new apartment in a popular neighborhood near Warsaw's Kabaty Forest, splurged on foreign-made beauty products, and spent a weekend in Paris before attending a seminar financed by her university. "None of this was available before," she says.

Meet Central Europe's fast-rising consumer class. From white-collar workers like Gladziuk to factory workers in Budapest to hip young professionals in Prague, incomes are rising and confidence surging as a result of four years of economic growth. In the region's leading economies—the Czech Republic, Hungary, and Poland—the new class of buyers is growing not only in numbers but also in sophistication. Although they earn only a fraction of the wages of their counterparts in Western Europe, half of all Czechs consider themselves middle class, according to a recent poll. In Hungary, ad agency Young & Rubicam Inc. labels 11% of the country as "aspirers," with dreams of the good life and buying habits to match. Nearly one-third of all Czechs, Hungarians, and Poles—some 17 million people—are under 30 years old, eager to snap up everything from the latest fashions to compact disks.

These rising wants and needs offer big opportunities to companies from Polish food group Agros Holding to Citicorp. Whether they are selling beauty aids or leisure activities, companies are delivering the idea that their products can improve—or transform—the lives of Central Europeans. That's an alluring message in a region that spent most of the past 50 years cloaked in communist drabness or, more recently, faced the harsh realities of the transition to capitalism. Although cash is still king, companies and banks are teaching Central Europeans how to expand their purchasing power through consumer borrowing. With annual inflation dropping from triple digits to under 15%, credit is fueling increases in the sale of big-ticket items such as appliances and autos. Indeed, car sales in Poland raced ahead by 30% last year alone.

TUMBLING TABOOS. In such a frenetic environment, marketers are spending big to capture—and hold—the attention of consumers. "It used to be as simple as putting your product out there and putting up a few billboards," says John K. Sheppard, president of Coca-Cola East Central Europe. No longer. This year, companies will pour $2.3 billion into advertising, twice as much as just three years ago (chart, page 125). Central Europe is awash in sweepstakes appealing to consumers' get-rich-quick fantasies as these companies test new products. Old taboos are falling, too. In communist days, sexual images were banned in the media. Now, in Prague, ads for an energy drink called Erektus depict a Pope-look-alike eyeing a woman's bare legs. "For the man who wants what he can't have," says the copy.

The shopping spree is remaking Central Europe's distribution networks. Traditional mom-and-pop shops are disappearing as hypermarkets and malls spring up in major cities. In December, German retailing giant Metro opened Poland's largest shopping center, a $56 million behemoth in Czeladz, in the industrial heartland. The company will plow $555 million into Poland in the next five years. Similarly, a venture headed by Lehman Brothers Inc., the U.S. investment bank, is sinking $150 million into 10 new malls in the Czech Republic, Hungary, and Poland.

Meanwhile, service companies such as DHL International are seeing their business take off—as they expand networks for distributing goods for foreign importers and local manufacturers alike. "We are predicting growth of at least 25% a year in the region for the next five years," says Douglas West, commercial director for Central, Eastern, and Southern Europe.

In and around Warsaw, the surge in consumer spending is rising from the very ground: Young professionals are building thousands of new houses on the outskirts of town. Others are renovating their socialist-era apartments, adding sparkling new kitchens, built-in wooden cabinets, and expensive double-paned windows. Ikea Holdings, the Swedish furnishing company, is cashing in big on that trend, as is Potten & Pannen, a Czech marketer of high-end Western cookware and cutlery.

CASHLESS. But the region's hottest marketing opportunity these days is clearly financial services. Until now, many Czechs, Hungarians, and Poles have been reluctant to open bank accounts. Some worry the banks are too shaky. Others deplore the abysmal service. To combat that image, Bank Handlowy, a big commercial lender in Poland, has launched a new consumer division that will soon be offering everything from life insurance to car loans. Salespeople for Citibank in Poland are calling on customers at homes to pitch credit-card services. And in Hungary, debit cards are taking off. OTP Bank, the nation's largest savings bank, plans to issue 1 million cards by yearend. Katalin Szekely, 30, a manager at L.M. Ericsson in Budapest, uses her new OTP debit card to buy groceries at Tesco PLC. "I feel a lot better because I don't have to carry around all that cash," she says.

Plastic is just the beginning, however. Next to come is an explosion in mutual funds, as governments begin to reform their overburdened state pension systems. Starting next year, for example, $2 billion in Polish pension contributions will begin to go to private companies for the first time. Three dozen mutual-fund and insurance companies are seeking licenses to set up pension funds. Some 6 million workers will have to sign up with a private fund manager, starting on Jan. 1, 1999. "Every company will spend millions of dollars on commercials and advertising," says Tomasz Orlik, director of Pioneer Investment, Poland's new pension-fund department.

Central Europe's surging financial industry is contributing to the growth of the new consumer class. Just as in the West, the region's financial types are becoming role models for some workers and professionals lower down the consumer pyramid. With incomes of $30,000 a year and often much more, they are indulging in purchases they once could only dream of. Take Dusan Tejkal, 25, owner of Private Investors, a Prague brokerage. With a yearly income exceeding $80,000, Tejkal can afford to spend freely on exotic vacations, fancy restaurants, and fine clothes. This past spring, he took time off to ski in Austria and dive in the coral reefs off the coast of Belize. "When you want to escape, it' s worth paying extra," he says. "It's worth making sure that everything will be perfect."

Although such high rollers still make up a minute percentage of the population in Central Europe, more companies are targeting

(Cont.)

them. Czech mobile-phone company Euro-Tel saw its sales double last year, to $297 million, as it pushed its phones as symbols of worldliness for the country's young business class. Profits rose 89%, to $111 million. Travel companies, local nightclubs, auto makers such as BMW, and design houses such as Versace have all begun to cater to Central Europe's new rich.

TEEN ANGELS. With family incomes rising, Central Europe's youth are also a big new target. Since young people tend to live at home until they get married, they have money to spend on food, fashion, and fun. Coca-Cola Co. has gone to great lengths to grab their attention. One scheme: the Fanta Fun Taxi in Hungary. Coke joins local radio stations around the country to sponsor a weekly promotional event. Contestants peel the label off a bottle of Fanta and send it in to the station with their name, address, and phone number. The prize for the drawing: a 12-hour, chauffeur-driven joyride along the streets of the contestant's hometown in an orange, tail-finned, vintage Cadillac, with "Fanta" splashed in bold letters across the hood. On a recent Saturday night, Adam Szorenyi, 20, and three pals whooped and waved as they tooled around Budapest in their Fun Taxi.

In two years, Coke's marketing budget will have shifted from 90% advertising to a 50-50 split between advertising and promotions such as the fun taxi. "You've got to capture [consumers] with an experience," says Paul Garrison, managing director of Coca-Cola in Hungary. The strategy is paying off. Two years ago, Coke was neck and neck with Pepsi. Now, the company says, it sells 40% more soda than its leading rival.

Sportswear companies are also courting Central Europe's youth. Warsaw and Krakow are dotted with outlets of Nike Inc. and Reebok International Inc., selling shoes and other gym gear. In Hungary, mobile-phone companies such as Westel are chalking up sales among the under-20 crowd, as they offer service limited to domestic calls, along with low rates in the evening and on weekends.

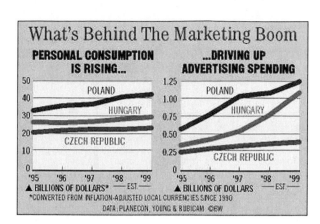

While young people and professionals represent an important market for many companies, manufacturers of household goods are going after a much broader spectrum. Procter & Gamble Co. and Unilever Group have poured millions of dollars into selling detergent, shampoo, and deodorant since they entered the region in the late 1980s. Their advertisements are partly geared to explaining their products to consumers who previously couldn't afford them. "People have an extreme interest in how products work," says Stef G.H. Kranendijk, P&G's chief executive in Poland.

In some cases, Central Europeans snap up pricey, foreign brands for special occasions but rely on cheaper, local products for everyday use. Despite the efforts of P&G and Unilever to unseat Hypo as the No.1 bleach in Hungary, it still commands a 65% market share because it costs one-fourth as much as rival brands. "In low-end products, it is price loyalty, not brand loyalty, [that motivates consumers]," says Jeno Andics, head of Mareco, a Budapest market-research company.

Indeed, low-cost local brands are giving Western companies headaches. In response, P&G, for example, slashed the cost of its new Bonux laundry detergent in Poland by selling it in plastic bags rather than boxes. "Poles said they didn't need expensive packaging," says Kranendjik. The marketing message trumpeted the savings: "Bonux cleans everything except your pockets." Now, the company's Bonux and Vizir are top sellers in the detergent market, where P&G commands a 40% share. P&G's total sales in Poland are expected to hit $500 million this year.

The fight between foreign and local brands isn't only about price, however. As

WHAT THE MERCHANTS ARE BOOSTING		
PRODUCT/SERVICE	**COMPANIES**	**THE SELL**
FINANCIAL SERVICES	Citibank, Pioneer, AIG, Handlowy Bank	Buyers should use less cash and more plastic, keep their savings in banks, and invest for the future as safety nets crumble.
HEALTH, BEAUTY, FASHION	Unilever, Procter & Gamble, Toma, L'Oréal, Hugo Boss, Johnson & Johnson	The new consumer has the money and time to care about appearance, by buying everything from toothpaste to designer clothes.
LEISURE ACTIVITIES	Malev, Lot, Lufthansa, Bonton, Gemini Group	Make up for time lost when borders were closed under communism. See the world, have fun.
HOME	Ikea, Potten & Pannen	If you can't afford to build a new house, redo your old apartment.

DATA: BUSINESS WEEKDATA: BUSINESS WEEK

(Cont.)

confidence grows, the appeal of exotic products from the West is fading. Local companies are using patriotic pitches to win back customers. In Hungary, Zwack Unicum Co., a distiller and wholesaler of spirits, airs TV spots that trace the 200-year history of Unicum, its big-selling after-dinner drink. In the Czech Republic, beverage producer Toma has knocked Pepsi into third place in the cola market by hawking its "Czech made" soft drinks as an antidote to the stresses of urban life. Says Zofia Gaber, president of food producer Agros, which makes popular Fortuna juices: "The inscription 'Polish product' brings us more consumers" than foreign rivals can attract.

As a result, Western companies are having to step up efforts to develop products—and marketing campaigns—that are geared to local needs and attitudes. That in turn is creating a demand for local talent to fill advertising and marketing positions, which can pay as much as $180,000 a year. One of the new breed is 28-year-old Szymon Gutkowski, strategic director at Corporate Profiles DDB, a joint venture between a local company and DDB Needham Worldwide Communications Group Inc., based in New York. Back in the early 1990s, Gutkowski was a political organizer for the forerunner to today's Freedom Union party. Now, however, he advises foreign companies to replace dubbed-over TV spots with commercials conceived with Polish tastes in mind. One ad he created, for example, features characters from novels of Henryk Sienkiewicz, the Polish author who won the Nobel prize for literature in 1905.

As more manufacturers, distributors, and marketers pile into Central Europe, consumers will be the winners. They'll benefit most from price competition, as companies jostle to tally up sales. Perhaps more important is that Central Europe's long period of painful economic reform is starting to pay off. The growing middle class promises to be not just the source of new business for companies. It also offers Central Europe the hope that some day its prosperity will match that of its neighbors to the West.

TREATING THE CLIENT RIGHT IN BUDAPEST

It's a typically hectic afternoon at the office of McCann-Erickson Budapest. Janos Serenyi, director of the operation, calls out to his creative chief: "When does the Gillette campaign begin?" On the phone, the chief executive of Opel Hungary, a subsidiary of General Motors Corp., is waiting to speak to him. And mock-ups for a Hungarian Insurance Co. advertising campaign clutter Serenyi's desk, ready for his approval.

NO SHARK. McCann-Erickson is Hungary's top ad agency. Since it set up shop here a decade ago, it has led the pack in billings. Last year, the Budapest office bought $47 million in media time and space for its clients—63% more than No.2 Initiative Media International and 100% more than Zenith Media Services Inc., media buyers for Bates Saatchi & Saatchi.

Serenyi's client list is a who's who of big business in Hungary: Coca-Cola, Johnson & Johnson, Unilever, plus local advertisers such as mobile telephone company Pannon GSM. To stay ahead as competition grows more intense, Serenyi relies heavily on local talent. And he's spinning off special units to cater to the demands of clients for online selling as well as events, direct, and health-related marketing. "We have to offer a range of marketing and communications services and really tailor it to the client," he says.

With his fuzzy hair and thick mustache, Serenyi doesn't look like an eastern version of a Madison Avenue shark. But he has come a long way. He was editing a karate magazine and working as a freelance public-relations specialist when McCann-Erickson asked him to open its Budapest office in 1988. Although he had no advertising experience, he was a natural salesman. "We started small. I did the media and production. I was the manager and my own secretary," Serenyi recalls.

From those humble beginnings, Serenyi built up to a staff of 125, all but four of whom are Hungarian. He taught them how to bend over backwards for customers and paid them well once they learned the ropes. Nowadays, a 24-year-old account executive can take home three times the $325 a month Serenyi earned when he first started.

Looking ahead, Serenyi sees more competition among agencies and even higher demands from clients, foreign and local alike. But Serenyi has always enjoyed coping with the challenges of the local scene. He remembers his first lecture at Dresden's University of Economics 30 years ago. "There are two dangerous things for an economy: computers and advertising," his Marxist professor declared. The streetwise adman is determined to keep ignoring conventional wisdom and stay out in front.

By Christopher Condon in Budapest

By David Woodruff in Warsaw, with James Drake in Prague, Christopher Condon in Budapest, and Peggy Simpson in Warsaw.

51

Where Are the Gloves ? They Were Stocklifted By a Rival Producer

Many Vendors Pay Big Sums To Get Competing Goods Off Major Chains' Shelves

The Origins of Close-Outs

By Yumiko Ono

Staff Reporter of The Wall Street Journal

ATHENS, Ga. — At the giant Lowe's Home Improvement Warehouse store here, in aisle 23 near the lawn mowers, hundreds of garden gloves recently vanished.

The missing merchandise was manufactured by Wells Lamont, the nation's largest garden-glove company. And almost overnight, the empty shelves were restocked last January with gloves made by Wells Lamont's archrival, Midwest Quality Gloves Inc. The same scene played out in 100 other Lowe's stores: Wells Lamont gloves were replaced by Midwest gloves — floral, pigskin, cowhide and others.

Behind the inventory switch was Midwest. It had struck a deal with Lowe's to buy 225,000 pairs of Wells Lamont gloves and clear them all out so it could fill shelf after shelf with its own product.

Spreading Tactic

This shadowy retail tactic — called a stocklift or buyback — is spreading. Makers of everything from party napkins to bicycle chains are lifting truckloads of competitors' products everywhere from Kmarts to Revco drugstores. Then they dump the merchandise into a sprawling underground pipeline for resale by faraway, and sometimes foreign, retailers.

Few products are exempt from the shelf switcheroo. Gemini Industries Inc., which makes power adapters and leather cases for cellular phones, says it has stocklifted products made by rival Katy Industries Inc. The First Years Inc., a baby-products company, says it recently stocklifted bibs and toys made by the Gerber Products unit of Novartis AG of Switzerland and Safety 1st Inc. The list of the stocklifted includes pet toys, humidifiers, flashlights, faucets and glue. As retailers consolidate into larger, fewer chains, suppliers are working harder to get into stores and get rivals out — taking an initial

hit in the hope that a buyback will pay off in the long run.

"Buybacks are a necessary evil in gaining market share," says Michael Brooks, chief executive of International Purchase Systems Inc., an Elmsford, N.Y., liquidator that disposes of stocklifted merchandise. "You get the market share immediately, but at a price."

Legal Risk

Legally, the tactic is dicey. A company may violate federal antitrust laws if it stocklifts from a competitor so often as to shut it out of a market, says Richard M. Steuer, an antitrust lawyer at Kaye Scholer Fierman Hays Handler LLP in New York. But such cases, brought under the century-old Sherman Antitrust Act, are difficult to prove, he adds.

Nonetheless, some legal experts deplore the tactic. Marianne Jennings, a professor of legal and ethical studies at Arizona State University's business school, worries that consumers don't know why some products vanish — or turn up — in a store. "You've taken away what should drive the market, which is the preferred product," she says.

Companies are generally reluctant to discuss stocklifting. When pressed, they frequently point fingers at one another. Retailers say new suppliers bombard them with offers to clear out rival products, and they add that retailers don't make any money on the deals because products are usually sold off at wholesale. Still, for retailers, a stocklift can help them avoid selling remaining inventory at a discount, potentially at a loss, while letting them quickly add a product that they think may sell better.

"With more competition, it's more likely that vendors will come to the table with buybacks as an option, just to try to lock in" a contract, says Greg Bridgeford, senior vice president for merchandising at Lowe's Cos. in North Wilkesboro, N.C. The No. 2 home-center chain after Home Depot Inc., Lowe's participates in "hundreds" of stocklifts a year, he says.

Costly Maneuver

Manufacturers say store managers increasingly consider stocklifts the normal way to do business with vendors. "It costs a ton of money," says Nicolaus Bruns, group product manager for humidifiers and other housewares at Bemis Manufacturing Co. But "if you want to land a major [retail] account, you're going to have to do it."

Driving the covert tactic is the emergence of product hit men, contracted to discreetly dispose of competitors' products. In many cases, the firms that do the job are barter companies or liquidators, which normally help route overstocked or flawed goods to close-out stores.

Their logistical expertise — expertise in disposing of merchandise cheaply — has become a sophisticated, powerful tool for stocklifting. Genco Distribution System, a Pittsburgh warehouse operator, has 40 warehouses nationwide and an army of 2,000 "teammates" who, among other things, use

scanners to inventory stocklifted products and then stack them in new boxes. Genco can handle the most ambitious of projects, such as a recent stocklifting of 29 trailer loads of light bulbs.

In a huge, dimly lighted warehouse in Fogelsville, Pa., Genco has special machinery to erase any sign that products once sat in a store. Price tags, for example, are instantly removed with electric sanding machines. One recent day, a few palettes in one corner were stacked with boxes filled with tick collars, flea spray and other items stocklifted from Kmart Corp. by a pet-products maker.

Some companies have an internal disposal system for stocklifted products. Magid Glove & Safety Manufacturing Co., a Chicago work-glove maker that sometimes stocklifts work gloves, says it routinely sells off the rival gloves along with its own brands to industrial customers. The buyers, usually factory workers, "don't care which brand it is," says Gigi Cohen, Magid's executive vice president of the retail division. The gloves are "like commodity items."

A detailed tracking of the stocklifted Wells Lamont gloves reveals how the tactic works. For years, Lowe's, which now has 450 blue-and-white stores, had primarily sold gloves made by Wells Lamont, a unit of Chicago's Marmon Group. But last year, it decided to try out another supplier in about 100 stores in the South.

Two Approaches

Lowe's typically has two ways to get rid of inventory. The new supplier, Midwest, could have paid Lowe's a "markdown allowance" to sell off the Wells Lamont gloves gradually, at discounted prices. But with the crucial gardening season approaching, Lowe's opted for a stocklift, to clear the shelves in one sweep. "It just gives a better presentation to the customer than mixing two different vendors," says Theresa Anderson, a Lowe's merchandising vice president.

Stephen Franke, Midwest's chief executive, declines to discuss specific stocklifts by his Chillicothe, Mo., company. But in general, he says, Midwest works hard to meet retailers' requests, including hanging the gloves on metal rods attached with clips, called "clip strips," for better shelf display. "We try to make it as easy as possible for the retailer to take our product in," Mr. Franke says, adding that such efforts have helped the company expand aggressively into new retail chains and increase sales an average of 35% a year.

Wells Lamont, the stocklift victim, had no immediate recourse. "Of course we mind it, but that's not illegal," shrugs Richard Stoller, a Wells Lamont vice president, referring to any stocklift. "We sold the product to the customer," the retailer. "It's their inventory, not ours."

So, last winter, the Wells Lamont gloves were pulled off the shelves, packed up and whisked away to a storage room. Meanwhile, Midwest arranged to sell all the gloves to Mr. Brooks, the 32-year-old liquidator. His

(Cont.)

International Purchase Systems derived 40% of last year's $6 million of sales from stocklifts and has a long list of clients that routinely dump stocklifted products in his rented Railroad Terminal Warehouse in Yonkers, N.Y.

Wells Lamont gloves arrived in the warehouse and, for weeks, sat in a dark corner. Some were stuffed into a hodgepodge of boxes that once held refrigerators and washing machines. Others, still sealed in Wells Lamont boxes, bore a sign that said "Buyback" in magic marker.

With rap music blaring from a radio hung from a pillar, four workers sorted out the gloves, discarding the shop-worn ones and separating them into about a hundred new cardboard boxes according to size and style — Cotton Hob-Nob, Vinyl-Coated KWrist, Work No Sweat and Yard & Garden with extra-long protective cuffs. Mr. Brooks calculates that 10 people working eight-hour shifts took about six weeks to sort out and count the gloves before they were resold. Time was running out. "The season is now. Spring and fall are when people do gardening," he says.

Midwest paid about $700,000 for the 225,000 pairs of gloves, Mr. Brooks says; he believes that is about the wholesale price. In turn, he says, he bought the gloves for about $280,000; the difference, about $400,000, may indicate just how eager Midwest was to get its gloves into Lowe's stores. (Midwest's Mr. Franke disputes the figures but won't say what they were.) Then, Mr. Brooks sold the gloves to an array of close-out stores, including National Wholesale Liquidators Inc. in West Hempstead, N.Y., and Building 19 Inc. in Hingham, Mass. He took in about $70,000, before his own operating expenses.

That may seem slim, but Mr. Brooks expects to be rewarded in the long run. In his tiny office on Warehouse Lane in nearby Elmsford, he shows off framed thank-you letters from customers. "When buybacks or slow-moving inventory occur, we know where to find you," says one 1996 letter from Masco Corp., which makes Peerless and Delta faucets. He has also expanded business by tapping the revenge impulse: After purchasing stocklifted products, he puts in "courtesy calls" to the victims, encouraging them to "return the favor" by working with his company.

More-Profitable Deals

Since his first stocklifting deal four summers ago, when he personally sorted paper plates and napkins in an unventilated warehouse, Mr. Brooks says these labor-intensive assignments have often led to some more-profitable deals, such as companies' excess inventory. Those products are more profitable because they are "factory fresh," free of store tags or other markings that have to be erased.

Two weeks later, with the gardening season in full bloom, some of the Wells Lamont gloves surfaced in downtown Manhattan's National Wholesale Liquidators store, amid a jumble of photo albums, vacuum cleaners, cordless telephones and $3.97 salad spinners.

In the basement of the close-out store's home-improvement department, an open box marked "Lowe's" sits next to coiled garden hoses. It is filled with Wells Lamont's purple Yard & Garden gloves. The "regular" price tag of $2.99 is crossed out. The gloves are on sale for $1.49.

52

E-tailers dash to wild, wild Web

Legions of anything.com mean tougher competition, gimmicks

By Chris Woodyard
and Lorrie Grant
USA TODAY

There's a new battle cry on the Internet: "You've got sales."

But the raft of would-be retailers rushing to the Web may end up with cyber-bruises.

Entrepreneurs and established merchants alike, emboldened by sizzling holiday Web sales, are stampeding to introduce or enhance on-line offerings.

"This industry is the wild, wild West all over again, and we love it," says Scott Blum, founder of Buy.com, a site for cut-rate merchandise on the Internet.

Yet stock prices slid on major Internet stocks Tuesday as the markets took a brief reality check. And when it comes to e-commerce, here's another dose of reality: The onslaught of on-line shopping services that will pick up steam this year are sure to make life harder for all Web merchants. Competition will stiffen, price wars will break out and sales gimmicks will abound.

"Everyone is going to want in," says James Mc-Quivey of Forrester Research, which tracks Internet trends.

Already, the Internet is filling up fast with shopping choices. The proportion of retailers selling on the Internet rose from 12% in 1997 to 39% in 1998, Ernst & Young reports.

The goal: capture shoppers such as David Smith, 52, of Narberth, Pa., anesthesiologist and Internet shopper, who says: "My real big goal in life is to never walk into a store."

Most of the more than 100 Internet shoppers who shared their holiday experiences with USA TODAY said they liked shopping on the Web. There are still plenty of potential shoppers to lure. The estimated $7.8 billion in sales over the Internet in 1998 will climb to $108 billion by 2003, Forrester predicts.

With those kinds of expectations, it's no wonder that a company such as Compaq Computer was willing to pay $220 million Monday for Shopping.com.

POTENTIAL PROBLEMS AHEAD

As sites multiply, on-line shopping may lose some of its investment allure. Potential problems include:

▲ Increased competition. As the Internet matures, consumers could face more on-line shopping choices than they want or need. Sites that aren't backed by major names, or those that just haven't figured out what works, will disappear. "A shakeout is inevitable," says Ford Cavallari of consultant Renaissance Worldwide.

▲ Discounting. Internet sellers are doing their best to establish their names and grab market share — even if it means deep discounting or big losses.

It's already happening. While most Internet retailers focus on taking advantage of their lower overall costs to beat the prices in traditional stores, other sites are trying to undercut Internet prices.

For example, while Amazon.com and Barnesandnoble.com surprised the book world by offering 30% off most hardcovers, upstart rivals, such as Buy.com,

Web eases shopping load

Marjorie Remland wanted a compact disc player for the holidays but not the hassle of going in stores and dealing with "obnoxious" sales representatives.

She started with Value America's Web site and never turned back.

"I bought a Panasonic CD player on the Internet. I paid shipping but no sales tax, and I didn't have to go near any chain stores. I figured I made out like a bandit," says Remland of Lincoln Park, N.J.

The former AT&T financial manager bought her computer last year.

Since then she has also purchased personal finance software, such as TurboTax, on line without any problems.

Aside from the ease of it all, she likes the range of goods offered on the Internet, particularly unique items.

"We celebrate Hanukkah, and I went to some of the Judaic sites on the Web and found some Disney character dreidels for a friend's grandson. I was also able to find a soft sculpture that said 'Happy Hanukkah.'"

She spent $400 to $500 shopping on line.

Remland, 55, likes the "tactile experience" of in-store shopping. But convenience will keep her browsing the Net.

"I have sent out get-well presents for people who have had surgery," she says. "You couldn't do that with real ease before on-line shopping."

'In more control' on Web

For all of his computer savvy, Richard Poje, an information technology analyst fo BP Amoco in Cleveland, first tried to get tickets to the Cleveland Indians' April 18 square-off against the Minnesota Twins the old-fashioned way: by telephone.

"I kept calling the 800 number and the local number and got busy signal, busy signal," Poje, 40, says.

He had to have the tickets in time for Christmas in order to surprise his wife, Maria, and ensure that she gets a refrigerator magnet of the season schedule—a promotion scheduled be given out at that game—to add to her collection of five years. "So I said, 'Let me try the Web.'"

At www.ticketmaster.com, he selected seats and received confirmation of purchase within 10 minutes. A week later, the tickets showed up in the mail with plenty of time to spare for Christmas.

The process was so smooth that Poje plans to shop more often on the Web. "I'm getting tired with calling numbers to order things and going through voice-response systems. You're pushing buttons from now 'til doomsday to get where you need to go. Having everything in front of you to point and click is nicer. You're really in more control over the Web."

are offering 50% off best sellers.

The privately owned Buy.com is subsidizing product sales with advertising on its site.

"We have no intention of making money on selling products," founder Blum says. "But we do have the intention to make money on advertising."

▲ Price comparisons. While low prices are critical in any phase of retail, one of the Web's unique features, the ability to allow instant price comparisons, will make life even harder for retailers.

Now, in an instant, consumers can find the lowest price on items among competing retailers — and be directed immediately to that site — by using such comparison search engines as Pricescan.com or Compare.net.

A new Internet shopping search engine being developed by Inktomi will allow on-line retailers to show the competition's price on a product, so the shopper doesn't have to visit a comparison site.

▲ Gimmicks. Retailers will use programs to try to engender buyer loyalty from Internet users who are always just a click away from the competition.

One of the most potent is the ability to learn more about a customers' likes or dislikes and use them to pitch products to them directly through e-mail or when they visit the site.

Sears, for example, is trying to figure out how to use its database of credit card purchases by 70 million households to aid its Internet efforts. Sears wants to "provide solutions, not just in single products," says Jane Thompson, president of Sears Direct, which includes Internet sales efforts. "This is about building lasting relationships."

Frequent-clicker programs, buyers' clubs, on-line buyers' guides and other gimmicks will capture high-frequency shoppers.

To draw in new buyers, Web commerce marketers are going to lengths to post their advertising on the Web. One idea: Some retailers are offering personal Web page creators a cut from sales from ads posted on their sites.

Costly promotions, sure to proliferate as competition toughens, eat into profits. No wonder Forrester found 69% of the sites it surveyed are losing money.

For their part, the sites don't sound worried. Amazon.com founder Jeff Bezos says the investment is necessary as long as the Internet is growing. "You will see these companies invest less when growth rates start to slow," he says.

E-tailers are finding ways to set their sites apart from rivals.

With the Web rived by stories of botched merchandise orders, some sites are investing in better service. Amazon.com, for instance, will open its third distribution center outside Reno, which should cut a day off

Efficiency satisfies customer

Kathryn O'Neill of Taylors, S.C., shook off fears of sending her credit card numbers over the Internet and shopped for the first time for Christmas gifts from Amazon.com and CDnow. She spent about $125 on books, music and videos and received all but one gift.

"One of the books that I ordered from Amazon, they could not get in time for Christmas, but they notified me four or five days before Christmas by e-mail. So I knew in time that I wouldn't get that particular item," the 32-year-old computer programmer says.

To win her loyalty, however, Amazon.com sent O'Neill an electronic gift certificate for use on another purchase.

Unnecessary. O'Neill was already hooked, mainly because of the ease of checking orders.

"You don't have to call and try to get someone from customer service. They come to you," she says.

First, she received confirmation that the order was placed, then another e-mail saying when it would be shipped.

Further, the hour spent shopping on line beat the stress of traffic, waiting in lines and going from store to store desperately seeking a single item, she says.

(Cont.)

delivery times to West Coast customers. "Our goal is to be (focused on) the customer and to build a better customer experience," Bezos says. "If we see our competition watching us while we watch our customers, that's our strategy."

Catalogers have an edge on the Web because of their customer service experience. "Catalogers know the business cold and don't make mistakes," Cavallari says.

BRAND NAMES GET EDGE

Lands' End, for example, has a "personal model" feature on its Web site that lets women try on tailored clothes without ever leaving the computer. A 3-D silhouette is created after answering a few questions about hair color, height and body proportions. Then, in a sort of electronic dressing room, the customer can outfit the model to see how certain fashions would look.

In the hustle for sales, the edge goes to brand names. Consumers will flock to the names they know, says Tom Tashjian, retail analyst for NationsBanc Montgomery Securities.

But despite growing competition and looming risks, soaring holiday sales "proved the skeptics and cynics wrong," says Bob Pittman, president of America Online, the Internet service provider that accounted for about half of all Internet holiday sales. "We're moving to a world that is transitioning to sales on line."

Gift of English china arrives via Web site

William Hausler had not touched a personal computer until 15 months ago. Though now adept at trading stock and buying everything from jewelry to flowers, it was not until shopping for a gift for his daughter Anne that he realized the true reach, convenience and price competitiveness offered by the World Wide Web.

Anne wanted Portmeirion dinnerware, made in England. She saw it in U.S. stores, but it cost about $150 a setting.

"I did a search on Portmeirion," says Hausler, 64, a retired data processor in Wichita, Kansas. "It listed a lot (of information), and I kept refining it. Then I entered 'discount' as part of my search and found one place in the Unted States, mround.com, with 25% off. Then I found a place in England, portmeirion.net, where they were half price."

Hausler placed a $1,000 order and avoided paying taxes and shipping costs to get them from England to Kansas City, Mo., because his order was more than $500.

He says he did not need to see the dishes first, likening the experience to catalog shopping.

"The only concern was that the dishes would be damaged. But the site gave a full warranty on it, and they arrived in Kansas City with no problem."

JUST FOR FEET IS MAKING TRACKS

Its "big-box" shoe stores have walked all over rivals

Anita Mollica is obsessed with tennis shoes. The mother of two used to spend days scouring stores in Birmingham, Ala., for the perfect pair until she discovered Just For Feet Inc. On a recent visit, Mollica browsed the toddler section for her 2-year-old. Nearby, while rock music blared, a boy practiced his jump shot on the store's half court. "The selection is great, and the kids have a ball," says Mollica.

That's music to the ears of Harold Ruttenberg, Just For Feet's CEO. From a single store 10 years ago, Ruttenberg has built the fastest-growing athletic-shoe retailer, averaging 104% annual growth since 1994. His "big-box" stores stock 4,000-odd styles—10 times as many as most rivals. Combining choice, service, and entertaining promotions, Ruttenberg has doubled his share of the $12.4 billion U.S. athletic- shoe market in the past two years, to 4%, according to analyst Marcia L. Aaron of BT Alex. Brown Inc.

As industry giants such as Ventacor's Foot Locker struggle with management problems and outdated merchandise, Just For Feet has bucked a four-year, 23% decline in industry sales to hit a record $479 million in revenue in 1997. "They've revolutionized this industry," says Renny Smith, managing director of Thomas H. Lee Co. Smith's buyout firm recently sold its Sneaker Stadium Inc. chain to Ruttenberg and now holds 1.8 million shares of Just For Feet. Aaron expects the 293-store chain to earn $54.4 million this year, up from $34.3 million in 1997. She thinks sales will jump 43% in 1998, to $682.5 million.

The stock has not had as smooth a climb. A move last year into smaller stores worried Wall Street and combined with industrywide weakness to depress the shares from 31 in January, 1997, to 12 1/2 last August. A change in accounting on store-opening expenses—from an aggressive 12-month write-off period to a more conservative practice of taking all charges at the time of the opening—forced the company to restate earnings. That didn't help the stock, either. Steady results since have aided the shares' climb back to a recent 29.

BOOTING UP. Just For Feet's advantage is its speed in recognizing shifts in taste. In 1996, when shoemakers offered a daunting number of styles linked to the Olympics, Just For Feet stocked the widest selection. The next year, when hiking boots hit big, most sneaker chains lost out. But Just For Feet had only to stock up its existing boot selection.

A typical Just For Feet store is 15,000 to 25,000 sq. ft. Mall-based rivals such as Foot Locker and Footaction USA Inc. average 4,000 to 6,000. Such size lets Just For Feet buy in bulk and negotiate discounts, Ruttenberg says, of 15% to 20%. That is passed on to customers in each store's Combat Zone, where discounts can reach 70%.

To humanize his big spaces, the CEO has designed stores-within-a-store—booths filled exclusively with one maker's apparel and footwear. At the Las Vegas store, goods from Nike Inc. are housed beneath a video wall broadcasting the brand's commercials. Elsewhere, Timberland boots climb a mock waterfall. "In-store presence like that is just as important an asset to us as an athlete endorsement," says Bill M. Sweeney, senior vice-president and general manager of Reebok International Ltd.'s North America division.

Ruttenberg doesn't stop with selection. He spends hundreds of thousands of dollars a year training his staff. Managers must graduate from Just For Feet University, a three-week program that includes everything from foot anatomy to setting up store displays. A $750,000 two-way satellite system lets manufacturers such as New Balance Athletic Shoe Inc. beam training tutorials to Just For Feet salespeople. New Balance, which offers an average of four different widths per sneaker—compared with one at Nike Inc.—

says training was a big factor in boosting the brand, No.6 nationally, to the No.3 seller at Just For Feet.

Selection and training have helped the chain outpace the competition. According to analyst David G. Magee of Robinson-Humphrey Co., an Atlanta investment bank, Just For Feet store sales average $650 per sq. ft., more than twice the $250 that mall stores average. But there have been challenges: A sharp growth in inventory was a problem until Just For Feet installed information systems to help bring the stock level down. It fell 22%, from $152 per sq. ft. in 1996 to $119 in 1997.

"A MIRACLE." Ruttenberg says he works by trial and error. Plenty of ideas have vanished like out-of-style sneakers. Gone are the in-store nursery ("Too busy for it," says Ruttenberg) and a $100,000 drive-through window. "Things weren't well planned in the beginning," he says. "When I look back on it, it was just pure luck and a miracle that it worked."

A South African native who started by selling Levi's jeans out of his car, Ruttenberg came to the U.S. in 1977 at the age of 34 with only $30,000. He opened a sportswear store in a mall a few years later, but after five years couldn't afford the rent. That's when he built a 10,000-sq.-ft. store right outside the mall stocked only with his best-seller: athletic shoes.

After a decade following this successful model, Ruttenberg is heading back to the mall. In 1997, he bought two regional chains, adding 86 smaller stores. Called Athletic Attic, these stores maintain many of Ruttenberg's big-box traits—including a smart staff, the store-within-a-store pattern, and a generous stock of 1,500 styles. Located in strip malls, they are meant to open up regional markets but avoid intra-mall competition.

Analysts expect the mall-based stores, starting from a small base, to grow twice as fast as big boxes this year. "I get accused all the time of being too risky," says Ruttenberg, "but you have to take risks in this business in order to succeed." So far, the risks are paying a nice premium.

By Nicole Harris in Birmingham, Ala.

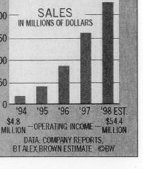

JUST FOR FEET'S FAST BREAK

SALES
IN MILLIONS OF DOLLARS

'94 $4.8 MILLION '95 '96 '97 '98 EST. $54.4 MILLION

OPERATING INCOME

DATA: COMPANY REPORTS, BT ALEX BROWN ESTIMATE ©BW

Why Wal-Mart Sings, 'Yes, We Have Bananas!'

BY EMILY NELSON

Staff Reporter of THE WALL STREET JOURNAL

To understand how Wal-Mart Stores Inc. makes sense of the zillions of pieces of information it has on the thousands of purchases it rings up, think about bananas.

Bananas, according to Wal-Mart's research, are the most common item in America's grocery carts — more common even than milk or bread. So even though Wal-Mart Supercenters sell bananas in the produce section, they also crop up in the cereal aisle to help sell a few more corn flakes.

Wal-Mart's banana-placement skills will be put to the test this week when it opens its first Wal-Mart Neighborhood Market, near the retailer's headquarters in Bentonville, Ark. The suburban-style supermarket is the first of four Wal-Mart plans to open this fall. If Wal-Mart expands the concept — nicknamed "Small Mart" — on a large scale, it will put the giant retailer in head-to-head competition with Kroger Co., Safeway Inc. and other seasoned grocery rivals.

Many retailers talk a good game when it comes to mining data collected at cash registers as a way to build sales. Wal-Mart, the nation's largest retailer, has been doing it since about 1990. Now, it is sitting on an information trove so vast and detailed that it far exceeds what many manufacturers know about their own products.

Wal-Mart's database is second in size only to that of the U.S. government, says retail analyst Daniel Barry, of Merrill Lynch & Co. Along with raw sales, profit margin, and inventory numbers, Wal-Mart also collects "market-basket data" from customer receipts at all its stores, so it knows what products are likely to be purchased together. The company receives about 100,000 queries a week from suppliers and its own buyers looking for purchase patterns or checking on a product.

Wal-Mart plans to use the data in its new Neighborhood Markets. Equipped with a drive-through pharmacy and selling both dry goods and perishables, the stores are a little smaller than typical suburban supermarkets. They are much smaller than Wal-Mart's Supercenters, the massive grocery-discount store combinations that Wal-Mart began opening in 1987. At 192,000 square feet, Wal-Mart Supercenters are about the size of four football fields.

Wal-Mart quickly found customers have trouble navigating them. Lance Garms, a Dallas marketing executive, dreads shopping at the supercenter in Plano, Texas. Either he or his wife, Kathy, shops there about every two weeks for baby formula, diapers and other items for their eight-month-old twins, usually racking up a bill of $75 to $125. "The stores are too big. It takes too long to get around," Mr. Garms complains. Wal-Mart's "really good prices" keep him going back, he says, but warns, "We've just about decided we'll go somewhere else and pay more not to have to go through all the hassle."

To address customers' frustrations, Wal-Mart dug through heaps of purchase data from its supercenters and unearthed lots of ways to help people find things they didn't even know they needed. Kleenex tissues are in the paper-goods aisle and also mixed in with the cold medicine. Measuring spoons are in housewares and also hanging next to Crisco shortening. This month, flashlights are in the hardware aisle and also with the Halloween costumes.

Since January, the famously secretive Wal-Mart has opened up its data vault to its buyers and, to a limited extent, suppliers. The move gives both sides direct access to some of the same data — and cements Wal-Mart's power over vendors.

Sales managers at big suppliers like Procter & Gamble Co. and Johnson & Johnson can check average Wal-Mart receipts for their products from their own office computers. Wal-Mart's buyers can sift through the market-basket data, to see what else the people who use Pampers or Tylenol tend to buy.

As a result, "when a supplier talks to a buyer, they're not debating information," says Randy Mott, Wal-Mart's chief information officer. Checking takes "less than a couple of minutes," he says.

At the supercenters, rather than displaying popular items at the end of an aisle in flashy displays, Wal-Mart often puts hot-sellers on interior shelves. That brings traffic down the aisle. Other suppliers want to be near the popular items — even if it means sitting on lower shelves instead of at eye level.

Wal-Mart managers can use a handheld computer that scans bar-codes on store shelves and gets a real-time report on sales, profitability and inventory position. The information is crucial for pricing and shipping decisions, but it doesn't leave much room for creativity: "Everybody thinks they have a

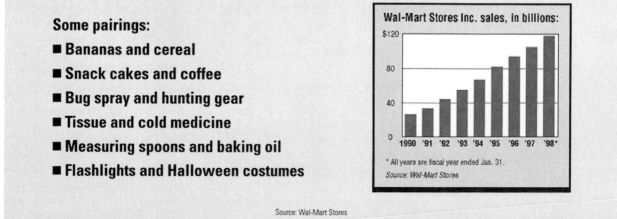

Good Neighbors

Wal-Mart Stores Inc. uses its computer system to help decide where merchandise belongs on its shelves to increase sales.

Some pairings:

- **Bananas and cereal**
- **Snack cakes and coffee**
- **Bug spray and hunting gear**
- **Tissue and cold medicine**
- **Measuring spoons and baking oil**
- **Flashlights and Halloween costumes**

Wal-Mart Stores Inc. sales, in billions:

* All years are fiscal year ended Jan. 31.
Source: Wal-Mart Stores

Source: Wal-Mart Stores

(Cont.)

feel for what people like, but we keep data," Mr. Mott says.

For customers, seeing products in unexpectedly logical places — Little Debbie snack cakes next to the coffee, for instance — cuts down on time spent wandering aimlessly. If people learn an item they want is in a remote corner of the store, "they won't go back," says Britt Beemer, chairman of America's Research Group, a consumer-research company.

Tailoring displays is a big reason why sales at Wal-Mart stores open at least a year usually rise faster than at other discount stores, Mr. Beemer says. Supermarket customers want to spend 18 to 30 minutes shopping. At a supercenter, shoppers might be willing to give up 25 to 45 minutes, Mr. Beemer says.

Still, Wal-Mart resists the temptation to fiddle too often with the layout, says Nick White, Wal-Mart's executive vice president for the supercenters. Supermarkets can expect to lose about 15% of their customers if they change their layout abruptly and customers can't find products, Mr. Beemer says.

At the Wal-Mart in Farmers Branch, Texas, another Dallas suburb, Olivia Yates was shopping for house-cleaning supplies, and a Spice Girls doll and notebook — birthday presents for her nine-year-old daughter. Ms. Yates, a telephone-repair center manager, also picked up new Maybelline blush — something she stumbled on while checking out the bath sponges. "We always end up getting at least one more thing than we plan," Ms. Yates moans.

Much of retailing is in the timing, and Wal-Mart leans on vendors to cooperate. For example, Wal-Mart anticipated heavier-than-usual traffic in the music and video section of its stores after the Sept. 22 release of "Supernatural," a new album from the Christian band dc Talk. Bill Hearn, president and chief executive officer of EMI Group PLC's Christian music group timed the release of a debut album, "Wide Eyed" by Nichole Nordeman, for the same day. Wal-Mart "preaches timing when you get your product on the shelf," he says.

The data also help Wal-Mart time merchandise deliveries so that its shelves stay stocked — but not overstocked. The supercenters have cut back on how high they stack merchandise, making stores feel less crowded. The data also has helped keep inventory levels leaner and turning faster — a must for a retailer of perishable produce as well as of perishable fashion.

Another neat trick is the way transaction data helps Wal-Mart lead shoppers out of low-margin merchandise and into more profitable sections. At the supercenters, mops and brooms — two "hard goods" used in the kitchen — turn out to be a good segue between low-margin food and higher-margin household items, like gardening tools. Then, it is on to electronics and clothes. Wal-Mart also sprinkles high-margin products in with the staples: Wal-Mart's baby aisle now often features baby food, formula and diapers along with infant clothes and children's medicine.

But Mr. Mott, the information executive, warns computer systems can only go so far in playing matchmaker. "If you looked at every item affinity," he says, "you'd say everything has to be next to bananas."

eBay erupts

Net auctioneer's volcanic success looks unstoppable

By Kevin Maney
USA TODAY

SAN JOSE, Calif. — The superhot Internet company of the moment is hidden inside an aging three-story complex that could easily be doctors' offices or garden apartments. To get here, scoot in the door of 2005 Hamilton Ave. Then hop on the excruciatingly slow elevator, which is lined with tacky wood veneer and announces each floor with a bell that clangs so loudly it makes visitors jump.

The reception area is no less low-budget. The walls are bare. The desk is 1960s metal. The woman behind it frantically punches buttons on a phone, saying, "Hello, eBay!" about once a second. After all, this is a day when the stock is shooting up more than 80 points.

It is a phenomenon, this eBay thing. Of course, it's a sizzling Internet stock, but you can pick those by the armload these days. EBay is held up as so much more. On a basic level, eBay is an on-line flea market, where everything is sold by auction. That's a brand-new kind of business, made possible only by the Internet. But eBay also has created a slice of life in late-1990s America. People go gonzo over eBay. They get hooked. They find mates while using the service. They quit good jobs to sell products full time on eBay.

"EBay is not only a business," says Ginger Willis, 41, of Pascagoula, Miss., who used eBay to find dolls to replace some she'd lost in a flash flood when she was 11. "It's a place for all of us to bring back a part of our past and regain the memories of our childhood."

Such enthusiasm for eBay explains why the company has been able to brush off recent embarrassments. Stories keep surfacing of rip-off schemes on eBay and New York City's Consumer Affairs Department is investigating a series of consumer complaints. (The complaints are almost always about sellers who list bogus products on eBay, not about eBay itself.) In December, the software running eBay's massive computer system had a seizure, bringing auctions to a halt and angering users.

Yet nothing, it seems, can slow eBay. A year ago, only the Internet underground knew what it was. In September, eBay offered its stock to the public at $18 a share, and it immediately went to $47. Today, the stock is at $239 after dropping 39 1/4 Thursday — a price swing that's almost humdrum for this company. EBay has more than 1 million registered users, processes 700,000 auctions a day and ranks as the No. 2 site in time spent on the service per month, according to Media Metrix. No. 1 is Yahoo. "The market opportunity is monstrous, the business model is much more profitable than almost any other on the Web, and the stock may reach unprecedented levels," says a report from Keith Benjamin, Internet analyst at BancBoston Robertson Stephens.

So eBay has hyper growth, controversy and the spotlight that comes with being THE stock of the moment. You might think the company would be manic, concerned only with keeping up with events. That would be wrong. Go into eBay's inner offices, and employees talk about how much room they still have to grow and how they're building a strong, unique culture that will guide the company to long-term success. Like almost everything about eBay, the culture and long-term plans are more than a wee bit quirky.

THE STUFF OF LEGENDS

By now, the basic story of how a Pez dispenser collection led to the creation of eBay is practically Internet legend.

In 1995, Pierre Omidyar, a brilliant Zen kind of character, had already started and sold one software company. He was working at General Magic. He had a girlfriend. She had a Pez dispenser collection. She remarked to Omidyar that it would be neat if there were a place on the Net where she could buy and sell Pez dispensers with other like-minded people.

Omidyar whipped up a Web site, for fun. Remember, this was in the frontier days of the Web. Soon, collectors of non-Pez stuff found the site and started using it as a place to trade. At the time, listing an item for sale on the site was free. But as trading increased, maintaining the site became burdensome. Omidyar figured he'd charge 25 cents per listing to slow use of the site. Didn't work. Envelopes carrying checks started piling up at his home. He hired someone to open and tally them. Within six months of putting up the site, Omidyar realized he'd accidentally started a company and quit his job.

By 1997, eBay was a growing, profitable niche company. Omidyar wanted to turn it into a barnburner. To do that, he sought venture capital, but not because he needed the cash. In fact, here's one of the all-time conversation stoppers in the Silicon Valley: eBay got $3 million in venture money from Benchmark

(Cont.)

Capital in June 1997 and never touched a cent. It's still in the bank. EBay has made enough money on operations to fund its own growth. Benchmark's stake, after an additional $2 million investment, is now worth $2.3 billion and is the best return on investment in the history of venture capital.

Omidyar took Benchmark's money for two reasons: the networking it could get from being a Benchmark company and the respectability that comes with landing a big venture check. Both have helped eBay bring in top talent and win over Wall Street when time rolled around for it to go public.

With Benchmark's support, new hires from the toy industry and Pepsi, and good word-of-mouth, eBay started doing some real marketing in 1998. That was all it took. "We blew on the embers that were there," says Brian Swette, senior vice president of marketing. "And it just exploded."

ONE OF A KIND

Nothing like eBay had existed before, and really nothing else like it exists yet. While there are other sites for auctions, analysts say nothing truly competes with eBay.

Two groups of people come to eBay's site: sellers and buyers. People sell everything: shotguns, Elvis autographs, old G.I. Joe lunchboxes and rare stamps worth $2,000. The site has become a hotbed for the Beanie Baby trade. Many sellers are people who use eBay as an on-line garage sale. Others are pros. They turn eBay into on-line extensions of antique stores and music shops. Tales pop up of people such as Judy Williams of Atlanta, Texas. She is making $2,000 to $3,000 a month selling odds and ends on eBay — enough so she could finally move off welfare.

The sellers are eBay's source of revenue. The company charges a graduated fee for listing an item: 25 cents for items priced at up to $10, 50 cents for items priced at $10 to $20 and so on. Then there's a final transaction fee of 5% for the first $25 of an item's selling price, 2.5% of the next $975 and 1.25% of any amount over $1,000. In the past quarter, those fees added up to $19.5 million in revenue and earnings of 7 cents a share. Earnings are rare among Internet companies.

Buyers flock to the site for the eclectic selection and the chance to grab bargains. But the secret sauce of eBay goes beyond products and transactions. "A big part of it is that it's a game. It's fun," says David Ticoll of Alliance for Converging Technologies, which studies the Net's effect on business. "But it's not as hard as the on-line games your teen-age kids play."

Users also go to eBay's site for socializing. Elvis fans who bid for the same items find each other and

How to buy

1. On eBay Web site, click through categories or search for items you might want.
2. When you find an item, check out background of seller.
3. Place bid or proxy bid.
4. If you win, eBay sends you an e-mail. Bidding is considered a binding contract: If you win, you must buy.
5. Send check to seller. Seller sends you item.
6. When transaction is complete, post feedback and rate seller.

chat in chat areas on eBay. The woman who runs eBay's Elvis area, Rockin' Robin Rosann, has become their leader. Rosann and a bunch of eBay users recently met in Las Vegas to play some new Elvis slot machines. Those people have bonds to eBay that go far deeper than products and auctions. "The site is alive," says Keith Antognini, a manager at eBay.

As Internet folks say, once a site comes alive, it takes off — and it can't easily be duplicated.

A GROWTH BUSINESS

The challenge for eBay is to prove its success is not just as fleeting and faddish as the Beanies and Furbys sold on its site.

Growth should not be a problem. EBay's market, as analyst Benjamin points out, is wide open.

If you put into one basket the U.S. market for auctions, garage sales, flea markets and purchases through classified ads — all of which are in eBay territory — you get a $100 billion market. If eBay does nothing different, its growth opportunities exceed those of Amazon.com.

Ask around at eBay, and the company doesn't sound like it plans to do much different. "Our core business is helping people trade," says Michael Wilson, a vice president. "That's where we're going to look. We're not going to go into e-mail or news or anything like that."

For the near term, eBay will expand its product categories to lure new buyers and sellers. It has launched versions of its site for Canada and the United Kingdom and plans to continue an international push. And the company is stepping up marketing. It's running ads on

136

(Cont.)

radio for the first time and sending representatives to more than 100 collectibles trade shows.

The company has some rough areas to work on. It is missing a huge opportunity by failing to get into localized auctions, analysts say. For some products, such as furniture and cars, buyers want to be near sellers so they can pick up what they've bought. EBay has not announced plans to move into local auctions.

EBay also has to fix its fraud problem. The company says that only a tiny fraction of deals is fraudulent, but a reputation as a buyer-beware marketplace could scare potential users. EBay already has a number of clever mechanisms to catch bad guys or warn users away from them. It's introducing more, such as ways to certify that sellers have had background checks. In fact, eBay's safety mechanisms are becoming a strength. The company is amassing a huge database of users, which anyone can access to find out whether a buyer or seller is trustworthy. "That knowledge capital makes eBay a powerful force," Ticoll says.

BANKING ON TRUST

Inside eBay, the company's culture is focused on long-term success. This is not the generic Silicon Valley nerd culture. Many of the 138 employees come from outside the technology industry. CEO Meg Whitman had previously been at Hasbro, FTD and Walt Disney. Swette spent 17 years at Pepsi. Managers such as Rosann come out of the collectibles industry.

Omidyar ties the company together. He is the author and keeper of the only corporate mission statement that would be at home on a Hallmark card. "EBay was founded with the belief that people are honest and trustworthy," the statement says. "We believe that each of our customers, whether a buyer or a seller, is an individual who deserves to be treated with respect."

EBay operates that way, too. It's democratic and open. "I came in with my MBA and said, 'Where's the organizational chart?' But it's not like that," Vice President Steve Westly says.

Employees revel in the idea that they're helping people make a living or find old friends. It seems to drive them more than the stock price, which is making most of them rich. Omidyar is now worth $3.6 billion; Whitman, $574 million. Most employees have stock options. Yet on the day of the $80 stock surge, no one chattered about personal net worth. They did, though, talk about the eBay Foundation. Omidyar dumped 100,000 eBay shares into a fund to start the eBay Foundation before the IPO. The foundation, which plans to give money to communities, has stock worth more than $23.9 million.

Omidyar's cultural guidance even figures into why eBay is still here in this raggedy office complex. As eBay grew, the company looked for more expansive digs. An officer found a sleek office tower in San Jose that would be the perfect size. Omidyar squashed it. Too sterile. Too corporate. "It wasn't eBay enough," spokeswoman Jennifer Chu says.

EBay will move soon, but to a bigger area in the same complex. Just as funky. Just as eclectic. Definitely eBay enough.

Promotion

56

COLA WARS ON THE MEAN STREETS

The battle heats up in Gotham— and the rest of the country

Until recently, the northern edge of Central Park was a weary, rundown spot. But in the past few months, the look of the place has changed. Suddenly, five convenience stores sport red awnings and one store features a new mural with a bright-yellow sun. The latest urban beautification program? Hardly. It's part of an aggressive new push by Coke into New York, long a Pepsi-Cola stronghold. After hanging the awnings and supervising the mural job, Coke's forces have taken to promoting the corner as a sign of their victory. Says Deborah Stokes, a longtime resident: "It looks like Coca-Cola Land now."

Harlem, a four-square-mile neighborhood, may seem like small potatoes. But these days, as Coke and Pepsi rev up their marketing rivalry, no fight is too small and no market too local to take on. With $30 billion in beverage sales between them, Coca-Cola Co. and PepsiCo Inc. have long battled each other with multimillion dollar ad campaigns and country-by-country marketing coups. And on July 20, Pepsi tackled Coke on a new turf, paying $3.3 billion for Tropicana Products Inc., a rival to Coke's Minute Maid.

But to make sure all that marketing money translates into bottles sold, both Coke and Pepsi are intensifying their efforts at the local level. With each pushing hard to improve U.S. market share, top managers are calling on the troops to redouble marketing and sales efforts as they duke it out in a storefront-by-storefront battle for soda supremacy. And nowhere is the fighting more heated than in the intensely competitive, intensely difficult New York market. "Many soft-drink executives think New York is the toughest market in the country," says John Sicher, editor of industry newsletter Beverage Digest. "The traffic is huge, the population is dense, the neighborhoods are complicated."

But it's also a huge prize—and one PepsiCo, headquartered in Purchase, N.Y., would be loath to lose. Pepsi has always spent big to stay ahead on its home turf. New York is one of only four U.S. markets where Pepsi-Cola outsells Coca-Cola Classic. Nationwide, Coke—along with its portfolio of other brands, such as Sprite and Diet Coke—controls 44.1% of the beverage market, against a stagnant 30.1% for Pepsi products.

But in New York, Coke's lead in total sales is less than half that much.

BELLWETHER. New York is only the starting point. Both cola kingpins know there are plenty of underexploited opportunities in other big urban markets, making the battle a forerunner for others beginning to unfold across the country. "The model of New York is pretty much the model of what's going on in the U.S. right now," says Philip A. Marineau, president of Pepsi-Cola Co. North America.

The showdown over the Big Apple began a year ago when Coke's largest bottler, Coca-Cola Enterprises Inc. (CCE) moved into the New York market. CCE has since added 600 more marketing people and 60 new trucks to its delivery fleet, in addition to a multimillion dollar investment in infrastructure. That comes two years after a buy-up of truck routes to improve control over distribution.

The efforts are evident on the streets. Each marketing representative visits up to 120 small stores a week, pushing for snazzier displays, better placement, and more promotions. When the owner of the 10th Avenue Gourmet store on Manhattan's Upper West Side told 26-year-old sales manager Rebecca Flores that he was planning a promotion for Pepsi's Mountain Dew in three days, for example, Flores called headquarters and set up a giveaway of Surge, Coke's competing product, the next day.

The Surge push is also part of CCE's effort to align its marketing programs with those of Coca-Cola itself. For Coke, which owns 44% of CCE, going local means working closely with the bottler, since their delivery force is in the stores every day. "We can't do this on a macro basis," explains Henry A. Schimberg, chief executive of CCE. "We have to do it on a micro basis."

LOCAL SAVVY. So far, the results of Coke's Harlem push—and of redoubled efforts in all of New York—are impressive. In the hotly contested Harlem small-store segment, sales of Coke's high-margin 20-ounce bottles have doubled. Throughout New York this year, they're up 56%, well above Coke's 30% goal. Harlem supermarkets have seen a boost too, with sales up 20%. Even William

NEW YORK, NEW YORK

As Coke tries to snatch Pepsi's lead in this key market, the two are fighting it out

COKE	PEPSI
BUSINESS: Pumps millions into trucks and infrastructure, adds 600 marketers	**BUSINESS:** Boosts investment and works with distributors to sharpen marketing
IMAGE: Pays for new awnings and new coolers at stores featuring its logo	**IMAGE:** Refurbishes landmark East River sign and launches an in-store campaign
PROMOTION: Gives away 2 million Coca-Cola Cards to build up its teen market	**PROMOTION:** Gives away 1 million Pepsis in one day, 600 Mets tickets every Friday

(Cont.)

TROPICANA: A WAY FOR PEPSI TO SQUEEZE COKE

When PepsiCo Inc. announced on July 20 that it would pay $3.3 billion for juice giant Tropicana, there were plenty of reasons to wonder why. Unlike soda pop, juice is subject to commodity markets and vulnerable to bad weather and crop failures. Juice margins of 1% to 3% are far lower than Pepsi-Cola Co.'s 16% rate for soda. Even delivering the product is tough. Perishable fresh juice can only be transported and stored using costly refrigeration.

But for all its headaches, the juicemaker offers Pepsi the possibility of a sweet payoff. As the world's largest juice company, analysts say, Tropicana arms Pepsi—stymied in its core soft-drink market—with a powerful weapon in the war against archrival Coca-Cola Co. "Tropicana gives Pepsi a chance to beat Coke at something," says Standard & Poor's Corp. analyst Richard Joy. In the $3 billion market for orange juice, Tropicana's 42% share blows away Coke-owned Minute Maid, which has 24%. Indeed, Tropicana has done so well selling its top-of-the line fresh juices that last year Minute Maid pulled out of that $1.3 billion slice of the market.

O.J. also promises growth. Sales of Pepsi beverages grow about 3% a year in the U.S. But orange juice sales are expanding at a much better 8% annual pace thanks to O.J.'s health appeal among adults and a fruit-drink fad among teenagers. PepsiCo Chairman Roger A. Enrico is banking on huge overseas opportunities.

Already, Tropicana has boosted international from 3% of sales in 1988 to 19% today by upping advertising dollars and expanding distribution—and there's still more running room. The average American consumes 15 gallons of O.J. per year, compared with six in Europe and only one-half gallon in Asia. A victory overseas would buoy Pepsi, which has long trailed Coke internationally.

Still, a leg up in what will now become the broader beverage wars didn't come cheap. Although Pepsi anted up $200 million less than Tropicana seller Seagram Co. initially wanted, analysts say it appears to have paid a full price. Seagram, which will use the money to fund its purchase of music company Polygram, first tried an initial public offering but abandoned that for the Pepsi offer.

In 1997, Tropicana earned $81 million on $2 billion in sales. Wall Street reckons that with Pepsi's financial and marketing powerhouse behind it, Tropicana has good long-term prospects. "It brings great brand-name recognition," says James Fleischmann, research director at pension fund TIAA-CREF, which owns 20,000 Pepsi shares. An acquirer's stock often falls the day a deal is announced; Pepsi's rose 1/4 point, to 39 3/4.

Short term, though, the all-cash deal may call on Pepsi to sacrifice $500 million of its ongoing $3 billion stock buyback. Still, if Tropicana helps Pepsi beat Coke, that may be a small price to pay.

By Larry Light in New York

W. Wilson, president of Pepsi's New York bottler, describes the Harlem effort as "a good attempt at tactical marketing." But, he adds, "these things are hard to sustain."

Just in case, Pepsi is pushing its own New York campaign to the hilt. But rather than send out fresh new troops, Pepsi is relying heavily on its bottler's local distribution force to boost its presence in stores, with new racks, coolers, and giveaways. It is also making a big push to get the most from its sponsorships of Lincoln Center, Radio City Music Hall, and the Bronx Zoo with ticket giveaways and advertising tie-ins. Pepsi executives believe that Coke will regret the decision to buy out distributors. By hiring out its truck fleet, Pepsi keeps costs low and adds local savvy. Indeed, after the buyouts, many of Coke's old distributors defected to Pepsi, taking their connections—and crucial knowledge of the city's traffic patterns—with them. The result: Sales of Pepsi's 20-ounce bottles in New York are up 77% over the past 18 months, thanks largely to big gains in Mountain Dew. Patrick J. Mannelly, group vice-president of CCE's New York territory, concedes that Coke is still fighting to recapture hundreds of small-store accounts.

MOXIE. That's not the only way Pepsi is using the street smarts of its entrenched distribution force—and its own connections—to trump Coke's efforts. When Pepsi's sports-marketing office learned that Coke's sponsorship agreement for Yankee Stadium was filled with loopholes, for example, it pounced. Now, even though Coke signs festoon the outfield and vendors hawk it in the stands, Pepsi's All Sport brand is in the dugout, where yellow coolers stand in full view of fans and TV cameras. Coke-North America President Jack L. Stahl can do little but sniff: "If you wandered in there, not a lot would be consumed."

Pepsi's renewed push reaches all the way to the top. Pepsi CEO Roger A. Enrico is using his friendship with Yankees owner George Steinbrenner to lobby for a switch when the sponsorship comes up in 2002. One promising sign: Steinbrenner did voice-over narration for a claymation ad for Pepsi's new Lipton Brisk tea that was set—of course—in Yankee Stadium.

Elsewhere, too, Pepsi has kept up the heat. It snatched the Shea Stadium contract from Coke this year, and now a group called the Pepsi Party Patrol uses a shoulder-mounted air cannon to launch T-shirts as high as the upper deck between innings. "Pepsi's interest and energy about this is palpable," says Mark Bingham, marketing chief of the New York Mets. In this hard-fought battle, Coke and Pepsi are doing everything they can to come out on top.

By David Greising in New York

57

'Wobblers' and 'Sidekicks' Clutter Stores, Irk Retailers

By Yumiko Ono

Staff Reporter of THE WALL STREET JOURNAL

It's the greatest show in the grocery store.

Sales of Barnum's Animals jumped more than 15% in the past year — and half the cookies sold were munched even before people got to the checkout counter.

The reason? A 76-inch gorilla-shaped cardboard tower that greets supermarket shoppers right at the front door. The gorilla towers, along with their tiger and elephant predecessors, have prompted children to pester parents for Barnum's new cookie shapes, flavors and back-of-the-box prizes. "The tower is really the cornerstone of Barnum's in terms of marketing," says Michael Senackerib, a business director for cookies at Nabisco Holdings.

All over the grocery store, food and beverage makers are laying eye-catching promotional traps to snare impulse purchases. "We're the last five seconds of marketing before a consumer purchases," says Rob Olejniczak, director of promotional services at Miller Brewing, the Philip Morris unit.

Marketers insist that as much as 70% of purchase decisions in grocery and drug stores are made on the spot, in store aisles. The goal, says Gwen Morrison, a managing director of Frankel, a Chicago-based agency that specializes in store promotion, is "to intrude into the environment."

But the intrusion is raising merchants' hackles. Store aisles, ceilings and refrigerator cases have become so cluttered with novelty displays that some retailers have drawn up strict rules about what kind of signs they'll accept. The backlash is forcing marketers to become more creative in staking out store turf.

"We do have to bob and weave a little bit," says Neal Larkin, a promotion director at Triarc's Snapple unit. Snapple recently decided against flooding certain stores with three different signs — an easel display, a sign for showcases and a "pole topper" mounted on a pole. Instead, Mr. Larkin says, Snapple developed a big cardboard poster that can be converted into any of the three types of displays.

The proliferation of in-store advertising come-ons has sparked a jargon all its own. A seven-foot-tall cardboard cutout of the Marlboro Man is called a "standee." A little plastic stage to display sunglasses is called a "glorifier." The coupon hanging around the bottle of Coca-Cola's Powerade drink is a "necker." Thomson-Leeds, a New York ad agency, recently patented the "Y.E.S. unit," a foot-long product fact sheet for TV sets and vitamins that can be pulled down like a window shade. Y.E.S. is short for "Your Extra Salesperson."

Above the fray is the "ceiling breakthrough." In some convenience stores, above the cashier, PepsiCo has placed hard-to-miss Mountain Dew signs with legs dangling through the ceiling, as though someone had tried to crash through but got stuck. Another Mountain Dew sign is designed to look like a mountain biker dropping through the ceiling.

Now, as the all-important holiday season approaches, advertisers are gearing up to bombard retailers with more signs and displays than any other time of the year. Spending on in-store advertising rose 5.8% to $12.7 billion in 1996, the most recent figures available, according to the Point-of-Purchase Advertising Institute, a trade group. Industry watchers have detected no slowdown in store promotions this year or last.

There's nothing random about the placement of neckers and glorifiers. Nabisco's in-house designers spent 14 weeks fashioning just the right kind of gorilla tower, called a "dump-fill tower display," that catches the attention of toddlers.

After Nabisco discovered that rushed shoppers circle only the periphery of the store and skip the snack aisle, it set up elaborate "waterfall" displays (tall triangular arrangements that look like cascades of cookies) at the ends of the aisles. PepsiCo busily works on dispersing displays, too, figuring that about two-thirds of soft drinks are sold outside the soft-drink aisle.

Others use eye-catching freebies. Clearly Canadian Beverage recently attached to its

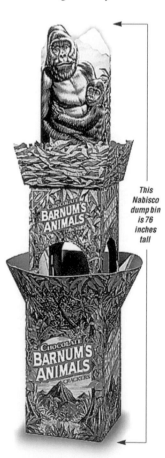

This Nabisco dump bin is 76 inches tall

A Miller Brewing wobbler

Sign Language

Aisle Interrupter	Cardboard sign that juts into the middle of the aisle
Dangler	Sign hanging down from a shelf that sways when shoppers pass
Dump Bin	Box-shaped display holding products loosely dumped inside
Glorifier	Small plastic 'stage' that elevates one product above the rest
Wobbler	A jiggling sign
Lipstick Board	Plastic surface on which messages are written with crayons
Necker	Coupon hanging on a bottle neck
Y.E.S. unit	'Your Extra Salesperson,' a fact sheet that pulls down like a shade

(Cont.)

one-liter bottles of sparkling water elaborate neckers shaped like plastic pouches, each containing a free pack of Trident cherry-flavored gum.

Marketers negotiate with retailers months in advance about placing their in-store advertising. Big retail chains keep a schedule of which product displays go where, and when. Because many of the displays are accompanied by discounts, retailers try to prevent simultaneous promotions for rival products. Manufacturers often pay stores to display their ads, especially if they occupy prime retailing real estate, like end-aisle displays.

But this rush to stand out from the clutter has produced its own clutter. So some retailers have begun imposing strict rules. Duane Reade, which has more than 80 drug stores in the New York area, says it typically rejects "danglers," (hanging signs) and big "aisle interrupters" (signs that jut out of the middle of an aisle).

"In terms of letting them do mobiles and waterfalls and God knows what else they want to do, we just stay away from them," says Gary Charboneau, Duane Reade's senior vice president of sales and merchandise.

Sensitive to such concerns, Miller Brewing last year started offering retailers signs it calls "wobblers," one of them featuring a football player in a blocking stance. Miller insists that its wobblers jiggle more than other moving signs and thus are more fun than annoying.

But some retailers just won't bite. Rite Aid Corp. of Camp Hill, Pa., shuns most in-store advertising from manufacturers in its 4,000 stores. Rite Aid's own designers work up the chain's coordinated store advertising, concentrating on such things as racks that latch onto end-aisle displays, called "sidekicks."

"We're really trying to control the retail environment to make sure it doesn't get cluttered with a circus of colors," says Beth Kaplan, Rite Aid's executive vice president of marketing.

GOT MILKED?

After a $385 million campaign, sales are declining

Those cute milk-mustache ads are causing a nasty food fight. After a two-year audit, the Agriculture Dept. has declared that the dairy industry's campaign to promote milk consumption has "serious problems" and has been badly mismanaged. The audit recommends suspending the dairy group running the program because of sloppy record-keeping, overpayments to the program's administrator, and awarding of contracts to groups with ties to the campaign.

But there's an even bigger problem: During the course of the four-year-old campaign by the International Dairy Foods Assn. (IDFA), which will have spent $385 million by next June, milk sales have declined—at an accelerated pace. U.S. per capita consumption has fallen almost 4.8% since 1994, says the USDA, vs. a 3.5% decline in the four years before the campaign started. "If any government agency was run like this," says Senator Patrick Leahy (D-Vt.), "Congress would call them before it and ask what the heck they're doing."

Why is the government involved? Under a 1985 law, food-commodity suppliers can require all companies in their industry to kick in to a promotional campaign. Agriculture ensures compliance and oversees the program.

But the milk campaign's executive director, Kurt Graetzer, calls Agriculture's report "an outrageous hatchet job." IDFA, he says, has fixed some of the problems by hiring a full-time direc-

tor and producing formal progress reports. The other criticisms, Graetzer says, "are nit-pick procedural issues." He concedes that some record-keeping was weak but says no money went where it should not have. Leahy has jumped on the bandwagon, Graetzer says, to make the IDFA look bad—because it opposes price floors that Leahy and Vermont farmers want.

An Agriculture spokeswoman said the inspector general would let the audit speak for itself. Leahy says he criticized the campaign only after seeing the report.

The milk campaign has certainly been a grabber. About 100 celebrities, from President

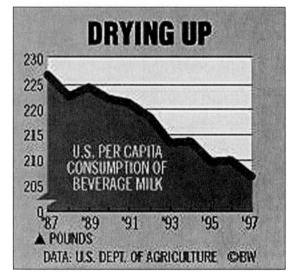

Clinton to the cast of Frasier, have donned the mustache. But Americans have continued to cut back on dairy to reduce fat intake—or make room for more soda. With bad weather producing high milk prices in both 1996 and 1998, Graetzer says consumption would have fallen even faster without the ads.

Perhaps—but it's also clear that campaign organizers have tried to twist the numbers to trumpet the program. "After a 30-year decline, milk consumption is trending up," Jay Schulberg, chief creative officer of Bozell Worldwide—the New York agency that designed the spots—said in a newspaper interview this summer. The agency says Schulberg was referring to total, not per capita, consumption—but even that has fallen in the past four years. And the USDA went so far as to tell Congress annual sales were 5.9% higher than they would have been without the milk ads.

The USDA has until Nov. 22 to respond. Enrique E. Figueroa, administrator of the branch overseeing the campaign, says it may ask for more changes but won't fire the IDFA. And the IDFA says it's confident milk processors will vote next month to extend the almost 2 cents-a-gallon fee to fund the campaign. So they're not going to cry over you-know-what.

By David Leonhardt in Chicago

Samplers and Getaways Help Push Black Books

BY LEON WYNTER

Staff Reporter of THE WALL STREET JOURNAL

TO PROMOTE books to an African-American audience, some experienced authors and publishers recommend finding a gimmick because traditional marketing tactics often miss the mark.

Denene Millner and her husband, Nick Chiles, plan to push their new book, "What Brothers Think, What Sistahs Know," published by William Morrow & Co., with a multicity series of parties starting this month in New York. They figure black singles and couples will mingle, play games like "The Dating Game" and talk about relationships with them.

The two believe reaching the young professional black "grapevine" is the most efficient route to the "Blackboard," a list of top-selling black-oriented books that appears in Essence magazine and usually generates

additional sales. "We're trying to draw people who might not necessarily go to a signing or a book store but will go to a party," Mr. Chiles says.

To boost "Just Between Girlfriends," a celebration of black female friendships published by Simon & Schuster, author Chrisena Coleman organized a getaway weekend in the Bahamas for "200 of my closest girlfriends" with backing from such corporate sponsors as Tommy Hilfiger.

One World Books distributed more than 10,000 "samplers" of book chapters to a list of over 1,000 black beauty parlors to pump the romantic novels "Waiting in Vain" and "Gingersnaps" last summer. Cheryl Woodruff, associate publisher of the Ballantine African-American imprint, was responsible for the approach. She cites a recent Gallup survey that found African-Americans buy 39.7 million books a quarter and tend to be college-educated women. "Waiting in Vain" has now sold 25,000 copies in hardcover. "Gingersnaps" has sold 22,000 and recently made the "Blackboard" list.

Ms. Millner experienced the shortcomings of traditional marketing when she was promoting her first book, a semi-satirical romance guide for African-American women

called "The Sistahs' Rules." Last Valentine's Day, she recalls, she was booked "on a radio show with a woman who thought she was the female Howard Stern" and spent the segment making anatomy jokes and eliciting Ms. Millner's feelings about O.J. Simpson and white women.

"I was just infuriated," Ms. Millner says. "It was obvious these people had no idea what I'd written." Though her book eventually sold a respectable 70,000 trade-paperback copies, she believes it would have done better if her publisher had paid more attention to details like booking her on the black-oriented New York station WBLS on Valentine's Day to talk about real relationships.

Mr. Chiles says he realizes that authors of all colors are left on their own, and everyone has a tough time getting an audience for traditional book promotions. But, he says, "what works for white authors won't necessarily work for us. You have to make sure they aren't putting you on radio shows where you hear the Beach Boys playing before the interview starts."

ENTERTAINMENT MARKETING:
Before its first visitor, Kingdom exec primes pool
Travel agents, cross-promotions, videos drive new Disney park

by Polina Shklyanoy

Entertainment perfectionist Walt Disney Co. took no chances with Animal Kingdom, its newest and biggest-ever theme park, five times the size of Disney's Magic Kingdom.

A project of this scope requires the right balance of traditional and nontraditional marketing, says Linda Warren, senior VP-marketing for the Animal Kingdom in Lake Buena Vista, Fla.

To get visitors to include Animal Kingdom in their plans, Disney used every bullet in its marketing arsenal, she says.

Drawing on 20 years of experience as the head of marketing departments for both Walt Disney World and Epcot Center in Florida, Ms. Warren has overseen marketing efforts for the park beginning five years before it opened—two years before Disney even broke ground on the project.

CAST OF THOUSANDS

To put the giant scale of the project in perspective: Animal Kingdom features more than 1,000 animals, 4 million plants and a "cast" of more than 2,000 employees. It will include five distinct environments when the fifth and final one, Asia, opens this spring.

Attractions inside the park include real-life safaris in Africa, up-close encounters with animals in Safari Village, games and rides for kids in Camp Minnie-Mickey, a time-travel ride into the past in DinoLand USA and a whitewater raft trip in Asia.

Winding trails and safari trucks lead travelers through landscaping so real that Franklin Sonn, the South African ambassador to the U.S. reportedly said, "This is the bush veldt. This is my home."

"The reason this launch was so successful was because we fully integreated marketing and communications plans. That's definitely where the future of marketing is going—the whole is greater than the sum of its parts," Ms. Warren says.

BURNETT ADS PREPARED

Before the first potential visitor saw the first Leo Burnett USA-created TV and print advertising in the late fall of 1998, Ms. Warren had already primed the pool with one of the best marketing tools Disney has—travel agents.

A Disney-produced video mixing rah-rah PR with informative travel facts is sent to any agents that "raise their hand," Ms. Warren says.

Cross-promotions with other Disney parks and Mc-Donald's Corp. restaurants surrounding the movie "A Bug's Life" helped rope in kids.

By the time parents and grandparents—an increasingly important target audience—popped the video into their VCRs, or read one of the ads in a magazine, their little tykes were already convinced on their own level of the need to visit the park.

Three of the park's five areas feature characters from popular animated Disney films including "The Jungle Book" and "The Lion King."

MCDONALD'S VIDEO WALL

A key element in Animal Kingdom's marketing plan is a 10-year sponsorship deal with McDonald's, which includes a video wall in two McDonald's restaurants in Disney World in Orlando that show spots for the restaurants and clips from Disney movies.

McDonald's is the fast-food franchise sponsor of DinoLand USA and has a restaurant in the park called Restaurantasaurus.

"Walt Disney is big on synergy," she says, "It has to work with all the businesses. It has to work for TV, video, consumer publications. McDonald's is a great way to

(Cont.)

extend the message. On the heels of our own promotion, it gives us a very broad reach."

Marketing will target consumers in 15 major cities this spring when Disney opens the new area of the park, Asia, on its one-year anniversary. Animal Kingdom plans a kind of traveling trade show, sort of like an Animal Kingdom camp.

"It's going to [have] hands-on entertainment and live stage shows," she says.

Disney has toured similar shows in the past, but never on such a large scale, Ms. Warren says. "This is the first time we've ever done anything this big—it's very, very interactive."

In addition, the Internet has been an important piece in the marketing puzzle for Animal Kingdom, Ms. Warren says, starting with a virtual grand opening.

TOO MUCH OF A GOOD THING

But is this too much of a good thing?

Ms. Warren says there is no danger in overmarketing Animal Kingdom to the point where it cannibalizes patrons from other Disney parks. Having more parks to choose from is "causing people to stay longer," she says. "People who have been here before want to see what's new, and we find that guests who are brand new hit the hot spots and then want to come back again."

61

Internet Advertising, Just Like Its Medium, Is Pushing Boundaries

Targeting Gets More Precise; Wall Separating Content From Ads Gets Wobbly

The Dilbert Stock Portfolio

BY GEORGE ANDERS

Staff Reporter of THE WALL STREET JOURNAL

OAKLAND, Calif. — Tony Nethercutt points to a big white swatch of emptiness as his computer pulls up a page on the World Wide Web. Then he coyly tells his audience: "All that space is still available. It can still be yours. But there's a great land rush going on for advertising space on the Internet. Eventually, there will be a bidding war for sites like this."

Across the table, two Clorox Inc. executives listen eagerly to the ad salesman's presentation. They are looking for new ways to promote their Armor All line of car cleansers. Online advertising is new territory for them, but Mr. Nethercutt beckons with a $50,000 opportunity to reach a targeted audience. His proposal: Put their message on the Web pages of Kelley Blue Book Inc., the bible of used-car data.

After a moment's pause, Clorox marketing manager Cary Rosenzweig nods his head. "I'm very supportive," he says. "This is the right thing to do."

Mr. Nethercutt's triumph is part of a wider coming of age for cyberspace advertising. Just 18 months ago, much of his pitch would have been laughable. Few companies outside the technology field wanted to advertise on the Internet, and those that tried were hardly dazzled by the results. By some estimates, more than 80% of the Internet's available ad slots in 1997 went unsold.

Now, online advertising is booming. First-half spending in the U.S. totaled $774 million, double the year-earlier pace, according to Pricewaterhouse Coopers. Full-year 1998 outlays are expected to reach $2 billion, says Salomon Smith Barney Inc. Online ad spending isn't just keeping pace with increased use of the Internet — it is rising appreciably faster.

Blurring Some Lines

This surge is happening in part because advertisers see new ways cyberspace can fit their strategies. Some global marketers, such as General Motors Corp., are spending more online as they hunt for alternatives to television. Meanwhile, dozens of start-ups want to make a splash in online commerce, and their business plans practically force them to buy Internet ads.

Moreover, the online world is accommodating advertisers in ways that print and broadcast media would find impossible. Some of these ways are technological, including an exceptional ability to target specific customers. Others involve a willingness to blur the division between content and advertising, which traditional media regard as almost sacred. If the money is right, many online publishers are willing to strike whatever sort of partnerships an advertiser might want.

"There are so few rules here," says Anil Singh, senior vice president, sales, at Yahoo! Inc., the Internet directory company in Santa Clara, Calif. Mr. Singh, who oversees a cyberspace sales force of about 100 people, relishes the way his company can help advertisers meet their goals. "Creativity is crucial," he says.

The Unknowns

Still, whether online advertising can live up to its champions' hopes is unclear. Rates are steep enough that some marketers wonder whether they can get enough response to justify the cost. Most advertisers pay at least as much to reach an Internet audience — typically $10 to $40 per 1,000 viewers — as they would for TV or magazine ads.

And online audiences often greet ads with a yawn, as measured by "click-through rates" of sometimes 1% or less. The rates show how often computer users point their mouse at an ad and ask for more information. "A lot of Internet banner ads are like billboards on the side of the highway," says Martha Deevy, a senior vice president at Charles Schwab & Co., a brokerage firm. "People drive right past them and don't bother to look."

Still, the people who sell space on the Internet often have something new and supposedly better than last month's way of advertising. These days, many are promoting "sponsorships," which cost more than simple banner ads at the corner of a Web page but showcase a message much more prominently. Also popular are "rich media" ads with video-like images, including flying golf balls and wiggling fingers, that are meant to engage Web surfers.

The brash, chaotic nature of the Internet-ad business comes through clearly in daily sales calls. Computers periodically freeze up or crash in the midst of demonstrations. Negotiators dicker over ad rates as if at a used-car lot. And even low-level managers can't seem to conduct a meeting without a speech about their unique vision of where the Internet is headed.

A week on the road with the 40-year-old Mr. Nethercutt shows both the allure and the limitations of online advertising. A lifelong

Tony Nethercutt

salesman, Mr. Nethercutt abandoned his old career in TV-ad sales last year after a corporate restructuring cost him his job. Now he helps cover northern California for DoubleClick Inc., an ad-sales network based in New York. It represents more than 70 sites on the Internet.

In practically every call, Mr. Nethercutt woos advertisers with the notion that he can deliver just those parts of the vast Internet audience most valuable to them. If they want to reach women, he plays up DoubleClick clients such as foodtv.com, an offshoot of cable television's Food Network. If they want small-business owners, he plugs the Web site for Fast Company magazine.

If customers want even-more-precise targeting, Mr. Nethercutt can often oblige. At AirTouch Communications Inc., ad manager Paul Whitbeck wants to reach people in Sacramento, Calif., but not the nearby San Francisco suburbs, where his cellular-phone company can't deliver service. No problem, Mr. Nethercutt says. In the brief moment when Internet users wait for a Web page to be delivered to their screen, Doubleclick's computers can identify the area code being serviced. People in Sacramento's 916 area code would get the AirTouch ad; those elsewhere wouldn't. "Nice," Mr. Whitbeck says. "The customer has been targeted before he knows it."

Cookie Trail

Craftier techniques are about to arrive. Many Web sites already tag visitors' computers with small files, known as "cookies," that help identify users on return visits. If they never come back, though, they vanish. No more. Starting next year, DoubleClick will introduce powerful software that will let advertisers spot those visitors weeks later on other Web sites. Then people can be greeted with more ads for the original merchant.

(Cont.)

On a recent morning, Mr. Nethercutt and several DoubleClick colleagues introduce this new service to Lot21 Interactive, a San Francisco ad agency representing the NationsBank unit of BankAmerica Corp. It is clear that the new service, called Boomerang, is enticing. When DoubleClick executives briefly fumble about quoting a price for the service, a Lot21 executive chides them: "Come on, I brought my checkbook for you."

Boomerang gets a chillier reception on Mr. Nethercutt's next stop. "I'm worried about a privacy issue here," says Elizabeth Duff, a marketing manager for the Discover brokerage unit of Morgan Stanley Dean Witter & Co. Customers might be uneasy about so many of their online habits being shared with strangers, she says. Her bosses give her a lot of leeway to try new ideas in cyberspace, she says, but they don't ever want to find Discover in hot water over its business practices.

Finding What Works

A look at click-through rates shows why targeting is becoming such a key part of online-ad strategy. In extreme cases, only one viewer in 2,500 clicks on a banner-ad site. The advertiser could end up spending an astronomical $1,500 to recruit each new customer online.

But a savvy salesman like Mr. Nethercutt knows how to comb through data to find a happier story. One morning, he visits BSC Inc. to discuss the results of a shotgun campaign in October, when the Burlingame, Calif., company plastered the entire DoubleClick network with ads for its GetSmart online-loan service. Many of the sites turned out to be duds, generating click rates of 0.6% or less.

Mr. Nethercutt isn't perturbed. He has singled out some of the top-performing sites — such as Autobytel.com Inc., an online car-buying service — where click rates are as high as 1.7%. It is a logical home for GetSmart ads, he says, because many car buyers need financing. He proposes that GetSmart spend heavily to increase visibility on such sites.

"Can I try it for a month?" asks Shane Spitzer, GetSmart's vice president of business development.

"Yeah," Mr. Nethercutt replies. "They want a longer term, but I'll give you a typical one-month exit."

"OK," Mr. Spitzer replies. He spends the next few weeks pressing for a discount from DoubleClick's rate card, but he embraces the basic idea of experimenting with many sites, then sticking with the winners. "You get an incredible amount of information on what sites work well and what sites don't," he explains. "And you get it fast enough that you can react to it."

Maximum Flexibility

Increasingly, online advertisers aren't just moving money to the sites they like; they are stepping forward with ideas about how to change the sites into better vehicles for their messages. And the people who run Web sites aren't taking offense, the way their cousins in print and television might. Instead, they are braiding advertisers' stories into the central message of their sites.

DoubleClick, for example, persuaded Scott Adams, the cartoonist who draws Dilbert, to include a "financial section" on his Web site, with stock portfolios for his favorite characters. This new section appears in the center of dilbert.com's home page, surrounded by cartoon strips and background facts about Dilbert. But it is paid advertising, packed with plugs for Datek Securities Inc., the online stock-trading firm.

How does Mr. Adams feel about this? The answer appears on his site. "Many people have asked why the Dilbert Zone has sold out and accepted advertising," he writes. "The reasons are complicated, involving many philosophical and ethical issues. For the slower students, I can summarize it this way: They give us money. We like money."

So Change the Site

At other times, the online boundary between advertising and content is wiggling in ways hard to pin down. One morning, Mr. Nethercutt visits AllApartments.com Inc., a San Francisco rental service, to suggest that it advertise on a section of the MindSpring Enterprises Inc. Internet directory labeled "Home and Auto."

That idea doesn't quite click with Andy Jolls, the head of marketing at AllApart-ments. "The category is too broad," he says. "We'll get a lot of people wanting to buy a house who aren't our customers. But if they renamed it 'Apartments,' we'd probably be interested." Mr. Nethercutt says he will encourage MindSpring to make the switch and will come back if he can oblige.

"We all grew up in this environment where publishers had this strict, church-and-state separation between content and advertising," says Mr. Nethercutt's boss, David Gwozdz. "In the online world, it's different. Users are more attuned to advertising, and publishers are less choosy."

Mr. Nethercutt won't say how many ads he has sold this year or what his pay will be. But colleagues say that after one year on the job, he has become a star in DoubleClick's most productive office. Mr. Gwozdz says his top salespeople have base salaries of about $70,000 a year and earn commissions on every sale. Competent salespeople earn at least $100,000, he says. Top producers can exceed $200,000.

There are cases where even a star can't sell Internet advertising. Mr. Nethercutt made repeated efforts to sign up California Milk Processors' Association, which spends a hefty $22 million a year on TV, print and outdoor ads. It got nowhere. Milk is already a familiar product, an association official notes, and it can't exactly be bought online. Some manufacturers say online advertising's real strength is helping specialized products find the right customer. Car cleansers and home loans may meet that test; soap and soft drinks don't.

Mr. Nethercutt says he can do just fine bringing online advertising to whatever markets seem appropriate. "I was born way too late to be part of the pioneers in television," he says. "But I used to think a lot about how much fun it must have been to be the first person to figure out how to sell Folger's coffee on television in the 1950s. Now I'm getting a chance to be one of the pioneers in this new medium."

62

Victoria's Secret to success?

17 minutes of flesh and lace may change face of on-line retailing

By Greg Farrell
USA TODAY

Sex sells, but Victoria's Secret sells more. The lingerie company strutted its models on Wall Street and onto the Internet Wednesday to show investors what the future of on-line retailing could look like.

Victoria's Secret broadcast its New York fashion show live on the Internet to an audience estimated to be more than 100,000. The number of people who watched the 17-minute show simultaneously won't be known until today, but the total will "blow away" the previous record of 50,000 simultaneous views of a Webcast, says Mark Cuban, president of Broadcast.com, the company that produced the Webcast.

By getting that many people to go on line to its Web site at one time, Victoria's Secret has untied the Gordian knot that has thwarted all on-line marketers: how to draw masses of people to a commercial Web site.

Until now, the most successful on-line retailers have been companies like Amazon.com that have sold commodities like books and CDs over the Web. If Victoria's Secret records a big jump in sales for its Valentine's Day push, other retailers might start thinking of ways to draw traffic to their sites.

Maybe not right away. For many novice Web users who caught the fashion show via computer it may have seemed like watching TV on a 4-inch screen.

And there were traffic problems. "Unless it's a fashion show in a snowstorm, I'm not seeing anything," said Internet consultant John Aravosis, as he tried to log on, only to be confronted by a blank space where the show should have been.

Experienced Web users probably didn't expect much more than they got: a tiny image with jerky, blurry pictures. But people new to the Web, drawn by the storm of publicity in this case, could have been disappointed if they expected TV-quality video. In fact, analysts had worried that pushing streaming pictures to too many people before the technology is mature could actually generate a backlash. New users might get turned off to the technology if this was one of their first experiences.

But fears of any huge meltdowns turned out to be unfounded. "It was a wonderfully successful effort and a historic night for the Web," says Ed Razek, chief marketing officer of Intimate Brands, Victoria's Secret's parent company. An audience greater than 100,000 would compare with that of The Weather Channel. Razek says the only technical glitch occurred in the Texas-based computer that tried to count all the traffic to the site. It crashed with the surge in visits that started at 6 p.m. ET, about 90 minutes before the show began.

Despite the technical shortcomings, Victoria's Secret's Webcast was a masterful marketing stroke. A lightning-strike $5 million ad campaign, launched during the Super Bowl, and culminating in full-page newspaper ads in Wednesday editions of national and international newspapers, stoked interest. A public relations blitz, which saturated media with TV appearances by the company's superstar models, drew unprecedented attention to this year's show at Cipriani Wall Street, a ritzy restaurant.

"Sex sells on the Internet," says Farhan Memon, co-founder and executive producer of Yack, a programming guide for Web chats and broadcast. "It's a 60-minute infomercial for Victoria's Secret on the Net."

The technology behind such an undertaking is daunting. Internet surfers flocked to the live feeds of two major events last fall: John Glenn's space shuttle trip and President Clinton's videotaped deposition in the Monica Lewinsky case. For Glenn's space ride, 50,000 on-line viewers flooded the sites that featured the video feeds, driving most viewers to TV news.

The fashion show's live video-stream was handled by Broadcast.com. The company's stock, which is traded on Nasdaq, could soar if Wednesday's event is deemed a success on Wall Street. After the Webcast, Cuban declared the event a breakthrough and said that "95% of the viewers had a great experience."

Even before the Webcast, Victoria's Secret's high-profile ad campaign had driven enormous traffic to its Web site, victoriassecret.com. According to Razek, the site recorded more than 1 million hits within an hour after the company's commercial aired on the Super Bowl.

"For 1 million people to move to a completely different medium is unprecedented," Razek says. "We were thunderstruck with customer response."

The surge of interest in the site grew this week: 15 million hits were registered on Monday, 25 million hits on Tuesday and close to 50 million hits Wednesday leading up to the Webcast.

James McQuivey, a senior analyst at Forrester, is impressed with the number of people who logged on to the Victoria's Secret Web site Sunday. "You wait until the computer and the TV are in the same appliance," he says.

"I don't believe that this event will have any long-term effect on the on-line retail industry," says Brian Sugar, director of new media at J. Crew. "We do not have immediate plans for a Webcast, but it is on our list of possibilities. We are going to concentrate more on providing our on-line visitors with the best possible experience in buying clothes, not in driving huge amounts of traffic to our site."

"This might be as important for fashion as it was for the Internet when Kenneth Starr put the Clinton documents on line," says trend tracker Tom Julian of ad agency Fallon McElligott. "It's creating a whole new genre for the fashion experience."

"This is a very powerful way for them to market, and it's the biggest runway show ever," says Ben Narasin, president of Fashionmall.com, an on-line mall that has produced Internet fashion shows.

Victoria's Secret received a lot of buzz about its runway show, but it's not the first to put one on the Web. Designers Dolce & Gabbana and Helmut Lang have done it. But it could be awhile before cyber-fashion shows are common. Some high-end designers, such as Ralph Lauren, don't yet have Web sites.

"Viewing on a computer, obviously, is not the same experience as watching something like Playboy TV on a big screen television," says Tony Lynn, president of the Playboy Entertainment Group. "If and when pay-per-view comes to the Internet, we expect to enjoy similar success on line as we now have with our worldwide television and pay-per-view business."

What are the consequences of Victoria's Secret's Webcast?

▲ **Enormous increases in traffic to the Web site.** Launched with no fanfare on Dec. 4, the Victoria's Secret Web site proved to be a big hit during the Christmas season, racking up orders from 37 countries worldwide only hours after its debut. The Webcast was advertised in *International Herald Tribune*. International sales are important to the company, since it has no stores overseas and doesn't distribute its famous catalog outside the USA.

▲ **A big boost on Wall Street.** It's no coincidence that supermodel Stephanie Seymour rang the closing bell on the New York Stock Exchange Wednesday night and that the fashion show was held around the corner at 55 Wall St. Intimate Brands is using its e-commerce strategy to convince investors that its stock has enormous growth potential in the USA and overseas. Wall Street has listened. Wednesday, the stock of Intimate Brands jumped 10% to $44 3/16 after the company said its fourth-quarter earnings beat Wall Street estimates.

▲ **Luring men into the den.** According to Razek, women make more than 90% of Victoria's Secret purchases in retail stores and through catalogs. But since the Web site launched in December, men have accounted for about 35% of on-line sales. "This is becoming an effective way to reach the boyfriend," says Evie Black-Dykma, an analyst at Forrester. "It's a lot more comfortable for men to buy on line."

The show's popularity left some shaking their heads.

"The company shows ridiculous beauty standards that very few women can meet," says Patricia Ireland, president of the National Organization for Women. "The notion that everything has to be fixed, with bras that push up and hips pushed in. It's all supposed to be sexy. But it's an image that creates a lot of dissatisfaction and insecurity and self-loathing among women."

"For those who would be outraged, I would remind them that there's more nudity on the shows they're sponsoring," said L. Brent Bozell III, chairman of the Media Research Center. "I've seen more flesh on *Melrose Place* than on these ads. Is it a blatant attempt to sell sex? Yes. And so are ads from Levi's and Benetton. Just maybe more obvious. There's nothing radical or different about it: You can't single out Victoria's Secret."

What's the view on Wall Street? Two thumbs up, says Mark Friedman of Merrill Lynch. "The Super Bowl ad and the Web presence have increased the company's reach to the consumer," he said as he stood along the runway near the start of the show. "This show has a big impact on building the brand."

Contributing: Janet Kornblum, Kevin Maney, Cesar G. Soriano and Melanie Wells

63

Yikes! Mike Takes a Hike

How Jordan's exit is shaking the world of sports business

On Jan. 13, when His Airness—aka Michael Jeffrey Jordan—officially stepped down from his throne, the earth didn't stop spinning and the stars stayed in the sky. The world of sports business, however, did register a seismic tremor on its Richter scale.

> More than a basketball star, Jordan became a powerbrand with peerless commercial reach

Life Without Michael will be tough on NBA fans as they file back to a truncated basketball season. But they're not the only ones who will be hurting. His decision to retire after 13 extraordinary years of skywalking across the NBA has shaken the league. After narrowly averting a shutdown of the entire season, the NBA now faces the formidable task of trying to win back fans without its No. 1 draw. The void will be felt by the TV networks, too, as they brace for an inevitable drop in ratings, and by corporations, long buoyed by Jordan's massive appeal, as they struggle with how to replace arguably the most perfect player—and certainly the most perfect pitchman—of his generation.

Jordan is more than a basketball star. As marketers say, he's a powerbrand—a player whose popularity and reach is peerless in the history of sports business. "Michael Jordan is greatness," says Rick Burton, director of the Warsaw Sports Marketing Center at the University of Oregon.

FIRST PAIN. The NBA is likely to suffer the earliest and biggest blow. Jordan has pumped about $1 billion in revenue into the league by beefing up attendance, stoking merchandise sales, and increasing the value of broadcast rights, according to Andrew Zimbalist, a Smith College economist who advised the players' union during the lockout. The NBA was already reeling from the effects of its five-month lockout before M.J. hung up his Air Jordans. Many fans, who viewed the feud as quibbling among millionaires, have grown apathetic and say they are less likely to attend games this year. For example, only 75% of Detroit Pistons season-ticket holders have renewed their packages, down from the usual 85%, the team says. And only 30% of people with partial-season plans have re-upped. The Pistons expect both numbers to rise, but

neither will reach its usual level.

Clearly, the Chicago Bulls stand to lose the most. Since a group led by Jerry Reinsdorf bought control of the Bulls for $9.2 million the year after Jordan arrived in 1984, the team's value has grown more than 2,000%, to over $200 million. The first pain will be from falling ticket sales. Jordan's retirement could end an amazing streak in which every Bulls game since Nov. 20, 1987, has been sold out. At up to $80 a ticket, "I don't know if people are going to come back to watch an average team," says Chicago sports agent Stephen Wade Zucker.

And the Bulls won't be the only team to suffer. Jordan has been a top draw wherever he plays. In his last visit to the Georgia Dome to play the Atlanta Hawks, Michael pulled in 62,000 fans—an NBA record. And 5,000 had no view of the court. They paid up to $10 to watch the game on a video board suspended from the roof, says Hawks President Stan Kasten. The Vancouver Grizzlies had two sellouts last year—games against the Los Angeles Lakers and the Bulls. Laments Orlando Magic Senior Vice-President Pat Williams: "Our No. 1 product just decided to walk away."

Jordan's absence is sure to suck profits from the NBA's lucrative licensing deals. The Bulls generate more apparel dollars than any team in the league, and Jordan long accounted for as much as a third of the league's sales, according to some estimates. While merchandise licensees didn't expect Jordan to play much longer, the '98–'99 season will be a lost year for an industry that was already seeing sales drop 50% to 60% in the second half of '98, says John Horan of Sporting Goods Intelligence, a Glen Mills (Pa.) newsletter.

As ticket sales decline, so will television viewership. This year, NBC, which has aired NBA games for the past eight years, begins a four-year $1.75 billion contract, and it's bracing for a ratings dip. In 1994, when Jordan forsook the basketball key for the baseball diamond, NBC's season ratings slumped from 4.9 to 4.6. And last year, ratings for NBC, TNT, and

TBS were as much as 70% higher for Bulls games than for others. During the playoffs—not even the finals—games with Jordan pulled down a 10.9 rating vs. a 5.4 for games without him.

Despite the imminent challenge, the network brass remain cool. "We've been here before," says Dick Ebersol, chairman of NBC Sports. "When we acquired the NBA in 1990, there were those who wondered where we'd find a defining superstar on the level of Larry Bird or Magic Johnson, who were about to retire." But despite such stiff upper lips, there is no obvious Jordan successor. And his departure has to be a blow to efforts aimed at luring back viewers. After the NBA lockout ended, Ebersol noted that the league has its work cut out. "There's no question in my mind that the real long-term basketball fan will be back almost immediately," he said. "The casual fan will take us some time."

THE KING OF THE PITCHMEN HAS DEALS WITH:	
BRAND	**EST. 1998 VALUE (MILLIONS)**
NIKE	$16
GATORADE	5
BIJAN	5
MCI WORLDCOM	4
HANES	2
BALL PARK FRANKS	2
RAYOVAC	2
OAKLEY	2
WILSON SPORTING GOODS	2
WHEATIES	2
AMF BOWLING	1
CBS SPORTSLINE	1
CHICAGOLAND CHEVROLET DEALER ASSN.	1
TOTAL	$45

DATA: *IEG ENDORSEMENT INSIDER*

(Cont.)

Time is about the only thing that stands a chance of dulling Jordan's highly polished image. His slam-dunk appeal as an endorser will change little in the short term. Even though Jordan's agent, David Falk, long ago signed Jordan to multiyear deals with corporate partners, marketers still show the same zeal for the superstar today.

Gatorade is typical: It doesn't plan any immediate changes in its marketing program because of Jordan's announcement. The brand—which has more than doubled its sales during Jordan's tenure as an endorser—will continue using him in about one-fifth of its commercials, showing him both on and off the court. "Michael has a work ethic and competitiveness that transcend the court," says Susan D. Wellington, president of Quaker Oats Co.'s U.S. Gatorade division, which has used Jordan as an endorser for eight years. "Right now, I'd like to meet the idiot who stops using him."

SECOND SHOCK. Nike Inc., Jordan's first and most important major corporate partner, also says it plans to deepen the relationship. The athletic-shoe company has made elaborate preparations for Life Without Michael on the court, creating a separate Team Jordan brand that could be expanded beyond athletic wear, says Larry G. Miller, president of Nike's Jordan Brand.

Still, Nike certainly didn't need another hit to its sports-marketing machine. Even before the Olympics scandal in Salt Lake City started giving sponsors like Coca-Cola, U S West, and UPS the jitters, sports-star saturation was starting to show. Nike annually spends $500 million on endorsements and sponsorships that range from Jordan to the Brazilian national soccer team. Yet its earnings are off by more than 50% in its just concluded second quarter, in part because of higher endorsement expenses and the NBA strike. Nike recently said that it would trim $100 million from its endorsement budget for 1999.

Its sales, already battered by Asia's economic slump and shifting fashions, are likely to suffer as Jordan's retirement and ill feelings from the NBA lockout keep fans away from the game. The retirement effect hit as early as Jan. 12, when news stories about Jordan's expected announcement were all over the daily papers and TV. Nike shares slipped more than 4%, to 42 5/16, as investors worried that sales of the company's athletic shoes and apparel would take a bad bounce upon Jordan's exit.

The biggest question for Nike is whether Jordan's brand can endure over the long haul. "People fade in retirement," says Jim Davis, chairman and CEO of New Balance, which does not use endorsers. "His name will be out there for a year or two, but after that, it won't mean a hell of a lot—at least in terms of endorsements. When an endorser is not seen in action, his value diminishes."

Most athletes who have maintained a high profile after retirement—like Joe Namath or Arnold Palmer—have done so by endorsing adult products. Jordan is far more popular than Palmer ever was, particularly globally, and he could continue endorsements that don't directly relate to sports. Nike has portrayed him as a fleet-footed CEO and will focus more on his core values of hard work and dedication in future ads. Sara Lee Corp. pays him to promote Hanes underwear and Ballpark Franks and almost never shows him on the court. "You can still use Michael Jordan the person," says Jim Andrews, editor of IEG Endorsement Insider, "but you may need to change the message."

CORPORATE PLAYER. Still, a huge part of Jordan's appeal has always been to kids. That's why he starred in Space Jam, a Warner Bros. live-and-animated movie that brought in $250 million globally. By 2010, though, there will be an entire generation of kids who have not watched His Airness play a single game. To them, he may have more in common with Joe DiMaggio and Joe Montana—

legends of yesteryear—than with the stars of the moment. "If he's not positioned well, it's just a question of a couple of years before he loses the power of being a credible and meaningful endorser," says Seth M. Siegel, co-chairman of Beanstalk Group, a New York firm that negotiates licensing deals for companies, including Coca-Cola.

Even so, Jordan will still have much to offer Corporate America. His uncanny connection to consumers could translate into a job as a corporate adviser or even director. "He could provide consumer-marketing advice at the top of the company and an increase in the company's image," says Charles A. Tribbett III, managing director for headhunters Russell Reynolds Associates Inc. in Chicago.

Looking businesslike in a black suit and gold tie at his farewell press conference, Jordan said he will indeed look to the corporate world to satiate his "competitive juices." And he barked: "A lot of people say Michael Jordan doesn't have any challenges away from the game. I dispute that."

The first challenge for Jordan and his advisers is to decide quickly how to position him. He could do another movie and hit the speaking circuit. He could become a part-owner of an NBA team, as former Pistons star Isiah Thomas was until he sold his share of the Toronto Raptors. Or maybe he could get involved in public-interest causes or politics, as former New York Knicks star Bill Bradley did. Senator Jordan. Now there's a mountain Michael hasn't conquered.

By Roger O. Crockett, with David Leonhardt and Richard A. Melcher in Chicago, Mark Hyman in Baltimore, Ronald Grover in Los Angeles, Linda Himelstein in San Francisco, and Richard Siklos in New York

A SLAM-DUNK FOR RANDOM HOUSE?

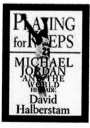

In sports-book publishing as in sports itself, timing is everything. And like a pinpoint pass to a cutter in the lane, Michael Jordan's retirement could mean a big score for two recently published books.

For the Love of the Game: My Story, by the No. 1 hoopster himself (with a little help from book producer Mark Vancil), is an opulent coffee-table volume published this fall by Crown Publishers Inc., an imprint of Bertelsmann's Random House Inc. David Halberstam's *Playing for Keeps: Michael Jordan and the World He Made,* which carries the Random House colophon, will be in stores on Feb. 1—just as the scaled-back NBA season starts.

Executives at Crown acknowledge that Jordan's retirement was on their minds all along. The idea of *For the Love of the Game,* which has a cover price of $50, came from Vancil, president of Rare Air Ltd. in Chicago. "Vancil had a sense that Michael's retirement would mean a flurry of unauthorized and not-so-good books," says Chip Gibson, Crown's president and publisher. "So he said to Michael, 'You want to control this and have it come from you.'"

NEW MUSCLE. The volume hit No. 2 on *The New York Times* best-seller list, but the almost-canceled basketball season hurt sales during the critical holiday period. Now, a book that Gibson says was "somewhat overdistributed"—700,000 copies were printed—could soon show new muscle.

Halberstam and Random House officials

say there was no calculation regarding the release of *Playing for Keeps.* According to Halberstam's editor, Scott Moyers, the author wrote a lot of the book during the last NBA season. "David wrote as fast as he could," says Moyers, but "couldn't get it done for Christmas—February seemed all in all a good date for us."

But even if the author and publisher of *Playing for Keeps* weren't clairvoyant in choosing a pub date, they find no fault with the timing. Observes Moyers: "It was nice of the NBA to start the season on our publication date: Jordan is in the air, the NBA is in the air, and this book is likely to be the first and last word on Jordan's career." Well, with 76 Jordan books since 1987, at least some of the last words.

By Hardy Green in New York

64

The Tricky Business of Rolling Out a New Toilet Paper

By Tara Parker-Pope

Staff Reporter of The Wall Street Journal

Marketers of bathroom tissue have used everything from puffy clouds to cuddly babies to advertise their products. Now **Kimberly-Clark** wants to talk about the real reason people use toilet paper.

Testing the limits of how much consumers want to hear about what goes on in the bathroom, the maker of Kleenex Cottonelle is spending $100 million to promote the brand as the toilet paper that wipes better than regular tissue, thanks to a new "rippled texture." New ads begin today and ten million free samples will be hung on doorknobs in the eastern U.S., where the product will first appear.

The new texture is "designed to leave you feeling clean and fresh," promise the ads from **WPP Group's** Ogilvy Mather in Chicago. Another ad claims that "discriminating toilet paper users" prefer the tissue because it "left them feeling cleaner than the leading brand." The name, Kleenex Cottonelle, will remain the same, as will the price. The tagline: "Your fresh approach to toilet paper."

Talking about the way a toilet paper performs is a major departure for a category that for years has focused on squeezable softness, quilted softness and cottony softness. Are consumers who remember seeing Mr. Whipple squeeze the Charmin ready to hear even a hint of what he did with the product?

Kimberly-Clark is convinced that they are. And the ads call it by the name most consumers use: toilet paper. This is, after all, familiar territory for the maker of Kotex, the first feminine-care product ever advertised. The company also pushed the boundaries of personal-care advertising when in 1981 its Depends brand launched the first national-television advertising for an adult-incontinence product. More recently, the company has tacitly acknowledged the unpleasant task of cleaning baby bottoms as it boasts that its Huggies baby wipes "clean like a washcloth."

"If we have news that's important for a consumer, then we can find a way to tastefully communicate it," says Tom Falk, group president of Kimberly-Clark's North American tissue, pulp and paper business. "It's graphic, but [the textured tissue] really feels very different."

This is Kimberly-Clark's biggest push ever in the $3.5 billion-a-year U.S. toilet paper business, where it is a relative newcomer. Its original Kleenex toilet-tissue brand struggled after its introduction in 1990. The company merged with Scott Paper, maker of the Scott and Cottonelle brands, in 1995 and created Kleenex Cottonelle, which helped Kimberly-Clark gain a 23% share of the market. But it trails rival **Procter & Gamble's** Charmin, which has 30%. Among premium tissues, Kleenex Cottonelle still ranks a distant fourth behind Charmin, Fort James's Northern and Georgia-Pacific's Angel Soft.

Overall, bath-tissue sales are flat and premium brands are losing share to economy-priced tissue. Many toilet-paper consumers treat the brands as interchangeable and simply shop for the best deal. Even the industry's most recent innovation — the triple-sized roll from Charmin — is about value, rather than improved performance.

Kimberly-Clark hosted focus groups to talk to consumers about toilet paper, and asked them to compare leading brands with the new Kleenex Cottonelle textured tissue. They discovered that even though tissue advertising doesn't talk about how well a toilet paper wipes, that is what customers are thinking about.

Nonetheless, Kimberly-Clark marketing executives quickly discovered there were limits to what they could say. In advertising focus groups, it became clear that words such as "hygiene" and "cleansing" conjured up unpleasant images about the "process" of using toilet paper, rather than the final benefit.

"You can quickly cross a line where consumers say, 'Yeah, that's what the category is all about, but please don't go there,'" says Kent Willetts, marketing director for Kleenex rolled products. "Our big challenge was how do you talk to people about it."

The advertising solution is an anthropomorphic roll of toilet paper with a heavy British accent (the voice of London actress Louise Mercer from the old NBC sitcom "Dear John"). "I'm new Kleenex-Cottonelle toilet paper, and I understand you have a cleaning position available," the tissue says. "I have a unique, rippled texture designed to leave you feeling clean and fresh. I'd love to show you what I can do."

In another ad, the tissue brags that consumers prefer it to the leading brand. "Looks like all my bottom-line thinking is paying off," the tissue says. For now, the ads will claim only that consumers say the new tissue leaves them feeling cleaner than other brands, but Kimberly-Clark is "working on a way to objectively measure cleaning better," says Mr. Willetts. "There's no method right now."

The rippled texture is the result of a patented technology that dries the tissue during manufacturing without crushing it flat and later embossing it, the older approach. This method also allows the tissue to hold its rippled shape when wet, allowing it to clean better, the company says.

Thanks to a $170 million investment in a Beach Island, S.C., manufacturing site, the process uses less fiber while improving the bulk and strength of the tissue. As a result, the company's manufacturing costs per roll are 20% less than those for other premium tissues.

Bathroom Brawl

Kimberly-Clark hopes a new rippled texture will boost its Kleenex Cottonelle brand. Here are sales of toilet-tissue industry leaders, in billions of dollars for 52 weeks ending Nov. 23.

COMPANY	TOTAL SALES	CHANGE FROM 1996
Charmin	$1.052	− 2.4%
Northern	0.481	+ 0.6
Scott	0.434	− 2.6
Private Label	0.387	+ 4.2
Angel Soft	0.373	+ 8.6
Kleenex Cottonelle	0.360	(n/a)[1]
TOTAL CATEGORY	3.487	+ 0.3

[1]New brand following merger of Kimberly-Clark and Scott Paper

Source: Information Resources, Inc.

(Cont.)

With the price to consumers remaining the same, the extra margin will help Kleenex Cottonelle better withstand the price wars plaguing the tissue category and let the company spend more on marketing and advertising to grab market share.

"It's a very delicate thing, but it has the potential, if it's done right, of taking a major share of the toilet paper market," says George Rosenbaum, chief executive of Chicago market researcher Leo J. Shapiro Associates. "When you revisit cleaning, you're opening up a number of issues that years of product promotion have been silent about."

The $100 million launch budget is more than double what Kimberly-Clark spent on the brand last year. About $20 million to $30 million will go toward national television advertising, including 18 weeks of prime-time TV. In addition to the door-to-door sampling, another million single rolls will be available in stores for 50 cents each in the Eastern U.S.

As is typical in the paper-products industry, it probably will be at least 18 months before the product is available elsewhere, because Kimberly-Clark will have to build a new tissue-making plant to supply the remaining two-thirds of the country.

In the meantime, the company will launch a new, softer version of Kleenex Cottonelle in the rest of the U.S. Those more-traditional ads show a bubble drifting onto folds of toilet tissue. But the product package includes the "clean, fresh feeling" promise, in an effort to prime consumers for the eventual appearance of the textured tissue nationwide.

Pore Strips Clean Up With Grimy Pitches

BY YUMIKO ONO

Staff Reporter of THE WALL STREET JOURNAL

It wasn't the easiest of ad assignments: The product's name was hard to pronounce. Consumers didn't know how to use it. And sales depended on convincing people that their noses are unbearably dirty.

Biore Pore Perfect is a white bandage strip. Basically, it yanks grime from pores on the nose, the way Scotch tape lifts lint from clothing. What **Deutsch,** a midsize advertising agency in New York, came up with for the Biore (pronounced bee-OR-ay) strip is a print ad that bluntly promised to extract "more dirt, oil and blackheads than you ever knew you had."

Developed by **Kao,** a Japanese consumer-products giant, Biore Pore Perfect has racked up an estimated $55 million in U.S. sales since its launch last summer. Despite the price, $5.99 for a box of six strips, some drugstores have reported shortages of the product.

In September, giant **Unilever** launched a similar product called Pond's Clear Pore Strips. Unilever says sales are going "phenomenally well," but declines to give specific figures. One of its print ads — part of a campaign created by **WPP Group's** Ogilvy & Mather — shows a magnified photograph of a sample extraction, which looks like a forest of tiny dark hairs.

This in-your-face approach, complete with grimy images, is a novelty in the skincare industry, accustomed to ads with airbrushed faces and promises of radiant or rejuvenated skin. Many benefits of skin-care products are hard to illustrate, but the nose strips seem to have gained popularity expressly by showing results that are dramatically visible. And ugly.

The intended first reaction is, "That's so gross!" says Jeff McCurrach, director of new business at Andrew Jergens, the Kao unit that is distributing Biore Pore Perfect in the U.S. Then, he adds, comes relief that the skin is clean.

Although the Jergens brand has long been known for skin lotions and soap, Mr. McCurrach says the company chose to market the product under its Japanese brand name, Biore. It was thought to be hipper than Jergens, and thus more suitable for its target audience of women in their teens and 20s.

The hype draws caution signals from some dermatologists, who warn that the benefits of cleansing pores are cosmetic and temporary. Besides dirt, pores contain natural oils and proteins that are oxidized on the skin surface, turning them dark. And after a few weeks, clean pores clog up again.

"It doesn't mean you're dirty," says David Becker, an assistant professor of dermatology at the New York Hospital-Cornell Medical Center. "It just means that you're a normal human being."

Normal or not, women use a host of crude remedies, from steaming to scrubbing, to get rid of dirty pores. Albert M. Kligman, a dermatology professor at the University of Pennsylvania School of Medicine who invented Retin-A, an antiwrinkle lotion, has even used Krazy Glue on patients' noses.

Sophia Nissen, a 21-year-old college student in New Paltz, N.Y., first tested a sample Biore strip in Cosmopolitan magazine, and then ran out to buy more. "They're addictive, regardless of whether they're good for you," she says. One satisfying ritual, for her: holding up a grimy strip to the light.

Both strips require water. The Pond's strip is moistened, applied to the nose, then peeled off 10 to 15 minutes later. The process is the same for the Biore strip, except a user moistens her nose before applying the dry strip.

But the two companies employ different technology. Jergens says the Biore strip uses a patented molecule called polyquaternium-37, or C-bond, part of a family of molecules used as softening agents in hair conditioners. Because C-bonds are positively charged, they attract dirt and blackheads, which are more negatively charged than the skin, says Richard Maksimoski, Jergens's director of research and development.

Michael Indursky, a category director at Unilever's U.S. home and personal-care division, says the Pond's product uses a different adhering ingredient called PVM/MA Copolymer. He adds that Unilever's internal tests showed that the Pond's and Biore strips were "comparable" in effectiveness.

Kao, Japan's largest consumer-product company, launched Biore Pore Perfect there in 1996, to capitalize on a pore-cleaning craze that sparked more than a dozen new creams, masks and look-alike bandages.

The decision to introduce the product in the U.S. was risky, given Kao's checkered history here. Its fizzy bath solvent called ActiBath fizzled, and its shower gel, Jergens Refreshing Body Shampoo, was quickly washed away by heavily marketed products from Unilever and **Procter & Gamble.**

To create a buzz, Jergens first gave away samples on college campuses, in magazines like Glamour and Self, and at last year's Lilith Fair, an all-women's rock tour. It stacked postcards affixed with samples in trendy restaurants. And it persuaded Howard Stern and his staffers to try the Biore strip during his irreverent radio show. (His nose was fairly clean, more so than some staffers'.)

With a modest ad budget of $20 million, says Jergens's Mr. McCurrach, "You've got to market differently than P&G or Unilever."

To develop the Biore ad, Jergens and Deutsch conducted focus groups with hundreds of women. The research showed the need to demonstrate the effectiveness of the strips vs. facial cleansers. The problem: Showing a magnified used strip on the air would repel many viewers.

In the end, Jergens decided to show a cartoon diagram of a cross section of skin, with the strip prying debris from the pores. The commercial also shows a self-confident woman who peels off her strip, takes a peek and grimaces. She says the results are evident on the strip, "if you like looking at that sort of thing."

Despite the heavy targeting of women, word has also spread to some adventurous men. Seeing the results of using nose strips he got from his sister, Daniel Brescoll, a 29-year-old New Yorker, said his reaction was, "Wow, that's really intense." Both Pond's and Biore recommend once-a-week application, but Mr. Brescoll found he didn't need them that often.

If the cleanliness fascination begins to fade, Jergens is already prepared with its next grime fighter. This month, the company began shipping Biore Pore Perfect Face Strips, for the chin and forehead.

Biore and Pond's go nose-to-nose in print ads for pore strips

The Virtual Ad: On TV You See It, at Games You Don't

BY WILLIAM POWER

Staff Reporter of THE WALL STREET JOURNAL

Philadelphia Phillies fans often couldn't believe their eyes as their baseball team bumbled in recent years.

This year, even though the team is better, fans watching at home really can't believe what they see.

On the wall behind the batter, TV viewers see large advertisements for Coca-Cola or for the team's Web site. But the ads aren't really there. They are generated by computer for the TV audience by a company called Princeton Video Image. Fans at the ballpark see just a blank wall.

The Phillies are only the latest sports team to venture into "virtual signage," which was first used in a minor-league baseball game in 1995. Now, even 3-D promotional objects like giant, inflated soda cans or floating blimps can be added to the scene on screen, visible only to TV audiences.

Unbeknownst to many viewers, the virtual ads are proliferating in TV sports these days, in baseball games, bullfights and the international TV feed of January's Super Bowl. Walt Disney's ESPN network says the virtual signs could be appearing soon in boxing, basketball and tennis coverage as well.

ESPN used the technology during the national broadcast of the Yankees-Mets interleague game on June 28 — one ad was for Disney's "Armageddon" — and plans to use it again for the Braves-Giants game in San Francisco on Aug. 9. This weekend, the ABC broadcast of the Brickyard 400 motor race in Indianapolis will show logos for Pennzoil, Chevrolet, Miller Beer and NAPA, looking like they have been mowed into the grass on the fourth turn. Several National Football League teams will use them in preseason games in coming weeks. Look for virtual billboards between the goal posts — seemingly obliterating some fans — during extra-point attempts.

For advertisers, virtual signs offer an array of benefits — including state-of-the-art graphics and a way to hold a viewer's attention during key plays, rather than waiting for commercial breaks. They are also cost-effective. A half-inning of national exposure can run about $20,000, or roughly the same as a 30-second conventional commercial.

The technology also allows advertisers to target ads regionally. A TV feed to one city can have one ad behind the batter, for example, while a feed to another city shows a different ad simultaneously.

"It reminds me of when everyone started playing around with the audio of games," boosting the sound on TV," says David Klatell, a Columbia University professor who has written books on sports television. Teams and broadcasters "may think of this as nothing more than a video version — 'We've been fooling with the sound for years; now we'll fool with the picture.'"

What's next? Can the computer put more fans in the seats? Sure, but there are no such plans, says ESPN's vice president of special sales, Bob Jeremiah. Could it change one team's uniforms to another's? Or bring Babe Ruth, Henry Aaron and Roger Maris up to bat? Not quite yet, insist the technology experts, but such feats are not impossible one day.

What the technology can do is deftly insert fake signs behind, or even underneath, real athletes in motion. Fans of professional wrestling, for example, will soon see virtual signs on the mat, complete with wrestlers "wrestling on top of them," says Mervyn Trappler of Imagine Video Systems, a competitor of Princeton Video's in Norwalk, Conn.

Princeton Video's technology starts with a microwave-oven-size computer called L-VIS (pronounced Elvis). Before a game, the company's technicians use L-VIS to scan a wall or other object where the ads will go. The computer, inside a phone-booth sized TV production console, looks for high-contrast landmarks like cracks in padding. It creates a "digital canvas" of the blank wall that is stored in its memory.

When the game starts, the computer can rapidly "recognize" the blank wall and insert the static ad, or a 3-D object or video clip, exactly over the blank wall in less than two-tenths of a second. The virtual ads look real because the computer compensates almost perfectly when the camera zooms in or out, and lets objects pass in front of the ad. (The techies call that ability "occlusion.") One of the most impressive effects is when a virtual sign is created on a race track, and cars or runners pass right over it.

Theoretically, such technology could also be used to do so-called ambush ads, wiping out "real" signs at a sporting venue and replacing them with a virtual one. But because the teams control the sale of space to both kinds of advertisers, "that doesn't happen," says Princeton Video's Sam McCleery, marketing and sales chief. The company, based in Lawrenceville, N.J., went public on the Nasdaq Stock Market in December and is still 12%-owned by investment bank Allen & Co.

Mr. McCleery says that viewers "don't seem to make the distinction" between real and virtual ads or to be "bothered by it." One reason, clearly, is that few viewers realize the ads are virtual to begin with.

Early on with the technology, one or two teams ran disclaimers in their broadcasts, to disclose that some ads viewers would see would be "virtual." But that practice has stopped. "There's no need to even bring it up," says David Buck, the Phillies' advertising-sales director, who says there has been

What fans at Philadelphia's Veterans Stadium (top) and at home see

"maybe one complaint so far" from viewers.

ESPN's Mr. Jeremiah says his network has used the virtual signs "very cautiously, with the full understanding that . . . the commercials shouldn't compete with the event." But that fine line is already being crossed, or at least flirted with elsewhere. On Phillies broadcasts, for example, the sign behind the batter suddenly comes alive to show a few seconds of animated fireworks, to promote Fireworks Nights at the ballpark. Even novice viewers could deduce that the ad wasn't real — otherwise, the pitcher on the mound would be very distracted.

The Phillies don't seem to mind, though they were notoriously slow to embrace even conventional ads behind the plate. "Times change," says the team's Mr. Buck. Now, "the whole point of 'virtual' gives us flexibility to do things — Coke now, diet Coke the next night. The regular fan won't even know."

Imagine Video, whose technology is called Imadgine, has put virtual signs in overseas broadcasts of rugby, cricket and soccer and will work with the NFL's Philadelphia Eagles this year, among others. ESPN says it is talking about ice-hockey signs with the company, which is owned by Swiss sports-marketing firm ISL and Orad, an Israeli-based technology company.

The technology is starting to be used in non-sports settings, too, such as making special video effects on talk shows. There are ideas for its use during rock concerts, news broadcasts and pledge drives. If you're in Spain watching soap operas on TV, by the way, don't believe that Ruffles bag you might see in the scenery. It's not really there.

Advertising drama: Ad rates, viewers down as network season starts

By Melanie Wells
USA TODAY

NEW YORK—The Big Four networks are battling declining viewership and escalating programming costs. And, if that's not bad enough, cautious advertisers and a lackluster fall schedule mean the networks have been unable to significantly increase ad rates for the 1998-99 season.

The average cost of a 30-second commercial on prime-time TV for the season that starts today is an estimated $153,000, down 3% from a year ago.

No prime-time show on ABC, NBC, CBS or Fox will break *Seinfeld*'s record $575,000 for 30 seconds of commercial time. NBC hospital drama *ER* now claims the highest advertising price tag on network TV with an estimated $565,000 for 30 seconds. But that's only a slight increase over last year.

Since 1980, prime-time network ad rate increases typically have hovered around 6.5% a year, media buyers say. Even in recent years, as a growing number of viewers flipped to cable TV, network ad rates have climbed. This year's drop in the average prime-time rate appears to be the first since the early 1990s and comes despite large increases for a handful of return hits.

According to *Advertising Age*'s annual survey of media buyers and networks, ABC and Fox posted increases in average ad rates, but not enough to offset lower averages at NBC and CBS. Details:

▲ **NBC.** The average prime-time ad rate dropped 10.2% to $168,000 from $187,000 a year ago. Blame it on the loss of *Seinfeld*. Even with the four most expensive shows — and a 78% increase in *Frasier*'s rates as it moves to *Seinfeld*'s Thursday night slot — the network wasn't able to compensate for the loss of that powerhouse.

▲ **CBS.** Prime-time ad rates average $129,000, down 11% from last fall. The drop could be due to reduced demand for some return hits, such as *The Nanny* which, at $145,000 for 30 seconds of ad time, cost advertisers 38% less than last year.

"I promise you the numbers are wrong," says Joe Abruzzese, CBS president of sales. "From last year, our rates are up." But Abruzzese confirmed *Advertising Age*'s estimates for CBS' four most expensive shows. And he wouldn't disclose what the network calculates its average rate to be.

▲ **ABC.** ABC has the season's highest average, $172,000, a 5.5% increase over last fall. It also boasts the most highly regarded new offerings.

▲ **Fox.** Fox's average ad rate grew the most this season, 7.9% to $137,000. Its return hit *Ally McBeal* posted the fall's biggest gain — 121% to $265,000 for 30 seconds of ad time.

Some media buyers, citing concerns about the continued strength of the economy, predict advertisers will be even more parsimonious in 1999.

"It's getting a little weird out there," says Jon Mandel, chief negotiating officer for MediaCom. "The money is still there, but advertisers are being hesitant to commit." Adds Abruzzese: "Advertisers are a little more conservative."

A show's average ad rate is difficult to determine. That's because most advertisers don't buy a specific show. Instead, they negotiate rates for a mix of shows. Different advertisers often end up paying different rates, depending on their clout and the package of

Advertising drama

Television networks begin a new season today. These shows have the highest estimated rates for a 30-second commercial:

Show (Network)	Ad Rate (1998–99)
1. *ER* (NBC)	$565,000
2. *Frazier* (NBC)	490,000
3. *Friends* (NBC)	425,000
4. *Veronica's Closet* (NBC)	380,000
5. *Drew Carey* (ABC)	375,000
Monday Night Football (ABC)	375,000
6. *The X-Files* (Fox)	330,000
7. *Jesse* (NBC)[1]	325,000
8. *Touched by an Angel* (CBS)	275,000
9. *Ally McBeal* (Fox)	265,000
10. *Dharma & Greg* (ABC)	250,000

1—New show

Source: *Advertising Age*

(Cont.)

Most expensive new shows

Show (network)	Ad rate (1998-99)
1. *Jesse* (NBC)	$325,000
2. *Pre-Game Blast* (ABC)	$230,000
3. *Secret Lives of Men* (ABC)	$210,000
4. *Sports Night* (ABC)	$185,000
The Hughleys (ABC)	$185,000
5. *Encore! Encore!* (NBC)	$175,000
That '70s Show (Fox)	$175,000

Source: *Advertising Age*

Ad rates

How rates for 30-second ads for this season's most expensive shows changed from last season.

Show (network)	Change from '97-'98 season
Ally McBeal (Fox)	120.8%
Frasier (NBC)	78.2%
Drew Carey (ABC)	36.4%
The X Files (Fox)	20.0%
Dharma & Greg (ABC)	19.0%
Touched by an Angel (CBS)	17.0%
Monday Night Football (ABC)	4.2%
Friends (NBC)	3.7%
ER (NBC)	0.9%
Veronica's Closet (NBC)	−5.0%

Source: *Advertising Age*

shows they pick. Even so, estimated ad rates reflect which new shows advertisers and networks believe will be most popular.

And while the average ad rate has dropped, falling viewership actually means advertisers are paying more for each viewer they reach. "The cost of doing business is going up for advertisers — they look at what they pay per viewer. But the networks look at revenue per commercial and see dollars decreasing," Mandel says.

DESPERATE FOR HITS

To be sure, the networks need hits more than ever. The Big Four networks saw their prime-time market share fall from 68% in the 1992-93 season to 59% last year. Meanwhile, cable channels collectively rose from 24% to 36%.

Networks also are scrambling to offset rapidly escalating programming costs. NBC is cutting jobs in part to offset more than $280 million a year it has agreed to pay Warner Bros. for *ER*. And ABC and CBS will pay more than $4 billion each over the next eight years for the rights to air professional football. But advertisers will not pay significantly more for commercial time just to support network business deals.

"The rights fees were not passed along to advertisers," says Peter Chrisanthopoulos, president of broadcast and programming at Ogilvy & Mather. "That's not how the supply and demand works. Rights fees are a network cost."

There are 28 new shows on the Big Four networks' schedules this season. Ad price tags range from $60,000 for ABC's *Vengeance, Unlimited*, a show about a vigilante who tracks criminals, to *ER*'s $565,000.

Some Madison Avenue media buyers are skeptical this will be a winning season. "There seems to be a plethora of sitcoms that all look very much the same,"

says Steve Grubbs, director of TV buying for BBDO. "It's very difficult for a new sitcom to stand out."

A few ad buyers complain that more new offerings than usual include gratuitous foul language and violence. They cite *Vengeance, Unlimited* and Fox's *That '70s Show*.

"Finding high-quality, family-oriented programming is a challenge," says John Costello, head of advertising and marketing for Sears. The retailer spent $231 million on network TV advertising last year, Competitive Media Reporting says.

NBC's new comedy *Jesse* commands the highest ad rate for a freshman offering — $325,000 for a 30-second commercial — thanks to its Thursday night hammock between *Friends* and *Frasier*.

Last year's most expensive new show was *Veronica's Closet*, with an average ad rate of $400,000. This season, the Kirstie Alley comedy is still among the 10 most expensive shows, but its ad rate is 5% lower than last year. That drop may reflect Thursday night's loss of *Seinfeld*, which it followed.

"I think *Jesse* is the best property NBC has tried to put in the Thursday night 8:30 time slot," says Visa ad chief Liz Silver, who spent $150 million on network advertising last year.

BETTING ON EXCITEMENT

"We like the excitement generated by the new fall season every year," says Sears' Costello. "Whether or not shows succeed, they do generate a lot of trial and early interest."

(Cont.)

Sears, which targets women ages 25 to 54, bought ad time on *Frasier* and *The Nanny*, as well as on new shows such as ABC's wholesome *Two of a Kind* and campy *Fantasy Island*.

Indeed, ABC has the most shows among the fall's 10 most expensive new offerings. Among them:

▲ *The Secret Lives of Men.* At $210,000 for 30 seconds of commercial time, this is the fall's third most expensive new show. Ad buyers like the premise — the travails of three thirtysomething male friends — and that it follows top-rated *Drew Carey* on Wednesday.

▲ *The Hughleys.* This show, about an urban African-American family's adjustment to suburbia, has an advertising price tag of $185,000. Advertisers hope it will catch fans of *Home Improvement* and *Spin City*, which sandwich the sitcom.

▲ *Two of a Kind.* ABC's Friday night lineup is one of its strongest because of its youth appeal. This new show, about twin girls, kicks off the evening. Ad buyers are ponying up $130,000 per commercial.

Stratospheric ad rates don't guarantee a show's success. Last fall, ABC's *Hiller & Diller* commanded the third-highest ad rate of all new shows — $270,000 for a 30-second commercial — but the show was short-lived. Only four of the 26 new shows the Big Four networks rolled out last fall appear on this season's schedule. They are NBC's *Veronica's Closet* and *Working*, ABC's *Dharma & Greg* and Fox's *Ally McBeal*.

"Most shows fail," Grubbs notes. "The success rate is about one in four or five shows."

68

Recreating advertising

Many marketers, frustrated by giant agencies, look elsewhere for cutting-edge ideas, talent

By Melanie Wells
USA TODAY

NEW YORK—Before Reebok introduced its DMX running shoe this year, the sneaker maker's marketing chief rang up presidential political consultant James Carville.

After two conversations, Reebok had its new ad pitch: "The best running shoe in the world."

"There's no limit on where great ideas come from," says Reebok marketing director Brenda Goodell, explaining why she looked beyond Madison Avenue. "The more smart, insightful out-of-the-box thinkers, the better the end result."

Madison Avenue's giant advertising agencies once had a lock on advertising and marketing ideas. But as Reebok's call to Carville illustrates, that era is over. Signs of advertisers' discontent:

▲ ABC, Anheuser-Busch, First Union, BankAmerica and Visa are among an increasing number of companies hiring consultants for marketing advice.

▲ The USA's two leading advertisers are attacking the advertising industry's revered commissions. For decades, clients paid agencies a flat percentage of a campaign's advertising budget, often 15%, whether the campaign improved sales or not. General Motors and Procter & Gamble, joining other companies, next year plan to introduce fee-based formulas under which agencies will be paid for specific services. They will receive bonuses if their work results in higher sales.

▲ Anheuser-Busch and Reebok now have a long roster of small ad agencies. They say they get faster, more efficient service than big agencies deliver.

▲ Between January and October, about 30 advertising accounts with more than $30 million in annual billings — and collectively worth more than $1.5 billion — changed agencies. Over the past two years, some companies have dropped agencies they've used for years, including Domino's, United Airlines, Kodak and Delta Air Lines.

The gripes are not new, but Madison Avenue's clients are expressing them more loudly and more publicly than ever before. Marketers say traditional ad agencies no longer have the talent or the cutting-edge ideas for 30-second commercials.

"Madison Avenue is in need of a serious over-

> "Madison Avenue is in need of a serious overhaul. Its creative process is out-dated. the marketplace we're in moves at the speed of light, and they move at the speed of a train."
>
> —Cheryl Bachelder,
> vice president of marketing at Domino's

haul," says Cheryl Bachelder, vice president of marketing at Domino's. "Its creative process is outdated. The marketplace we're in moves at the speed of light, and they move at the speed of a train."

In a recent survey of 50 marketers — including titans such as Procter & Gamble, Philip Morris, Citibank, Nike and Burger King, which each spend more than $100 million a year on advertising — half said traditional full-service advertising agencies are obsolete. The companies, surveyed for USA TODAY by executive recruiter and management consultant Gundersen Partners, collectively spent more than $10 billion on advertising last year.

Their beef? Marketers say they're frustrated by agencies' loss of focus and a dearth of talent, particularly among account managers who they say lack the ability to develop sound marketing strategies for the brands they advertise.

"Most agencies have the capability to do good, C-plus work, but there's not enough time spent trying to find a way to really break out and hit a home run," says Phil Guarascio, head of advertising and marketing for General Motors, the nation's largest advertiser. "The business, quite frankly, needs a talent upgrade."

Dissatisfaction is not evident in the big agencies' financial results. Overall, business is booming on Madison Avenue. The strong economy has fueled steady growth in ad spending and agencies' revenue and profits. But some of the industry giants' growth is coming from aggressive acquisitions of public relations agencies, direct-marketing companies and Internet advertising shops.

Signs of marketers' discontent and . . .

Marketers are taking out their frustrations with ad agencies mainly in three ways. Here's a look at each.

1. SWITCH AGENCIES

Companies have been flipping ad agencies for more than a year at what many industry watchers say is a record clip. Fewer longtime marriages have come unhinged this year than last, but there's still a lot of churning. Among the 29 accounts that migrated to new agencies this year: Little Caesars, Ernst & Young, Sprint and Compaq Computer.

"You can't keep bouncing your business around, but, from time to time, you need other people to take a look at things," says Phil Guarascio of General Motors.

2. MORE CONSULTANTS

First Union tapped a consulting firm to help the company name a new product. BellSouth has used consultants for brand positioning. Disney's ABC TV network is working with a London consulting firm called Red Spider on a long-term strategic study that could result in a different ad campaign.

"We're always looking for different ideas," says Alan Cohen, ABC executive vice president of marketing.

The assignments that marketers give consultants aren't always ones that agencies might handle, but they often affect advertising plans. Agencies complain that they have provided advice on corporate strategy, sometimes for no additional fee, for decades.

"A lot of agencies provide that but what they do best is produce advertising," says BellSouth ad chief William Pate. "You may sit down to talk about brand positioning but you end up talking about how the advertising works."

Bain & Co. Vice President Vijay Vishwanath says management consultants can provide more comprehensive marketing expertise than agencies: "They're looking for strategies to win. Ad agencies provide a piece of the puzzle," he says. "What we provide is a more comprehensive approach."

3. SMALL AGENCIES BENEFIT

Many small agencies have benefited from the account churn that started with Coca-Cola's infatuation with Michael Ovitz in 1992.

First, the company tapped Ovitz, then the head of Creative Artists Agency, Hollywood's top talent agency, as a consultant. Shortly thereafter, Coke handed the firm creative responsibility for its main brand, Coke Classic. Advertising executives were incensed that Ovitz, a Madison Avenue interloper, could spirit away one of advertising's most coveted accounts.

Some industry watchers believed other marketers would follow Coke's lead and flock to Hollywood. That didn't happen. But now other companies are tossing assignments among a smattering of mostly small ad shops.

"There will always be businesses that are better served by having one central agency, but in highly competitive businesses, such as the sneaker and beverage industries, there will be more agency arrangements structured like ours," predicts Brenda Goodell, Reebok's marketing director.

She uses five agencies for creative work and one for media buying.

Marketers' love affair with small agencies has helped fuel a buying frenzy on Madison Avenue. For the past two years, the publicly held advertising parent companies such as True North, Interpublic and Omnicom have been snatching up smaller, independent shops and specialty agencies.

There were about 30 acquisitions between January and October, according to a tally by the American Association of Advertising Agencies.

Among them: Interpublic Group acquired Carmichael Lynch and Hill Holliday Connors Cosmopulous; Publicis snapped up Hal Riney & Partners; Boznell bought Avrett Free & Ginsberg.

While some big marketers, such as AT&T and Citibank, say they like the global resources of a big firm like Young & Rubicam or McCann-Erickson Worlwide, other companies believe they get more efficient service from smaller shops.

Anheuser-Busch has not relied on just one agency for all of its advertising needs since it parted ways with D'Arcy Masius Benton & Bowles several years ago.

Since then, Anheuser-Busch brand management chief Bob Lachky says the company has gotten more creative advertising, such as the well-recognized commercials for the Budweiser frogs and lizards. (DMB&B, however, created the first frogs commercial.)

"If an agency has a Madison Avenue address, I don't want to pay for it; I want to pay for the minds that go up and down the elevator," says Lachky, who taps 14 mostly small shops outside New York for creative work. "We'd never, never go back to using a single big agency."

(Cont.)

> **"Most agencies have the capability to do good, C-plus work, but there's not enough time spent trying to find a way to really break out and hit a home run. There needs to be more edge. The business, quite frankly, needs a talent upgrade."**
> *—Phil Guarascio,*
> *General Motors' head of*
> *advertising and marketing*

Some marketers knock large agencies for being too distracted by those other services instead of concentrating on what clients want most from them — creative advertising.

Says Pepsi marketing chief Dawn Hudson: "One-stop shopping, on paper, is a great thing, but I just haven't seen it play out in reality where one source is the best. When it comes to PR and Internet advertising, there are other sources that are more creative than ad agencies."

MADISON AVENUE'S VIEW

In interviews, few Madison Avenue executives disputed marketers' view of a talent crunch. They've admittedly been struggling to attract and hold onto talented people. Talk of drawing new blood into the business is Topic A at ad agency functions.

One problem, most agency executives agree, is that college grads overlook Madison Avenue for more lucrative careers elsewhere. At Harvard, Stanford and Dartmouth, 30% to 40% of MBA graduates go into management consulting, where the median starting salary hovers around $90,000. About 10% pursue careers in marketing, where the median is about $70,000. Hollywood's outsized salaries also draw creative talent.

"Advertising isn't seen as exciting or glamorous as it once was," says O. Burtch Drake, CEO of the American Association of Advertising Agencies, which represents about 500 agencies. "Also, when we went through the 1990-91 recession, agencies made severe cutbacks. They stopped recruiting and many stopped training."

Agency executives see their industry's credibility on the line. Martin Sorrell, chief executive of WPP Group, which owns ad agencies Ogilvy & Mather and J. Walter Thompson, has said that marketers "don't think we're smart enough" to hire for projects.

"Agencies don't try hard enough to hire top people," Sorrell says, pointing out that "consulting companies and investment banks try very hard to attract the best talent."

Some agencies are trying to build relationships with job prospects before they graduate from college. Leo Burnett, in a new program, takes 50 students a year from the Miami Ad School for internships. P&G marketing chief Bob Wehling says ad agencies need more diversity.

"In the future, the agencies that access a wider array of talent — it doesn't necessarily have to be on their payroll — but agencies that have relationships with poets and psychologists and people who can provide perspective from a lot of different angles will (have the) advantage," Wehling says.

P&G and General Motors, the nation's two largest advertisers, are making their frustrations known.

Wehling and Denis Beausejour, P&G's worldwide vice president of advertising, want P&G's seven ad agencies to assign smaller teams to P&G's accounts, execute ideas faster and produce more advertising that makes a strong impression on consumers. They're also getting ready to test fee-based compensation plans that link agency pay to company sales. Fee-based compensation is growing as an alternative to commissions. IBM, Kmart, Levi Strauss & Co. and MasterCard are among those that already use some type of fee-based pay. With the commission system, the more money a client spends placing ads, the more the agency gets paid. That means an agency earns more for buying expensive TV ad time than for buying billboards, which might be more effective.

Like their counterparts at General Motors, P&G executives hope a new compensation system will embolden ad agencies to experiment with media other than TV.

"We're looking for thinking that on Brand X we should have a chat room on the Internet, or we ought to be in dentist offices or we ought to suspend advertising and put money into a PR effort with beauty editors at magazines. The agencies that do that the best over the next 10 years will do the best (financially)," Wehling says.

Wehling says the company decided to re-evaluate its agency relationships when it realized that fewer than 2% of its brands were building market share.

"We need 80% to 90% building share," he says. "We think great advertising will drive that. We're going to monitor the progress on a continuing basis. I do expect to see some significant success stories."

P&G executives accept some of the blame for lackluster advertising.

"Streamlining has to occur at our end as well as at their end," Wehling says. "It's both of us that have built up too much bureaucracy."

Contributing: Christine Sparta

69

Technology is changing face of U.S. sales force

By Beth Belton
USA Today

Iowa native Morrie Norman Jr. has selling in his blood.

He's been a salesman all his life, just like his father and grandfather before him. Two of his brothers are in sales, and his sister used to be. He has won many top awards for selling Dale Carnegie courses, which teach people how to sell. But, uncharacteristically, he hesitates when asked whether he wants his children to go into sales.

"Selling used to be selling," Norman says. "But in the last five years, I'd say there have been dramatic changes. I mean very dramatic."

As the new millennium approaches, globalization, an explosion of communications technology — including telemarketing and Internet commerce — and the ability to sell almost anything as a commodity are starting to demolish a way of life that has defined the infrastructure of corporate America for most of this century.

Wednesday evening is the 50th anniversary of the Broadway opening of Arthur Miller's timeless play *Death of a Salesman*. But while the play is being revived, the salesman of American lore is, in many ways, a dying breed.

It is still possible for bright upstarts without college degrees or the right connections to earn fantastic wages using a bit of moxie and the gift of gab and refusing to take no for an answer. But technology and competition are rapidly encroaching. The old school model of the fast-talking, backslapping salesman is becoming as outdated as Willy Loman, the tormented and pathetic protagonist in Miller's drama.

Just last week, Rite-Aid Drug Stores, third-largest U.S. pharmacy chain, announced it no longer would deal with salespeople in an attempt to reduce costs and speed up its buying process. Late last month, copier giant Xerox announced a sweeping reorganization of its sales division, renaming the direct sales force the "industry solutions operation."

Even the legendary Dale Carnegie course, *de rigeur* training for four decades of salespeople, has been revamped and relaunched for the first time to reflect changes in how the selling process works.

"A few decades ago, salespeople were taught that they should talk fast and dominate the conversation for fear that the prospect might ask a question they couldn't answer," says famed sales coach Zig Ziglar, author of two hit books on how to sell. "We now understand we must probe not as a prosecuting attorney, but as a concerned individual who wants to become an assisting buyer."

Whether hard sell or soft, the role of sales hasn't disappeared. Far from it. There are 15.5 million salespeople out there, according to government data. That's about 12% of the workforce — a percentage that has held steady for at least 15 years. It is the role of the salesperson that is undergoing a radical shift.

Roger Hirl, president and CEO of Dallas-based Occidental Chemical, has given speeches about how different it is now than when he started out in the '60s: "I covered a 10-state territory that ran from Louisiana all the way to Idaho and Montana. I had no pager, no laptop, no cellular phone, fax or e-mail. I used pay phones that took coins. I kept track of appointments with a pocket secretary and a ballpoint pen, and customers with an index card file."

Today, a salesperson who sells just products or services is being displaced by a new breed of *uber*sales types. They have titles like "global sales and marketing consultant," and many follow tried-and-true, company-approved scripts instead of ad-libbing. This salesperson of the 21st century is expected to develop ways for clients to create profit and gain market share, dubbed "value-added sales," because yesterday's clueless customer has turned into today's formidable buyer.

Now, even before the first sales call, customers, via e-mail, can get price quotes. The Internet arms them to the teeth with product information. A global economy has created a 24-hour business cycle, connecting buyers and sellers around the clock. Automation is eliminating the need for traveling salespeople.

Says David Cole, a University of Michigan professor who studies sales in the transportation industry: "There's been a revolution that has almost escaped unnoticed we've been moving so fast."

SALESMAN OF THE 21ST CENTURY

On a given day, the fairways of the nation's classiest golf courses still are filled with sales executives on the hunt for a big deal.

But increasingly, that personal relationship is considered less and less, says Norbert Ore, head of purchasing at paper-products maker Chesapeake Corp. in Richmond, Va.

"We've gone from the age of the golf course buyer to the spreadsheet buyer," Ore says. "Before, buying was done on a relationship-built basis among companies that probably had done business for years and years together. Now, business is done on an evaluation of quality, price and delivery."

At the heart of the change is a transformation of the salesperson, from job description to gender (nearly half of today's sales force is female, up from less than 35% female 25 years ago).

"The day of the lone wolf is gone," says Marvin Jolson, retired vice president of sales at Encyclopedia Britannica, who still teaches personal selling at the University of Maryland. "You're talking about salesmen who don't have a one-on-one conversation with someone. They're facing a team of buyers that includes engineers, two lawyers and an accountant."

And before that presentation, they're better prepared than ever.

Salespeople are more educated than in the past and receive more training than many executives. The typical salesperson gets 38 hours of training a year — 10 hours more than senior executives, according to a December survey of 3,703 U.S. companies by *Training* magazine.

"The good ol' boy has been left by the wayside," says Patrick Egan, vice president of purchasing at drugmaker Pfizer. "He doesn't know enough technically, and he also doesn't know enough about how his company works."

"It used to be we got five different proposals (to pitch a product) and they were all the same and we would pick one," Egan adds. "Now proposals are customized."

Mass customization is the paradigm of the 21st century just as mass production was the paradigm of the 20th century, experts say.

"At one time all you had to worry about was getting a bunch of deals closed," says Lynn Brubaker, vice president of sales and service in the aerospace division of Morristown, N.J.-based AlliedSignal. "Now you have to worry about the (customer's) overall business. You have to be a market leader; you need to be able to identify trends."

Today's sales reps are plugged in — to headquarters and their customers. They're walking electronic wonders, virtual offices of laptop computers, cell phones and pagers. But just as technology has made their job easier, it also has created obstacles. Salespeople must contend with phone mail, e-mail and stressed-out prospective buyers who no longer have the time or the boss's blessing to conduct business over an afternoon of golf or a three-martini lunch.

"It's a 24-hour sales cycle," says Marshall Smith, an account manager at Silicon Valley-based Cisco Systems, which sells computer networking equipment. Smith says he takes his laptop home with him every night and checks his e-mail right before he goes to bed.

THE MIDDLEMAN'S DEMISE

Changing tactics and technology don't tell the whole story, experts say. Most of the biggest changes are affecting the biggest companies. Smaller businesses must still use tried-and-true selling strategies to survive.

Small-business owners know better than anyone that "selling hasn't changed," argues Oliver Crom, president and CEO of Garden City, N.Y.-based Dale Carnegie Inc. "Selling has always been trying to find out what the customer needs, then determining and demonstrating that what you have to sell fits that need."

"What has changed," Crom says, "is the customer. Today the customer is much more knowledgeable. Through the Internet and other sources, the customer has a tremendous amount of information available."

The result, in many instances, is that the traditional role of the salesperson is being eliminated or changed so dramatically as to be unrecognizable. The December issue of *Sales and Marketing Management* magazine terms it the "invisible sales force," because companies increasingly are transferring duties that used to be handled by salespeople to telephone representatives, direct mail and the Internet.

> "And for a salesman, there is no rock bottom to the life. He don't put a bolt to a nut, he don't tell you the law or give you medicine. He's a man way out there in the blue, riding on a smile and a shoeshine. And when they start not smiling back— that's an earthquake."
> —*Death of a Salesman,* by Arthur Miller

Here's how some of the new or transformed ways of selling are working:

▲ **Computer technology.** Consumers can now buy a new car on the Internet without ever having to face down a car salesman. Stocks of retailers that sell their goods on line have skyrocketed in recent months due to the forecast that more and more consumers will shop on line. Businesses, too, are ordering raw materials and other supply staples over the Internet.

▲ **Consultation selling.** Historically, most selling was transaction-based, the one-time sale of a good or product without regard to a buyer's future needs or

(Cont.)

overall corporate vision. Volume was power and it didn't matter who you sold to as long as you kept selling.

But transaction-based selling has gone from 90% or more of all sales down to 65% and the percentage is expected to continue declining sharply, says Bob Davenport, vice president of the sales force effectiveness practice at the Philadelphia-based Hay Group consulting firm.

"Today, we do much more of a consultative sale and we're looking really to figure out what are (the customer's) critical business processes and how can we add value," says Xerox's Joe Valenti, newly named chief of staff for North American solutions. "It's much more than just selling a box."

At the same time, competition and cost-cutting mania have made companies more interested in keeping their biggest customers satisfied. Procter & Gamble, for example, has its Wal-Mart salespeople living in the retailer's headquarters in Bentonville, Ark., devoted to the singular task of keeping Wal-Mart happy.

▲ **Indirect selling.** In the mid-'80s, mainframe computer giant IBM had a sales force 400,000 strong. Today, it's been reduced to 275,000. And it's not just smaller: 15% of the sales force never leaves the office because they're involved in so-called indirect selling, calling smaller customers on the phone to pitch products and take orders. Indirect selling is one of the biggest growth areas in sales as companies grapple with the ever-rising expense of sending people out into the field. A decade ago, none of IBM's sales force did indirect selling.

▲ **Corporate selling.** There's been an explosion of so-called "executive selling," according to sales industry trade magazines. This means a chairman or chief executive will make a personal visit to prospective CEOs to discuss doing business — alongside the traditional salesman. Chairman Manny Fernandez of the Gartner Group, a Stamford, Conn.-based information technology consulting firm, spends more than half his time traveling on sales pitches.

THE FATE OF THE MAVERICK

In the midst of these changes, something quintessentially American, something unique, may be getting snuffed out.

More and more salespeople now are required to use a blueprint — a step-by-step manual that a sales rep must carry at all times. It's generally a compilation of what has been proven to work for the company's top salespeople. Banter with the customer is discouraged.

Oracle, the giant software supplier based in Redwood Shores, Calif., began using a blueprint in mid-'97 and sales have since rocketed. It's a seven-page, six-phase outline of the sales process that includes up to 21 steps under each phase on how to sell Oracle products.

That's the kind of selling that demoralizes the mavericks. In most companies, salespeople traditionally were kept separate from other areas of a company's operation, partly because they typically were cut from a different cloth than the accountants, technicians and factory line workers.

Behind a desk, they were useless. But out on the road, they were king, doing what they wanted when they wanted and how they wanted — as long as they produced revenue.

But in today's world, they need new skills.

"There is a . . . fundamental change in the type of person who will be successful," says Davenport, vice president of the consulting firm. "When an organization runs into trouble and the job changes but you've got the same old person, it's like the analogy: you can teach a turkey to climb a tree, but if you need tree-climbers, you hire a squirrel."

Price

70

GOOD-BYE TO FIXED PRICING?

How the wired economy could create the most efficient market of them all

Coca-Cola Co. has a bold idea: Why should the price of a can of Coke be the same all the time? Would people pay more for a cola fix on a sweltering summer day than they would on a cold, rainy one? The beverage giant may soon find out when it begins experimenting with "smart" vending machines that hook up to Coke's internal computer network, letting the company monitor inventory in distant locales—and change prices on the fly.

Sure, consumers might balk if Coke's prices were suddenly raised. But they also might be persuaded to buy a cold soda on a chilly day if the vending machine flashed a special promotion, say 20 cents off—the digital equivalent of the blue-light special. Says Sameer Dholarka, director of pricing solutions for Austin-based software maker Trilogy Systems: "List pricing is basically irrelevant."

Forget sticker prices. Forget sales clerks, too. There's a revolution brewing in pricing that promises to profoundly alter the way goods are marketed and sold. In the future, marketers will offer special deals—tailored just for you, just for the moment—on everything from theater tickets to bank loans to camcorders.

Behind this sweeping change is the wiring of the economy. The Internet, corporate networks, and wireless setups are linking people, machines, and companies around the globe—and connecting sellers and buyers as never before. This is enabling buyers to quickly and easily compare products and prices, putting them in a better bargaining position. At the same time, the technology allows sellers to collect detailed data about customers' buying habits, preferences—even spending limits—so they can tailor their products and prices. This raises hopes of a more efficient marketplace.

Today, the first signs of this new fluid pricing can be found mostly on the Internet. Online auctions allow cybershoppers to bid on everything from collectibles to treadmills. Electronic exchanges, on the other hand, act as middlemen, representing a group of sellers of one type of product or service—say, long-distance service—that is matched with buyers.

The pricing revolution, though, goes beyond the Net. Companies also are creating private networks, or "extranets," that link them with their suppliers and customers. These systems make it possible to get a precise handle on inventory, costs, and demand at any given moment—and adjust prices instantly. In the past, there was a significant cost associated with changing prices, known as the "menu cost." For a company with a large product line, it could take months for price adjustments to filter down to distributors, retailers, and salespeople. Streamlined networks reduce menu cost and time to near zero.

This will clearly benefit consumers. Already, many are finding bargains at the hundreds of online auction sites that have cropped up. And on the Net, it's a cinch to check out product information and compare prices—thanks to a growing army of shopping helpers called "bots" (page 170). That, says Erik Brynjolfsson, a management-science professor at Massachusetts Institute of Technology, "shifts bargaining power to consumers."

But that doesn't mean sellers get a raw deal. Businesses can gather more detailed information than ever before about their customers and run it through powerful database systems to glean insights into buying behavior. While the concept of point-of-sale promotions, such as Coke's, is not new, in a wired world, it takes on a whole new dimension. Suddenly, marketers can communicate directly with prospective buyers, offering them targeted promotions on an individual basis. Says Yanni Bakos, a visiting professor at MIT's Sloan School of Management: "It's like an arms race, where you give a more powerful weapon to both sides."

As buyers and sellers do battle in the electronic world, the struggle should result in prices that more closely reflect their true market value. "The future of electronic commerce is an implicit one-to-one negotiation between buyer and seller," says Jerry Kaplan, founder of Onsale Inc., a Net auction site. "You will get an individual spot price on everything."

The notion of fixed costs is a relatively

(Cont.)

recent development. A couple of hundred years ago, when a person went to the cobbler to order a pair of shoes, they negotiated the price face-to-face. It wasn't until the arrival of railroads and canal systems, which allowed products to be distributed widely, that uniform prices came into being.

The Net brings us full circle. "We've suddenly made the interaction cost so cheap, there's no pragmatic reason not to have competitive bidding on everything," says Stuart I. Feldman, director of IBM's Institute for Advanced Commerce based in Hawthorne, N.Y. Someday, you might haggle over the price of just about anything, the way you would negotiate the price of a carpet in a Turkish bazaar. Except it's likely to take place on an electronic exchange, and it may be a computer bidding against another computer on your behalf.

WIN-WIN. For a preview of what's to come, just look to the financial markets. Take the NASDAQ stock market, or Instinet's even more automated system, after which many Net entrepreneurs are modeling their businesses. NASDAQ, for example, uses a system of dealers, or market makers, who trade shares of stock for brokers or individuals. The dealers are linked by an electronic network that matches buy orders with sell orders, arriving at the value of a stock for that moment in time.

Like NASDAQ dealers, the new Internet market makers must set up mechanisms for clearing transactions and for making sure that both buyers and sellers are satisfied. As electronic exchanges are established to trade everything from advertising space to spare parts, the true market value of products will emerge. "All of this brings you closer and closer to the efficient market," says Robert MacAvoy, president of Easton Consulting in Stamford, Conn.

The most widely used form of this today is online auctions. In the world of virtual gavels, Kaplan's Onsale is the kingpin. The Web site runs seven live auctions a week where people outbid one another for computer gear, electronics equipment, even steaks. Onsale buys surplus or distressed goods from companies at fire-sale prices so they can weather low bids. And customer love it. Grant Crowley, president of Crowley's Yacht Yard Inc. in Chicago, bought 14 old-model desktop PCs for his business via Onsale. He figures he saved 40% over what he would have paid in a store. "It's a great deal for people in small businesses like mine," Crowley says.

So far, the lure of a bargain has proved powerful: More than 4 million bids have been placed since Onsale opened its doors three years ago. It sold $115 million worth of goods last year, up nearly 300% from 1996. "Suddenly, consumers are active participants in price-setting," says Onsale founder Kaplan. "It's infinite economic democracy."

For every couple dozen online auctions, though, there is an entrepreneur applying the new Net economics in ways that will ultimately transform entire industries—from telecommunications to energy. These companies are setting up exchanges for trading things such as phone minutes, gas supplies, and electronic components, a market Forrester Research projects will grow to $52 billion by 2002. Their approach is such a departure from the past that analyst Vernon Keenan of Zona Research Inc. says they represent the "third wave" of commerce on the Net—companies that are moving beyond simple marketing and online order-taking to creating entirely new electronic marketplaces.

EQUAL FOOTING. Who are these trailblazers? Some are established companies, while others are born of the Net. But they all share a radical new vision of electronic commerce. "This is the model of the future," says Eric Baty, business-information manager at Southern California Gas Co.

You might not think of a stodgy utility as being in the vanguard of cyberspace, but that's exactly where Southern California Gas is. A couple of years ago, it saw an opportunity in the dovetailing of two sweeping trends—the deregulation of the energy industry, which lets customers shop for energy suppliers the way they shop for long-distance phone service, and the rise of the Web. So, last fall, it launched Energy Marketplace, a Web-based exchange that lets customers shop for the best gas prices.

The system has something for everyone. Small and midsize gas providers list their prices on the exchange. That lowers their marketing costs and gives them access to a broader market—putting them on equal footing with big energy suppliers. Customers, mostly businesses, save money by shopping for the best price, or locking in long-term deals when prices are low. And Southern California Gas, as a distributor, increases its volume of business and collects a subscription fee from gas providers that use the exchange. In coming months, SoCalGas will offer residential customers the same opportunity and expand the service to include electricity.

Does it work? Using Energy Marketplace, Sumiden Wire Products Corp. in Stockton, Calif., found a new supplier, Intermarket Trading Co., and now saves $500 a month—about 20% of its $3,000 a month energy bill. "They're cheaper than the other guys," says Wayne Manna, plant manager at Sumiden. "It's much simpler and easier than before."

Energy Marketplace is typical of the early electronic bazaars. Like the pork bellies or wheat traded in the financial markets, the first goods to be bartered in the new electronic markets are commodities. Whether No.2 steel or No.2 pencils, price—not features or how something looks, feels, or fits—is the determining factor in a sale. And if the commodity happens to be perishable—such as airline seats, oranges, or electricity—the Net is even more compelling: Suppliers have to get rid of their inventory fast or lose the sale.

Alex Mashinsky sees similar qualities in long-distance phone minutes. A former commodities trader, Mashinsky's New York-based

---

DIARY OF A DIGITAL SALE

FastParts matches buyers and sellers of computer electronics

1. **A COMPUTER MAKER** finds itself with a shortage of a memory chip needed to assemble a circuit board. It needs to buy 20,000 chips—fast.

2. **A PURCHASING EXEC** logs on to FastParts, an Internet trading exchange, and enters information about the chip he's seeking. The system returns a list of available lots, with price, quantity, and other details. One lot looks like it fits the bill: 20,000 of the needed chips are available at 36 cents a piece.

3. **THE BUYER** puts in a lower bid: 29 cents apiece. The supplier and other buyers interested in the same part are notified of the bid by E-mail.

4. **THE SELLER** lowers the price to 33 cents. The computer maker is alerted by E-mail. It's a good price, and he accepts.

5. **FASTPARTS** confirms the details of the sale, and the payment is held in a special escrow bank account. Once the buyer receives the chips, he has five days to inspect and accept them. After five days, the payment is released to the seller.

ArbiNet (short for Arbitrage Networks) is building an exchange for routing phone calls over the lowest-cost networks—on the fly.

Most telecommunications carriers have built massive networks to handle peak loads. The problem is, much of the capacity goes unused. AT&T, for example, typically uses just 20% of its global network capacity. In a fiercely competitive market that has seen margins erode, "that excess capacity is becoming

(Cont.)

extremely sensitive," says Mashinsky. "It can be the difference between making money and losing money." ArbiNet's exchange lets carriers optimize their capacity by accepting lower-cost calls over their networks during off-peak hours. There are other companies that broker long-distance minutes. But Arbi-Net is the only one attempting it in real time.

The ArbiNet Clearing Network works this way: Network carriers, such as AT&T, supply information about their network availability and price at a given time. Carrier customers send calls through ArbiNet's clearinghouse—say, a phone call from New York to Hong Kong that must travel over secure lines. ArbiNet's powerful computers and phone switches match the request with the lowest-cost carrier for that particular call, check to make sure the capacity is in fact available, and route the call—all in a mil-lisecond. "We arbitrage the capacity available at any given time," says Mashinsky.

ArbiNet's focus today is on the whole-sale, or carrier-to-carrier, business. But Mashinsky thinks that two years from now, the market will be ripe for consumers. A "smart" phone, for example, could automatically check for the lowest carrier on each call that is placed. Such a scenario could be unnerving to the giant phone companies. "The

A CYBERSHOPPER'S BEST FRIEND

Amy Rommel uses the Web a lot at work. But the 25-year-old public-relations director doesn't have time to compare prices when buying CDs online. Not, that is, until she discovered Lycos Inc.'s shopping service. Using the search engine's technology to scour the Web, Rommel found a way to come up with deals at the click of a mouse button. "I knew there were other music sites, but the Web is so big, it's hard to keep up," she says.

Shopping services, which include helpers, or "bots," are popping up all over the Web. They range from true bots—such as the one Lycos uses—that comb sites for prices each time a request is made, to hybrids, such as Compare.Net, a Web site that lists comparative product information.

These clever programs promise plenty of bargains for consumers—and headaches for merchants. Early online merchants often charged higher prices than physical stores because customers would pay for convenience. But bots undercut the convenience premium. A recent Ernst & Young study found that 87% of the 30 consumer products tracked could be bought online at the same price or cheaper than in retail stores. "Margins are going to be pushed down and down," says Walter A. Forbes, chairman of Cendant Corp., which runs an online shopping club.

The timing is right. Web shopping is on the rise—10.3 million people bought online last year, up from 6.3 million in 1996, according to Jupiter Communications Co. That's prompting Web sites to add bots to their lineups. Search engines Yahoo! and Lycos offer shopping bots through partnerships with Junglee and Info-Space. Last fall, Excite Inc. acquired shopping service Netbot. And this month, Microsoft Corp. bought Firefly, which recommends products based on a consumer's tastes.

How do they work? Once a request is made, the agents hunt down product information as well as prices and reviews. Excite, for example, tracks products from 500 merchants. Consumers visiting the Excite shopping area type in the name of a specific product. The service then goes to different merchants' sites and hunts for current data and prices.

Yet bots have flaws. These first-generation agents can sometimes misidentify data on retailers' sites. A search for a Tickle Me Elmo doll on Yahoo! Inc. brought back information on that toy—as well as Elmo sheets, Barbie dolls, and Tickle Me Cookie Monster. Accuracy will improve in the coming months with a new language called XML, which lets site designers create "tags" to define data on a site, making it easier for bots to pick out the right information.

And there's a new generation of bots in the works. Massachusetts Institute of Technology's Kasbah can negotiate based on price and time constraints that it is given. And companies such as AgentSoft Ltd. create software that lets corporations build their own bots.

So what will happen when bots are really let loose on the Net? Sure, there will be bargains. But in computer simulations at IBM's Institute for Advanced Commerce, bots set off price wars. Some concerned companies already are blocking bots' access to their sites. But experts say the best solution is product differentiation and bots that take into account more than price. If that doesn't work well, bots may just turn out to be too much of a good thing.

By Heather Green in New York

WHERE THE BOTS ARE

In Web parlance, "bots" are software "robots" that do your bidding. Among the more sophisticated are digital bargain-hunters.

JUNGLEE Searches databases and Web sites, including job listings from 450 employers, such as AT&T and IBM. Also lists prices and products from 70 merchants. Partners Yahoo! and America Online offer the service for free and share with Junglee a percentage of the revenue they get from merchants.

EXCITE'S SHOPPING SEARCH Available on Excite's site, the free service seeks out products, prices, and reviews from 500 merchants. The technology is Netbot's Jango, which Excite bought for $35 million last October.

AGENTSOFT Develops software that lets companies build their own agents for comparison shopping of suppliers and subcontractors. It has four test services on the Web, including book shopping on the Amazon.com and Barnes & Noble sites.

big carriers don't want to do this," says Mashinsky. "It would undercut their prices."

Indeed, big businesses are sensitive about falling prices. Some entrenched companies already are fighting the idea of electronic markets that make it easy for customers to compare products and prices. Houston-based energy giant Enron Corp., for example, last month filed suit against SoCalGas and its Energy Marketplace. Enron, which plans to enter the California market, alleges that Energy Marketplace unfairly favors local suppliers that are better known. SoCalGas calls the suit a blocking tactic.

BEYOND SURPLUS. Other big players are embracing the Net, but half-heartedly—using it to dispose of surplus goods while protecting margins on their core products. Not that surplus inventory is anything to sneeze at. Chicago-based FastParts Inc. and FairMarket Inc. in Woburn, Mass., operate thriving exchanges where computer electronics companies swap excess parts. All told, U.S. industries generate some $18 billion in excess inventory a year—around 10% of all finished goods, says Anne Perlman, CEO of Moai Technologies Inc., a Net startup that makes software for creating online bartering sites. "Excess and obsolete equipment is a big and painful problem," she says.

Or a huge opportunity. Perlman knows firsthand about surplus goods. Before joining Moai, she ran Tandem Computer Inc.'s personal computer business. When Intel Corp.'s 386 microprocessor came out, she found herself with a boatload of earlier-generation 286 chips that were instantly obsolete. Afraid that she might have to write off the inventory as a loss, Perlman made some calls and found a customer willing to buy the stock—though she was left with the nagging feeling that she could have gotten a better price. Now, at Moai, along with co-founders Deva Hazarika and Frank Kang, she sells a $100,000-plus package to companies that want to run their own auctions to generate revenue from aging merchandise.

Most of the Net pioneers had to build their own systems—a time-consuming and costly task. The availability of off-the-shelf software packages from Moai and others should help jump-start more electronic exchanges.

"THIRD WAVE." That could pave the way for fluid pricing to reach beyond commodity products and surplus goods to popular, even premium-priced items. Electronic markets could be just as effective selling unique items, such as a Van Gogh painting or a company's core product line. "The move away from surplus goods to primary goods will be the real thrust of the third wave," says Zona's Keenan.

There's just one snag: When anyone on the Net can easily compare prices and features, some high-margin products could fall in price. And a strong brand name alone may not be enough to make a premium price tag stick. Some branded products may even prove to be interchangeable. You might not trust your phone service to an outfit you have never heard of on the basis of price alone. But you might be willing to swap among AT&T, MCI, or Sprint for a better deal. And do you really care if your credit card is from MasterCard or Visa? "There's a commoditization at the top level of brands," contends Jay Walker, CEO of Priceline, a new Web service that lets consumers name their price.

One way companies can respond is by cooking up creative ploys to distinguish their products. That could include personalizing products or offering loyalty programs that reward frequent customers. "Inventiveness in marketing is going to be very important in this world where people can go out and compete on price," says IBM's Feldman. That's happening in online brokerage services, a cutthroat market. Thanks to Internet brokers, trading fees are already rock-bottom. Now, companies such as E*trade are mulling loyalty programs that reward frequent traders.

There are other ways to sidestep the effects of the ultra-efficient Net market. Just look at the airline industry. It was one of the first industries to go online, starting with American Airlines Inc.'s Sabre automated-reservation system in the 1960s. When other airlines followed suit, American introduced the frequent-flier program to keep customers loyal.

Three decades after Sabre, airlines still manage to get many passengers to pay rich fares. The secret: knowing whom to gouge—in this case, the business customer who has to get somewhere and is less price-sensitive. Airlines also have perfected the science of yield management, concocting complicated pricing schemes that defy comparison. The price for an airline seat can change several times an hour, making it virtually certain that the person sitting next to you paid a different fare. "Airlines are using the Internet to raise the average price of a fare," says Ken Orton, CEO of Preview Travel, an online ticketing site.

Now, airlines are tapping into the Net—but mainly as a way to sell unfilled seats. They routinely send out E-mail alerts of last-minute fare specials. And several major airlines have signed up with Priceline, which lets consumers specify when and where they want to travel, and name their price. Priceline then forwards the bids to participating airlines, which can choose to accept the request or not. The company makes its money on the spread between the bid and the lower airline price. "It empowers the buyer," says Walker, "but also the seller. They can plug in demand to empty flights."

As long as Priceline is clearly targeted at the leisure—not the business—traveler, airlines are willing to go along. "It's not for frequent fliers but to get people out of cars without affecting the airlines' retail price structure," says Walker.

In the end, such tactics may simply delay the inevitable march of the Internet. And the truth is, Net-based markets may not be such a bad thing for sellers. They produce a price that fairly reflects demand. Some companies may be surprised by the results.

Look at AucNet, an online auction for used cars. Dealers and wholesalers flock to AucNet's Web site to buy and sell some 6,000 cars a month. Surprisingly, sellers fetch more for their used cars than they might on a physical lot. That's partly because of the larger audience they get on the Net. But dealers also have come to trust the quality ratings that AucNet inspectors assign to each car after physically examining them, and they are willing to pay more for that seal of approval. Moai's Perlman has seen similar results in other online marketplaces. Most of the time, she says, "the market will bid a better price than the vendor was expecting."

Or at least, the right price. So why fight the perfect market?

By Amy E. Cortese, with Marcia Stepanek in New York

71

Web's Robot Shoppers Don't Roam Free

BY REBECCA QUICK

Staff Report of THE WALL STREET JOURNAL

Shopping "robots" — computer programs that scan the Internet for bargains — are supposed to transform cyberspace into a consumer paradise. But don't try telling that to Jason Olim, founder of CDNow Inc., one of the hottest music retailers on the Web.

Mr. Olim doesn't like the invasive "bots," and he routinely blocks them from the CDNow Web site to prevent them from taking his prices and stacking them up against his competitors.

"We're simply not interested in working with the bots," says Mr. Olim. "It's too expensive to try and serve a customer who's only going to shop with us one out of every three times because of a 50-cent savings."

Internet pundits and venture capitalists have long claimed that comparison-shopping programs will help turn the Web into a nirvana of "frictionless capitalism," where middlemen are obsolete, markups are pared to the bone and consumers rule. With the aid of the bots, the theory goes, a shopper could find the cheapest price for everything from books to flowers to spark plugs, with just a few clicks of the mouse.

Trouble is, the bots are only as good as the information they collect, and there are plenty of ways for uncooperative Web stores to thwart and confuse the digital comparison shoppers. Some bots charge merchants for listing their products, thereby excluding those who refuse to pay. There is even the specter that on-line merchants themselves may operate shopping bots that avoid competitors' products.

Why are retailers balking? Some worry that shopping robots will turn the Internet into a virtual wholesale warehouse, where the lowest price wins, and other expensive features they have built into their sites will be devalued. CDNow, for example, offers not only hundreds of thousands of albums but also dishes out music reviews and commentary from critics and fans, as well as recommendations based on a customer's past purchases. Some retailers also claim the bots can clog their Web sites by requesting page after page of data as they gather prices.

Catalog-sales giant Lands' End Inc. in Dodgeville, Wis.,

doesn't block bots. And Thane Ryland, a spokesman for the company, acknowledges that the comparison-shopping they offer is convenient. Still, he says that is only part of what customers want. The Lands' End Web site, for instance, offers essays on rural life, clothing-care tips and a folksy newsletter in addition to the retailer's full catalog.

The shopping bots blow by all that window dressing. They are programmed to home in on specific bits of information, such as model numbers and prices. The bots know how most Web pages are designed, and can sift out the needed data from the jumble of software coding and fancy graphics.

Here's how they work: Say you want to buy a videotape of "North by Northwest," the classic Alfred Hitchcock thriller starring Cary Grant. You could go to the Webmarket site (http://www.webmarket.com), select the "movies and videos" section and type in the movie title. In seconds, back comes a list of a half-dozen Web stores offering the tape for prices ranging from $14.64 to $19.49.

Some Web sites simply slam the door on shopping bots, refusing to answer requests for Web pages that come from known bot sites. (Web retailers can see the address of a visitor.) Or they try to confuse the robots by changing the Web site's format or appearance, so the bot doesn't know where to look for pricing information. Another trick that can foil the bots is to lower a product's base price, but then raise hidden costs such as shipping and handling.

"It's easy to break the legs of the virtual shopper at the virtual door," says John Sviokla, a partner at Diamond Technology Partners, a Chicago technology consulting firm. And Web retailers should be afraid, Mr. Sviokla warns, because well-informed shop-

ping bots could spark a cutthroat pricing war in cyberspace.

Despite these concerns, shopping robots are a hot technology, and Web giants are clamoring to offer them to attract visitors. Search site Excite Inc. offers a comparison-shopping guide called Jango. Last month, competitor Infoseek Corp. shelled out $17 million for Quando Inc., which makes a shopping robot scheduled to debut later this year.

That deal came just after Internet book seller Amazon.com Inc. paid $180 million for Junglee Corp., operator of one of the Web's biggest bargain-hunting sites. And just this week, Inktomi Corp., a maker of search-engine technology, agreed to acquire C2B Technologies, a maker of comparison-shopping software, for stock valued at $92.7 million.

In addition to charging merchants, shopping bot sites can earn money by selling advertising space. Some also enter partnerships by providing their search software to other companies' Web sites. A Junglee "shopping guide," for example, appears on a site run by Compaq Computer Corp. It offers users information on apparel, books and electronics, but not personal computers.

The first shopping bot to gain widespread notice was BargainFinder, which was built by Andersen Consulting back in 1995 as a research project to persuade its retailing clients to prepare for electronic commerce. BargainFinder, which still exists, allows consumers to search a half-dozen on-line music stores and returns with a list of titles arranged by price.

But from the very start, the technology was mangled by suspicious retailers that refused to cooperate.

"A lot of the sites saw our robots coming in and refused them entry. Other sites asked

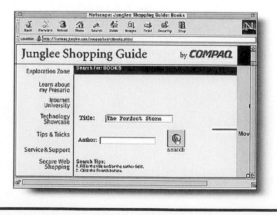

Windows Shopping

On-line shopping guides are often incomplete. A search on Compaq computer's Junglee shopping guide for the book 'The Perfect Storm' did not reveal several on-line sites that carried the book.

Among those left out:

- **All Book Web**
- **Bargain Book Warehouse**
- **Barnes & Noble**
- **Bolen Books (based in Canada)**
- **The Book Pl@ce (based in the U.K.)**
- **Books-A-Million**
- **Powell's Books**

(Cont.)

us not to send the robots in," says Glover Ferguson, director of the electronic commerce program at Anderson. Why would the retailers balk at being included in a project that could drive traffic to their sites? "If you spent a gazillion dollars coming up with a great site, then [the shopping robot] is just not attractive to you," says Mr. Ferguson. "Nobody wants to be reduced to a commodity."

The shopping bot sites are quick to point out that they are driving traffic to retailers, and that the benefits to them outweigh the risks. "There are people who are afraid not to be included," says Kirstin Hoefer, product manager for Jango.

And even if some retailers won't cooperate now, they will eventually bow to the bots, say the comparison-shopping concerns. "As consumers start moving to a medium, you have to follow them if you're a retailer," says Venky Harinarayan, a vice president at Junglee.

The Web retailers, though, may not be the only impediment to comparison shopping in cyberspace: Some of the shopping bots may be undermined even by their owners. The acquisition of Junglee by Amazon.com, for example, will give the book seller control of one of the most well-known shopping bots. That worries critics, who note that it isn't in the best interests of Amazon.com to have traffic driven to competitors should Amazon.com fail to have the lowest prices.

A book search using Junglee on the Compaq Web site missed a number of on-line vendors that offer the title, including Barnes & Noble Inc. Junglee, which lists only vendors that have paid it a fee, says that it does not currently have a relationship with Barnes & Noble, but it is in discussions with it and other booksellers. A spokesman for Barnes & Noble denies that the two companies are talking.

Amazon has pledged that Junglee won't play favorites and will make as much information as possible available to consumers. Nonetheless, Junglee is now playing down the idea that cheaper prices are the main reason to use a shopping bot.

"You don't buy based on price alone. There are multiple aspects, like the convenience of having everything in one place," says Mr. Harinarayan. "That's the way we've started looking at this — as one-stop shopping."

72

Low cost drives modular vehicle assembly

Automakers are saving millions using a relatively new manufacturing process. The biggest winners may be consumers, who could pay less for cars and trucks.

By Earle Eldridge
USA TODAY

Mercedes-Benz puts together its M-Class sport-utility vehicle at a plant in Alabama. But aside from the engine, little is manufactured by Mercedes.

The dashboard comes from General Motors' Delphi unit. The frame comes from Budd; the gear box from Dana.

The M-Class is an example of the hottest trend in automaking, modular assembly, through which suppliers design and build major chunks of vehicles — whole interiors, for example — before they reach the automaker's assembly line.

U.S. and European automakers have enthusiastically embraced modular assembly. Almost every new auto plant — from the Mercedes plant in Alabama and BMW's plant in South Carolina to Chrysler, Ford and Volkswagen plants overseas — uses modular assembly. Components pre-assembled by suppliers, especially seats and dashboards, can be found in most new cars.

The dissenters are the Japanese automakers, who shun modular assembly because, they say, it gives suppliers too much authority.

But supporters say the benefits are huge for everyone.

▲ For automakers there are big savings. They spend less on design, engineering, inventory, labor and manufacturing costs.

▲ For suppliers, there are long-term contracts and opportunities to grow through mergers.

▲ And consumers get better quality and lower, or at least stable, prices on new cars.

At the Mercedes-Benz plant in Vance, Ala., Delphi Packard Electrical Systems builds the dashboard for the M-Class sport utility. Complete dashboards with temperature knobs, radios, glove boxes, air bags, instrument panels — everything except the steering wheel — arrive at the plant just in time to slide inside M-Classes rolling down the assembly line.

Doors with windows, arm rests, speakers and locks also are trucked to the plant ready to be bolted on the M-Class. So are axles, exhaust systems, seats and other components pre-assembled by suppliers and sent to the plant.

"We took the vehicle and divided it into sections," says Robert Birch, vice president for purchasing and logistics at Mercedes. "Each section had a team to develop those parts of the vehicle."

In Brazil, Dana works with 70 other suppliers providing more than 220 parts — from tires to electrical wiring — to build the chassis for the Dodge Dakota pickup.

Only the engine, transmission and body are added to the chassis to complete the vehicle. In all, Dana builds about a third of the Dakota before it even reaches the Dodge plant.

"Modular helps us get products to market faster and at the lowest possible cost," says Jonathan Maples, director of supplier management for Chrysler.

Automakers can save millions. Ford estimates modular assembly and just-in-time parts delivery from suppliers (which it calls in-sequence delivery) have produced annual savings of more than $9 million at its Wixom, Mich., factory, which builds the Lincoln Continental and Town Car and soon will begin building Lincoln LS6 and LS8 sedans.

Ford expects modular assembly and in-sequence delivery to save the company more than $200 million over 10 years as the concept is rolled out to other plants.

The automakers' big savings come because no designers are needed to develop the interior; fewer assembly line workers are needed to build the interior; no floor space is needed to stock parts before they are assembled; and the supplier takes responsibility for testing and certifying the parts.

For example, instead of asking a supplier to build a console, an automaker will ask for a design of the whole interior. If the design is approved, the automaker will have the supplier build the interior, coordinating the assembly of parts from several other suppliers.

Using computerized ordering from the automaker, the supplier can deliver the completed interior to the assembly plant in the right color and the proper sequence to fit into a pre-determined vehicle rolling down the line.

For suppliers, modular assembly has meant bigger

and longer-term contracts. Instead of having guaranteed work for just a couple of years, suppliers who can design complete sections of a vehicle for an automaker are getting seven- and eight-year contracts.

Major suppliers — Delphi, Eaton, Visteon Automotive Systems, Dana, Magna International, Johnson Controls, Lear and others — have that ability.

Suppliers also see the trend as a chance to make their names known outside the industry — if they can convince automakers that adding a supplier name to a component improves the value of the vehicle. Bose audio systems puts its name on sound systems in Cadillacs. And Cadillac brags that it uses Bose systems.

Eventually, supplier names on vehicles could become as commonplace as "Intel inside" on today's computers, identifying the chipmaker.

And modular assembly has sparked a consolidation boom among suppliers who are looking to buy or merge with other companies to help them build major sections of a vehicle. Brake suppliers are merging with axle suppliers, for instance. Dashboard suppliers are selling their suspension operations.

But the big benefactors of modular assembly ultimately may be consumers.

In a market where vehicle quality is essentially good across the board, consumers shop for value. That makes auto companies hungry for new ways to cut prices and beat the competition. Modular assembly may be the ticket.

Automakers also say quality improves with modular assembly because suppliers use fewer parts in a module, decreasing the chances of components breaking down and thus improving quality and reducing consumer complaints.

Ford says that when it began modular assembly of instrument panels for Lincoln Navigator and Ford Expedition sport-utility vehicles, panel repair work dropped by 95%.

But despite the benefits cited by proponents, Japanese automakers have avoided it. Toyota officials say the company is taking a "cautious approach" to modular assembly as it looks to reduce its manufacturing costs. But it is concerned that "the more you let go to the outside," the less control you have over the quality of the vehicle, says Barbara McDonald, a Toyota spokeswoman.

Suppliers join to meet carmakers' demands

By Earle Eldridge
USA TODAY

A consolidation boom is sweeping the auto supply industry as suppliers try to meet automaker's demands to build major chunks of their vehicles.

Nearly every week, a supplier announces it has bought another company or is selling some portion of its business.

Earlier this month, Lear, an automotive seat maker, bought Delphi Automotive's seat business from General Motors for $250 million.

The purchase will help Lear build more interior components for automakers.

In July, seat maker Johnson Controls bought Becker Group for $548 million. Johnson officials said Becker "strengthens Johnson's ability to build complete auto interiors."

Also earlier this month, Dura Automotive Systems, a latch, parking brake and jack maker, bought Tower Automotive's hinge business for an undisclosed amount.

Tower said it sold the hinge business so it could focus on its auto chassis and suspension components.

Since January, Eaton, an engine parts maker, sold its axle, brake and suspension divisions and bought companies that make fuel systems and cylinder heads.

Not all the acquisitions are friendly. AlliedSignal, a vehicle electronics supplier, is in the midst of a hostile takeover of AMP, another vehicle electronics maker. By buying AMP, Allied will be able to build computer mapping systems and crash avoidance devices for automakers.

Small suppliers are making deals, too. Chasco Systems, a suspension maker, recently bought Delphi Automotive Systems' coil spring operations for an undisclosed price.

Analyst John Hoffecker of A.T. Kearney estimates that the number of so-called Tier 1 or major suppliers to automakers will fall to about 1,000 by the year 2000 from about 2,500 in 1995.

"You are going to see more and more consolidation," Hoffecker says.

(Cont.)

Honda officials say that by doing most of its own assembly work, the automaker can maintain strict quality control.

Having suppliers pre-assemble major components "is not a methodology we are embracing," says Roger Lambert, a spokesman for Honda in Marysville, Ohio.

Other automakers counter that they maintain strict control over their vehicles even though large portions are pre-assembled by suppliers.

The automakers' engineers have the expertise to make sure all the modules from suppliers work together and give the vehicle the proper ride and feel. And responsibility for the exterior styling of the vehicle will remain with the automaker, they say.

And few automakers are willing to give up control over the engine and its performance, considered a core strength. But as automakers entrust suppliers to build major chunks of the vehicle, they do, in fact, give up some control over the final product, analysts say.

"When the supplier picks the kind of radio in the vehicle and other components, the automaker loses some control," says David Porreca, manufacturing manager for the Society of Automotive Engineers.

Suppliers say automakers needn't worry.

"Automakers have to be comfortable understanding that they give up some of their control, but they still have ultimate control over the vehicle," says Ann Cornell, a spokeswoman for Delphi. "We know it is not an easy thing for them to actually turn over control to a supplier. Part of it is trust."

73

Drug Makers Agree to Offer Discounts for Pharmacies

Deal to Match Institutional Prices May Boost Sales of Brand-Name Products

BY ELYSE TANOUYE AND
THOMAS M. BURTON
Staff Reports of THE WALL STREET JOURNAL

Prices for some widely used prescription drugs could be coming down at your corner drugstore. But that doesn't mean big drug makers are reaching for the painkillers.

Instead, by tentatively agreeing to a deal that gives independent pharmacies and small drugstore chains access to drugs at lower prices, drug makers could have an opportunity to enlist the friendly folks behind the pharmacy window in the promotion of brand-name remedies such as Rhone-Poulenc SA's Nasacort AQ allergy drug or Pharmacia & Upjohn Inc.'s anxiety drug Xanax. That's because the pharmacists' profit margins could be bigger.

The wholesale price discounts to the pharmacies could be substantial, up to 50% on some drugs. Will pharmacies pass along their lower prices? "Given the competitive nature of retail pharmacy . . . It would be a rare circumstance where they wouldn't be passing on the difference," says John Rector, general counsel for the National Community Pharmacists Association.

For doctors, however, such programs will add another source of pressure on their prescribing decisions. They already complain that managed care organizations badger them incessantly about sticking to the formularies; patients demand prescriptions for drugs they've seen advertised in magazines or on television; drug salespeople entice doctors with samples and other goodies; and now pharmacists will be calling to convince doctors to prescribe drugs that will get their stores bigger discounts.

But there is already intense skepticism among retail buying groups for independent drugstores about whether the smaller independents will have the ability to qualify for the potential windfall and pass the savings on to consumers. There are nitty-gritty practical obstacles, such as not having the necessary computer systems to document market-share shifts in a way that would convince big pharmaceutical companies.

There's a risk, too, that patients could be confused because pharmacists will have a financial incentive rather than a therapeutic one to ask them to switch prescriptions to other brands.

All this hinges on an agreement earlier this week by Abbott Laboratories, the Hoechst Marion Roussel unit of Germany's Hoechst AG, Pharmacia & Upjohn and the Rhone-Poulenc Rorer Inc. unit of Rhone-Poulenc to settle class-action price-fixing litigation brought by thousands of pharmacies and drugstore chains. The four drug companies earlier this week tentatively agreed to pay about $350 million and to give pharmacies the opportunity to earn the same discounts as managed care and other institutional customers. The agreement follows an earlier settlement agreement among a dozen other drug companies for $373 million, which also included an agreement to end a two-tier pricing system that the pharmacies charged violated antitrust laws.

At the heart of the massive litigation is the drug industry practice of giving managed care and other institutions discounts on their purchases of prescription drugs, but withholding such opportunities from pharmacies. A hospital or managed care organization could extract such discounts by threatening to exclude a company's drugs from its list of preferred drugs, or formulary. But drug companies argued that pharmacies didn't have such clout because they had to keep in stock whatever drugs a physician might prescribe.

Stunned by the sudden power of their managed-care customers, drug companies in the early 1990s capitulated with discounts to any managed care plan that asked. Pharmaceutical companies' sales and profit growth quickly shrank from 15% to 20% a year to less than 10%, triggering a frenzy of consolidation and downsizing in the pharmaceutical industry.

Even before the settlement, drug companies had begun to change their discounting practices to pharmacies responding to market forces rather than legal challenges. Pharmaceutical marketers noticed that only a small minority of health plans can truly influence physicians' prescribing choices. Most plans had "open" formularies that were so broad that discounting didn't give a drug any particular advantage, and most health plans didn't enforce the formulary with physicians anyway. Instead of giving discounts indiscriminately to all managed care plans, drug companies began to limit discounts to those plans that proved they could affect market share.

As part of the renegotiated settlement finalized in February, drug companies agreed to offer retail pharmacies the same opportunities for discounts as HMOs. Some manufacturers have begun sending contracts to drugstores under the same terms — discounts in return for market share increases. American Home Products Corp, Glaxo Holdings PLC, Warner-Lambert Co., Zeneca, and Pfizer Inc. offered pharmacies contracts, says Mr. Rector of the National Community Pharmacists Association.

In their lawsuits, pharmacies argued that they too could move market share, and gave vivid examples of individual pharmacies that

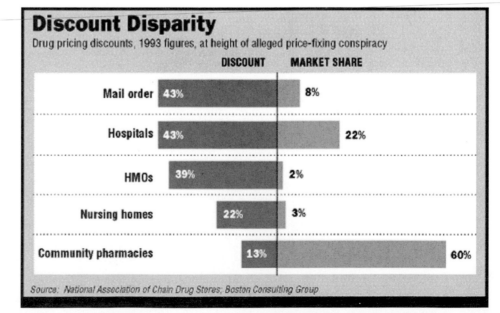

Discount Disparity

Drug pricing discounts, 1993 figures, at height of alleged price-fixing conspiracy

	DISCOUNT	MARKET SHARE
Mail order	43%	8%
Hospitals	43%	22%
HMOs	39%	2%
Nursing homes	22%	3%
Community pharmacies	13%	60%

Source: National Association of Chain Drug Stores; Boston Consulting Group

(Cont.)

had switched prescriptions in favor of particular drugs—for example, substituting the asthma medication Ventolin when prescriptions came in written for Proventil, and vice-versa. But moving market share is time-consuming: Pharmacists must call the prescribing physician each time and ask permission to switch one drug for another.

Still, some drug companies may see such programs as a way to put pharmacists' persuasive powers with doctors to work for them. And it may present a way around managed care formularies — pharmacists may be able to convince doctors to switch prescriptions to a company's drugs even if it isn't on health-plan formularies.

Zeneca's program, for example, offers pharmacies discounts that range from a couple of percentage points to more than 50% in return for market-share increases and participation in other programs.

About 39,000 pharmacies have signed up for Zeneca's programs, says Thomas Behan, Zeneca's director of U.S. market strategy and contract operations. But among smaller retailers, "maybe half are submitting data and participating actively—on a good day," he says. The discount program for managed care and retail stores has increased Zeneca's overall sales volume, he says. "No one is complaining that our margins are shrinking," he says.

Some analysts question whether small pharmacies can exert much influence on doctors' prescription decisions. "This could change the relationship of pharmacists and physicians, but only if the physicians are willing to listen to pharmacists," says analyst Hemant K. Shah. "But I don't know of any physicians who would take a call like that."

Mr. Rector of the pharmacy association, disputes this view: "If anybody can affect the prescribing practices of doctors, it's pharmacists."

74

ANYTHING YOU SELL, I CAN SELL CHEAPER

Buy.com uses stealth technology to undercut rivals

To Internet shoppers, price matters. A lot. Just ask Scott A. Blum. The 34-year-old founder and chief executive of Buy.com reprices the 30,000 or so products in his online computer store daily, if necessary, so that he always has the lowest price. That way, when Internet-savvy shoppers use price-comparing Web technology to search out the best deal, Buy.com always comes up on the top of the list.

It's working. In the first 11 months that Buy.com has been shipping computer gear—through Oct. 31—sales topped $86 million. They are currently running close to $1 million a day, and Blum expects they will reach $120 million to $130 million for the calendar year. That puts the fledgling Aliso Viejo (Calif.) retailer on a pace to beat Conner Peripheral's $113 million record, set in 1987 in its first full-year sales.

Now, Blum has a plan aimed at extending the startup's torrid pace. On Nov. 16, he changed the name of his company to Buy.com from Buycomp.com and got into the book, movie, and video game markets, going head to head with the likes of Amazon.com and Reel.com with his Buybooks.com and Buymovies.com. To get a leg up, Buy.com is acquiring Internet retailer SpeedServe Inc. from Ingram Entertainment Inc., the country's largest video and video game distributor. In exchange, Ingram will get a 5% stake in the company, now worth about $20 million.

Buy.com is betting that its best-price guarantee will work as well for $15 books and movies as it does for $500 hand-held computers. Blum reckons that if he dispenses with Web niceties—say, the community-like feel of book reviews and chats on rival Amazon.com's site—and sticks with bargain-basement deals, Buy.com will carve out new ground. "We're

going for someone who knows what they want and wants it for the best price," he says. "We're trying to keep our site simple, effective, and easy to use—not cluttered with a lot of links and long reviews and stuff." In short, Blum figures cybernauts may browse at Amazon but plunk their money down at Buybooks.com.

Or will they? Some experts are doubtful. "The surveys we do say that price is a huge factor in getting consumers to buy online," says analyst Nicole Vanderbilt of market researcher Jupiter Communications in New York. "But with books and music, there's a different dynamic." Says Amazon.com CEO Jeffrey P. Bezos: "Customers want selection, ease of use, and a low price—in that order."

Who's right? To be sure, Blum is no novice to the startup scene, though his record is spotty. A college dropout, he started his

first company, Microbanks, when he was 19, making memory modules for Apple Macintosh computers. He sold that outfit in 1987 for $2.5 million and founded Pinnacle Micro Inc. with his father, a retired Hewlett-Packard Co. executive. But Pinnacle, which made optical-storage systems for computers, ran into manufacturing problems. Two years ago, Blum and other Pinnacle officials settled charges by the Securities & Exchange Commission that the company had used improper accounting practices to inflate sales and earnings. In the settlement, Blum neither admitted nor denied any wrongdoing.

CEO SEARCH. Today, Blum's backers shrug off his run-in with the SEC. "We like to invest in entrepreneurs with experience, good or bad. He ran into problems but learned a lot," says E. Scott Russell, a Buy.com director and general partner at Softbank Technology

BUY.COM ON THE MOVE

OCTOBER, '96
Company founded

NOVEMBER, '97
Buycomp.com opens for Internet business

JULY, '98
Former Apple CEO Sculley joins the board

AUGUST, '98
Softbank invests $20 million ($40 million more in October)

OCTOBER, '98
Sales reach $86 million

NOVEMBER, '98
Announces acquisition of Internet book, movie, and game business from Ingram Entertainment. Name changed to Buy.com

(Cont.)

Ventures, which spent $20 million for a 10% stake in Buy.com in August. In October, parent Softbank Holdings Inc. came up with $40 million for an additional 10%, valuing the company at $400 million.

The blemish on Blum's track record, however, has prompted him to launch a search for a CEO who would have credibility with Wall Street. The company, which plans to go public early next year, should have a new chief executive in place by then. "Because of my past, we're bringing in a new CEO with the intent of taking the company public early next year," Blum says. "And I assembled a great board so that I could go to them to get answers." Ingram Entertainment CEO David B. Ingram resigned Nov. 6 from the board of Ingram Micro Inc., which packs and ships Buy.com orders, so that he could take a seat on Buy.com's board once his deal closes. Other directors include former Apple Computer CEO John Sculley and PepsiCo co-founder Donald Kendall Sr.

SECRET WEAPON. Blum's success does not depend solely on selling goods. With computer gear, he uses low prices to drive customers to his site, which then sells advertising to the manufacturers it represents. BuyPrinters.com, for example, has an opening page with 12 ads that go for $3,000 a month each, and there are more than 600 such pages on the BuyComp.com site. The company stocks no inventory. Instead, it depends on Ingram Micro in neighboring Santa Ana, Calif., to fill orders the same day.

Buy.com's secret weapon, though, is a stealth technology that allows its computers to crawl through other Web sites and ferret out rivals' prices. Instead of landing on their sites with a high-speed connection from a single Internet address—which would alert them and let them block Buy.com—the company has set up hundreds of accounts with Internet service providers, using low-speed modem connections. Each one hits a rival site no more than seven times, looking only like a curious consumer. Once the lowest price is determined, Buy.com undercuts it and sends it off to price-comparing search engines, which present it to shoppers the next day.

Blum's ambitions don't stop at books and movies either. Coming next year: music, with BuyMusic.com and even BuyJazzMusic.com. He has locked up the Internet addresses BuyCars.com, BuyInsurance.com, and even BuyCheeseburgers.com—all told, 3,000 Web addresses starting with "Buy." And just in case there's any confusion about his game plan, he owns a couple of Web addresses that he's holding in reserve. One of them: 10percentoffAmazon.com.

By Larry Armstrong in Aliso Viejo, Calif.

'BUILD A BETTER MOUSETRAP' IS NO CLAPTRAP

Yes, companies can hike prices—if they reinvent their products

When Gillette Co. unveiled Mach3, the world's first triple-blade razor, it took a bold gamble. While deflationary pressure was making it impossible for most companies to charge high prices for new products, Mach3 cartridges were to sell for around $1.60 each, a 50% premium over Gillette's then-priciest blade, the SensorExcel. Skeptics predicted the personal-care giant would soon be forced to cut that price. But six months after Mach3 hit U.S. stores, the price is holding and Mach3 has become the No. 1 blade and razor. Gillette had 70.7% of the U.S. market in December, its highest share since 1962.

Most companies would kill for a product with this kind of pricing power. In a new survey by the Financial Executives Institute and Duke University, chief financial officers from all industries said they expect price hikes to average just 1.4% in 1999. Manufacturers say they'll manage a gain of only 0.2%. And some 25% of U.S. companies, in industries from breakfast cereal to autos, will have to cut prices, figures Gary Stibel, a founder and principal of the New England Consulting Group.

REALLY BIG SHOE PADS. But an elite few are bucking the trend by introducing "new products that provide benefits people think are worth paying for," says Gillette CEO Alfred M. Zeien. Colgate-Palmolive Co., for example, priced Colgate Total 25% above mainstream brands because Total is the first paste approved by the Food & Drug

> Pricey toothbrushes are appealing to aging baby boomers who want to enter old age with their own choppers

Administration to help prevent gingivitis. After a year, Total is the No. 1 brand, with a nearly 10% share. Dr. Scholl's, a unit of Schering-Plough Corp., has taken the lowly shoe-insert pad and used biomechanics to transform it into a remedy for leg and back pain. The new product, Dynastep, sells for as

much as $14 per insert, twice as much as older inserts—and since 1997, it has become the No. 1 device, with 29% of the market.

What's the secret to pricing power? For starters, a commitment to innovation. Gillette spent nearly $1 billion on the development and initial marketing of Mach3. Similarly, a stream of breakthroughs allows Sony Corp. to command a premium even for TVs, where prices have been falling. Thanks in part to the Wega, the world's first conventional flatscreen TV, Sony's TV sales rocketed 24% in the first half of its fiscal 1998.

Of course, pricing power is often fleeting. Intel Corp., for one, has had to cut prices of low-end chips as rivals have brought out similar products. But Intel remains "the only game in town" for high-end chips, says Ashok Kumar, senior research analyst for Piper Jaffray Inc. Intel is charging $3,692 for its latest Pentium II Xeon processor—or $3,271 above the production cost, according to MicroDesign Resources. "It's a license to print money," says Kumar.

It also helps to aim products at the affluent. They "are willing to pay a lot more to save time or obtain other significant benefits," says Christopher Hoyt, a marketing consultant in Stamford, Conn. Maytag Corp.'s environment-friendly Neptune washer is a hit among well-off consumers, even though at $1,100, it costs twice as much as conventional washers. Over the course of a year, it uses $100 less electricity than other washers and saves 7,000 gallons of water— as much as a person drinks in a lifetime.

BLITZKRIEG. Even the humble toothbrush has undergone a price-boosting metamorphosis—thanks to aging baby boomers who want to keep their choppers. Gillette's Oral-B Laboratories is betting that it can charge $5—50% more than current top-line rivals— for its new CrossAction brush, due in February. Oral-B claims its unique design will remove 25% more plaque than today's best-selling brush.

The pricing elite also back their products with lavish ad spending. Gillette is sinking $300 million into marketing Mach3 in its first year. Ian Cook, president of Colgate North America, boasts that an "unprecedent-

---

WHERE THE PRICING POWER IS

COLGATE TOTAL TOOTHPASTE
25% higher than conventional toothpaste, now No. 1 brand

GILLETTE'S MACH3 RAZOR
$1.60 per cartridge, 50% more than SensorExcel, now top seller

MAYTAG'S NEPTUNE WASHER
$1,100, double the average washer, now No. 2

---

ed" blitzkrieg on dentist's offices made Total "the toothpaste most recommended by dentists and hygienists" in its first four months.

Inevitably, some pricing power champs lose muscle. "Three years ago, Nike was a controlling factor," says Chet James, owner of Super Jock 'n Jill, a Seattle running-shoe store. But thanks to a style shift to brown shoes, a plunge in Asian demand, and Michael Jordan's retirement, "right now, it's not pricing power but buying power" that's at the forefront. In autos, a global capacity glut has meant that "prices have actually gone down," says DaimlerChrysler Co-Chairman Robert J. Eaton.

The message seems clear. While competing on price can work, the success of the pricing elite suggests there may be a better way. "Most companies don't take a bold enough position to invest in the development of superior products that can command a premium price," argues Jeffrey M. Hill, managing director of Meridian Consulting Group. Given the potential rewards, perhaps they should.

By William C. Symonds in Boston, with bureau reports

REVOLT OF THE EXECUTIVE CLASS

They're learning how to beat high fares and low service

The fourth quarter of 1998 should have been a glorious one for the airline industry. Fuel costs fell 18% for the year, saving carriers some $2 billion. Debt is down, the resilient economy has kept planes fuller than ever, and fare wars seem a relic of days gone by.

Yet carrier after carrier spent the week of Jan. 18 preparing to announce fourth-quarter earnings declines—for a combined 36% industry fall, projects Salomon Smith Barney. Northwest Airlines suffered the most, with a quarterly loss of $181 million, a hangover from its summer pilots' strike. Despite picking up Northwest's lost business, though, the other major airlines reported weak earnings. Delta Air Lines Inc.'s, for example, were up 2%, while at AMR Corp., parent of American, they were down 13%. And this year doesn't look any better. Salomon expects first-quarter pretax earnings to fall 25%. The stocks have been punished accordingly, down 20% since July even as the S&P 500-stock index has risen 7%. For airline executives, who have made a habit of boasting that they have overcome the industry's violent cyclical swings, it is a nasty sight indeed.

FARE FALL. What went wrong? The crisis in Asia continues to hurt, but the biggest problem was right here at home in the lucrative business-travel market. Though leisure travelers continued flying at roughly their usual pace, business travelers learned new ways around high-priced fares. By pushing up business fares far faster than inflation, the airlines have given Corporate America a huge incentive to find new ways to save. For the first time in two years, the average fare paid by American businesses actually dropped slightly in the fourth quarter. "Companies are fed up," says Eric J. Altschul, a corporate travel consultant, "and now more than ever, they are questioning what they can do."

That's not all—they're also taking action. Big companies sliced travel spending by 17%, according to the National Business Travel Assn. The result: The airline industry has been hit by a downturn even as the rest of the economy continues to grow.

Certainly, some of the cutback stems from the usual belt-tightening that comes when companies fear the economy may slow. But an equal share of the blame lies with the airlines themselves. Over the past three years, the cost of business travel has skyrocketed, while the quality of service has deteriorated. The average published fare for an unrestricted one-way ticket—those typically bought by Corporate America—climbed 31%, to $461, over the past four years, according to American Express Travel Related Services Co. Only at the end of last year did prices level off. Over the same period, air passengers have encountered more late planes, waited through longer airport lines, and been more likely to find themselves stuck in a center seat.

TAKE THE VAN. Now businesses are fighting back—in surprising and innovative ways. They're using new technology to find the cheapest fares, installing videoconferencing units, and with increasing frequency, even chartering their own planes. Companies are turning more often to alternative airports such as Oakland, Calif., Flint, Mich., or Providence where fares can be much cheaper. To avoid monopolistic fares, Black & Decker Corp. has started shuttling employees by van between its Towson (Md.) headquarters and a North Carolina plant 350 miles away for an annual savings of $50,000.

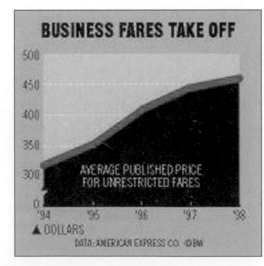

BUSINESS FARES TAKE OFF

500
450
400
350
300

AVERAGE PUBLISHED PRICE FOR UNRESTRICTED FARES

'94   '95   '96   '97   '98

▲ DOLLARS

DATA: AMERICAN EXPRESS CO. ©BW

> Road warriors' new cost consciousness has hurt the big airlines' profits

DaimlerChrysler and General Motors Corp. have taken the extraordinary step of underwriting an upstart airline to keep prices competitive on routes in and out of Detroit.

The airlines' problem isn't the number of people boarding planes. Instead, it's the newly aggressive steps that businesses are taking to avoid paying the highest fares. On average, corporate fliers now pay 63% of the published unrestricted fare, according to American Express, down from 74% in early 1996. Even airline executives, who remain bullish, admit to some worry: "There's tremendous concern about what demand levels are going to be in 1999," says James E. Goodwin, president of UAL Corp., United Airlines Inc.'s parent company.

That said, don't look for any *mea culpas* from the industry. Airline executives believe that globalization will keep demand for business travel strong—and deny that they overcharge for their services. "There has been a lot of brouhaha about the punitive nature of business travel costs that is just unfair," says Frederick W. Reid, chief marketing officer for Delta. He says that providing corporate travelers with plenty of direct flights and the ability to make last-minute changes justifies the higher fares.

Still, fares have gone high enough to attract the attention of senior management for perhaps the first time. "It's no longer just the travel manager who's concerned about the high level of airfares. It's the senior V-P of finance, it's the comptroller, it's the CEO," says Norman R. Sherlock, executive director of the NBTA, which represents 2000 companies that account for $65 billion in annual travel spending. An executive at ConAgra Inc. found that out the hard way when he was chewed out during a conference call by CEO Bruce Rohde. His crime: buying a first-class seat to Paris. "I just bitched at everybody about it," Rohde says.

A WEB OF SAVINGS. Ironically, many companies are beginning to use the same tactics airlines have long employed to squeeze every possible penny out of their customers. Call it reverse "yield management"—the flip side of the process that airlines have refined

(Cont.)

for steering fliers into higher-fare seats. Desktop programs allow travel managers to search the Internet for bargain fares normally snapped up by leisure travelers. Companies have also learned to use convoluted fare structures to their advantage. Hewlett-Packard Co., which has cut travel by 25% over the past six months, for a savings of $100 million, recommends that employees sometimes buy advance tickets even when they aren't sure if they'll make a trip—because on the whole, paying penalties for cancellations is cheaper than buying last-minute tickets. Quaker Oats Co. has upped the average number of days before a ticket is bought from 10 to 15, for a savings of $1 million over the past 18 months. It has lots of company: 62% of businesses say they are increasing their use of advance-purchase fares, according to the NBTA.

Then there's videoconferencing, which has long been hailed as a potential substitute for travel. While many functions require face-to-face contact, plenty of other tasks can be done via fiber-optic lines. Hewlett-Packard Chief Executive Officer Lewis E. Platt, for example, recently opted to skip a speech in Singapore and deliver it instead by real-time video. A March NBTA survey found that 52% of companies are using the technology—almost double the 1996 level.

Even when corporations do have to conduct business in person, they're finding new ways to avoid the commercial carriers. Outright ownership of a private plane is still hard to justify on cost alone, but charters and fractional ownership may add little additional expense—and offer far more convenience. The number of hours flown by charter planes climbed 35% last year, according to the National Air Transportation Assn. Boston Consulting Group Inc., for example, often charters an eight-seat plane for $3,000 for trips between Toronto and Boston, saving an hour each way. With round-trip fares on a commercial carrier running $800, it doesn't take many passengers to break even. Executive Jet Inc., the Montvale (N.J.) company owned by Warren E. Buffett's Berkshire Hathaway, will sell companies as little as one-16th of a plane. Last year, it flew 145,000 hours, up from 95,000 in 1997.

All of these steps to cut corporate travel costs can hurt the major airlines, but they are unlikely to rewrite the rules for the nation's skyways. That would take an influx of new competitors—something the major carriers may finally be more vulnerable to, though starting an airline remains immensely difficult. Already, discount giant Southwest Air-

lines Co. has increased its market share by 44% in the past five years, according to GKMG Consulting Services, and it will soon enter the metropolitan New York area.

Meanwhile, Midwest Express—the full-price Milwaukee carrier that caters to business travelers with wide all-leather seats and cookies that are freshly baked on board—saw profits rise about 40% last year, according to analyst's estimates. And in Detroit, 18-month-old Pro Air Inc. is being under-written by DaimlerChrysler and GM, which are eager to keep fares competitive in a city dominated by Northwest. In January, Pro Air starts service to New York.

THE FEDS STEP IN. The government may soon make it easier for upstarts, most of which have struggled mightily in the '90s. Measures that industry critics have long pushed are finally getting attention from a group of bipartisan heavyweights, including Vice-President Al Gore and Senate Commerce Committee Chairman John McCain (R-Ariz.). They worry that the major airlines no longer compete with each other in many markets and have effectively chased new-comers off their routes. After President Clinton's impeachment trial, Congress and the Administration will mull an array of steps aimed at spurring competition and defining predatory behavior.

There's little doubt that the market could handle more competition. Of the nation's 1,000 most traveled routes, 500 lack low-fare service, the Transportation Dept. says. That's created a lot of unhappy business travelers eager to pursue alternatives. If their dissatisfaction causes them to step up their efforts, the airline industry's future could be as unpleasant as standing in line at the airport.

By David Leonhardt in Chicago, with bureau reports

77

CHEAPER EXPORTS?
NOT SO FAST
Manufacturers face soaring materials and financing costs

When East Asia's currencies started crashing last summer, Vigor International President Wang Yu-len smelled opportunity. Like many Asian middlemen who export garments and handicrafts to big retailers in the U.S., Taipei-based Vigor had been relying heavily on low-cost factories in China. With the Indonesian rupiah, Thai baht, Malaysian ringgit, and Philippines peso all suddenly trading at less than half their old values against the dollar—while China's renminbi remained stable—Wang figured Southeast Asia would be awash with bargains.

It seemed like a no-brainer. But after a swing through the region in early January, Wang returned empty-handed. Why? Most Southeast Asian manufacturers were hungry for foreign orders but so strapped for cash that they couldn't buy the imported materials needed to fill them. "Suppliers face a very embarrassing situation," says Wang.

TOUGH SLOG. To officials in Asia's most battered economies, the situation is downright depressing. They had hoped that cheaper currencies would translate into a major boost in export competitiveness in everything from toys to computer chips, allowing their countries to emerge quickly from the crisis. But for many, this silver lining is proving to be a mirage. That's because the fuel needed to

---

> ## CASH CRUNCH
> ## Many suppliers no longer accept the Indonesian rupiah, so manufacturers can't buy fabric

---

power these export machines—dollars—is in short supply. Whether they are small Indonesian shoemakers or South Korea's largest conglomerates, the region's manufacturers are having a hard time raising the cash to buy raw materials. Skittish foreign banks and overstretched domestic lenders are refusing to extend letters of credit. Local suppliers, fearful of further currency devaluations, are demanding dollars up front—or are bankrupt themselves.

To be sure, Asia's exporters will register gains as the months roll on. Thai producers

of computer components report surging sales, while South Korean conglomerates such as Samsung, Daewoo, and Hyundai are canceling plans to expand in the U.S. and Europe and are shifting production of some electronics goods back home in order to capitalize on the cheaper won. Factories that are either owned or financed by multinationals also stand to benefit.

But for most exporters, it will be a tough slog. Judging from the problems Asian traders and manufacturers are having so far, it seems doubtful that the increase will be enough to enable Korea, Thailand, and Indonesia to export themselves back to health. World markets for cars, chemicals, and many electronics components are already glutted. China, with its vast base of suppliers and efficient infrastructure, remains a ferocious competitor in many industries. And the new advantage of devalued wage rates in Korea and Southeast Asia is more than offset by higher import costs. Most Southeast Asian producers buy most of their raw materials and components from abroad.

Financing costs are also soaring. Interest rates in some countries have tripled, to around 30%, as panicked central bankers try to stabilize currencies. The area's currency devaluations may hurt Asian exporters much more than they help, says Toby Brown, managing director of General Oriental Investments (HK) Ltd. "The tidal wave of cheap exports isn't going to happen," Brown predicts.

Yet buyers for big stores in the U.S. have heard so much about the collapse of Asian currencies that they are already counting on huge price cuts of 35% to 75%. Manufacturers say they can't afford much more than a 10% cut. A Nike spokesperson notes that because 65% of the materials of shoes made in Indonesia are imported, prices on U.S. retail shelves won't change much. "Customers don't understand," says Lydia Hsu, a sales manager at Fairtrade Co., a Taiwan company that exports luggage and handbags made in the Philippines and China. Hsu says one of her big U.S. retail customers wants to renegotiate contracts that were struck a few months ago, hoping to get a better deal. But inflation of raw-materials costs makes that impossible, she says.

The gyrations in the currency markets are adding to the problem. Some Indonesian fabric suppliers, for example, have become so nervous about another dive in the rupiah that

---

---

they won't quote prices for their products. "Every day, the prices from the mill are changing without notice," says Flor Cayanan, a merchandise manager for Hong Kong trading house Swire Maclaine, which buys garments in Indonesia. The 70% plunge in the rupiah has actually pushed up the price of Indonesian fabric by 20%, Cayanan says, because of the higher costs for financing and imported yarn. And suppliers no longer accept rupiah.

Meanwhile, banks are pulling back on credit, adding to the paralysis. For many normally sound manufacturers, getting export financing from shell-shocked Asian banks is nearly impossible. A manager at a trading arm of an elite Korean conglomerate says his company is facing difficulty in all export areas, including textiles, electronics, cars, and machinery. Moon Kye Ho, assistant manager at furniture maker Fursys Inc., says he hasn't been able to buy any imported raw materials since December. To fill export

(Cont.)

orders, he has been drawing down inventories. "If the situation continues for one more month, exports will be hard hit," Moon says. **LENDING FREEZE.** For Asia's export logjam to ease, its currencies must stabilize, and governments must make progress in cleaning up bad debts. Then they can start lowering interest rates and inject liquidity back into the system. But relief won't come soon. Many of the region's indebted banks simply can't lend because they remain far short of the 8% capital-adequacy ratios required by the International Monetary Fund as part of bailout packages. "If we don't meet the requirements, we get shuttered," explains a Korean bank exec.

Some Asian manufacturers are so starved for finances that Hong Kong trading giant Li

> ## NO BARGAINS
> **U.S. retailers expecting 35% to 75% discounts will be sorely disappointed**

Fung Ltd., which buys garments and other goods from vendors across the region, says it may have to take on the burden of buying raw materials itself and delivering them to factories. "We may have to do business in a totally different way," says Managing Director William K. Fung.

Not that less-than-expected export growth in Asia will be bad news for everyone. Predictions that a flood of cheap imports will push the U.S. trade deficit to $300 billion this year may turn out to be far overblown. And China could be under less pressure to devalue the renminbi if its competitors falter. A Chinese devaluation would shake financial markets worldwide. But for many Asian exporters that are barely hanging on, time is running out.

By Jonathan Moore in Taipei, with Moon Ihlwan in Seoul

78

Value Retailers Go
Dollar For Dollar

If you thought the corner five-and-dime had succumbed
to the Wal-Marts of the world, think again. Three hot retailers
strike gold with small, "extreme value" stores.　■ *by Anne Faircloth*

The Madison Square shopping center on the outskirts of Nashville has clearly seen better days. A couple of stores sit vacant; the parking lot is far from full. Yet one small, unpretentious storefront is abuzz. At 10 A.M. on a Wednesday morning Dollar General store No. 2392 is doing brisk business on items like 75-cent-a-gallon bleach, $10 cookware sets, and two-for-a-dollar cans of Vienna sausage. John Brown, a maintenance technician at the Nashville airport, is eyeing the $1.50 deodorant. "Sure, it's cheaper here," he says. "They don't call it a dollar store for nothing."

The corner five-and-dime was supposed to have succumbed to the superstore blitzkrieg long ago. But it hasn't worked out that way. Several strong players are proving that there's plenty of money to be made by simply "living off the crumbs of Wal-Mart," says Dan Wewer, an analyst at Robinson-Humphrey. Indeed, the strongest, and many believe the last, growth segment in retailing is the so-called extreme-value category, which includes three of today's hottest retail stocks: Dollar General, Family Dollar, and Dollar Tree.

About as glamorous as three-for-a-dollar paper towels, these stores have nonetheless caught the attention of Wall Street, which believes they are hitting an economic and demographic sweet spot. While in today's category-killer world most suburbanites trek to stores the size of your average island nation to buy everything from linoleum flooring to Barbie dolls, many people are put off by such big-box shopping experiences. In particular, low- and fixed-income customers are drawn to value retailers , which offer easy access, small stores (at an average 6,400 square feet, a Dollar General is about the size of one department in a superstore), and a narrow selection of basics like washing powder and toothpaste. And, of course, excellent prices; although Dollar Tree is the only real dollar store (everything literally costs no more than $1), all three manage rock-bottom pricing.

According to analyst Barbara Miller of BT Alex. Brown, "Dollar-store customers think Wal-Mart is expensive. They go into these supercenters and ask, 'Do I belong here?'" A small neighborhood convenience store suits these shoppers perfectly. A dollar store is to Wal-Mart what a 7-Eleven is to Safeway—except that in dollar stores, the customer doesn't pay a premium for convenience.

> ## DOLLAR TREE
> **With its shipshape look, the chain has shed the image of a junky close-out shop.**

Dollar General and Family Dollar, the grandes dames of this niche, have been around since the 1950s, yet today's numbers indicate that there's never been a better time to be in this business. About 40% of the country's households earn less than $25,000—the target income level of these two chains. And thanks in part to the recent increase in the minimum wage—20% over the past two years—these folks have more money to spend. And they will buy, says Miller. "These customers spend every extra dollar they have."

She estimates that households earning $30,000 or less drop a whopping $55 billion each year on basic consumables—canned meat, snacks, cleaning supplies, and health and beauty aids. This sales potential has not been lost on the dollar stores, which have significantly boosted their offerings in these categories. Last year value retailers as a group rang up $8.3 billion in total sales; of that, $3.8 billion was generated by consumables. There is a lot of room left for growth.

As major discounters continue to shift toward the supercenter format, broadening their customer base and increasing their offerings of higher-priced goods, they create an opening for value retailers to snap up shoppers from the low-income segment. In other words, for every middle-class mom Kmart attracts with its Martha Stewart bedding, it alienates a minimum-wage worker struggling to make ends meet on $5.15 an hour. By 2002, Miller predicts, value retailers will rack up $10.3 billion in consumables sales and total sales of $19.4 billion—18% compound annual growth over five years.

Martha Stewart would feel decidedly out of place in your average dollar store. Most have bare-bones fixtures—products like detergent are often stacked on the cardboard cartons they come in—and a cash-and-carry checkout (no credit cards). In keeping with the low-budget format, value retailers tend to go into locations left vacant by other tenants at rents of around $3 to $4 per square foot, less than half the discount-store average.

Thanks to these controlled costs, Miller estimates that in its first year of operation, a Dollar General produces a return on investment in excess of 50%, which in turn creates considerable cash flow. The company is thus able to sustain rapid growth—500 new stores slated for 1998—while incurring minimal debt. Family Dollar, which has never carried long-term debt, has a return on investment of 35% per unit as a result of lower sales. Still, that has been enough to fund a debt-free expansion into 38 states, with 350 to 400 new stores planned for the next fiscal year.

It's remarkable that in a niche so small, two such similar companies have competed successfully against each other for 40 years while overlapping significantly: In over half the towns where there's a Dollar General,

(Cont.)

there's also a Family Dollar. It works because these little stores draw from a very small radius, often less than three miles. Therefore, a town of 7,000 can easily support both.

Nevertheless, in the past five years Dollar General has emerged as the clear winner in the dollar-store wars, surpassing Family Dollar in both number of stores (3,360 vs. 2,970) and revenues ($2.6 billion vs. $2 billion). Along the way, its stock increased sixfold since 1993 and is currently trading around $40. Key to its success was Dollar General's recognition in the late '80s of the importance of everyday low prices, a concept pioneered by Wal-Mart. Although the company now offers goods at prices other than a dollar, more than 1,500 items are still sold at that price point, and others are fixed at prices between $1.50 and $20. This strategy has allowed Dollar General to eliminate advertising circulars, once the backbone of its business.

Cal Turner Jr., CEO of the Nashville-based chain, has spent his life courting the low-income customer. His father opened the first Dollar General in 1955. But Cal Jr. had a hankering to enter the ministry and today, at 58, looks every inch the lanky Southern Baptist preacher. His mission, however, is Dollar General: "I've had more of an impact on people in this business than I ever would have had from the pulpit."

Family Dollar was slower to act on the pricing and merchandising trends that drove Dollar General's growth. The retailer, based in Charlotte, N.C., emerged from a prolonged slump in 1994 when it phased in everyday low prices and cut circulars—which cost $2 million to produce each time—from 22 to nine this year. As a result, its ad budget has shrunk to less than 1% of sales for 1998. Following Dollar General's lead, it has shifted its merchandise mix from clothes to household basics—a move that is paying off in strong

same-store sales: 9.3% growth last year. Apparel and other soft goods account for just 34% of sales. Shoppers replenish cleaning supplies and food more frequently than they do clothes; therefore, although prices are lower, traffic and sales are up. The stock, responding to the turnaround, has doubled in the past year, from $8 to $16.

Much of the credit goes to President Howard Levine, 38, who in 1996 returned after a nine-year hiatus to the company his father founded. Leon Levine, 60, who remains chairman and CEO, has long been respected and feared as a merchant. He understood that to sell merchandise at Family Dollar's low price points, you had to first buy it at the right price. A trade publication described him as possessing "bargaining skills that would put a...bazaar trader to shame."

In the early '80s, Procter & Gamble refused to cut Family Dollar a deal on Pampers diapers, arrogantly assuming that the store could not do business without the brand. Family Dollar dropped Pampers and continued to feature its own private label. Even though today vendors like P&G can no longer afford to ignore the buying power of extreme-value retailers, "we still don't sell Pampers," chuckles Howard.

Dollar Tree is the type of single-price-point store that's long been considered a glorified junk shop, packed with closeout goods nobody wants. Yet since going public in March 1995, Dollar Tree stock is up more than sevenfold, from $6.67 to $51. Last year the company made $49 million on sales of $635 million and now operates 924 stores, with 205 to open in 1998. Wall Street loves Dollar Tree's store economics—it boasts a return on investment of nearly 100% per unit, allowing the company to open hundreds each year through cash flow alone.

How does a company get returns like

that when it sells everything for $1? Rather than focusing on schlocky closeouts, Dollar Tree strikes relationships with first-run vendors—often producers of so-called parallel brands—so instead of Fantastik, Dollar Tree sells Fabulous. It imports 40% of its merchandise directly, eliminating the costly middleman, and relies on closeouts for less than 15% of the mix.

FAMILY DOLLAR
The company's founder is famous for his skill at squeezing suppliers.

With its slightly more upscale real estate—25% of its stores are in shopping malls—Dollar Tree targets a higher-income customer than the other value retailers. By locating stores alongside Wal-Marts and Targets, Dollar Tree is going after their $35,000 to $40,000 household-income demographic. It lures these customers to make impulse purchases with what analyst Jim Stoeffel of Smith Barney calls the "wow factor"—the excitement of discovering that an item costs only a dollar. Just 30% of its merchandise mix consists of core consumables; the rest is a hodgepodge of toys, garden tools, holiday decorations, and ceramic angels.

Still, the same trends that have played so favorably for Dollar General and Family Dollar have worked for Dollar Tree as well. CEO Macon Brock emphasizes the convenience aspect: "You can find every category we sell at Wal-Mart, but you'll pay more, and it will take you longer to find it and longer to pay for it," he says.

Value Retailing's Big Three

A look at the numbers behind the leaders in Wall Street's favorite new retailing category

Retailer	Sales 1997	Income 1997	Same-store sales growth	Number of stores	New stores for 1998	Number of states	Average store size	Sales per sq. ft.	Average sale total
Dollar General	$2.6 billion	$145 million	8.4%	3,360	500–525	24	6,400 sq. ft.	$141	$7.90
Family Dollar	$2.0 billion	$75 million	9.3%	2,970	350–400	38	6,500 sq. ft.	$127	$8.04
Dollar Tree	$635 million	$48 million	7.8%	924	205	28	3,900 sq. ft.	$224	$5.50

(Cont.)

rock estimates that there is room for at least 3,000 stores in Dollar Tree's existing 28-state base. The other players, too, see room for a lot more outlets. Dollar General has six stores on an 18-mile stretch of highway in Orlando—each is generating $1 million in sales, above the company average of $900,000.

For now, no one seems eager to go after value retailers' small-box, convenience-oriented turf. This fall Wal-Mart intends to open three prototype small-format convenience stores that will include drive-through pharmacies; however, Turner dismisses these stores as "a different animal." Indeed, at 40,000 square feet, they can hardly be considered as accessible as the dollar-store for-

DOLLAR GENERAL
Food staples are flying off the shelves, driving sales growth.

mat. Pat McCormack, who covers Wal-Mart for BT Alex. Brown, believes the discount giant is hardly worried about the extreme-value segment. Dollar General's total revenues equal one week's sales for Wal-Mart, he points out.

And yet the dollar stores are pesky creatures. Argues Tom Tashjian, an analyst at

NationsBanc Montgomery: "They are taking a nickel here and a quarter there from everybody"—the local variety stores, traditional discounters, grocery stores, and drugstores. The danger, he says, would be to "steal too many nickels from any one of those competitors. Then someone would retaliate." For now, they have stayed safely under the big players' radar by offering value to a segment of the population that traditional discounters have largely ignored. As Sam Walton was fond of saying, the customer votes with his feet, and low-income shoppers are clearly casting their lot with the dollar stores.

Marketing Strategies: Planning, Implementation and Control

79

Brewing a British coup

Starbucks follows couple to Europe

By Marco R. della Cava
USA TODAY

LONDON — If Europeans wake up to find a Starbucks on every high street, *via, rue* and *strasse*, there will be two ways to account for this coffee coup.

One is to accept that, despite popularizing the drink, the Continental crowd really wasn't living until it sipped a triple half-caf skinny mocha latte.

The other is to blame Scott Svenson. He'll take it with a Seattle-bred, Harvard-refined smile, proud of his critical role in planting yet another American corporate icon in an Old World dense with McDonald's, Gap, Disney and Planet Hollywood outlets.

Svenson, 32, and his wife, Ally, 31, moved here in 1990. Five years later, desperately missing their hometown staple, they opened their first Seattle Coffee Co. shop. An instant hit, it spawned 55 U.K. branches, capitalizing on a trend away from traditional tea and dank pubs.

Starbucks, long interested in the European market, had been following the success story and in May snapped up the Svensons' labor of homesickness for $84 million. The couple unwittingly had served as Starbucks' reconnaissance team. Now comes the army.

On Thursday, the first European Starbucks store will open on London's famous King's Road, followed by two dozen others across Britain — added to the conversion of all Seattle Coffee Co. locations.

Starbucks has 1,582 stores in North America and 54 in Asia. The Seattle-based company has plans for 500 European sites by 2003.

Wall Street is bullish. Starbucks stock rose when the sale was announced, "meaning that investors perceive (them) as a global brand, and the quicker they get there, the better," says Lehman Bros. restaurant analyst Mitchell Speiser.

"It won't be a cakewalk, but we can own this market," says Svenson, a casual yet confident man who prefers a Rolex, khakis and loafers to the Seattle grunge look. A former investment banker, he now owns about $20 million in Starbucks stock and has stayed on as CEO of Starbucks U.K.

"We have to be very sensitive to the feel of the local markets," he says over a grande latte in his Fulham Road shop. "Setting up in Germany isn't like going from Washington state into Oregon."

A lovely understatement that captures the challenge facing Starbucks in Europe: Will it be able to take a drink people here have enjoyed since long before our states were united and repackage it successfully enough to lure locals from their cafes and coffee-based bars?

Perhaps surprisingly, the odds are excellent.

In England in the '70s, tea still outsold coffee 4-to-1, thanks to centuries of tradition behind the former and a lowly instant form of the latter. But in the past five years, an economic boom has fed into a Continentalization of Britain. Coffee sales have soared and now outpace tea by 35%.

PUBS PAY A PRICE

A young, well-traveled and somewhat monied new generation created a seismic shift in British nightlife. As the posh nightclubs and restaurants mushroomed, so did hip outlets for those seeking caffeine-and-chat pit stops.

The venerable British pub has been shocked into reform. For example, the Stargazer pub in trendy Chelsea featured a black exterior and dour interior. Chairs sat empty. A wrecking crew came and went last spring, leaving behind a white-walled glassy replacement called The Fine Line. Now one stretches out the door nightly. Starring on the menu: java.

"The aroma of coffee is like a magnet, and it's often better than that of lager," says Caroline Stacey, who recently indulged her coffee habit to report a cover story on "Cafe Society: Where It's Hip to Sip" for a London edition of the weekly entertainment guide *Time Out*.

"Londoners are now upmarket grazing instead of sitting for long meals," she says. "There's a lot more standing around outdoors talking, a lot more moving around. Coffee fits into that."

There are 250 coffee-focused shops in Britain (60% outside London). Analysts believe there is room for 1,500 stores to thrive. Far from seeing Starbucks' arrival as a threat, existing retailers welcome it as brethren.

"They will expand the market for everyone," says Bobby Hashemi, who co-founded Coffee Republic with his sister in 1995. He hopes to add 15 stores to his 20 by the spring.

Most Londoners don't see coffee in nationalistic terms. Starbucks will be judged not as a slice of Americana but on its ability to serve up a good product, Stacey says.

(Cont.)

"America to us is corporate, it's chains, it's a lack of individuality," she says. "That said, as long as Starbucks stores are not offensive and tacky, people will buy their product if it's good."

WILL IT PLAY IN PARIS?

Starbucks isn't saying when it plans to open its first store on the Continent. But when it does, the idea is to become so enmeshed in a given community that, as Starbucks executives like to parrot, someone born in Europe 20 years from now will come to the USA and say, "Oh, I didn't know you had Starbucks here, too."

"Our opportunity lies in offering people a place to come in and take a break in their day," says Jane Melvin, Starbucks International marketing director. "If it was just about selling a cup of coffee, we'd never be who we are."

Truth is, the coffee alone could spell success.

The British passion is evident, yet daily coffee consumption averages about two cups per day, similar to that in the USA. In Finland, Europe's top coffee market, fans swallow up to eight cups a day. That lofty figure also applies to other northern European nations. Blame the weather. And imagine the market.

In the Netherlands, coffee is so much a part of daily life that a popular midday entertainment-oriented TV show is called *Coffee Time*. The country's leading supermarket chain, Albert Heijn, offers shoppers free coffee.

"Women especially want to sit and have a coffee and talk and not be in a bar with loud music," says Jacha van Hout, a mechanical engineer from Arnhem, Netherlands. "Some such shops have opened, but we need more."

In France, the steady decline of cafes offers Starbucks a perfect opportunity. About 6,000 cafes a year have closed since their '60s heyday, prompting owners to convert their stores to themed eateries ranging from cybercafes to discount sandwich shops.

One nation, however, may prove a tough sell: Italy, the home of espresso, king of coffee.

"I think Italians will just laugh at Starbucks," says David Schomer, owner of Seattle's Espresso Vivace shops. His coffee research trips have taken him to hundreds of Italian coffee bars.

Although he acknowledges being a Starbucks detractor ("We call them Charbucks here in Seattle because of the way that they over-roast their beans"), he centers his argument on the sophistication of Italian coffee fans, much as the French tout haute cuisine and Americans pride themselves on their barbecue.

In a land where ordering a cappuccino after noon is the mark of a tourist, the chain has its work cut out.

"My family is divided on the subject," says Milanese ad representative Lucio Aliotti. "My daughter goes to school in Virginia, and my wife, Bonaria, always asks her to bring back vanilla-flavored coffee. Starbucks will never get me, but they'd have my wife from the start."

THANKS TO THE TENOR

When Scott and Ally Svenson opened the doors on their first Seattle Coffee Co. shop, the prospects looked grim.

"The shop was too small, its design was bad, and it was a brutally hot summer," Scott says.

And it made money hand over fist. Contributing heavily was an Italian tenor who performed that season at the nearby Royal Opera. He came in for triple shots of espresso three times a day, often singing along to the arias on the store stereo.

A few months later, the couple decided to open their second shop in London's financial monolith, Canary Wharf. Another score.

Scott decided to quit his job as a senior executive of a health care company to concentrate on the growing business. Besides, he liked the offices better.

But there were some hurdles. Applying for planning permits often became a matter of explaining that "coffee shop" was not a synonym for "greasy spoon." And after Seattle Coffee struck a deal with a local paper cup manufacturer for a variety of sizes, the firm initially refused to deliver the largest cup because it just couldn't believe anyone would drink that much. "As hard as the work got, we'd sit back and think, 'This is great; we've brought a little bit of Seattle to London.' And we missed Seattle so much. Still do," Scott Svenson says.

The Svensons remain eager to return to Bellevue, Wash., and the inspiring vistas of Elliott Bay and the Olympic Range. But not soon; their and Starbucks' futures lie here.

"I've been gone from Seattle since I left for college, so when I finally return, I think to a lot of people I'll still be the high school quarterback," Svenson sighs. "I've done a few things since then."

80

How a Pasta Maker Used Its Noodle To Whip the Giants

AIPC Reflects Power Shift Within Food Industry To Private-Label Firms

Hit: Lemon-Pepper Penne

By Rekha Balu

Staff Report of The Wall Street Journal

American Italian Pasta Co.'s plan to steal pasta sales from the likes of Hershey Foods Corp. was so audacious that its backers suggested it locate in a prime spot in Kansas City, Mo. If the operation failed, they reasoned, the real estate would be easy to unload.

But the company set up in the suburb of Excelsior Springs for cheaper labor and raw materials and easy access to railroads. Instead of unloading its property, it is now expanding.

In the past 10 years, AIPC has grabbed more than 25% of U.S. retail pasta sales, even though few shoppers know it by name. Its products sell under private labels such as President's Choice spaghetti and Albertson's linguini. One measure of AIPC's surge: Hershey and Borden Foods Inc. have decided to trim their pasta businesses. And Bestfoods, owner of the No. 1 branded pasta, Mueller's, recently hired AIPC to make the brand-name product.

"If I had said five years ago we'd have this kind of market share, people would have carted me off to the funny farm," says Timothy Webster, AIPC president and chief executive officer since 1991.

Power Shift

The success of AIPC is part of an enormous power shift taking place in the $430 billion U.S. food industry. Losing market share are the products — such as Kellogg cereal and Nabisco cookies — that showed how powerful a brand can be. Gaining shelf space are the private-label makers, whose products now account for 21% of sales at the top 15 grocers, up from 17% in 1992. While the food industry as a whole grew less than 1% last year, private-label brands grew 4% — and growth looks set to continue in good times or bad.

Store brands, also known as private-label brands, are typically made by an outside manufacturer according to specifications set by the retailer. They're often sold under the store's name and marketed by the retailer.

Branded products are typically marketed and made by the branded company. That is changing as more companies begin to assign production to some of the same companies that make private-label goods — partly in response to the strides those companies are making. Kellogg, which has publicly criticized private-label makers for inferior quality, relies on Keebler Foods Co., the largest private-label cookie maker, to produce about half of all of Kellogg's Pop-Tarts pastries.

Private-label makers are defying the widespread perception of the food industry as sluggish and short on innovation. Branded-food companies like Kellogg Co., H.J. Heinz Co., Nabisco Inc., Quaker Oats Co. and others are firing employees, shutting down plants and selling off businesses. And the market capitalization of many branded-food companies has declined sharply.

By contrast, AIPC is adding capacity and distribution centers from coast to coast, while its stock has climbed to $22.75, yesterday's close on the New York Stock Exchange, from $18 when it went public last year. Ralcorp Holdings Inc., which makes private-label cereal and snacks, saw its share price rise 80% over the past two years.

Fundamental Change

What is especially worrisome for branded companies is that private-label competitors such as AIPC have stolen market share during a decade of strong consumer spending. Historically, store brands grew only during hard times, when consumers watched every penny.

But the growth of private labels this decade indicates a fundamental change in consumer perception. Buying a store brand no longer necessarily means sacrificing on quality. When Jeff Moffatt was growing up, the "private label was frowned upon" as inferior, he says. But now, the San Francisco travel agent treats his pierced tongue to Safeway Co.'s bran flakes and salsa because, he says, the quality is better than that of the Kellogg or Pace brands.

Appearance also has improved. Private-label products evolved from generics, and used to come in black-and-white cans that resembled government rations. But a great deal of design and packaging expertise is devoted to today's private-label products. Amberlyn Nelson, 33, says she buys Safeway Verdi pasta sauce over higher-end Classico largely because of the packaging. "It has a lot to do with the graphics," she says.

Big Advantages

In placing its products on retailers' shelves, the private-label maker boasts some big advantages over branded-food companies. At a time when retailers are losing market share to discounters such as Wal-Mart Stores Inc.'s Supercenters, private-label makers offer a way for supermarkets to compete on price. Store-brand products often are priced 10% to 24% below branded products.

An even bigger marketing advantage than

customer savings is the cut that private-label makers offer retailers: Supermarkets earn an average of 25% more on store-brand products, according to Merrill Lynch. Little wonder that retailers are starting to place their own products at eye level and in prized aisle-end displays, instead of on the lower shelves. Packages, shelf signs and even taste-test tables loudly boast that the store's product tastes as good as the national brand. The store-brand box of Apple Cinnamon Tastees at Iowa-based HyVee supermarkets says, "If you like Apple Cinnamon Cheerios, try this!"

Private-label makers also are going after regional markets. Heinz, the largest producer of private-label soup, recently introduced an "Italian wedding soup" for Pittsburgh-area stores and the Southwest Classics line of bean soups for the Southwestern U.S. For the 52 weeks ended Oct. 11, unit sales of private-label soup grew by 17.7%, compared with 1.5% growth from leader Campbell Soup Co.

Some supermarkets are pulling away from outside brands altogether. "We don't use our energies to advertise other people's labels," says Ira Cohen, director of merchandising at California-based Trader Joe's, which gets 85% of its sales from private-label goods.

The consolidation of the supermarket industry is only enhancing the private-label advantage. Back when most supermarkets were local, national brands carried a lot of clout. But now, the hot pace of acquisitions by a few supermarket chains such as Safeway Inc. and Kroger Co. has helped them gain a near-national presence. And bigger chains, in particular, are enlarging and enhancing their private-label offerings — partly because their size gives them the sort of marketing clout that used to be wielded only by branded-food companies.

All of this raises the question of whether a store brand becomes a national brand when the store itself goes national. More than just semantics, the issue points to the logical goal of the private-label juggernaut. As grocers grow into national chains, they invariably create national brands, just as Sears Roebuck & Co. did. In England, where four supermarket chains control 75% of the market, store brands account for nearly 44% of sales.

The changes in the pasta aisle reflect those throughout the supermarket. As recently as 10 years ago, branded pastas dominated the market. They came from giants like Hershey, Borden and CPC International Inc. Profit margins were sizable.

Then, in the mid-1980s, a Kansas college dropout named Richard Thompson vowed to create a pasta that was both lower in price and superior in quality. Mr. Thompson, an entrepreneur who had prospered in real estate and oil, spent months in Italy studying pasta making, from shapes and flavors to the art of cooking it to al dente perfection. Along with an Italian partner, he lined up investors including Morgan Stanley and Citicorp Venture Capital Ltd.

(Cont.)

AIPC's first customer was Sysco Corp. the big food-service distributor. Mr. Thompson faced the task of delivering premium-quality pasta at a low price — while taking over from Sysco's 30 other suppliers. AIPC soon discovered the upside of its fledgling status.

For one, prices are so high on branded products that a new player can afford to offer quality at a discount. In the store, AIPC pasta typically sells for 69 cents a pound, about 30 cents less than premium brands. Yet the store earns between 15% and 25% more on AIPC pasta. Moreover, new companies can invest in the latest technology, gaining an edge over competitors saddled with old plants and processes.

So AIPC was able to pare its overall costs — the company says its costs are 20% lower than its competitors' — even as it spent more than its branded rivals on higher-quality ingredients and produced more pasta shapes and flavors. AIPC ended up with a large menu of proprietary products that enabled it to offer each of its buyers a unique product. The payoff for Sysco: After signing on with AIPC, its pasta volume rose 16% during a time when Sysco's total unit sales grew only 8%.

Supermarkets generally won't discuss their private-label business, for fear of offending branded suppliers. But Peter O'Gorman, executive vice president of the New Jersey-based A&P chain, which is operated by Great Atlantic & Pacific Tea Co., says AIPC met his pasta wish list: "I wanted European quality, something that didn't get mushy or fall apart," and at a competitive price. The result, he says, has been improved profits and image for A&P.

Calling on supermarkets around the country, AIPC won some enormous accounts. Nearly 40 grocers have hired it to make store-brand pasta. They include eight of the 10 largest chains as well as Wal-Mart. With many of these accounts, AIPC also has won the highly desirable contract to set up the pasta aisle, allowing it to give its products the best display.

AIPC expects its 25% market share to grow as sales rise. Earnings for fiscal 1998, boosted by the Mueller's contract, soared 53% to $15.3 million, on a 46% surge in sales to nearly $189 million. For 1999, earnings and sales are expected to settle down to still-hefty and industry-leading growth rates of 30% and 20%, respectively.

Other big changes are shaking the pasta establishment. Hershey, which sells $400 million a year of pasta under a variety of brand names, has put its business up for sale, saying it wants to focus on its more-profitable confectionery business.

And then there's AIPC's Mueller's coup. Bestfoods recently hired it to make the brand-name pasta, the top-selling label in the country. In doing so, Bestfoods acknowledged that AIPC made a lower-cost product, despite using processes and ingredients that typically cost more. Until now, for instance, Bestfoods didn't use durum wheat for its Mueller's pasta. Already, AIPC's flavored pastas for Mueller's, such as lemon-pepper penne, are a hit.

For branded-food companies, the AIPC story doesn't necessarily represent a threat. It can offer a solution, since there's no rule against branded companies making store brands to compete against their own. Some category leaders already are doing it. Spice maker McCormick & Co. now makes Safeway's spices. Tyson Foods now makes private-label breaded chicken items just like its branded product.

Heinz owns the 9-Lives cat-food brand and also makes private-label canned cat food. "If we don't do it, somebody else will," says Steve Whitaker, Heinz Pet Products regional-sales director.

81

SOUPING UP THE SUPPLY CHAIN

Today's supercontractors are turning manufacturers into models of efficiency

Even in this "just-in-time" age, the production line that churns out Hewlett-Packard ink-jet printers in Newark, Calif., is impressive. In response to electronic orders from customers around the country, parts trucked in moments earlier are loaded onto a 110-foot assembly line. Finished printers fly off the other end—and soon are aboard another truck heading to a distributor. The operation is seamless and speedy. But then, what would you expect from one of America's premier high-tech corporations?

You might think the factory belongs to Hewlett-Packard Co. Instead, it's owned by Solectron Corp., a contract manufacturer. What's more, even as Milpitas (Calif.)-based Solectron pumps out HP's printers, its 24 production lines are simultaneously assembling everything from pagers to television decoding boxes for some of the biggest brand names in electronics.

Solectron is part of a new breed of U.S. supercontractors that promise to revolutionize manufacturing well into the next century. They command dozens of factories and supply networks around the world. Increasingly, they also manage their customers' entire product lines, offering an array of services from design to inventory management to delivery and after-sales service. Their unusually flexible operations are surprisingly profitable, producing returns on assets in the range of 20%.

"Outsourcing," a practice that has been around for decades, doesn't begin to describe the phenomenon. In place of traditional contracting relationships between client and supplier, arrangements with companies such as Solectron represent a sort of extended enterprise—a set of partnerships between product developers and specialists in components, distribution, retailing, and manufacturing.

The resulting organization can be so tight as to behave like a single, closely knit company—only better. Its strategies can slash time and costs out of the supply chain, the process between the invention of a new product and the time it reaches the consumer. Customers say they have achieved cost efficiencies of 15% to 25% already. And that, says James E. Morehouse, a logistics expert

at A.T. Kearny Inc., is only 5% to 10% of U.S. industry's potential savings.

BUSTED BARRIERS. The effect on innovation could be huge. Spinning off manufacturing and other noncore functions allows industrial titans to focus new investment where it gets the most bang: on research and marketing. Because the strategy reduces the need for capital and in-house operations expertise, moreover, startups face far lower barriers in bringing new technologies to market.

In 1996, for example, Egyptian-born engineers Zaki and Shlomo Raqib came up with a modem, capable of advanced services such as teleconferencing, that could be deployed over any cable system without needing costly upgrades by cable operators. But while their Santa Clara (Calif.) company, Terayon Communications Systems Corp., had $45 million in venture capital, it lacked manufacturing facilities. So it went to Solectron, and four months later Terayon's modems were being shipped to cable operators in the U.S. and abroad. In terms of manufacturing capability, boasts Zaki Raqib, "this puts us on a par with the Motorolas of the world."

COST BENEFIT. Far from eroding American industry, the new manufacturing paradigm is one of the surprise strengths of America's high-tech economy. Because independent contractors can better meet demands for quick delivery, the U.S. is actually becoming more competitive as a production base—even in mass-volume assembly work. As Asia's cheap wages are offset by higher shipping costs, "the cost difference between the U.S. is now virtually gone," says Michael E. Marks, chief executive at Flextronics International USA Inc., a major contract manufacturer.

Not everyone is abandoning their factories. Compaq Computer, Intel, National Semiconductor, and Merck are among the corporate giants that keep manufacturing in-house to protect their competitive edge. They fear losing control over intellectual property and quality, or that secrets will leak to competitors. They also worry about losing touch with clients and industry trends.

But in many industries, vertical integration is giving way to virtual integration. General Motors Corp.'s Aug. 3 decision to spin off its $31 billion Delphi Automotive Systems components unit is part of the auto industry's

---

Faster, Cheaper, Smarter

How the new manufacturing model boosts U.S. competitiveness

INNOVATION Startups can get their products to global markets without having to build their own factories—so barriers to entering many industries drop away

EFFICIENCIES Because contract manufacturers manage much of the supply chain, companies can slash inventory and distribution costs while radically shrinking time to market

CAPITAL Product companies get higher returns on investment since they can focus spending on R&D and marketing rather than on capital-intensive production facilities

COMPETITIVENESS Time to market is superceding labor costs in determining market success, giving the U.S. a big advantage for goods made and sold in North America

(Cont.)

shift toward "modular" production, where prefabricated chunks with scores of parts are supplied by outsiders and bolted together at the last minute. Delphi, for example, makes full instrument panels for M-class sport-utility vehicles assembled at Mercedes Benz's modular plant in Vance, Ala. Some experts believe the Big Three also will eventually sell off their engine and auto assembly plants.

The same trend is emerging in pharmaceuticals, where the cost of bringing a new drug to market—as high as $500 million—and the high risk of failure have long been barriers to entry. Covance Inc., one of the world's largest contract research organizations for drugmakers, has just opened a $55 million plant in North Carolina's Research Triangle Park that CEO Christopher A. Kuebler likens to a "sterile version of a microbrewery," capable of making up to five biological drug products simultaneously. Among its first customers is seven-year-old StressGen Biotechnologies Corp. of Victoria, B.C., which has hired Covance to make its new vaccine for treating cervical cancer.

The movement is much further along in electronics, where a $90 billion contract manufacturing sector is growing three times faster than overall electronics sales, according to Technology Forecasters Inc. of Alameda, Calif. Semiconductor startups can turn to a growing number of silicon-wafer foundries—highly flexible shops willing to produce small runs of a few thousand units at first and ramp up to mass production if demand takes off. That allows "fabless" Silicon Valley design houses like Xilinx Inc., 3Dfx Interactive, and Broadcom Corp. to market innovative telecom, graphics, and video chips that power the myriad multimedia gadgets of the Digital Age. With billions of dollars in new capacity coming online, analysts expect the supply of new chips to explode.

As virtual integration evolves, futurists envision a time when product developers, manufacturers, and distributors will be so tightly linked through data networks that inventory will all but disappear. Companies will make goods based on the daily needs of retailers. Even automobiles will be assembled to a customer's specifications within days, just as Dell Computer Corp. and Cisco Systems do now with computers and networking equipment. A sunset industry no longer, manufacturing will help drive innovation.

By Pete Engardio in Milpitas, Calif.

82

INVOICE? WHAT'S AN INVOICE?

Electronic commerce will soon radically alter the way business buys and sells

Ever since Wal-Mart Stores Inc. revolutionized retailing by linking its computers to those of suppliers, executives in every other industry have been dreaming of doing the same. They've seen how Wal-Mart's pioneering use of computer networks to conduct business electronically squeezed costs and time out of clunky supply chains and helped it outgun just about all of its rivals.

Well, hang on. Electronic commerce, once little more than a management buzzword, is about to radically alter how all companies sell to and buy from each other. The techniques that Wal-Mart and giants such as General Motors, Eastman Kodak, and Baxter International have been perfecting on private networks for the past decade are evolving and are now about to move to the wide-open Internet.

SIZZLE. U.S. companies already buy $500 billion worth of goods electronically each year, reckons Torrey K. Byles, a director at market researcher Giga Information Group. That's a small fraction of their total purchases, but it shows why Internet experts believe that business-to-business links—rather than glitzy online malls—will be the first form of Web commerce to pay off. Doing business on the Net is "a cost-reduction and efficiency-improvement play," says Jim Sha, vice-president, new ventures at Netscape Communications Corp., the sizzling Web software maker.

E-commerce could have profound effects on efficiency. As more transactions move from the numbing pace of paper to the lightning speed of electrons, economists predict that a new era of nearly friction-free markets will arrive. Companies that don't move quickly to the new technology risk being left behind. "Electronic commerce will happen," says Brad Wheeler, professor of information systems at the University of Maryland. "People can't stick their head in the sand or they'll be dealt right out."

Take something as simple as a purchase order (table). Even though manufacturing giants such as GM have used a scheme called electronic data interchange (EDI) to order parts automatically from suppliers since the concept was proposed in the early 1970s, most business-to-business sales still are done with paper forms—a reminder, in triplicate, of outdated methods. If you eliminate paper, you spend less time and money re-keying information into different computers and correcting the resulting errors. By some estimates, E-commerce could slash the cost of processing a purchase order from $150 to as little as $25.

Once the software—and security measures—are available, the Internet's World Wide Web will become the global infrastructure for electronic commerce. IBM, General Electric Information Services (GEIS), Dun & Bradstreet, Microsoft, and a raft of others are scurrying to build what's needed—everything from software for securing payments and building electronic catalogs to services that authenticate a new trading partner's electronic identity. One company, Industry.Net Corp., headed by former Lotus Development Corp. CEO Jim P. Manzi, is developing a sort of industrial mall to help companies find customers and suppliers in cyberspace.

EARLY BIRDS. "I really see the Internet as an explosion of electronic commerce," says Hellene S. Runtagh, president and chief executive of GEIS. That company is rushing to extend its EDI services, currently delivered over a private network, out to the Internet so it can reach thousands of new businesses. By putting global markets at virtually anyone's fingertips, Runtagh says, the Net should trigger the creation of a multitude of new companies worldwide. "This is the most exciting sea change to hit commerce globally in the last 100 years," she says.

In the meantime, some companies are already rigging E-commerce systems on the Net. Fruit of the Loom Inc., until recently a self-confessed technology laggard, is using the Net to make up for lost time. Led by computer executives hired away from Federal Express Corp. and elsewhere, the apparelmaker is using the Web to one-up Hanes Cos. and other brands in the market for blank T-shirts and other items sold through novelty stores and at special events.

Fruit depends on some 50 wholesalers nationwide to ship its goods in bulk to thousands of silk-screen printers, embroidery shops, and similar outfits. And now, it's offering to put those wholesalers on the Web, at virtually no charge to them. Fruit's plan is to give each one a complete computer system, called Activewear Online, that's programmed to display colorful catalogs, process electronic orders 24 hours a day, and manage inventories.

One of Fruit's major goals is to avoid losing customers when a wholesaler is out of stock. If, for instance, a silk screener needs 1,000 black T-shirts in a hurry for a Megadeth concert and the wholesaler is low, Fruit's central warehouse can be notified to ship the shirts directly to the customer. "We'll make Fruit's inventory a virtual inventory for our wholesalers," says Charles M. Kirk, Fruit's chief information officer.

Until now, it would have taken years to build such a rich E-commerce system—even if it were possible on the closed, mainframe-based EDI networks run by companies such as GE and IBM. But for Fruit of the Loom, Connect Inc.'s software, called OneServer, and a catalog program from Snickleways Interactive helped it get online in just a few months. And its retailers need only an ordinary PC with a modem and Web-browsing software.

Along with Connect, players such as TradeWave, TSI International, OpenMarket, Netscape Communications, and Microsoft are chasing a Web commerce software market that should hit $750 million in 1999, according to Forrester Research Inc. New software from Premenos, GE, and Sterling Commerce, meanwhile, is starting to move traditional EDI traffic over the Internet, too—at a fraction of the cost that the private EDI nets currently charge.

For large-scale E-commerce initiatives, however, the private EDI setups still have the edge for now. Campbell Soup Co., for instance, has just spent $30 million to redesign its order-processing system around EDI. Called Compass, the new setup is scheduled to go live in August. One goal: Double the portion of paperless orders that the food

---

Less Paper, More Electrons

1. Browsing an electronic catalog, the customer clicks on items to purchase. A computer sends the order directly to the merchant's machine.

2. The merchant's computer checks the customer's credit and determines that the goods wanted are indeed available.

3. The warehouse and shipping departments are notified and goods readied for delivery.

4. The accounting department bills the customer electronically.

(Cont.)

company receives to 80%, whether from salespeople's laptop computers or the "continuous replenishment" systems that companies such as Flemings Cos. use to automatically restock warehouses.

Compass should reduce Campbell's costs by $18 million a year and speed deliveries, says Ronald W. Ferner, vice-president for low-cost business systems. Just cutting out the errors would be a boon. Mistakes now creep into 60% of the orders that Campbell gets by fax and phone. The result: Sales-people spend 40% of their time straightening out problems instead of selling. Compass, which relies on software from Industri-Matematick, a Swedish firm, and an IBM SPsuperscript/2 computer, will turn around orders within 18 hours, down from 48 now. It will even book space on delivery trucks and reserve time at customers' loading docks. Says Ferner: "Even the trees are happy. We're not chopping them down to make paper."

BIG SAVINGS. As impressive as that is, the Web promises to take E-commerce much farther. AMP Inc., for instance, has put up a multilingual catalog of more than 40,000 connectors and other electronic parts on the Web. Eventually, the Web site may take orders, but for now that's being left to distributors. But CEO William J. Hudson Jr. says the catalog is already saving money compared with the $8 million a year it costs to print and mail paper catalogs. And the Web catalog's fresher data should generate more orders.

Ultimately, E-commerce will take place in virtual marketplaces. These trading posts will allow buyers and sellers who may not know one another to meet electronically and trade in goods and services without the aid—or cost—of traditional agents and brokers. Industry. Net now collects fees from more than 4,000 makers of all kinds of industrial gear in return for listing their products and services in a large electronic catalog. Purchasing agents and engineers from all over the world browse the data for next to nothing. Now, purchases continue to go through local distributors. But CEO Manzi wants Industry. Net to process orders and transfer payments, too—for a service fee on each transaction. To develop a system capable of handling thousands of transactions hourly, he hired Mark Teflian, a computer expert who helped to design United Airlines Inc.'s reservation system.

Meanwhile, a consortium that includes D&B, AT&T, Digital Equipment, and SHL Systemhouse has created International Business Exchange, or IBEX. It's a sort of electronic bulletin board on which companies in any country can list goods they want to buy or sell. The system lets them negotiate anonymously and, if a deal gets far enough, helps them initiate credit checks, arrange financing, and get legal and customs paperwork completed by local companies. "Electronic commerce is really a massive information management job," says Mady Jalinous, president and CEO of Global Business Alliance, IBEX' major investor.

The Web is seeing all sorts of specialty markets sprout up, too. EarthCycle Inc. in Woodland Hills, Calif., runs one that deals in chemicals recycled from industrial waste. In September, an online market for buying and selling electricity is to go online. Sponsored by a consortium of 170 utilities and cooperatives, it's intended to help meet a federal mandate to increase competition in the wholesale power market and smooth out price imbalances across the nation. The system is being designed to support futures contracts and other sophisticated commodity trading.

As powerful as the E-commerce concept is, it won't spread evenly across the economy. "People who are powerful sellers may be able to delay the development of electronic markets," says Thomas Malone, head of the coordination science department at Massachusetts Institute of Technology's Sloan School. After all, despite NASDAQ, a vast electronic market, the New York and American stock exchanges rely on humans and paper, and they're still entrenched. But, warns Malone: "Those who try to delay it will be fighting a losing battle. In the long term, buyers migrate to the market that's better for them." Get ready, there's an electronic market coming to a screen near you.

By John W. Verity in New York

83

Firms aim for Six Sigma efficiency

By Del Jones
USA TODAY

The engineer who invented Six Sigma died of a heart attack in the Motorola cafeteria five years ago never knowing the scope of the craze and controversy he had touched off.

Today, depending on whom you listen to, Six Sigma either is a revolution slashing trillions of dollars from corporate inefficiency, or it's the most maddening management fad yet devised to keep front-line workers too busy collecting data to do their jobs.

Leading the revolutionaries is General Electric, the company most smitten with Six Sigma, which announced another quarter of record profits this month and became the first company worth more than $300 billion based on its stock price. But Six Sigma's founding company, Motorola, this month said its second-quarter operating profit shrank to almost zero. It is cutting 15,000 of its 150,000 jobs.

Six Sigma is "malarkey," says Bob Pease, an analog circuit engineer with Texas Instruments. "All they are is brainwashed."

Counters enthusiast Larry Bossidy, CEO of AlliedSignal: "The fact is, there is more reality with this than anything that has come down in a long time in business. The more you get involved with it, the more you're convinced."

Six Sigma may sound Greek to you, but it's sweeping industry to such an extent that you may soon find yourself in intensive and expensive training. After four weeks of classes over four months, you'll emerge a Six Sigma "black belt." And if you're an average black belt, proponents say you'll find ways to save $1 million each year.

It's expensive to implement, so it has been a large-company trend. About 30 companies have embraced Six Sigma including Bombardier, ABB (Asea Brown Boveri) and Lockheed Martin. But it's capturing widespread attention because of two heavyweight disciples: CEOs Jack Welch of GE and Bossidy. They are arguably the most influential executives in business today; they talk to each other on the phone weekly and encourage their employees to share Six Sigma discoveries between companies.

It was Bossidy who sold Welch on Six Sigma, and they both now aim to retire with it as their legacies. AlliedSignal says it's halfway toward $3 billion in annual savings. GE says it spent $200 million in 1996 on Six Sigma to save $170 million. But it saved $700 million by spending $380 million in 1997 and expects to save $1.2

Magic wand or malarkey?

Six Sigma, a sort of Holy Grail for managers, is the level of quality where errors nearly vanish. To devotees, it's a statistical process that can improve quality and reduce waste. To critics, it's a very expensive corporate fad.

AlliedSignal: Figured out a way to recycle 200 million pounds of stained carpet a year — which saves $30 million–$50 million a year.

Lockheed: Saved 200 man hours per C-130J Hercules transport jet by identifying one problem part.

GE: Reorganized satellite access time to increase usage to 97% of the time instead of 63%.

By Genevieve Lynn, USA TODAY

---

billion by spending $450 million this year.

GE's army of 4,000 black belts completed 17,000 quality-improvement projects last year. This year they'll do 37,000, and starting this month, nobody gets promoted to an executive position at GE without Six Sigma training. All white-collar professionals must have started training by January. GE says it will mean $10 billion to $15 billion in increased annual revenue and cost savings by 2000 when Welch retires.

When customers complained that they weren't reaching the right person when they called GE Capital Mortgage Insurance, GE collected data to measure the impact of variables ranging from lunch breaks to the use of voice mail. It found that 24% of callers were hanging up, an "abandon rate" that was slashed to 0.5%.

Raytheon figures it spends 25% of each sales dollar fixing problems when it operates at four sigma, a lower level of efficiency. But if it raises its quality and efficiency to six sigma, it would reduce spending on fixes to 1%.

DEVELOPED AT MOTOROLA

Six Sigma began back in 1985. Motorola was facing extinction, having lost its radio and TV businesses to Japanese competition and was within a few years of losing pagers and semiconductors as well. Bill Smith, a studious midlevel engineer who had never caught much attention, came up with the idea. By 1988,

(Cont.)

Motorola had won the first-ever Malcolm Baldrige award for quality.

If old quality methods were a hammer and a wrench, Six Sigma proponents say they have taken a quantum leap into power tools. For example:

▲ AlliedSignal became the first company to find a way to clean dirt, oil and stains from old carpet so that 100 million pounds will be recycled back into new rugs rather than dumped into landfills. It's more than an environmental success. It will keep the company from having to build an $85 million plant to fill increasing demand for caperolactan used to make nylon, a total savings of $30-$50 million a year. The company may have eventually stumbled upon the solution, but leadership probably would have run out of patience as experiments failed, says Ed Duffy, manager of recycling technology.

▲ GE makes plastics like that molded into telephones. One of its customers is United Technologies Automotive, which molds the plastic into casings for car sideview mirrors. Environmental laws prevented United Technologies from making more casings because they were limited by pollution caused by the painting. Using Six Sigma, GE found a way to add a carbon-based conductor to the plastic, causing far more paint to stick and cutting United Technologies pollution by 35%. Why go to such lengths to help a customer? United Technologies can now make more mirrors, so it orders more plastic from GE.

▲ GE also manages access time to 12 satellites, mostly for TV and radio programming. It found it assigned time haphazardly, much like an untidy person puts things in a closet, says Senior Vice President Walter Braun. Using Six Sigma to organize the closet, GE added $1.3 million a year in revenue by utilizing the satellites 97% of the time vs. 63%.

▲ Lockheed Martin builds the C-130J Hercules, a large transport jet. Lockheed used to spend average of 200 worker-hours trying to get a part that covers the landing gear to fit. For years, employees had brainstorming sessions, which resulted in seemingly logical solutions. None worked. The statistical discipline of Six Sigma discovered a part that deviated by one-thousandth of an inch. Now corrected, the company saves $14,000 a jet.

Six Sigma may sound new, but critics such as quality consultant Jim Smith say it's really Statistical Process Control in new clothing. Others say it dates even further to the 1950s when it was known as multivariate analysis. "What's unique about Six Sigma? They get to charge more money," Smith says.

The 4-year-old Six Sigma Academy in Scottsdale, Ariz., is run by former Motorola quality experts Mikel Harry and Richard Schroeder, who rope steers in their spare time and pose for publicity pictures in cowboy hats and boots. Their fees start at $1 million per corporate client.

In April, the American Society for Quality decided to make Six Sigma training affordable to small and midsized companies. But even though trainees from different companies are grouped together, it costs $35,000 to $40,000 a person. There's a waiting list.

Six Sigma has not always delivered the intended results. Lockheed Martin took a stab at Six Sigma in the

---

Process relies on methodical tests

So what is Six Sigma?

Sigma is a letter of the Greek alphabet used as a symbol by statisticians to mark a bell curve showing the likelihood that something, like a pot of coffee, will deviate from the norm. The narrow definition of six sigma is 3.4 defects (sour pots of coffee) per 1 million opportunities, or 99.9997% perfect.

The Six Sigma movement attempts to insert the science of hard-nosed statistics into the foggy philosophy of quality.

Rather than just striving to, say, make a better cup of coffee, Six Sigma requires testing thousands of variables such as the temperature of the water and the strength of the grounds to find out why some pots are good, others sour, says AlliedSignal quality expert Carl Berry. It halts guesses and gut instincts about what makes good coffee.

A good company operates at less than four sigma, or 99% perfect. That might not seem much worse than six sigma. But think of the savings for an automaker that has to repair 6,210 cars for every 1 million it made at four sigma, but at six sigma it would repair 3.4.

Solutions vary depending on the product and problem. But armed with data, action is taken to increase revenue (sell more coffee to satisfied customers) or cut costs (eliminate throwing out sour pots).

(Cont.)

Why such high goals?

Six Sigma means being 99.9997% perfect. That may seem like overkill until you consider that settling for 99% perfect — closer to 3 or 4 sigma — means:

▲ 20,000 lost articles of mail per hour.
▲ Unsafe drinking water almost 15 minutes each day.
▲ 5,000 incorrect surgical operations per week.
▲ Two short or long landings per day at each major airport.
▲ 200,000 wrong drug prescriptions each year.
▲ No electricity for almost seven hours each month.

---

early 1990s, but the attempt so foundered that it now calls its trainees "program managers," instead of black belts to prevent in-house jokes of skepticism.

"We're trying to stay away from anything that smacks of slogans and T-shirts," says William Kessler, vice president of enterprise productivity for Lockheed Martin Aeronautical Systems, who says Six Sigma is a success this time around. The company has saved $64 million with its first 40 projects, he says.

NOT A CURE-ALL

John Akers promised to turn IBM around with Six Sigma, but the attempt was quickly abandoned when Akers was ousted as CEO in 1993.

Motorola says Six Sigma saved $2.2 billion from 1987-91. But the company has stumbled badly, which only shows that Six Sigma can't control events outside the company such as an economic crisis in Asia and sagging semiconductor demand, says Dennis Sester, Motorola's vice president of quality.

Others are unconvinced. "Our customers don't measure six standard deviations," says Gordon Bethune, CEO of Continental Airlines, in an industry with perhaps the most to gain with 99.9997% perfection. "They just say 'I want my bag and I kind of liked the pasta and the flight attendant was cute.' That's the definition of success."

Wall Street analysts familiar with Six Sigma say it can have a significant impact on earnings, but admit that it's difficult to quantify because internal numbers are not disclosed.

Critics say that's because Six Sigma is really a promotional ploy aimed at making customers think the companies are more devoted to quality.

"Marketing will always use the number that makes the company look best," says Doug Kimzey, a software engineer at PC Engineering. "Promises are made to potential customers around capability statistics that are not anchored in reality."

Because managers' bonuses are tied to Six Sigma savings, it causes them to fabricate results and savings turn out to be phantom, Smith says.

But Jay DesMarteau, a master black belt with GE Capital Mortgage, says that can't happen. Managers who dared to overestimate savings would dig themselves a hole because promised savings must materialize at year's end. "If we don't deliver, we're in trouble," he says.

Smith says Six Sigma will eventually go the way of other fads, but probably not until Welch and Bossidy retire.

History will prove those like Smith wrong, says Bossidy, who has been skeptical of other management fads. "Six Sigma is not more fluff. At the end of the day, something has to happen."

The customized, digitized, have-it-your-way economy

Mass customization will change the way products are made—forever. ■ *by Erick Schonfeld*

A silent revolution is stirring in the way things are made and services are delivered. Companies with millions of customers are starting to build products designed just for you. You can, of course, buy a Dell computer assembled to your exact specifications. And you can buy a pair of Levi's cut to fit your body. But you can also buy pills with the exact blend of vitamins, minerals, and herbs that you like, glasses molded to fit your face precisely, CDs with music tracks that you choose, cosmetics mixed to match your skin tone, textbooks whose chapters are picked out by your professor, a loan structured to meet your financial profile, or a night at a hotel where every employee knows your favorite wine. And if your child does not like any of Mattel's 125 different Barbie dolls, she will soon be able to design her own.

> **People may soon walk into body-scanning booths that can determine their exact 3-D structure.**

Welcome to the world of mass customization, where mass-market goods and services are uniquely tailored to the needs of the individuals who buy them. Companies as diverse as BMW, Dell Computer, Levi Strauss, Mattel, McGraw-Hill, Wells Fargo, and a slew of leading Web businesses are adopting mass customization to maintain or obtain a competitive edge. Many are just beginning to dabble, but the direction in which they are headed is clear. Mass customization is more than just a manufacturing process, logistics system, or marketing strategy. It could well be the organizing principle of business in the next century, just as mass production was the organizing principle in this one.

The two philosophies couldn't clash more.

Mass producers dictate a one-to-many relationship, while mass customizers require continual dialogue with customers. Mass production is cost-efficient. But mass customization is a flexible manufacturing technique that can slash inventory. And mass customization has two huge advantages over mass production: It is at the service of the customer, and it makes full use of cutting-edge technology.

A whole list of technological advances that make customization possible is finally in place. Computer-controlled factory equipment and industrial robots make it easier to quickly readjust assembly lines. The proliferation of bar-code scanners makes it possible to track virtually every part and product. Databases now store trillions of bytes of information, including individual customers' predilections for everything from cottage cheese to suede boots. Digital printers make it a cinch to change product packaging on the fly. Logistics and supply-chain management software tightly coordinates manufacturing and distribution.

And then there's the Internet, which ties these disparate pieces together. Says Joseph Pine, author of the pioneering book Mass Customization: "Anything you can digitize, you can customize." The Net makes it easy for companies to move data from an online order form to the factory floor. The Net makes it easy for manufacturing types to communicate with marketers. Most of all, the Net makes it easy for a company to conduct an ongoing, one-to-one dialogue with each of its customers, to learn about and respond to their exact preferences. Conversely, the Net is also often the best way for a customer to learn which company has the most to offer him—if he's not happy with one company's wares, nearly perfect information about a competitor's is just a mouse click away. Combine that with mass customization, and the nature of a company's relationship with its customers is forever changed. Much of the leverage that once belonged to companies now belongs to customers.

If a company can't customize, it's got a problem. The Industrial Age model of making things cheaper by making them the same will not hold. Competitors can copy product innovations faster than ever. Meanwhile, consumers demand more choices. Marketing guru Regis McKenna declares, "Choice has become a higher value than brand in America." The largest market shares for soda, beer, and software do not belong to Coca-Cola, Anheuser-Busch, or Microsoft. They belong to a category called Other. Now companies are trying to produce a unique Other for each of us. It is the logical culmination of markets' being chopped into finer and finer segments. After all, the ultimate niche is a market of one.

The best—and most famous—example of mass customization is Dell Computer, which has a direct relationship with customers and builds only PCs that have actually been ordered. Everyone from Compaq to IBM is struggling to copy Dell's model. And for good reason. Dell passed IBM last quarter to claim the No. 2 spot in PC market share (behind Compaq). While other computer manufacturers struggle for profits, Dell keeps reporting record numbers; in its most recent quarter the company's sales were up 54%, while earnings soared 62%. No wonder Michael Dell has become the poster boy of the new economy. As Pine says, "The closest person we have to Henry Ford is Michael Dell."

Dell's triumph is not so much technological as it is organizational. Dell keeps margins up by keeping inventory down. The company builds computers from modular components that are always readily available. But Dell doesn't want to store tons of parts: Computer components decline in value at a rate of about 1% a week, faster than just about any product other than sushi or losing lottery tickets. So the key to the system is ensuring that the right parts and products are delivered to the right place at the right time.

To do this, Dell employs sophisticated logistics software, some developed internally, some made by i2 Technologies. The software takes info gathered from customers and steers it to the parts of the organization that need it.

(Cont.)

When an order comes in, the data collected are quickly parsed out—to suppliers that need to rush over a shipment of hard drives, say, or to the factory floor, where assemblers put parts together in the customer's desired configuration. "Our goal," says vice chairman Kevin Rollins, "is to know exactly what the customer wants when they want it, so we will have no waste."

The company has been propelled by this thinking ever since Michael Dell started selling PCs from his college dorm room in 1983. The Web makes the process virtually seamless, by allowing the company to easily collect customized, digitized data that are ready for delivery to the people who need them. The result is an entire organization driven by orders placed by individual customers, an organization that does more Web-based commerce than almost anyone else. Dell's future doesn't depend on faster chips or modems—it depends on greater mastery of mass customization, of streamlining the flow of quality information.

It's not much of a surprise that a leading tech company like Dell is using software and the Net in such innovative ways. What's startling is the extent to which companies in other industries are embracing mass customization. Take Mattel. Starting by October, girls will be able to log on to barbie.com and design their own friend of Barbie's. They will be able to choose the doll's skin tone, eye color, hairdo, hair color, clothes, accessories, and name (6,000 permutations will be available initially). The girls will even fill out a questionnaire that asks about the doll's likes and dislikes. When the Barbie pal arrives in the mail, the girls will find their doll's name on the package, along with a computer-generated paragraph about her personality.

Offering such a product without the Net would be next to impossible. Mattel does make specific versions of Barbie for customers such as Toys "R" Us, and the company customizes cheerleader Barbies for universities. But this will be the first time Mattel produces Barbie dolls in lots of one. Like Dell, Mattel must use high-end manufacturing and logistics software to ensure that the order data on its Website are distributed to the parts of the company that need them. The only real concern is whether Mattel's systems can handle the expected demand in a timely fashion. Right now, marketing VP Anne Parducci is shooting for delivery of the dolls within six weeks—a bit much considering that that is how long it takes to get a custom-ordered BMW.

Nevertheless, Parducci is pumped. "Personalization is a dream we have had for several years," she says. Parducci thinks the custom Barbies could become one of next year's hottest toys. Then, says Parducci, "we are going to build a database of children's names, to develop a one-to-one relationship with these

"Choice has become a higher value than brand in America," says marketing guru Regis McKenna.

girls." That may sound creepy, but part of mass customization is treating your customers, even preteens, as adults. By allowing the girls to define beauty in their own terms, Mattel is in theory helping them feel good about themselves even as it collects personal data. That's quite a step for a company that has stamped out its own stereotypes of beauty for decades, but Parducci's market testing shows that girls' enthusiasm for being a fashion designer or creating a personality is "through the roof."

Levi Strauss also likes giving customers the chance to play fashion designer. For the past four years it has made measure-to-fit women's jeans under the Personal Pair banner. In October, Levi's will relaunch an expanded version called Original Spin, which will offer more options and will feature men's jeans as well.

With the help of a sales associate, customers will create the jeans they want by picking from six colors, three basic models, five different leg openings, and two types of fly. Then their waist, butt, and inseam will be measured. They will try on a plain pair of test-drive jeans to make sure they like the fit before the order is punched into a Web-based terminal linked to the stitching machines in the factory. Customers can even give the jeans a name—say, Rebel, for a pair of black ones. Two to three weeks later the jeans arrive in the mail; a bar-code tag sealed to the pocket lining stores the measurements for simple reordering.

Today a fully stocked Levi's store carries approximately 130 ready-to-wear pairs of jeans for any given waist and inseam. With Personal Pair, that number jumped to 430 choices. And with Original Spin, it will leap again, to about 750. Sanjay Choudhuri, Levi's director of mass customization, isn't in a hurry to add more choices. "It is critical to carefully pick the choices that you offer," says Choudhuri. "An unlimited amount will create inefficiencies at the plant." Dell Computer's Rollins agrees: "We want to offer fewer components all the time." To these two, mass customization isn't about infinite choices but about offering a healthy number of standard parts that can be mixed and matched in thousands of ways. That gives customers the illusion of boundless choice while keeping the complexity of the manufacturing process manageable.

Levi's charges a slight premium for custom jeans, but what Choudhuri really likes about the process is that Levi's can become your "jeans adviser." Selling off-the-shelf jeans ends a relationship; the customer walks out of the store as anonymous as anyone else on the street. Customizing jeans starts a relationship; the customer likes the fit, is ready for reorders, and forks over his name and address in case Levi's wants to send him promotional offers. And customers who design their own jeans make the perfect focus group; Levi's can apply what it learns from them to the jeans it mass-produces for the rest of us.

If Levi's experiment pays off, other apparel makers will follow its lead. In the not-so-distant future people may simply walk into body-scanning booths where they will be bathed with patterns of white light that will determine their exact three-dimensional structure. A not-for-profit company called [TC^2], funded by a consortium of companies including Levi's, is developing just such a technology. Last year some MIT business students proposed a similar idea for a custom-made bra company dubbed Perfect Underwear.

Morpheus Technologies, a wacky startup in Portland, Me., hopes to set up studios equipped with body scanners. Founder Parker Poole III wants to "digitize people and connect their measurement data to their credit cards." Someone with the foresight to be scanned by Morpheus could then call up Eddie Bauer, say, give his credit card number, and order a robe that matches his dimensions. His digital self could also be sent to Brooks Brothers for a suit. Gone will be the days of attentive men kneeling on the floor with pins in their mouths. Progress does have its price.

Thirty years ago auto manufacturers were, effectively, mass customizers. People would spend hours in the office of a car dealer, picking through pages of options. But that ended when car companies tried to improve manufacturing efficiency by offering little more than a few standard options packages. BMW wants to turn back the clock. About 60% of the cars it sells in Europe are built to order, vs. just 15% in the U.S. Europeans seem willing to wait three to four months for a vehicle, while most Americans won't wait longer than four weeks.

Now the company wants to make better use of its customer database to get more Americans to custom-order. BMW dealers save about $450 in inventory costs on every such order. Reinhard Fischer, head of logistics for BMW of North America, says, "The big battle is to take cost out of the distribution chain. The best way to do that is to build in just the things a consumer wants."

Since most BMWs in the U.S. are leased, the company knows when customers will need a new car. Some dealers now call customers a few months before their leases are up to see whether they'd like to custom-order their next car. Soon, however, customers will be able to configure their own car online and send that info to a dealer. Fischer can even see a day when the Website will offer data about vehicles sailing on ships from Germany, so that people can see whether a car matching their preferences is already on the way. That does, of course, raise the question, Why not send the requests directly to BMW, circumventing dealers altogether? Says Fischer: "We don't want to eliminate their role, but maybe they should have a 7% margin, not 16%." Ouch.

Such dilemmas are inevitable, given that mass customization streamlines the order process. What's more, mass customization is about creating products—be they PCs, jeans, cars, eyeglasses, loans, or even industrial soap—that match your needs better than anything a traditional middleman can possibly order for you.

LensCrafters, for instance, has made quick, in-store production of customized lenses common. But Tokyo-based Paris Miki takes the process a step further. Using special software, it designs lenses and a frame that conform both to the shape of a customer's face

> **"Mass customization is novel today," says one Internet CEO. "It will be common tomorrow."**

and to whether he wants, say, casual frames, a sports pair, sunglasses, or more formal specs. The customer can check out on a monitor various choices superimposed over a scanned image of his face. Once he chooses the pair he likes, the lenses are ground and the rimless frames attached.

While we tend to think of automation as a process that eliminates the need for human interaction, mass customization makes the relationship with customers more important than ever. ChemStation in Dayton has about 1,700 industrial-soap formulas—for car washes, factories, landfills, railroads, airlines, and mines. The company analyzes items that are to be cleaned (recent ones in its labs include flutes and goose down) or visits its customers' premises to analyze their dirt. After the analysis, the company brews up a special batch of cleanser. The soap is then placed on the customer's property in reusable containers Chem-Station monitors and keeps full. For most customers, teaching another company their cleansing needs is not worth the effort. About

95% of ChemStation's clients never leave.

Hotels that want you to keep coming back are using software to personalize your experience. All Ritz-Carlton hotels, for instance, are linked to a database filled with the quirks and preferences of half-a-million guests. Any bellhop or desk clerk can find out whether you are allergic to feathers, what your favorite newspaper is, or how many extra towels you like.

Wells Fargo, the largest provider of Internet banking, already allows customers to apply for a home-equity loan over the Net and get a three-second decision on a loan structured specifically for them. A lot of behind-the-scenes technology makes this possible, including real-time links to credit bureaus, databases with checking-account histories and property values, and software that can do cash-flow analysis. With a few pieces of customized information from the loan seeker, the software whips into action to make a quick decision.

The bank also uses similar software in its small-business lending unit. According to vice chairman Terri Dial, Wells Fargo used to turn away lots of qualified small businesses—the loans were too small for Wells to justify the time spent on credit analysis. But now the company can collect a few key details from applicants, customize a loan, and approve or deny credit in four hours—down from the four days the process used to take. In some categories that Wells once virtually ignored, loan approvals are up as much as 50%. Says Dial: "You either invest in the technology or get out of that line of business."

She'd better keep investing. Combine the software that enables customization with the ubiquity of the Web, and you get a situation that threatens Wells' very existence. If consumers grow accustomed to designing their own products, will they trust brand-name manufacturers and service providers or will they turn to a new kind of middleman? Frank Shlier, a director of research at the Gartner Group in Stamford, Conn., sees disintermediaries emerging all over the Net to help people sift through the thousands of choices presented to them. In financial services, he suggests, there is "a new role for a trusted adviser, maybe someone who doesn't own any banks."

Shlier's middleman sounds a lot like Intuit, which lets visitors to its quicken.com Website apply for and purchase mortgages from a variety of lenders, fill out their taxes, or set up a portfolio to track their stocks, bonds, and mutual funds. Tapan Bhat, the exec who oversees quicken.com, says, "The Web is probably the medium most attuned to customization, yet so many sites are centered on the company instead of on the individual." What would lure someone to Levi's if she could instead visit a clothing Website that stored her digital dimensions and ordered custom-fit jeans from the

manufacturer with the best price and fit? Elaborates Pehong Chen, CEO of Internet software outfit BroadVision: "The Nirvana is that you are so close to your customers, you can satisfy all their needs. Even if you don't make the item yourself, you own the relationship."

Amazon.com has three million relationships. It sells books online and now is moving into music (with videos probably next). Every time someone buys a book on its Website, Amazon.com learns her tastes and suggests other titles she might enjoy. The more Amazon.com learns, the better it serves its customers; the better it serves its customers, the more loyal they become. About 60% are repeat buyers.

The Web is a supermall of mass customizers. You can drop music tracks on your own CDs (cductive.com); choose from over a billion options of printed art, mats, and frames (artuframe.com); get stock picks geared to your goals (personalwealth.com); or make your own vitamins (acumins.com). And you can get all kinds of tailored data; NewsEdge, for example, will send a customized newspaper to your PC.

These companies want to keep customers happy by giving them a product that cannot be compared to a competitor's. Acumin, for instance, blends vitamins, herbs, and minerals per customers' instructions, compressing up to 95 ingredients into three to five pills. If a customer wants to start taking a new supplement, all Acumin needs to do is add it to the blend.

Acumin's products address what Pine calls customer sacrifice—the compromise we all make when we can't get exactly the product we want. CEO Brad Oberwager started the company two years ago, when his sister, who was undergoing a special cancer radiation treatment, couldn't find a multivitamin without iodine. (Her doctor had told her to avoid iodine.) "If someone would create a vitamin just for me, I would buy it," she told her brother. So he did.

The Web will make that kind of response the norm. Sure, there are any number of ways for consumers to provide a company with information about their preferences—they can call, they can write, or, heck, they can even walk into the brick-and-mortar store. But the Web changes everything—the information arrives in a digitized form ready for broadcast. Says i2 CEO Sanjiv Sidhu, "The Internet is bringing society into a culture of speed that has not really existed before." As new middlemen customize orders for the masses, differentiating one company from its competitors will become tougher than ever. Responding to price cuts or quality improvements will continue to be important, but the key differentiator may be how quickly a company can serve

(Cont.)

a customer. Says Artuframe.com CEO Bill Lederer: "Mass customization is novel today. It will be common tomorrow." If he is right, the Web will wind up creating a strange competitive landscape, where companies temporarily connect to satisfy one customer's desires, then disband, then reconnect with other enterprises to satisfy a different order from a different customer.

That's the vision anyway. For now, companies are struggling to take the first steps toward mass customization. The ones that are

Says BMW's Fischer: "We don't want to eliminate their [car dealers'] role, but maybe they should get a 7% margin, not 16%."

already there have been working on the process for years. Matthew Sigman is an executive at R.R. Donnelley & Sons, whose digital publishing business prints textbooks customized by individual college professors. "The challenge," Sigman warns, "is that if you are making units of one, your margin for error is zero." Custom-fit jeans do come with a money-back guarantee. Levi's can't afford for you not to like them.

85

Amid Soda Giants' War Mr. Kalil Vies for a Spot On the Grocers' Shelves

In a Land of Coke and Pepsi, He Sells RC and Crush; Now, Even 7 UP Is Down

Of Wildcats and 'Big Dogs'

By NIKHIL DEOGUN

Staff Reporter of THE WALL STREET JOURNAL

TUCSON, Ariz. — George Kalil pulls into the parking lot of a Just for Feet shoe store. He immediately sees red.

A massive sign for Coca-Cola's latest summer promotion beams from the store window. Inside sits a brightly lit Coke vending machine. Mr. Kalil knows he has a difficult mission. For 50 years, the Kalil family has owned and run an independent bottling firm, which now distributes 7 UP, RC Cola, Crush orange soda and a panoply of other drinks not owned by Coca-Cola Co. or PepsiCo Inc. "The Good Guys at Kalil," the slogan plastered on Kalil Bottling Co.'s delivery trucks, is a common sight in this desert city.

A silver-haired bear of a man with an impish grin, the 60-year-old Mr. Kalil introduces himself to the manager and asks if the store would consider putting in a Kalil vending machine. The manager politely explains, "That's all decided by headquarters."

Mr. Kalil leaves his business card but isn't hopeful: These days, large chains often sign national contracts. His hunch is correct. Back in Birmingham, Ala., the head office of the 100-store chain confirms that it signed an exclusive contract with Coke last year.

Beneath the hype of the cola wars that Coke and Pepsi are waging rages another battle: the struggle by family-owned, "third tier" bottlers like Mr. Kalil to make gains behind the first two tiers of Coke and Pepsi. Those two behemoths together control 75% of the $54 billion domestic soda market, up from about 60% in 1980, according to Beverage Marketing Corp., a New York consulting firm. Formerly well-known soft drinks have diminished so drastically that finding them in retail stores can be a major undertaking. Even a brand like 7 UP, which in the early 1980s was the nation's No. 3 soft drink,

has eroded to No. 8, as Pepsi and Coke and their subsidiary brands take over.

Exclusive Deals

"Coke is an extraordinarily well-run company and so is Pepsi," says Mr. Kalil. But as they sign exclusive deals with movie theaters, delis, schools, even a shoe-store chain, "it gets closer and closer to what's next? Will there come a time when you go to a supermarket and get only one type of soft drink?"

At the same time, soft-drink pricing is cutthroat in supermarkets, with two-liter bottles often on sale for 69 cents and 12-packs of cans for $1.99. Profit margins for third-tier bottlers, who sell most of their drinks in supermarkets, get squeezed as they often need to price their drinks even more cheaply than the better-advertised brands. Mr. Kalil's selling price per 24-can case is just three cents more now than it was 10 years ago, he says.

It's a downward spiral. As volume falters for brands like Royal Crown Cola and Crush, it also means less money for brand owners to advertise. As products don't sell and are starved of advertising, retailers won't promote them.

Through all this, Mr. Kalil has enjoyed remarkable, if sporadic, sales growth. Kalil Bottling is one of the largest independent, third-tier bottlers in the U.S., boasting annual sales of $97 million, 720 employees and a franchise territory that stretches across Arizona, Utah and parts of New Mexico, Colorado and Texas. Mr. Kalil has managed to increase sales tenfold in the past 20 years by acquiring franchise territories and incrementally increasing sales of some brands.

Mr. Kalil won't disclose his salary, but says he is "modestly paid" and notes that four times in the past 20 years he has cut his salary to $100 a week for six months or so to save the company money.

Dim Profit Picture

The profit picture is dim these days. Though Kalil Bottling has managed to remain in the black overall, the main business — bottling and distributing carbonated soft drinks — isn't profitable. But it is crucial in spreading his costs and bringing in additional business. Instead, Mr. Kalil relies on distributing so-called New Age beverages, such as Snapple and Arizona tea, which have low volume but high margins. He also makes money by bottling and canning store-brand soft drinks, which are some of the same drinks he competes with for supermarket shelf space. His overall profits are less than 1% of sales, far below those of a similar-size Coke bottler, who makes profits about 5% of sales.

"This is the toughest year in the past seven years," he says. Making it tougher is the stock market, where Mr. Kalil says he owns the big soda stocks, which have been battered of late. "That's my hedge," he says, figuring that if his company is faring badly, they will be doing well.

The third-tier bottlers and brand owners, in many ways, are much to blame for the fix

George Kalil

they are now in. They failed to recognize business trends that have left them in their current predicament. Meanwhile, Coke and Pepsi were capitalizing on a consolidating corporate America by signing national accounts. They created a seamless distribution system by investing billions of dollars to lash together far-flung distribution systems, buy vending machines, advertise their brands and invest in technology. The top 10 Coke bottlers distribute more than 90% of Coke's U.S. volume.

By contrast, third-tier bottlers are highly fragmented. The top 10 bottlers for Cadbury Schweppes PLC's brands handled only 66% of Cadbury's volume. (Cadbury is the No. 3 soda company and owner of 7 UP, Dr Pepper, A&W, Sunkist, Crush and a host of other brands. It recently started to consolidate the third-tier system.)

"I'm bemused by people who say they're driven out by exclusive agreements; that's humbug," says Henry Schimberg, a former third-tier bottling executive who is now chief executive of Coca-Cola Enterprises Inc., which is the largest Coke bottler and is 42%-owned by Coca-Cola. Mr. Schimberg has little sympathy for soda companies that "ask for parity in the marketplace" regardless of how much they have invested in equipment, technology, advertising and employees. "As you cease to invest or as you lower your investment, you lose your viability," he says.

Double Cola

The second of seven children, Mr. Kalil joined at age 10 the business started by his father and Lebanese immigrant grandfather in 1948. Back then, the only brand the company bottled and distributed in Tucson was Double Cola, which bore the slogan: "Double measure. Double pleasure."

Even then, the business looked risky. "You won't last six months," an RC Cola sales manager told the family at the time.

But by dint of hard work and hustle, the business survived. That pessimistic RC manager even became a Kalil Bottling employee. Each of the children pitched in on weekends and the summers, sweeping floors, washing bottles, whatever was needed. The brood was told: Never complain about the blistering heat, for the hotter it gets, the more soda is sold.

As a teenager, George Kalil lugged 50-pound carbon-dioxide cylinders to restaurants for fountain-dispensed drinks. The calls came at all hours, and he kept a few cylinders at the back of his Chevrolet pickup. In four years, there was only one night when he wasn't on call. If he went to see a movie with friends, he would sit in the same seat so the theater owner would know where to find him should there be a delivery call.

The hours ruined dating; he never got around to marriage. Instead, Mr. Kalil's personal life has centered on basketball and he is known around town, where the University of Arizona Wildcats basketball team is considered a religion, as the team's No. 1 fan. He doesn't take vacations other than for basketball games and in the past 25 years he has missed only two of the university's games, both home and away.

In 1970, at the age of 32, he was named president. Soon, he was buying additional bottling franchises for Crush, Hires and RC Cola. At the time, the company had annual sales of $400,000.

In those days, bottlers duked it out on product quality and marketing. Kalil Bottling prided itself on producing consistently high-quality soft drinks. Bottlers got business by pressing the flesh in local circles and building strong relationships with retailers and restaurants.

Today, booming Tucson and Phoenix have far fewer mom-and-pop stores. They have been replaced by national chains like Just for Feet. Coke and Pepsi have legions of employees: In Phoenix, 80 Coca-Cola Enterprises salesmen handle cold-drink equipment, such as high-margin vending machines and clear-front refrigerators. Mr. Kalil has eight, but boasts 130 merchandisers, the people who stock the store shelves and arrange the displays.

Mr. Kalil himself now spends mornings making sales calls. He visits John Murphy, food and beverage manager of Baggin's, a local chain of gourmet sandwich shops. Mr. Kalil explains to a harried Mr. Murphy that he could offer 20-ounce bottles of Dr Pepper, 7 UP, RC Cola, A&W and others for a good price. For a brief moment, Mr. Kalil's strategy seems to be working. Holding a Dr Pepper in hand, Mr. Murphy raves about how much he loves Dr Pepper and promises to consider the offer. Mr. Kalil walks out into the glaring sun encouraged. Later, however, Mr. Murphy declines the offer. "I like Kalil," explains Mr. Murphy, "but the name of Coke and Pepsi is hard to beat."

Mr. Kalil heads to Canteen, a vending company that supplies corporations and factories with vending machines. Jeff Allen, district sales manager, is pleased Mr. Kalil is there, but teases him for not showing up before. "George, in the 20 years we've been doing business with you, I think this is the first time you've been down here," Mr. Allen notes.

Mr. Kalil is a little upset by the needling. But the meeting is a success: Mr. Allen agrees to place five more vending machines carrying Kalil products among his array of Pepsi and Coke machines.

The bigger challenge for Mr. Kalil is sales in grocery and convenience stores. Mr. Kalil believes customers will remain loyal to his brands if he can just keep his products around. Standing in the soda aisle of a local Safeway, a customer approaches him, proving his point. Thinking that he works there, she says she is looking for A&W cream soda, a Kalil-distributed product. Mr. Kalil helps her look. There is the store-brand cream soda on one shelf, Mug cream soda (made by Pepsi) on the next one down, but no A&W. Mr. Kalil gives up. The woman spends several more minutes looking and finally chooses private-label cream soda.

More than any other tactic, Coke and Pepsi's attempts to get more shelf space in food stores infuriates Mr. Kalil, for he believes such sales practices stifle competition. The cola giants sign what are known as calendar marketing agreements, or CMAs, with retailers. These agreements dictate marketing incentives and payments to get premium display and be advertised in retailers' weekly ad circulars. For instance, retailers can be rewarded per case of soda sold if they agree to grant end-aisle displays and allocate additional space on the store shelf or room for clear-front refrigerators. Mr. Kalil contends the levels of funding and incentives are designed to minimize his space.

"We try to be as fair as we can be," says a buyer for Tosco Corp.'s Circle K, a convenience-store chain. "It boils down to what's selling and what's not."

Pepsi and Coke dismiss Mr. Kalil's claims of unfair competition. "Vigorous competitive activity is the status quo in the soft-drink industry, and we continue to offer the best possible value to our customers," says a Pepsi spokesman.

'Your Diet Coke, Sir'

Mr. Kalil has been slow to keep up with some changes. After years of resistance, he is beginning to introduce 12-packs for some brands. He was reluctant because he can't make money on them and feels they eat into what little space he gets. To compete with Coke and Pepsi bottlers, he is investing aggressively: $500,000 to buy 165 hand-held computers for his sales staff; $200,000 toward a better routing system for delivery trucks; $600,000 for a factory cooling system that will save electricity and water and improve production speeds. To spread his costs, Mr. Kalil believes he could use his trucks, one of his largest assets, by adding other products, like pretzels.

Even so, it's hard for Mr. Kalil to get an advantage. At a late lunch at the El Padador restaurant, owned by decades-long family friends, he chats with much of the staff on a first-name basis as he confidently orders a diet cola. The Mexican restaurant serves only Kalil products. The waitress plunks down his glass and says in a chipper tone: "Here's your Diet Coke, sir." Mr. Kalil jerks up and says, "You mean a Diet RC." The waitress, puzzled, answers, "Whatever." Mr. Kalil later discovers she's new and didn't know El Parador served Royal Crown Cola.

Some days, Mr. Kalil experiences even harder knocks. When his beloved University of Arizona decides to consolidate its beverage contracts into one bid, Mr. Kalil puts together a bid of $5.05 million, with the help of the companies whose brands he bottles. Even at that price, Mr. Kalil knows he will lose money over the contract's life.

But Pepsi-Cola, which declines to say if it expects the deal to be profitable, slam dunks a $15 million bid to be the university's main beverage provider for 10 years, guaranteeing it 85% of all beverage sales at the 35,000 student school. Pepsi's bid includes $3.4 million for the student union and $1.9 million for athletics.

Kalil has lost another round. "If I were running the University of Arizona, I'd do the same thing," Mr. Kalil acknowledges.

Dan Adams, a university official, says that while university officials can be "empathetic" toward Mr. Kalil, they must accept the best offer. "The big dogs," he notes, "have bigger wallets."

86

DEATH BE NOT (SO) PROFITABLE

Lower mortality rates have left funeral players such as Service Corp. scrambling for new growth sources

From education to housing to health care, the arrival of the baby boomers has been the defining demographic event for many an industry. And few companies have anticipated the boomers' evolution as eagerly as \$2.7 billion Service Corp. International, the biggest and most profitable of the funeral home consolidators. Through the past two decades, the Houston company has assembled nearly 3,300 funeral homes around the world and recorded rich 25% operating profit margins, fueled by a steady 1% yearly rise in deaths.

But now, demographers see growing evidence that medical advances and healthier lifestyles are letting more of us defer the day of reckoning. In a dramatic change from past projections, age-adjusted deaths in the U.S. fell 3% last year on top of smaller declines the prior two years, according to the Centers for Disease Control & Prevention. Experts say the key causes are advances in HIV treatment, post-surgery heart care, and new strides in low-birthweight infant survival—and that the trend should continue. "The decrease in the death rate is based on solid progress that shouldn't reverse," insists Dr. Charles G. Hertz, chief medical director of Metropolitan Life Insurance Co. and editor of the demographic and health-care journal Statistical Bulletin.

That news, while encouraging for most of us, is forcing SCI to alter its growth strategy. After a torrid pace of funeral home acquisitions—SCI has bought more than 1,800 homes since 1995—the chain is downshifting its dealmaking and cranking up sales of "pre-need," or prearranged, funerals to boost revenues. It recently created a finance division as part of a plan to profit from selling life-insurance policies tied to funeral costs. Even with the market slowdown, "we can expand future revenues by expanding pre-need [sales]," insists SCI President L. William Heiligbrodt.

"BRILLIANT." While still enjoying growth from acquisitions, SCI's revenues per funeral home have slipped 5% since 1996 (chart). Earnings this year are still expected to rise 20%, to \$400 million, as a result of price increases and acquisitions. Others in the industry have been harder hit. In July, the second-largest funeral home operator, Loewen Group Inc. of Burnaby, B.C., put itself on the block, blaming "soft" mortality rates for a failed turnaround. Loewen's earnings fell 56%, to \$11.6 million, in the quarter ended June 30, on an 8% drop in revenues per funeral home.

Investors, meanwhile, have cooled on funeral-industry stocks. In addition to concerns about the improving death rate, the entire sector is sagging over worries that the consolidators' frenetic dealmaking has driven up prices for funeral homes to the point where many further acquisitions don't make economic sense. The Pauze Tombstone index of death-care stocks is up 1%, compared with the 6% gain in the Standard & Poor's 500-stock index. SCI, once a Wall Street darling because of its persistent 20%-plus annual earnings gains, is trading at 39 1/16, up 6% for the year.

It's not as if funeral homes can exactly expand their customer base. But SCI figures that it can grab some future business before it ma-

tures. That was the motivation behind two recent buys. On July 17, it purchased, for \$164 million, an American Annuity Group Inc. unit that underwrites prearranged funeral policies. Three weeks later, it agreed to pay \$830 million for rural funeral and cemetery operator Equity Corp. International, a spin-off SCI had only finished divesting in January, 1997. That spin-off had figured into SCI's plan for an unsuccessful attempt to buy Loewen; now, it may fit in with the new strategy.

Since 1995, SCI has boosted its annual sales of prearranged funeral policies from \$371 million to about \$700 million. Typically, such sales don't immediately add to revenues until the services are delivered. But owning the insurance unit enables SCI to profit immediately from the underwriting, taking transaction profits of 12% to 15% at the time of sale—and locking in future revenues. "This is a way to sell pre-need, service more families, and make this additional profit. It's absolutely brilliant," says Daniel M. Isard, president of Foresight Analysts Inc., a Phoenix death-care consulting company.

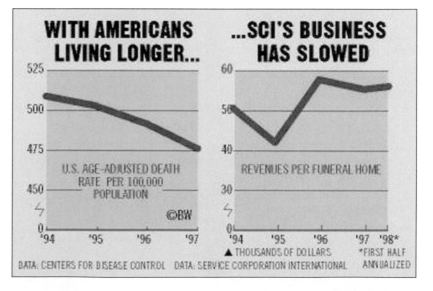

WITH AMERICANS LIVING LONGER...
U.S. AGE-ADJUSTED DEATH RATE PER 100,000 POPULATION

...SCI'S BUSINESS HAS SLOWED
REVENUES PER FUNERAL HOME

▲ THOUSANDS OF DOLLARS *FIRST HALF ANNUALIZED

DATA: CENTERS FOR DISEASE CONTROL   DATA: SERVICE CORPORATION INTERNATIONAL

(Cont.)

DEAD AGAIN. In the meantime, the run-up in funeral home prices is likely to crimp acquisitions. SCI recently broke up a corporate acquisitions group and shifted its employees into funeral, cemetery, and finance divisions. The intent is "to get better decisions and better business," not fewer deals, says Heiligbrodt. While acquisitions will play a smaller role in its future growth, "we're not going to abandon the acquisitions business," he insists.

Of course, improved health and medical care don't mean that we will live forever—and the numerous baby boomers will inevitably increase demand for funeral services. "This isn't a product you can walk away from," says J.P. Morgan Securities analyst Joseph Chiarelli. Even if the nation's mortality rate doesn't soon return to the past rate of annual increases, the aging of the boomers suggests that the number of deaths should begin to climb rapidly within a decade. The fastest-growing segment of the U.S. population is that which is 65 and older; it is expected to double, to 4 million, between 1990 and 2000. "A good management team will find a way to get through this period," says Chiarelli.

If he's right, the years of easy growth could quickly return. But that's assuming medical advances don't intrude on other key causes of death, such as cancer. Death and taxes are inevitable—but the timing of them may be another thing altogether.
By Gary McWilliams in Houston

Ethical Marketing in a Consumer-Oriented World: Appraisal and Challenges

NOW IT'S YOUR WEB

The Net is moving toward one-to-one marketing—and that will change how all companies do business

Soon after Jeri Capozzi logged onto the online nursery Garden Escape Inc. last winter, she was hooked. And it wasn't just because the World Wide Web site offered unusual plants, such as hyacinth beans, firecracker, and dog's tooth violet. It's because Garden Escape created a personal store just for her. Greeted by name on her personal page when she visits, Capozzi can take notes on a private online notepad, tinker with garden plans using the site's interactive design program, and get answers from the Garden Doctor. So far, the 41-year-old insurance caseworker from Litchfield, Conn., has spent $600 at Garden Escape and has no plans to shop at any other nursery. With service that personal, she says, "I probably will never leave it."

Personal service on the Internet? Isn't that an oxymoron? For most Web surfers, the Net has been just another aloof mass medium like television, radio, and newspapers, dishing up a morass of information that you then have to sift through. But as consumers such as Capozzi are discovering, the Net is finally beginning to cast off the mistaken identity of its youth and deliver on its original promise—the ability to tailor itself to every one of its 100 million users.

Don't think "mass." Think "me." Like no other mass medium or marketplace, the Net offers merchants the ability to communicate instantly with each one of their customers. The Net also lets those customers talk back, so that they can demand unique products and customized services. Until now, few Website operators have taken full advantage of this intimate link, but that's changing. Ac-

cording to a survey of 25 top online merchants by New York market researcher Jupiter Communications, 40% say they have begun to offer personalized features, with 93% saying they will within a year.

If personalization pops up all over the Net, it could usher in a new era in electronic commerce—one that threatens to shake the foundations of conventional mass marketing and mass production. Indeed, the real kick from the Net's personal touch will go far beyond marketing and sales. Ultimately, it could transform not just merchants' contact with customers but all their operations, from how they research and design products to how they're manufactured.

CHANGING FOCUS. For most of this century, mass marketing and production have held sway, thanks to both the exploding population and the incredible production efficiencies of the Industrial Age. It just didn't make economic sense to provide products and services customized to each buyer. And without a cost-effective way to track the purchases and preferences of individuals, marketers had to resort to inexact measures, such as demographics, to sell their wares.

Now, the Net—and its ability to reach the masses individually yet economically—may mark a historic swing back to one-to-one marketing. That could change merchants' focus from gathering a mass of customers for their products to getting products that fit individual customer demands. "The technology has caught up to the number of people in the world, and we've come full-circle," says Steve Kanzler, chief executive of LikeMinds Inc., a personalization technology company with the slogan: "Every individual is a market."

Early signs show personalization has a huge payoff. Jupiter reports that customization at 25 consumer E-commerce sites boosted new customers by 47% in the first year—and revenues by 52%. Even at a cost of $50,000 to $3 million for the personalization software, along with computers to store the customer profiles, personalization generally pays for itself within a year.

Music retailer CDnow Inc. already is singing its virtues. On Sept. 16, it launched My CDnow, which lets customers get a page designed just for them with music suggestions based on their stated preferences, past purchases, and ratings on artists and CDs. CDnow has seen an immediate benefit in consumer interest: The number of pages

---

PERSONALIZATION PACESETTER

Jason Olim
Founder and CEO of CDnow
CDnow's new personalized site, My CDnow, allows visitors to create a music store that's customized to their individual tastes. "Every single home page will be built on the fly," says Olim. "It really is a music store for each of our 600,000-plus customers."

A Day in the Life of a Wired Consumer

7 A.M. Stumble out of bed and log onto MyExcite (www.excite.com), which greets you with a cheery "Welcome Harry," for your local weather and info on your personal stock portfolio.

9 A.M. In the office, you're running low on floppy disks and printer paper. Log into your personal account on the company intranet with Office Depot (www.officedepot.com), click a few boxes, and the stuff's on its way.

10 A.M. Calling up your department's intranet page, you print out market research reports on rivals you had asked a software "agent" to search for.

11 A.M. American Airlines (www.aa.com) just sent an E-mail with a special fare on your usual business route next week.

12 P.M. While you're at the deli, your cell phone beeps. The digital readout says some stocks you own hit predetermined sell prices. Tap in your sell orders, and they go out instantly over the Net to your broker.

2 P.M. An E-mail from Amazon.com (www.amazon.com) tells you the John Grisham book you asked to be alerted about is out. You hit the hyperlink, land at Amazon.com, and with one more click, the book is on its way to you.

(continued)

---

viewed on one of its features, called "Wish List"—which appears on the customized pages and lets shoppers name CDs they may

(Cont.)

A Day in the Life of
a Wired Consumer
(concluded)

3:30 P.M. An alert on your customized contact service at PlanetAll (www.planetall.com) says your dad's birthday is next week. Log onto the comparison shopping service MySimon (www.mysimon.com), which sends out a personal "bot" to scour the Net for the lowest price on the Sinatra boxed set.

5:30 P.M. While listening to a supplier drone on about widgets, you surf Garden Escape (www.garden.com), check out landscaping plans you did online for your garden, click the Plant Finder for what will grow in that sunny border, and order the suggested marigolds.

7:30 P.M. The kids want a dog. Surf over Ralston-Purina's breed finder (www.purina.com), fill out the questionnaire on your life-style and the kinds of dogs you like, and the site provides a ranked list. Yikes—a St. Bernard's at the top.

9 P.M. You'll need a bigger house to fit that St. Bernard. Log onto Coldwell Banker's Personal Retriever homebuying site and peruse your personal portfolio of homes that meet your criteria.

10 P.M. Time to relax. At Imagine Radio (www.imagineradio.com), click on "Harry's Jazz Station," a Web audio feed programmed with your favorite artists, and let Miles Davis blow your tensions away.

buy later— jumped 200% almost immediately. "It really is a music store for each of our 600,000-plus customers," says Jason Olim, CDnow's CEO. "At the end of the day, it will mean more revenues."

Only if cybernauts are of the same mind as merchants, who think the upside of personalization outweighs the downside. So far, the answer to that is decidedly mixed. Because customizing requires people to cough up personal information and fill out sometimes lengthy forms, only a small fraction of Netizens have done so.

Worse, there are rising concerns about privacy, which could prove the Achilles' heel for personalization. Too often, sites step over the fine line between being personal and being nosy. And many Web surfers chafe at the very underpinnings of personalization: To build customer profiles, Web merchants often monitor an electronic trail that reveals all sorts of things about users—say, that you're a 28-year-old female Los Angeles office worker who likes vegetarian food, Jackie Chan movies, and mystery novels. "Personalization to many Web sites means, 'How can I sell you out to an advertiser so I can charge more for ads?'" says Steve Tomlin, CEO of PersonaLogic Inc. of San Diego, which makes personalization software.

Alarmed, government officials are threatening federal regulation that could severely limit the use of personal details merchants so badly need to offer tailored products. One encouraging sign: Most E-merchants seem increasingly aware that they have to be upfront with customers, and they're devising ways for cybernauts to surf incognito (page 215).

SNEAKY PEEPERS. Even if fears of sneaky peepers are assuaged, personalization faces yet another hurdle. For all its promise, it still is crude and cumbersome. Personal-recommendation technology, which uses complex mathematical formulas to match people's likely interests, has a long way to go before it lives up to your most trusted critic's suggestions. Buy a gift for someone whose tastes you abhor, for instance, and your future customized recommendations may never recover. And separate databases on your habits aren't always matched up: Amazon.com, for instance, sometimes suggests books you have already bought there (page 213).

Still, those who have taken the plunge seem pleased. Portal site Excite Inc. says people who use personalization come back five times as often as others and view double the number of pages. They also tend to stick around when they come. "It has kind of contained my surfing," says Hollywood producer Chris J. Bender, who has his stocks, movie news, and local weather on his customized MyExcite page.

How does personalization work? Buy a book at online retailer Amazon.com, and the next time you visit, the opening screen will welcome you back by name. Using recommendation software that analyzes your previous purchases, plus any ratings you have made on other books, it will suggest several new books you might like. And it will remember your personal information so you can buy a book with a single mouse click.

Or surf over to portals Yahoo! Inc. and Excite. Click on lists of what you want to see and do on the Net, and type in some personal information. Voila! Your MyYahoo! or MyExcite page displays your name and personal E-mail box, news you request, sports stats, the weather, and an alert about your spouse's birthday next week.

It's happening at work, too, where busi-

PERSONALIZATION PACESETTER

David Sze
Vice-president for programming, Excite
Web portal Excite intends to make personalization easier by letting Web surfers gradually reveal information instead of requiring them to fill out long forms. The result: Visitors stick around. "People who use MyExcite come back five times as often," says Sze.

nesses are getting just as up-close with each other online. This month, Office Depot Inc. began offering small-business buyers personalized online catalogs. And new software from Trilogy Development Group Inc. in Austin soon will enable these customers to craft unique Office Depot catalogs for each of their employees—based on their buying authority—and created instantly on demand.

There's a lot more to come. This fall, many of the best-known consumer sites, such as computer-seller Cyberian Outpost and N2K Inc.'s Music Boulevard, will launch personalized features to help kick off the holiday selling season. N2K, in a trial run of personalization this year, found that the recommendations prompted people to buy CDs 10% to 30% of the time—a huge leap over the average 2% to 4% rate on the rest of the site.

IN THE RED. Cybermerchants need just that kind of boost. After paying millions of dollars for real estate on portals and other high-traffic sites, few E-merchants are actually making money. Some big ones, such as Amazon.com, are expected to lose money until well after 2000. To earn profits, they have to get customers to buy not just once, but over and over.

For that, a personalized Web experience is critical. To keep coming back—or even to hazard an online purchase for the first time— customers need to feel they're getting something no one else in the brick-and-mortar world can offer. That's what Amazon.com is trying to do. By offering personal recommendations, which can change after every purchase and every visit, it hopes to get people to keep coming back. It worked for Christopher Mills, a marketing manager for a Torrance (Calif.) software company. He keeps buying at Amazon because, he says, "it has a real personalized touch." Indeed, repeat buyers accounted for more than 60% of Amazon's $203 million in sales in the first half of 1998.

Brand-building is just as important as sales for many merchants. They're finding that personalizing attracts more people and

(Cont.)

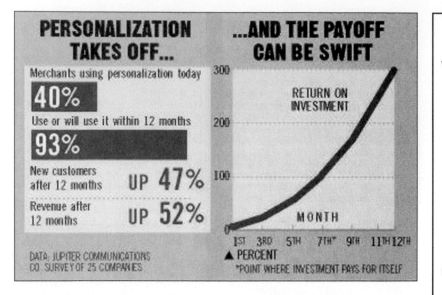

PERSONALIZATION TAKES OFF...

Merchants using personalization today
40%

Use or will use it within 12 months
93%

New customers after 12 months **UP 47%**

Revenue after 12 months **UP 52%**

DATA: JUPITER COMMUNICATIONS CO. SURVEY OF 25 COMPANIES

...AND THE PAYOFF CAN BE SWIFT

RETURN ON INVESTMENT

MONTH

1ST 3RD 5TH 7TH* 9TH 11TH 12TH
▲ PERCENT
*POINT WHERE INVESTMENT PAYS FOR ITSELF

NET PERSONALIZATION: A PRIMER

WHAT IT IS: Personalization is what merchants and publishers do to tailor a Web site or E-mail to a consumer based on past behavior, tastes shared with others, age, or location. Surfers either give the data to the site operator, or it can be gleaned by their movements or purchases on the site. Customization involves the active choices that Web site visitors make to specify which news, products, or other features they want to see regularly. The goal for merchants: One-to-one marketing.

HOW YOU USE IT: Shoppers can use a program called an intelligent agent—also known as a bot—that automatically scours the Net for information, such as prices on products. For customer service, a few Web sites feature a humanlike chatterbot, an intelligent agent that can answer questions in a conversational style. Many retail sites offer customers a recommendation service, which uses complex mathematical formulas to suggest products that match customer preferences.

THE TECHNOLOGY: Collaborative filtering compares customers' purchase history, stated preferences, or clickstream—where they go on a site—with those of other buyers to determine what they're likely to buy next. Another matching technique is neural networks—sets of programs and data that mimic the human brain to recognize hidden patterns in complex data, such as correlations between buyers of seemingly unrelated products.

keeps them on their sites longer. Ralston-Purina Co., for instance, has a Breed Selector on its purina.com site that guides people through a series of questions on their lifestyle and what canine qualities they prize. It then spits out a ranked list of dogs that fit their personal preferences. Since the feature was installed in June, the number of visitors has jumped 25%, and they stay twice as long—exposing them to more Purina marketing messages, says Mark S. Whitzling, director of Purina Interactive Group.

Loyal users are just as critical for merchants. They can use the data that members have revealed to help advertisers target the most likely buyers—and charge more for the ads. Right now, an untargeted Web site banner ad averages about $17 per thousand people reached—less than half the rate of consumer magazines. Kent Godfrey, CEO of the San Francisco Web marketing technology firm Andromedia Inc., thinks ad-driven sites need some ads to top $300 per thousand viewers. "To do that, you have to target on an individual basis," says Godfrey.

It will be an uphill struggle—and not because it can't be done technically. So far, few advertisers target ads online with any more precision than they do in conventional media because segmenting too finely may produce scant customers. "We can show ads to golfers in Kentucky with two kids," says Charles Ardai, president of Juno Online Services, which offers free Net access to people willing to accept ads. "But is it really worth your while doing a lot of work and analysis to target three people?"

Even so, early trials show some promise. Kraft Foods, Bristol-Myers Squibb, Kellogg, and others, for instance, saw an average 27% increase in sales when they ran a targeted banner ad on the grocery-shopping service, Peapod Inc. Even more impressive, San Francisco electronic coupon company planet

U found in a trial at Dick's Supermarkets in Wisconsin and Illinois that Web coupons targeted to shoppers' preferences were redeemed 20% of the time—more than 10 times conventional coupons.

For many earthly merchants, the Net's ability to personalize products and services with pinpoint precision adds up to a bowling ball aimed at the very foundations of modern-day commerce. It heralds wrenching change for how manufacturers, distributors, and retailers will be organized and run. Today, most companies organize themselves by products: Product managers are the basic drivers for marketing. In the future, companies instead will have customer managers, predicts Martha Rogers, co-author of *The One to One Future: Building Relationships One Customer at a Time* and a professor at Duke University. Their job: Make each customer as profitable as possible by crafting products and services to individual needs.

HALLOWED GROUND. The upshot is that actual customer demand—not forecasts—will drive production. Dell Computer Corp., for instance, has created some 1,500 customized home pages for its best customers so they get direct access to corporate-specified personal computers, negotiated discounts, and records of orders and payments. This is a big reason Dell's PC unit sales are growing over 70% a year, light-years ahead of the industry average of 11%.

The Web even allows customers to directly influence the most hallowed province of corporatedom: product research and design. Consider the case of Sapient Health Network. The site offers personalized information for some 115,000 sufferers of 20 different diseases, from breast cancer to hepatitis C. After filling out an extensive questionnaire on their unique conditions, each patient gets a personal "bookshelf" full of symptoms, treatments, and the like, specifically related to their

unique ailments.

Originally, Sapient charged subscription fees—but patients balked. So now, Sapient makes money from collecting patient data anonymously, compiling it into population studies, and selling it to drug companies. It also conducts focus groups and recruits willing patients into clinical trials of new treatments—often with unheard-of targeting, such as people who are incontinent and wet one pad a day. Asks Sapient product marketing

(Cont.)

director Michael S. Noel: "Where are you going to find these people in the real world?"

Ultimately, these ever-widening electronic links to the customer will lead to the Holy Grail for manufacturers and service providers: mass customization of products. For an early example, look to artuframe.com.

The art and framing site based in Lake Forest, Ill., started offering 1 billion possible combinations of posters and frames last May. Using recommendation software from Net Perceptions Inc. in Minneapolis, customers narrow down the vast choices—eventually coming up with their unique product. "We're giving total control to the customer," says artuframe.com President William A. Lederer. He expects $3 million in sales this year.

The Net's ability to reach millions instantly and individually is even creating products that couldn't be sold economically before. American Airlines Inc. recently beefed up its frequent-flyer member site using one-to-one marketing software from BroadVision Inc. Members can streamline their booking process by creating a profile of their home airport, usual routes, seating and meal preferences, and the like for themselves and their families. With these profiles and a way to reach members instantly, American can offer, say, parents whose children's school vacations start in a few weeks discounts on flights to Disney World. Says John R. Samuel, managing director of interactive marketing: "We're now able to create a

product that couldn't have existed before."

As the Net's ability to personalize products and services spreads, terra firma businesses will have to follow suit. How long will Compaq Computer Corp.'s customers, for instance, remain willing to wait longer for shipments and get less-customized PCs than competitors buying from Dell? "Consumers are going to have the big stick," says Eileen Hicken Gittens, president of Personify Inc., a San Francisco maker of Web customer-analysis software.

Does all this mean the end of mass marketing? Of course not. Many merchants aren't even ready to go online in a big way, let alone market one-to-one. But for all the perils of personalization, the real danger is pretending the Net is just another marketing channel. After all, why do you think they call 'em customers?

By Robert D. Hof in San Mateo, with Heather Green in New York and Linda Himelstein in San Mateo

SOME MATCHES ARE NOT EXACTLY MADE IN HEAVEN

Our reporter finds customizable Web sites are fun, but also a pain in the neck

I admit it. I'm a bit of a privacy freak. I memorize a fake phone number for nosy video-rental clerks. And I don't participate in supermarket rewards programs for fear of revealing my personal data (say, my weakness for Cheez-Its). So even if Web sites promise me personalized news or product recommendations, I often hesitate, or at least fudge data on the registration forms—O.K., so I lie. But to keep our readers informed (and to keep my job), I have sacrificed my privacy to check out customizable sites.

I began my search for My Web where just about everybody else does—at the Internet portals. Since last year, Yahoo!, Excite, Infoseek, Lycos, and others have offered ways to customize their sites in hopes of making you forget they were just supposed to be doorways to everywhere else. I tried MyYahoo first and, to my relief, it didn't ask for much personal info. But I got a cramp from spending a couple of hours scrolling through screen after screen, picking which news, sports scores, stock prices, and other features I want to see on my personal start page.

FIRST-NAME BASIS. An easier way

comes from Excite. Instead of forcing you to fill out a form, it asks that you type in your zip code for local weather, your birth date for your horoscope, and so on. Before you know it (that's the idea), you build up a profile that allows Excite to tailor material for you. You still have to make some choices to personalize areas such as news and stocks. But at least MyExcite has manners: It greets me by my name—not "robh56," like MyYahoo.

But I really came here to buy stuff on the company dime. Uh, I mean, I want to find out how well the so-called recommendation services work. Merchants like online bookseller Amazon.com use software that logs my interests and purchases and, using complex mathematical formulas to match them to other customers' habits, spits out suggestions for products people with similar tastes have bought. I've ordered only a few books from Amazon, on cooking, the Internet, and Jack Kerouac. So when I ask it for recommendations, I can't blame it for suggesting more books on the Net and cooking (but nothing, oddly, on Beat Generation writers).

To refine my profile, I dive into Ama-

zon's ratings section and, on countless pages of book lists, click either "I own it" or "Not for me" under each book. There's seemingly no end, so after 20 pages of this, I stop, rub my eyes, and ask for recommendations. In the literature and fiction category, the first six suggestions are by John Steinbeck, many of whose books I told Amazon I own. Not exactly rocket science. The nonfiction category brings up more Net and cooking fare, plus *Nightwork: Sexuality, Pleasure, and Corporate Masculinity in a Tokyo Hostess Club.* Whoa! Where did that come from? Several intriguing choices do pop up, one of which I buy (*Silicon Snake Oil,* by Clifford Stoll). But I bet the service would be more accurate if I could just type in some favorite books.

Still, Amazon does better than the competition. At barnesandnoble.com, the personal recommendation area is nowhere to be found on the site's first page. No wonder. Once I find it, I work through a dozen screens but find mostly contemporary fiction and only a few books I've read. Sure, make me feel like a philistine. Finally, a blank screen appears. What now? I go back
(continued)

(Cont.)

HURRY UP AND WAIT

Personalized Web sites can test your patience: You'll spend a couple hours clicking and scrolling, for example, with MyYahoo's page setup

and try the "Get recommendations" button—and it asks me again to rate all those books. Think again.

JOHN DENVER? I hope to have better luck with compact disks. My CDnow almost blows it by recommending a John Denver CD immediately after I register my music preferences. I suppose it couldn't know I hate John Denver, but it does know I chose neither country nor folk as a preference. However, after energetically clicking "not for me" on that one and clicking on others I did like—I also could type in my favorite artists and rate records I already own—the suggestions quickly improved. Otis Redding? Bingo.

Emboldened, I move on to movies. Video merchants such as cinemax.com and bigstar.com offer a few good suggestions but also some head-scratchers: C'mon, does anyone actually like the golf farce Happy Gilmore? That's why Reel.com Inc. is so refreshing. Instead of hoping that buyers will rate enough movies to build up an adequate database, a staff of 40 real people rates and matches movies before plugging them into a recommendation program. I ask for movies similar to Pulp Fiction, and "close" matches spit out Get Shorty

and Reservoir Dogs. Nice. But the "creative" matches were even better: Fargo, Trainspotting, and Blue Velvet (though after watching all those in succession, I might welcome Happy Gilmore).

Now, I'm ready for the big kahuna—buying a house. Coldwell Banker's Personal Retriever makes a decent attempt. Clicking through a series of choices on the type of house I want, the price range, the location, and the like, I create my personal portfolio of house listings in the locales I'm interested in. Hmmm—only four in my price range? (How about a raise, boss?) Once I find a listing I like, I click on a calculator to figure what my mortgage would be (ouch!) and get some information on local schools. I can save the listings and get updates via E-mail. It's handy, but limited to Coldwell Banker listings, and it's not all that tailored to my financial situation.

I'll have better luck once I have the house and can get started on a garden. Garden Escape's garden.com offers a raft of appealing personalized features, starting with a home page tailored to my climate (which it knows from the zip code obtained during a short registration). I also can store orders for plants and tools in a "wheelbarrow" for later purchase, jot notes about plants in an online notebook, and launch a Garden Planner program that lets me plug in plants on a grid representing my garden. A Garden Doctor even answers questions personally.

CHATTERBOTS. For pure fun, though, my favorite customizable site is Imagine Radio. It lets me create my own online radio station on the site, which can be heard by anyone through a PC using Real

Networks Inc.'s latest player. Clicking away on a long, though limited, list of artists (no classical, for example), I create my own personal station with just the music I like. No Yanni or Michael Bolton for me. Curious? Check out "Radio Rob": Click on the site's "personal" music button, and it's in the "Carnival" section.

Although these services are supposed to make the Web feel more personal, almost none of it feels as if there's someone at the other end of the wire. For that, I try a prototype service from Big Science Co.—a so-called chatterbot, or artificial intelligence character. One named Andrette is being tested as a possible cyberconcierge at Access Atlanta, a Cox Interactive Media city guide. Here's a sample (typed) conversation:

Andrette: "Tell me what you are looking for."

Me: "I'm looking for love."

Andrette: "Say that again, please?"

Me: "What are the best bars in town?"

Andrette: "To discover some great restaurants, click here."

Me: "O.K., how about music clubs?"

Andrette: "Click here for the Access Atlanta music calendar."

Not bad, I suppose, but a entertainment listings index of might work better.

What I initially feared most from all these personalization efforts was a deluge of junk E-mail. So far, that hasn't been a problem. I get more spam from two posts to a single Usenet group a year ago than from all my personalized Web adventures. On the other hand, the E-mail pitches I have received don't seem to make use of the personal information I've divulged. American Airlines Inc., whose frequent-flier program I signed up for online, has sent me several E-mails on last-minute Net SAAver Fares and hotel deals—none targeted to my home airport, let alone routes I specified.

Clearly, Web personalization has a long way to go. Navigating the Web's vast resources still requires a steady mouse hand, a big browser bookmark file, and a lot of patience. Oh, and I almost forgot, a good memory. I've created so many sign-on names and passwords for security on various sites that I can't remember them all. So I have to write them down—the worst security breach of all. Even so, my personal Web already is useful. I do get things done faster and sometimes discover things I didn't know I wanted—to the detriment of my credit-card balance. I tend to stick around some sites more consistently and even feel a little warm and fuzzy toward a few. Your results may vary. But then, that's the whole idea.

By Robert D. Hof in San Mateo, Calif.

Getting Personal

Like any new technology, the software behind personalization of Web sites can have some rough edges when it comes to getting your personal page set up or getting back what you want. Our review surveyed a few sites to see whether the experience was a pleasure, a pain, or just so-so.

WEB SITE	RATING
AMAZON.COM	
BARNESANDNOBLE.COM	
GARDEN.COM	
IMAGINERADIO.COM	
MY CDNOW (cdnow.com)	
MYEXCITE (excite.com)	
MYYAHOO! (yahoo.com)	
PERSONAL RETRIEVER (Coldwellbanker.com)	
REEL.COM	

(Cont.)

Fending Off Those Pesky Snoops

You're 55 years old, you make $50,000 a year, and you've been surfing the Web for athletic-shoe supports. Suddenly, Amazon.com starts urging you to buy safe-sport guides for aging joggers. Even more irksome, CDnow Inc. is recommending you buy '60s oldies by such artists as Iron Butterfly. Jeez. It's bad enough CDnow thinks you're a heavy metal fan. Do you really want these sites to know your salary, your age, and all about your fallen arches?

The trouble is, most of them already do. Consider "cookies," the deceptively sweet name for software that's downloaded into your PC's hard drive, usually without your knowledge. Sent by online merchants, advertisers, and Internet services, they quietly record your Web habits. Each time you visit a site, cookies are uploaded for review by the people who put them there, so they can pitch you products you may find too good to pass up.

Some cookies simply track what you read and buy on a single Web site. But more powerful software, called "tracking cookies," follow you everywhere. These hard-drive supersnoops, often used by advertisers, let marketers combine data from the cookie on your hard drive with the personal information you volunteer when filling out registration forms. Armed with such profiles, cybersalesmen may be able to get at your credit-rating, salary, and lifestyle.

BLOCKERS. What to do? You can block cookies entirely, using the preference settings in the pull-down menus of the two leading browsers, Netscape Navigator and Microsoft Internet Explorer. Or you can curb their snooping. With Netscape Navigator 4.0, you can set preferences so that your browser accepts only cookies that get sent back to the "originating server"—no more tracking cookies. The result: E-merchants and services are kept from tracing anything you do beyond their site. And there are other ways: Software, such as Kookaburra Software's Cookie Pal ($15), lets you list sites from which you'll accept cookies. And for $60 a year, Netizens can subscribe to The Anonymizer, a San Diego-based service that lets you surf the Web and send E-mail anonymously.

Some Net marketers argue that as long as your real name, address, and phone numbers are protected, it's impossible to overly intrude. "We don't need to know who a person is to customize the experience," says Dan Jaye, chief technology officer of Engage Technologies Inc., which sells anonymous user profiles to online marketers. Over the past five months, Engage has amassed a database of 38 million user profiles, which it sells to advertisers and E-retailers. Jaye says these "can't be used to track you down. If the government subpoenaed our database, we couldn't tell them who you are."

For those still worried, Engage is developing "trust labels," which reject any cookie that marketers or advertisers use to expose a Web surfer's real identity. Engage demonstrated the tool to the Commerce Dept. in June, and Netscape may add it to the next version of its browser, due late this year.

But the most ambitious privacy effort so far is called the Platform for Privacy Preferences (P3P). Software companies are working on a P3P standard that would let cybernauts choose how much personal information to disclose. Under the plan, cybernauts—by setting their browser preferences—may choose to block out every-

thing or agree to disclose only some data, such as their zip code and gender. Progress is slow, however, so consumers may have to wait a while for relief. Until then, the best advice might come from you mom: Don't accept cookies from strangers.

By Paul C. Judge in Boston

88

P&G'S HOTTEST NEW PRODUCT: P&G

A soup-to-nuts redesign aims for global speed and focus

At Washington State's Clark County Fair last month, coffee lovers got a front-row seat at a corporate revolution in the making. The local sales force for Procter & Gamble Co. was out in force at the Pancake Feed, distributing samples of P&G's Millstone Coffee. To the amazement of the Fred Meyer supermarket employees running the pancake breakfast, the Procter reps worked the crowd, chatting with customers, even taking turns in the full-size coffee-maker costume with the cup-and-saucer hat. "You don't generally see them out there doing that kind of grassroots work with customers," says Jeanne Lawson, a Fred Meyer buyer. Procter is better known for serving up advertising dollars and display-design tips, she says. "I'd never seen anything like it."

But then, P&G has never needed ordinary customers quite so badly. Battered by disappointing revenue growth and demanding retail customers, Procter & Gamble is a company in a bind. Two years ago, its executives boldly declared that the consumer-products giant would double its net sales by 2006, to $70 billion. P&G has consistently missed its growth targets ever since. Olestra, the company's high-profile fat substitute, more than a decade in development, is showing weak sales. And global economic turmoil is crimping overseas operations. Shares have dropped from $94 apiece in July to $70. The behemoth so used to leading the pack is looking lost.

So P&G, a company notorious for secrecy, has set itself on a remarkably outward-looking self-improvement plan. Breaking from decades of tradition, it has sought external advice. It is undergoing a structural shift prompted at least in part by outsiders—namely, its big chain-store customers. And it is already rolling out an aggressive global marketing blitz, from working the fairgrounds to marshaling the Internet.

Chief Executive John E. Pepper will step down about two years early to make way for President and Chief Operating Officer Durk I. Jager, who will drive the changes. It's a shift away from internal themes of recent years in which Procter focused heavily on such tasks as cost-cutting and shedding underperforming brands. But even as the giant revs its engines to push for faster sales growth, critics wonder if it can overcome both economic turmoil around the world and what will surely be cultural turmoil within its own ranks. "This is a very big deal, for Procter and for all the companies that watch Procter's moves," says Watts Wacker, chairman of consulting firm FirstMatter in Westport, Conn. "But great plans often come with great obstacles."

SIMPLIFY, SIMPLIFY. In preparation for the task, Pepper and other top execs have been traversing the country, visiting the CEOs of a dozen major companies, including Kellogg Co. and 3M, in search of advice. Pepper went to Jack Welch at General Electric Co. to learn how the company streamlined global marketing. He persuaded Hewlett- Packard Co. CEO Lewis E. Platt to share enough secrets about new-product development to make a 30-minute instructional video for P&G staffers. The message from all was clear, says Pepper: "What thousands of people have been telling us is that we need to be simpler and move faster."

The result of this unprecedented road trip is Organization 2005, a shuffling of the P&G hierarchy and a new product-development process designed to speed innovative offerings to the global market. The old bureaucracy, based on geography, will be reshaped into seven global business units organized by category, such as baby care, beauty care, and fabric-and-home care. The global business units will develop and sell products on a worldwide basis, erasing the old system that let Procter's country managers rule as colonial governors, setting prices and handling products as they saw fit.

SWIFT ROLLOUT. This new global vision has already had an accidental test run. Last year, P&G introduced an extension of its Pantene shampoo line. The ad campaign for the product was almost entirely visual, with images of beautiful women and their lustrous hair, and had a very limited script. That meant the campaign was easily translated and shipped to P&G markets around the world without the usual months of testing and tinkering. The result: P&G was able to introduce the brand extension in 14 countries in six months, vs. the two years it took to get the original shampoo into stores abroad. "It's

---

---

a success story that gets quite a bit of talk internally," says Chris T. Allen, a marketing professor at the University of Cincinnati, who spent his sabbatical year working in the P&G new-products department. "I see the reorganization as an attempt to do more Pantenes on a regular basis."

P&G didn't come to this global focus entirely on its own. Its biggest chain-store customers, such as Wal-Mart Stores Inc. and French-owned Carrefour, have been agitating for just such a program to mirror their own global expansion. It has been Topic A at retail conventions for months, says Robin Lanier,

(Cont.)

senior vice-president for industry affairs at the International Mass Retail Assn. While P&G craves an international image for its products, retailers want something more tangible: a global price. As it stands, prices are negotiable on a country or regional basis. What an international retailer pays for Crest in the U.S. could be considerably less than what it costs the chain in Europe or Latin America. A consistent global price gives big chains more power to plan efficiently and save money. Wal-Mart Chief Executive David D. Glass describes his company's goal as "global sourcing," which includes worldwide relationships on pricing and distribution. Moving P&G products from regional to global management is "pointing somewhat in that direction," Glass says.

In addition to marketing and pricing, global business units will supervise new-product development. P&G will move away from its long-used "sequential" method, which tested products first in midsize U.S. cities and then gradually rolled them out to the world. An example: Swiffer, a new disposable mop designed by P&G, is being tested simultaneously in Cedar Rapids, Iowa; Pittsfield, Mass.; and Sens, France, in hopes of sculpting a globally popular product right out of the box.

Jager concedes that it won't be a quick fix. The new regime won't start until January and won't really be functioning for about 18 to 24 months. He expects to see some top-line growth improvement within 12 to 16 months, with obviously better results two years out. Many observers doubt that will be fast enough to make the 2006 deadline. "[The plan] seems to work on paper, but it requires an accelerated sales growth in the final four years," says Constance M. Maneaty, an analyst at Bear,

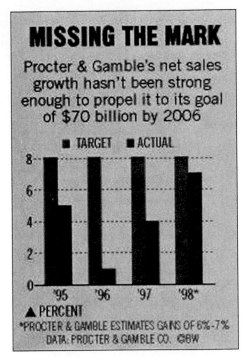

MISSING THE MARK

Procter & Gamble's net sales growth hasn't been strong enough to propel it to its goal of $70 billion by 2006

■ TARGET ■ ACTUAL

▲ PERCENT
*PROCTER & GAMBLE ESTIMATES GAINS OF 6%-7%
DATA: PROCTER & GAMBLE CO. CBW

Stearns & Co. "We haven't seen that kind of sales growth from them in a while."

Even if P&G could implement its strategy more quickly, it would still run into the ugly realities of global economic markets. For its extra $35 billion in revenues through 2006, Procter is counting on about $8 billion from emerging markets in Eastern Europe, China, and Latin America, says Clayton C. Daley Jr., P&G's treasurer, who becomes chief financial officer in October. Yet Asian emerging markets are likely to remain mired in deep economic slumps for at least two more years. Recent turmoil in Russia, which was a bright prospect for Procter just a year ago, has gotten so bad that the company has temporarily halted shipments there. "Growing in underdeveloped geographies is clearly questionable," says Jay Freedman, an analyst at Lincoln Capital, a big institutional holder of Procter & Gamble stock. "Whatever they thought the purchasing power of those new customers was going to be is less now."

"A LOT OF EX-CHIEFS." Procter has additional obstacles closer to home. How, for example, will tradition-bound P&G managers react to the new hierarchy? "You're going from 144 chiefs to 8. That's a lot of ex-chiefs," says consultant Wacker. And everyone will be affected by the change in tone that is sure to come from the corner office. Gentlemanly Pepper, 60, will be succeeded by Jager, a Dutch-born P&G lifer with a reputation for aggressive moves and abrasiveness. In the 1980s, he turned around Procter's failing Japanese business with such a fury that his Japanese managers called him "Crazy Man Durk" behind his back.

Crazy or no, Jager is sticking to the 2006 target date. He's wasting no time stepping into his new role as champion of the global focus: Already, even before taking on the official title of CEO, he has started preaching the new structure to P&G managers. After all, the clock is ticking.

By Peter Galuszka in Cincinnati and Ellen Neuborne in New York, with Wendy Zellner in Dallas

89

Ever Wondered Why Furniture Shopping Can Be Such a Pain?

Clues: Splintered Industry, Old-Time Technologies And Dubious Marketing

The Spring Table Falls Flat

By James R. Hagerty and Robert Berner
Staff Reporters of The Wall Street Journal

Visiting friends' homes can be painful for Evan Cole, whose family owns ABC Carpet & Home, a big home-furnishings retailer in New York. Often, says Mr. Cole, "They've got a $50,000 car, they wear Giorgio Armani — and you walk into the house and you say, 'What happened?'"

Perhaps the entire U.S. furniture industry should be asking itself the same question. Shabby chic is one thing, but millions of American homes are just plain shabby. Much of the blame lies with makers and retailers of furniture.

In an era when American consumers expect instant gratification — and generally get it — the furniture industry is a low-tech laggard, split into thousands of small retailers and manufacturers and frequently unable to deliver what people want, when they want it. While Americans splurge on cars, appliances and electronic toys, many approach buying furniture with the sort of dull dread that usually precedes an IRS audit.

Cathy Marshik, a 28-year-old inventory manager at a Minneapolis discount chain, twice has had to wait 12 weeks for furniture ordered at Pottery Barn. When she bought her 1998 Jeep Grand Cherokee, she was able to drive it home the same day. The furniture industry "needs to get in the ballgame," Ms. Marshik concludes.

Service With a Snore

Even big spenders get drowsy service. In June, Douglas McAuley, a management consultant in Chicago, hired a decorator and ordered $70,000 of furniture, including a hand-carved entertainment center. By November, only one of the pieces had arrived. "I'm still sitting here with an empty room," he says.

If customers got better service, this might be a golden age for the furniture industry. The average size of new houses in the U.S. has grown by 25% since 1980. Baby boomers are in their prime furniture-buying years. The American Furniture Manufacturers Associa-

tion projects a 13% jump in industry shipments this year. Still, furniture accounts for only about 1% of U.S. consumer spending, down from 1.2% in 1980. Motor vehicles and parts eat up 12.3% of consumers' budgets, up slightly from 12.1% in 1980.

Meanwhile, some of the nation's biggest furniture retailers are languishing. Heilig-Meyers Co., the No. 1 retailer, suffered a loss of $55.1 million in the year ended Feb. 28. Levitz Furniture Inc. is operating under Chapter 11 bankruptcy protection. Sears, Roebuck & Co. recently announced it may sell its lackluster HomeLife furniture stores.

What's the problem? Low investment in technology is part of it. Few companies in the residential-furniture industry have the financial muscle — or long-term vision — to invest heavily in the automation and computers needed to ship goods promptly and to accurately forecast demand.

In an industry with annual factory shipments of about $24 billion, only three manufacturers have sales of more than $1 billion a year: Furniture Brands International Inc. (owner of the Broyhill, Lane and Thomasville brands), LifeStyle Furnishings International Ltd. (Drexel Heritage, Henredon and Lexington) and La-Z-Boy Inc. The Big Three have U.S. market share of about 20%, says Furniture/Today, a trade paper; the rest is shared by more than 1,000 other manufacturers. In the U.S. market for cars and light trucks, the Big Three manufacturers hog more than 70% of the market, and invest heavily to keep it.

Research and Development

Capital spending at Ford Motor Co. totaled about 6.6% of sales last year. At St. Louis-based Furniture Brands, one of the more advanced furniture makers, the figure was 2.2%.

Because the larger furniture manufacturers haven't built up any overwhelming advantages in efficiency, it is easy for small competitors to pop up. Anyone wishing to set up a mainstream auto maker would need to invest billions of dollars. Mitchell Gold and partner Bob Williams nine years ago put down $90,000 to form Mitchell Gold Co., a trendy sofa and chair maker based in Taylorsville, N.C.

A few big manufacturers use computerized fabric-cutting machines that cost $250,000 or so. But in most upholstery factories, production of sofas and chairs remains a quaint craft. Workers use hand tools to slice fabric, bind together springs, stretch the fabric over wood frames and then staple the material in place. "A man and his wife can manufacture 10 sofas a week," says Bob McKinnon, chief executive of Century Furniture Industries Inc. of Hickory, N.C., which has annual sales of nearly $200 million, thus qualifying for the big leagues of furniture.

The large number of suppliers scrapping for orders helps keep prices low. But the small companies that predominate in furniture tend

to be short on capital. They often resist investments that would improve service. Most furniture retailers still communicate with suppliers by phone and fax rather than by zapping information instantly by computers.

Until a few years ago, customers typically had to wait several months for delivery of items that weren't in stock at retailers. Now the wait is more likely four to eight weeks, and some manufacturers say they make nearly all of their deliveries within a month. But even at four weeks, an impulse buy is out of the question. Cars go home the same day. Appliances are delivered the next day. A fine suit is tailored within two weeks. The furniture industry's delivery performance reminds ABC Carpet's Mr. Cole of "another century." Anne Marty, who recently moved to a Tudor-style home in Park Ridge, Ill., canceled an order for $7,650 of furniture after waiting 12 weeks for a shipment promised in four weeks. "I said, 'Forget it,'" she says. "Why does it take so long?"

One reason is the huge number of options. Century Furniture, for instance, has 3,500 different frames for sofas and upholstered chairs. If all combinations of fabric, skirts, pillows, springs and fringes are considered, company officials say, Century offers consumers 1.7 billion possibilities.

Making so many variations slows production and raises costs. "They don't have to have every single possible shade of green," says Richard Bennington, director of home-furnishings programs at High Point University in High Point, N.C., which is to furniture what Detroit is to cars.

Century's CEO, Mr. McKinnon, says the company is reducing the variations to gain efficiency, but believes customers still want lots of choices and crave more individuality in furniture than they do in, say, cars.

The industry's other conspicuous failing, say experts, is marketing. The nation's two biggest furniture-store operators, Heilig-Meyers and Levitz, stress low prices and easy credit in their advertising. "We've Gone Nuts!" announces a recent ad from a Heilig chain. "Don't Pay Anything Until April 1999!" shouts a Levitz ad depicting a four-piece leather living-room set on sale for $1,799.

The message many consumers read: The stuff must be way overpriced most of the time.

"We don't talk about how easy it can be to make your home more attractive," says Jerry Epperson, an investment banker in Richmond, Va., who specializes in the furniture industry. "All we talk about is sale, sale, sale and credit terms, credit terms."

Indeed, many consumers lament a seeming absence of new, appealing products. Christopher Shyers describes his recent furniture-shopping experiences as "abysmal." The 30-year-old trade-association manager moved into a condo in Chicago in August and needed new bookshelves and a couch. He shopped for a sleeper sofa at discount furni-

(Cont.)

ture stores. "They looked pretty shabby and flimsy and like they were covered in burlap," he says. "I would personally not ask someone to sleep on them."

The bookshelves he found were all made with particle board covered by veneer. "I was looking for something that was made of solid wood," he says.

He ended up driving to seven or eight stores. In the end, he bought a $1,000 sofa on sale at a Marshall Field's department store. He got three solid-wood bookshelves at store called Naked Furniture for $300 apiece — but had to add his own finish to the bare wood.

Furniture makers and retailers seeking "amazing" values also sometimes overlook simple elegance. An example is a glass-topped buffet table that rests on a half-moon sheet-metal frame, with a fiberboard wheel. Called the "Spring Table," it was designed by Russell Norton Buchanan of Dallas. The Dallas Museum of Art liked it so much that it installed one in its furniture collection in 1994. Mr. Buchanan has made just 32 of the tables and charges $4,500 apiece for them, though he admits materials cost him just $250 per table. He figures the table could easily be mass produced and sold for a small fraction of his price. So far, he has found no manufacturers interested in that idea.

Even when it does come up with tasty products, the industry often fails to get the word out to potential buyers. Dean Voiss, a 42-year-old consultant in Mountain View, Calif., is no miser. He owns three bicycles and four windsurfing boards. But he is still using the same living-room sofa he had two decades ago when he was in college. Mr. Voiss says he occasionally looks through furniture catalogs, but "nothing really jumps out

at me." He isn't even sure where he would look if he finally decides to replace his sagging sofa.

Many people in the furniture industry realize they have a problem. The American Furniture Manufacturers Association, based in High Point, is preparing a public-relations campaign to "encourage consumers to part with more of their disposable income on furniture," says the group's Doug Brackett.

A potentially more effective push for change is coming from some of the stronger retailers of furniture. Atlanta-based Haverty Furniture Cos., which operates about 100 stores in the Southeast, is weeding out its weaker suppliers. Suppliers that can't speed up delivery "probably will become history," says Haverty Chief Executive John E. Slater Jr.

To meet retailers' demands, some of the more ambitious furniture makers are scrambling. Century bought machinery formerly used to make aircraft parts and adapted it to carve wood. (The alternative, says Century executive Joseph M. Wisniewski, would be "15 people sitting under banana trees carving these things.") The company uses robots to punch fake worm holes in wood for artificial antiques. A study of one Century plant found that the stages of production were scattered so illogically that parts traveled 14 miles within the factory before exiting; a new system has trimmed the voyage to less than a mile.

Along with faster delivery, some retailers are demanding more attractive styling. Among the most demanding are the Crate & Barrel, Pottery Barn and Restoration Hardware chains. None offers a wide range of options. They narrow the choice to variations on a simple, contemporary style sometimes called "boomer casual," presented with coor-

dinated accessories.

These casual-furniture retailers don't have deep roots in the industry, and bring a consumer-friendly ethos to the game. Pottery Barn, a unit of Williams-Sonoma Inc., moved into furniture five years ago after one of its executives, Gary Friedman, discovered the frustrations of furniture. When Mr. Friedman moved into a one-bedroom condo in San Francisco, he called on a decorator for help in buying furniture. She proposed a budget of $100,000. Flabbergasted, Mr. Friedman decided to do his own shopping.

"I wound up schlepping around weekend after weekend," he recalls. In one furniture shop after another, he found, "there's a sea of stuff. You've got all kinds of fabrics and styles," many of them hideous. Sales people would hand him stacks of 100 or more fabric samples. By the time he had flipped through them, he was dazed.

The result of all this shopping: "For two years," he says, "I lived with no furniture. I had a bed and two chairs." On one of the chairs sat his radio alarm clock.

Mr. Friedman concluded that Pottery Barn should try to make things simpler for furniture buyers. Even so, he didn't rely entirely on his own stores for furnishings. Eventually, he went back to the decorator he had initially consulted, Kendal Agins, and she finished the job. The cost? "I don't even want to think about it," Mr. Friedman says. But for him, at least, there was a happy ending to the ordeal of home furnishing: He married Ms. Agins in July.

90

Antiacne Campaign Propels Birth-Control Pill

By Anne Marie Chaker
Staff Reporter of The Wall Street Journal

NEW YORK — Columbia University sophomore Lindsay Rachelefsky was flipping through some of her favorite fashion magazines a few months ago when she noticed an ad for a birth-control pill that also prevents pimples.

The 19-year-old student didn't have acne. But she asked her doctor to switch her pill prescription anyway, to "prevent me from ever breaking out."

The acne-fighting pill is Ortho Tri-Cyclen. It is made by Johnson & Johnson's Ortho-McNeil unit, and it is a hit among teenagers and 20-somethings nationwide. But its success poses a dilemma for health professionals, who say that many young women are being distracted from making the best birth-control choices because of their obsession with clear skin.

Ortho Tri-Cyclen is the only birth-control brand with Food and Drug Administration permission to advertise skin-clearing side effects. It won that approval in January 1997 after submitting clinical-test results of a six-month study involving 250 women. Ads in women's magazines such as Glamour, Marie Claire and Jane show a close-up of a young woman's face and pose a question riveting to teenagers: "Can a birth-control pill help clear up your skin?"

Since Ortho launched the campaign a year ago, the acne-clearing pill has surged past rivals, including other Ortho pills, to rank No. 1 among U.S. oral contraceptives, a $1.6 billion-a-year market.

At the Chautauqua County Health Department in New York state, counselors say, teens ranging from 14 to 17 years old arrive clutching the ad or scraps of paper scribbled with the Ortho Tri-Cyclen brand name. Adds Barbara Blizzard, a nurse practitioner at the University of Texas campus health center in Austin: Students "ask for it by name more than any other pill I've ever had."

Many health workers say anything that prompts teens to use birth control is a good thing. But some medical professionals are worried that the ad campaign is coaxing teens to use birth-control pills even though condoms can prevent sexually transmitted diseases. Each year 25% of sexually active teens contract such diseases, according to the Alan Guttmacher Institute, a New York research center on reproductive health.

"I'm really sick of this," says Martha Saez, a family-planning counselor at the Chautauqua health department. "Nine times out of 10 there's nothing wrong with their skin. I try to explain that this may not be the method they want" for birth-control, "but they don't want to hear the rest of it."

Ortho says its ad campaign serves a broader public-health purpose. Marc Monseau, manager of corporate communications, says it "is designed to encourage a dialogue between women and their health-care providers" and to "help adult women make informed decisions about the pill as well as Ortho Tri-Cyclen." He also notes that the company's ads say the drug doesn't prevent sexually transmitted diseases.

The company declined to respond in greater depth, saying that it doesn't comment on its marketing strategy.

Birth-control pills have lost market share to condoms and other forms of contraception in recent years. In addition to concern about sexually transmitted diseases, health worries about the pill are also driving some women away. A study by the National Center for Health Statistics in Hyattsville, Md., found that 27% of U.S. women used the pill in 1995, down from 31% seven years earlier. The decline was even more pronounced for teens. Forty-four percent were using the pill, down from 59%. In the same period, condom use among women overall increased to 20% from 15%.

But Ortho's ad campaign has helped boost the number of Ortho Tri-Cyclen prescriptions, which surged 73% to 3.8 million in the first half, compared with a year earlier. The number of rival pill prescriptions filled edged up less than 2%. And Ortho Tri-Cyclen now has a 12.1% market share, up from 8.5% a year earlier, says IMS Health, a health-care information company in Plymouth Meeting, Pa. Some of Ortho's other top brands lost market share, but the company's combined share of those brands climbed from 28.5% in 1996 to 31.9% in the 1998 first half.

Those numbers don't even include pills dispensed on college campuses and in public-health clinics, where many teens seek contraception. At the University of Texas, Austin, where advertising inserts for Ortho Tri-Cyclen appeared in the Daily Texan campus newspaper, the number of packages distributed to students more than doubled in the

MARKET LEADER

An aggressive ad campaign has led to surging sales of Ortho Tri-Cyclen

	Market share of oral contraceptives		
Brand/Company	**1996**	**1997**	**1998[1]**
Ortho Tri-Cyclen/Ortho-McNeil[2]	5.1%	8.5%	12.1%
Triphasil 28/Wyeth-Ayerst	10.7	11.0	10.4
Ortho-Novum 7/7/7 28/Ortho-McNeil	12.2	11.0	9.7

[1]Year-to-date June 1998
[2]Both 21- and 28-day products

Source: IMS Health

(Cont.)

1997-98 academic year from a year earlier, to 13,592. During the same period, college pharmacists say, Ortho Tri-Cyclen prescriptions tripled at Harvard University, Cambridge, Mass., and at the University of Michigan, Ann Arbor. Stanford University, Stanford, Calif., started stocking the pill this year because of high demand.

The ad campaign touting Ortho Tri-Cyclen as an acne treatment began in September 1997, with inserts in college publications and ads in beauty magazines. "Introducing a birth-control pill that's also a beauty aid," said the ads. But the pitch ran afoul of the FDA, which called the beauty claim "misleading." A month later, the company adopted its current slogan.

Magazine-ad spending for Ortho Tri-Cyclen nearly doubled to $18.1 million in 1997 from $9.6 million a year earlier, according to Competitive Media Reporting. Mr. Monseau says the CMR figures are "substantially higher" than the actual figures but declines to elaborate because the company "can't comment on financial matters." The ads were developed by Omnicom Group's DDB Needham, but Interpublic Group's Ammirati Puris Lintas has since taken over the account.

Ortho is currently the only pill company allowed to plug acne benefits, but doctors have been prescribing birth-control pills to improve skin for years. That is because the estrogen in the pills lowers natural levels of "free" testosterone, which can cause acne. "We spend a lot of time trying to explain to students that it doesn't mean that other contraceptive [pills] won't clear your skin," says Robyn Tepper, chief of medical services at Stanford's student-health services. "It's difficult to try to fight the kind of marketing that they see in print."

Ortho says its pill is different because it contains Norgestimate, a patented brand of progestin. Progestin is the other hormone in birth-control pills, and it can interfere with the acne-clearing benefits of estrogen. But Norgestimate doesn't have that effect, says Geoffrey Redmond, the lead investigator in the clinical trials that resulted in Ortho Tri-Cyclen's acne-treatment approval.

The success of the Ortho ad campaign may trigger some copycat ads from other pill makers. American Home Products Corp.'s Wyeth-Ayerst Laboratories says it plans to seek approval in Canada and the U.S. for use of its Alesse birth-control pill as an acne treatment. "Everybody in the category is looking at Ortho Tri-Cyclen and looking at its success," says David Rebey, group product director for female health care at Berlex Laboratories Inc., a unit of Schering AG of Germany.

91

For the Right Price, These Doctors Treat Patients as Precious

Their 'Consultancy' Signals Rise of a System Critics Say Favors the Wealthy

Practicing HMO-Avoidance

By Anita Sharpe

Staff Reporter of The Wall Street Journal

SEATTLE — Garrison Bliss and Mitchell Karton, like many doctors, were tired of insurance companies telling them how to care for their patients. Looking for a way around the bureaucracy, the two physicians discovered the price people will pay for peace of mind.

Their practice, Seattle Medical Associates, is an unusual medical consultancy, where people pay for a doctor's know-how. For a range of fees, patients get unlimited access to a doctor they know who will guide them through the maze of hospitals and medical specialists they may encounter if they do get sick. There are unlimited office visits, an annual physical and X-rays as needed, but no ties to the insurers and health-maintenance organizations that most Americans now encounter. It doesn't take Medicare or Medicaid either. Instead, SMA promises the kind of personal, around-the-clock attention that people used to associate with their family doc.

Why It's Worth It

Many of their longtime patients had to think hard about paying almost $800 more a year on top of other health costs, and a lot of their old patients have left. Others are happy that they stayed. "It's expensive, but this matters," says Julie Blacklow, a 51-year-old freelance television producer who recently called Dr. Karton at 1 a.m. complaining of chest pains that she feared signaled a heart attack. He talked her through her symptoms, then told her — correctly — not to worry.

"To give someone access, that may be the best medicine of all," Ms. Blacklow says. "That's priceless."

Maybe. But such added prices are too high for many Americans and point the way to a multitiered medical system in which the quality of care might depend even more than it does today on the thickness of the patient's wallet.

For years, patients have been clamoring for more personal service, for example by choosing HMO programs that allow them to spend extra money to gain access to more choices in doctors and treatments. Now, doctors themselves are devising ways to satisfy the growing demand for attentive care. Some offer added services, such as deluxe executive physicals or alternative medicine, that often aren't covered by insurance plans. Drs. Bliss and Karton are among a small but growing number who have found a way to dispense entirely with insurers' reimbursements.

Of course, there have always been the so-called Park Avenue doctors who charge high fees and cater to millionaires. But personal physicians tapping into the middle and upper-middle classes signals a significant change in the nation's health-care climate.

An Area to Explore

Robert Elkins, chief executive of Integrated Health Services Inc., a nursing home and health-care provider, says some sort of pay-it-yourself medical care is an area he will explore if he starts another company. "I think there is a huge market out there," says Dr. Elkins, who is also a physician. "We're going toward a two-tier medical system in a very dramatic way."

Some question whether a major change lies ahead. The American Association of Health Plans, which represents HMOs and other managed-care companies, notes that most U.S. doctors — about 90% now, compared with 61% in 1990 — contract with managed-care concerns.

Others, however, worry about an increasingly popular multitiered system. Critics argue that a private-payment system will steer the best doctors to people who can pay the most for treatment, and that will siphon off the wealthy, well-connected people who could sway lawmakers to reform the health-care system.

Drs. Bliss and Karton say they aren't making much more with their new setup, but feel they have made the right choice. The two men first worked together in the intensive-care unit of an inner-city Seattle hospital in 1979. A year later, Dr. Bliss went into private practice in Seattle. Dr. Karton, who was on the faculty at the University of Washington, joined him in 1986. "We enjoyed our practice enormously," says Dr. Bliss, 48 years old.

But in ensuing years, their traditional fee-for-service practice gradually moved toward more managed care. Insurers who had reimbursed the doctors based on what the doctors charge for procedures began slashing payments. Dr. Bliss says his reimbursement fell to under 50% of office charges in 1996, from around 95% in the early 1990s.

Quantity Over Quality

Worse, says Dr. Karton, 45, is that the employers and insurers responsible for most health plans began viewing doctors as interchangeable. "There was no reward at that point for better work or better patient satisfaction." The quantity of patients, not the quality of care, seemed like it was becoming the main criterion.

In 1994, the two men affiliated with a larger group of doctors, a move that promised better business management and economies of scale. But the group's contracts were soon taken over by a company intent on imposing even stronger managed-care discipline, including suggestions that the two increase their patient load. "We weren't about to start seeing 30 or 35 people a day," says Dr. Bliss, who was seeing around 25 people a day. Before long, "I'd come to work and want to run screaming," says Dr. Bliss. "Financially, I was doing fine, but I hated the practice."

In 1996, two colleagues at the practice left to become healers to the opulent. For about $20,000 a year per family, Drs. Howard Maron and Scott Hall would oversee all medical care, even flying to a client's vacation home, and keeping their cell phones turned on 24 hours a day. It was a hit: The two now work in art-filled offices where a select group of clients — just 50 families per doctor — are buzzed in through an intercom system.

Drs. Bliss and Karton were wary of such an ultra-exclusive practice, but were also intrigued by the successful move away from managed-care dictates. Pulling off the same trick at a more affordable level was hard, though; virtually all insurance contracts, including the government insurance for the poor and elderly, Medicaid and Medicare, forbid physicians from tacking on a surcharge to cover costs beyond what the insurer pays.

Dr. Karton pored over every insurance contract the doctors had ever signed, looking for ways to get paid for kid-glove treatment. He and Dr. Bliss talked with consultants, who discouraged their plans for a cash-based practice, and with patients who had legal and insurance expertise of their own.

After more than a year, the doctors hammered out a plan that worked by abandoning the traditional billing structure: SMA offers guaranteed access to a knowledgeable doctor with good connections in the health-care system. Patients over the age of 35 pay $65 a month for the service; those between the ages of 21 and 35 pay $35 a month; and children over 14 can be added for an extra $10 a month. They don't take patients younger than 14. Patients are also urged to buy health insurance that covers additional care, such as surgery, specialists and hospitalization, which the doctors often orchestrate as part of their service. There is no limit on the number of patient visits.

The doctors don't bill third parties, but maintain relationships with some insurance-related companies so they can refer patients to specialists affiliated with those plans. That personal guide through modern health care's maze of specialists and gatekeepers is what many SMA patients value most.

Glenn Fleishman, a 30-year-old self-employed technology consultant, took a variety of complaints, including fever, weight loss and night sweats, to Dr. Bliss last January. Within a few minutes, the doctor made a pre-

(Cont.)

liminary diagnosis of Hodgkin's disease, and his staff began looking for a top oncologist who could see Mr. Fleishman fast. Some cancer specialists didn't have an opening for more than a month, but SMA secured a rapid visit with a friend of Dr. Karton's who is a highly regarded local oncologist, plus another physician for a second opinion. Mr. Fleishman's diagnosis was confirmed, treatment was started, and he says he now is in remission.

A Good Bad Experience

"It's been pretty darn easy, the whole process," Mr. Fleishman says. "I've had the best-possible worst experience, and it's because of them."

In another nod to traditional family-doctor service, a few of the doctors' patients are able to negotiate discounts. One even pays in home-grown produce, according to the doctors. "Our demographics haven't changed," says Dr. Karton.

Still, some patients have had to make sharp adjustments to the new system. Geri Alhadeff, a 48-year-old teacher's aide, came to Dr. Bliss after losing Dr. Maron to the gold-plated practice. When Dr. Bliss began talking about launching his own fee-based service, she recalls thinking, "Oh, great, another one down the tubes." Dr. Bliss offered her a discount from SMA's normal fee, but Mrs. Alhadeff still pays a premium over her family's $500 a month in medical insurance. Her husband and children no longer see Dr.

Bliss. "We truly could not afford to have me do it and my husband and my two kids," she says. Still, she says, the extra fees are "kind of a reasonable rate. . . . I don't feel it's for the wealthy."

Doctors who feel trapped in the current system might envy the SMA setup, but consultants who worked with physician groups call the practice a rare success. Others have tried, but "when they ran the numbers, it just wasn't feasible," says Ann Pietrick with Scheur Management Group. "It's just not feasible in any market I'm aware of to make it work without a wealthy population."

Even Dr. Karton has his doubts about his kind of practice working on a widespread basis. "It's incredibly hard to structure," he says. "It requires a certain history with your patients." People who had been going to the doctors for years were more likely to be willing to pay a premium to keep their services. He and Dr. Bliss have about 1,300 patients, about one-third the number of patients they used to have, and a figure they think is optimal for their practice. They earn the average salary for internists, around $140,000 to $150,000 a year.

The doctors say they can now frequently leave their offices, which provide a panoramic view of Seattle's mountains and waterways, by 5 or 5:30 p.m. They have time to read medical journals and keep up with changes in medicine. There is a staff of about five, including nurses. The billing depart-

ment is a lone personal computer, where Dr. Bliss spends about four hours a month updating records.

A Deciding Factor

The service has also won improbable converts. Roland Jankelson, who co-owns a medical-devices concern in Tacoma, Wash., had his family and his employees with a managed-care company. There were complaints about managed care, even from his wife, but Mr. Jankelson says he thought "they were just complaining about inconvenience."

Last March, his wife was diagnosed with ovarian cancer. She was admitted to a local hospital, but Mr. Jankelson thought she would have been diagnosed much earlier if she had had more attentive treatment from just one doctor. His brother recommended his own physician, Dr. Bliss, whom the executive called that night.

"He got back to me within a matter of minutes," Mr. Jankelson recalls in awe. By 11:30 the next morning, Mr. Jankelson's wife was on her way via ambulance to a hospital in Seattle where Dr. Bliss helped assemble a team of specialists to work on her care.

When his wife got sick, "insurance wasn't an issue," says the 59-year-old Mr. Jankelson. "I would pay whatever it took."

92

How eBay Will Battle Sham Bids, Mislabeling

BY GEORGE ANDERS

Staff Reporter of THE WALL STREET JOURNAL

For the past three years, eBay Inc. has used the freewheeling culture of cyberspace to build up an online auction service with more than 1.2 million participants. Now it wants to introduce some law and order.

This morning eBay plans to announce five initiatives to combat fraud, misrepresentation and bidding irregularities by people using its service. The company will start checking some users' identities much more rigorously. It will expand insurance and escrow services so buyers are better protected against sellers who don't deliver what they promise. Finally, eBay will crack down on people submitting sham bids for merchandise.

The overhaul is likely to be felt immediately by the swarms of people who use eBay to buy or sell everything from Furby toys to cars purportedly driven by basketball legend Michael Jordan. The San Jose, Calif., company has become an Internet sensation, with more than one million items up for auction, day and night. Its stock, which was priced at $18 a share when it went public last September, currently trades at about $225.

Yet eBay's action suggests that rapid growth on the Internet can create a community with too many strangers. During much of last year, eBay was adding more than 30,000 new users a week. While that expansion was great for business, it also meant that by year end eBay had a lot of users who hadn't been involved long enough to establish their reliability.

"Think of what happens when a small community turns into a big city," says Margaret Whitman, chief executive officer of eBay. "That's applicable to us. We want to make eBay as secure and safe as shopping at the Gap. That means people will need more information about who they might be doing business with. And it means we have to get more aggressive about trust and safety issues."

Much of eBay's appeal comes from its ability to offer an old-fashioned flea market reincarnated as an endless series of auctions in cyberspace. EBay itself doesn't have any inventory for sale. People from around the world post listings, and potential buyers place their bids over the Internet. When an auction is over, the winning bidder contacts the seller to arrange payment and shipping. EBay collects a small commission on each listing and sale.

Devotees say they love the huge selection, spirited bidding and periodic bargains available via eBay. Even so, users have come to expect that deals will occasionally go astray. Tom Russell, a collector of Western memorabilia, says he got "stiffed" once when the seller of an antique lighter cashed his money order and never sent the goods. Joanne Felix, a seller of Disney memorabilia, says the high bidder in one of her 75 auctions walked away from his offer and wouldn't complete the transaction.

Officials at eBay maintain that such problems are extremely rare. "More than 99.9% of our trades go off fine," says Ms. Whitman. According to eBay's tallies, only 27 auctions per million generate a fraud complaint to the company. "Fraud isn't a big problem, but we want to drive that number down as low as possible," Ms. Whitman says.

The company hasn't exactly encouraged users to file formal complaints, though; nor has it offered much hope of restitution. By contrast, Susan Grant, an Internet fraud specialist at the National Consumers League, Washington, D.C., says her nonprofit organization gets 600 complaints a month about Internet fraud. Two-thirds of these involve online auctions — a field in which eBay towers over dozens of much smaller competitors.

"All the online auction houses need to get better at identifying problem users," says Ms. Grant. "They're adamant that they don't have legal responsibility for user fraud. But they're making a profit by running a listing service. With that, I think, comes a responsibility to detect fraud and to try to prevent it."

Until now, eBay's main way of gauging a member's reliability has been feedback from other patrons of the auction site. Members can submit short messages about one another, which are tallied as positive or negative feedback and then posted as a member's score. Ratings of plus 10 or better are rewarded with a star any time that the member's name appears in an auction. People with scores of minus four or worse are evicted from the system.

Pierre Omidyar, eBay's chairman, developed that rating system within the company's first few months. He considered it an essential tool in building a sense of close-knit community among eBay users. The desire to build up a good score — and thus be known as a trustworthy trading partner — would be strong enough in users, Mr. Omidyar argued, that they would treat one another fairly.

As eBay use has exploded, though, the feedback system has at times been strained. Some users have pumped up their scores by getting friends to submit positive feedback, even though they haven't actually done business together on eBay. Other users have been loath to leave negative feedback, even when

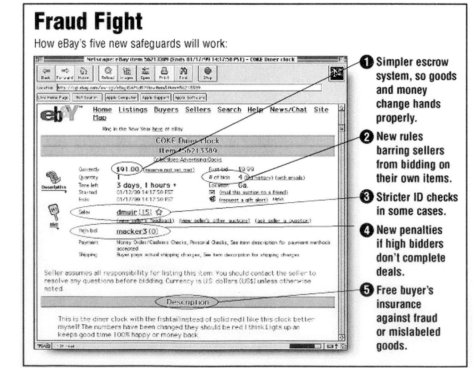

Fraud Fight

How eBay's five new safeguards will work:

❶ Simpler escrow system, so goods and money change hands properly.

❷ New rules barring sellers from bidding on their own items.

❸ Stricter ID checks in some cases.

❹ New penalties if high bidders don't complete deals.

❺ Free buyer's insurance against fraud or mislabeled goods.

(Cont.)

an auction went sour, for fear that recipients would strike back with a negative note that would tarnish their own online reputation.

To protect its rating system, eBay will change its score-keeping formula so that it counts only feedback related to actual transactions. Beyond that, eBay will:

• Give users the option of having their identities verified independently by an outside party, Equifax Inc., and then being certified on eBay as "accredited" users. Users would pay $5 and submit their driver's license and Social Security numbers. The data would be kept private, but participants would be rewarded with a special badge next to their names, indicating that their full identities had been verified. Ms. Whitman, eBay's CEO, predicts that if even a handful of the company's most active users embrace this service, it will quickly become the desired status throughout the system.

• Provide customers with free insurance against fraud or mislabeling of goods, with a $25 deductible and $200 of coverage. The insurance will be underwritten by Lloyd's of London. Customers who don't get their merchandise or feel they were materially misled about what was for sale will submit claims to eBay. It will forward the claims to Lloyds if they seem valid.

• Make it easier for customers to use third-party escrow services, particularly on large transactions. Currently, eBay offers online links to two escrow companies that will hold a customer's payment until word is received that the goods have arrived safely. But fewer than 1% of eBay customers use those services, regarding them as expensive and cumbersome. Company officials say they are seeking a closer, more economical alliance with an escrow company.

• Ban sellers from bidding on their own merchandise. The company has historically allowed one such bid, because sellers claimed to have friends who wanted to participate in an auction but weren't online. With the growing popularity of the Internet, though, that justification is fading, eBay officials say.

• Establish sanctions against bidders who walk away from auctions that they win without trying to collect the goods or pay for them. In one recent embarrassing case, a charity auction sponsored by eBay was hijacked by teenagers who submitted bids exceeding $100,000 with no intention of paying. Company officials say they will reprimand first-time offenders and will suspend users who repeatedly make frivolous bids.

Whether these initiatives will be enough to put an end to fraud remains to be seen. Eileen Harrington, director of marketing practices at the Federal Trade Commission, warns: "There's always an element of risk when buyers and sellers don't know each other. The Internet makes that sort of anonymity much easier."

But eBay executives hope that by taking a more activist role on the site, they can ward off problems. "In the past, we've been one or two steps removed from users," says Gary Dillabough, eBay's director of business development: "Now we want to do a little more hand-holding, to make sure that people have a good experience."

93

ENVIRO-CARS: THE RACE IS ON

Toyota's green machine will soon have lots of rivals

For more than a year, Toyota Motor Corp. has been cranking out the world's first mass-produced hybrid car. Under its hood are two power plants—a gasoline engine and an electric motor. In congested urban areas the motor is the full-time workhorse, while the engine keeps the batteries charged and kicks in extra oomph when passing.

Toyota's Prius goes a long way toward achieving the low-pollution benefits of electric vehicles. Yet it doesn't saddle drivers with a car that can only wander 100 miles or so before it must stop to recharge its batteries. In fact, because of the dual-energy approach, the Prius wrings 870 miles out of a tank of gas. "It represents a new value for the 21st century," boasted Toyota President Hiroshi Okuda when the car was launched.

Now, Toyota's backyard rivals are revving up their own hybrids. Honda, Nissan, and Fuji are gearing up to challenge Toyota's lead in "green" cars. The contest kicks off in the fall, when Honda Motor Co. aims to steal the spotlight with the first gasoline-electric hybrid car in the U.S., along with Europe and Japan. Toyota's Prius won't leave Japan until 2000, after an overhaul to give it more zip for foreign roads and to comply with various national regulations.

Honda's green contender will be a two-seat subcompact with an aluminum body. Code-named VV, it reverses the Prius recipe: The electric motor plays second fiddle to the gas engine, which runs constantly. Still, thanks largely to the VV's light weight— roughly 1,000 pounds less than the Prius— Honda promises the VV will one-up Toyota in fuel economy, cleanliness, and price. "We wanted to create a car so fuel-efficient it would shock everyone," says Hiroshi Kuroda, the VV's head engineer. Its engine will comply with California's tough Ultra-Low Emission Vehicle (ULEV) standard, the stage beyond the Low Emission Vehicle standard that the Prius meets.

Back in Japan, a third contender will enter the ring this fall: Nissan Motor Co. Its hybrid probably will be an offshoot of the new Tino station wagon. Come 2001, Fuji Heavy Industries hopes to mesmerize minicar fans with a hybrid Subaru minivan. **DISTANT PROFITS.** The race is on because Japanese drivers are snapping up 1,765 Prius compacts a month. That's shy of Toyota's

production capacity of 2,000 a month, but way over the initial target of 1,000. But it's still too few to be profitable. Analysts estimate that building a Prius costs many thousands more than its $19,000 price. Honda expects to

lose money, too. "It depends on the volume," says Honda President Hiroyuki Yoshino. "We don't know how many we will sell."

To trim their hybrid losses, Japan's carmakers hope to crank up volume by going

TWO TAKES ON HYBRID CARS

ON THE TRACK . . .
Toyota's Prius is selling well in Japan at roughly $19,000.

SPECIFICATIONS

Emissions rating	Low Emission Vehicle
Fuel efficiency	66 miles per gallon
Gasoline engine	1.5 liters, four cylinders, 58 hp
Electric motor	30 kilowatts, 40 hp
Range	870 miles per tank of gas

. . . AT THE STARTING LINE
Honda's VV will soon hit showrooms at an even lower price.

SPECIFICATIONS

Emissions rating	Ultra-Low Emission vehicle
Fuel efficiency	70 miles per gallon
Gasoline engine	1.0 liter, three cylinders
Electric motor	Not disclosed yet
Range	700 miles per tank of gas

(Cont.)

global. It will be a tough battle. Consumers haven't been eager to "buy" cleaner air—especially in the U.S., where gasoline costs less than bottled water. That's why General Motors Corp. is betting on hybrid buses and trucks. Fleet owners are willing to pay more up front if the outlay can be recovered from lower operating costs. GM plans to test a diesel-electric hybrid bus on New York City streets later this year. A hybrid car should be ready for production by 2001, GM says, but there's no timetable for actually building it. Ford Motor Co. and DaimlerChrysler don't expect to roll out hybrid cars before 2003, if then. Skepticism abounds in Europe as well. Although Volkswagen's Audi division has been road-testing hybrid cars since 1989, it hasn't found one that measures up to the Audi image.

BYE, BYE GAS? Japan's carmakers remain undeterred. They see hybrid technology as a bridge between the squeaky-clean, but unpopular, all-electric vehicles of today and tomorrow's ultimate green car—which probably will be powered by a fuel cell that chemically converts gasoline or hydrogen into electricity without combustion. With increasingly stringent pollution curbs spreading from country to country, gasoline engines seem doomed—but not for a decade or two. In the interim, better fuel efficiency could pay off in big market-share gains, just as it did after oil prices skyrocketed in 1973.

So Japan's carmakers are barreling ahead. Soon, the hefty subsidies for every hybrid may begin easing. Analysts expect Honda to buy its VV batteries from Panasonic EV Energy Co., the Toyota-Matsushita group joint venture that supplies nickel metal-hydride batteries for the Prius. If so, rising volumes could drive down battery costs—and batteries account for 20% of total hybrid costs. At 10,000 batteries a month, Panasonic EV Energy says it could slash its prices in half—reducing total hybrid production costs by 10%.

Nissan plans to use lighter lithium-ion batteries to offset the weight of its hybrid, which will be larger than the Prius. Nissan also is fine-tuning a new transmission to provide better handling, says Hiromasa Maeda, a senior engineering manager. The investments in new technologies mean "no one can make money for the time being," says analyst Koji Endo of Schroders Japan Ltd., a Tokyo securities firm. But he predicts some players will start earning returns "in three to five years."

This fall, look for Toyota to react strongly to Honda's challenge. Akihiro Wada, Toyota's executive vice-president for development, doesn't like being upstaged by Honda, so Toyota is working on a few performance-boosting schemes to trump the VV. For its U.S. debut, Wada wants the Prius to leap over California's ULEV standard and qualify as a super-ultra-low emission vehicle—which may make it slightly costlier in the U.S.

Pioneering green cars isn't easy or cheap. But the intense rivalry triggered by the Prius might end up helping to make the rush hour commute a healthier time to breathe.

By Emily Thornton in Tokyo, with bureau reports

HITTING THE ROAD IN TOYOTA'S PRIUS

There's just one hybrid car in production, Toyota Motor Corp.'s Prius, and it's sold only in Japan. But Toyota brought a handful to the U.S. recently, so I borrowed one for five days to see if this new breed of "green" car is easier to live with than all-electric vehicles.

I am pleasantly impressed. This is a no-compromise vehicle that behaves like a conventional small car. Thanks to its fuel tank, there's no need to remember to hook it up to the charger every night. No jitters over whether the battery has enough juice to get you home.

Still, the Prius is an electric car at heart. Get in, turn the key, and the "ready" light comes on. If the batteries are fully charged, the gasoline engine won't kick in until you approach 10 mph. At red lights, it shuts down.

Out on the road, though, it feels like an ordinary gasoline car. What reminds you otherwise is a 5-inch liquid-crystal display in the console. It shows whether the car is being propelled by the engine, the motor, or both. When you brake, the LCD lets you know that the excess energy is being converted into electricity. It's all a bit distracting, but I was soon just letting the Prius do its thing.

The Prius is three inches shorter than a Corolla, yet bigger inside—with generous headroom and legroom. Don't look for the speedometer through the steering wheel. Instead, it sits in a little pod on the dash, below the rear-view mirror. Looks weird, but I quickly discovered the location makes for quicker reading.

To see if the Prius could handle American freeways as well as Tokyo's traffic jams, I took it to San Diego—a 130-mile trek that's beyond the range of every electric vehicle now on the market. Acceleration was good enough, passing power was fine, and while the engine strained a bit, it kept up with traffic in the fast lane. And when I topped off the tank back home, I calculated the Prius got 47 miles per gallon, maybe half again as much as most 1.5-liter buggies.

By Larry Armstrong in Los Angeles